Privacy and Identity in a Networked Society

This book offers an analysis of privacy impacts resulting from and reinforced by technology and discusses fundamental risks and challenges of protecting privacy in the digital age.

Privacy is among the most endangered "species" in our networked society: personal information is processed for various purposes beyond our control. Ultimately, this affects the natural interplay between privacy, personal identity and identification. This book investigates that interplay from a systemic, socio-technical perspective by combining research from the social and computer sciences. It sheds light on the basic functions of privacy, their relation to identity and how they alter with digital identification practices. The analysis reveals a general privacy control dilemma of (digital) identification shaped by several interrelated socio-political, economic and technical factors. Uncontrolled increases in the identification modalities inherent to digital technology reinforce this dilemma and benefit surveillance practices, thereby complicating the detection of privacy risks and the creation of appropriate safeguards. Easing this problem requires a novel approach to privacy impact assessment (PIA), and this book proposes an alternative PIA framework which, at its core, comprises a basic typology of (personally and technically) identifiable information. This approach contributes to the theoretical and practical understanding of privacy impacts and, thus, to the development of more effective protection standards.

This book will be of much interest to students and scholars of critical security studies, surveillance studies, computer and information science, science and technology studies, and politics.

Stefan Strauß is Senior Researcher at the Institute of Technology Assessment at the Austrian Academy of Sciences in Vienna, Austria.

Series: Routledge New Security Studies

Series Editor: J. Peter Burgess,
École Normale Superieur (ENS), Paris

The aim of this book series is to gather state-of-the-art theoretical reflection on and empirical research into a core set of volumes that respond vigorously and dynamically to new challenges to security studies scholarship. This is a continuation of the PRIO New Security Studies series.

Transformations of Security Studies
Dialogues, Diversity and Discipline
Edited by Gabi Schlag, Julian Junk and Christopher Daase

The Securitisation of Climate Change
Actors, Processes and Consequences
Thomas Diez, Franziskus von Lucke and Zehra Wellmann

Surveillance, Privacy and Security
Citizens' Perspectives
Edited by Michael Friedewald, J. Peter Burgess, Johann Čas, Rocco Bellanova and Walter Peissl

Socially Responsible Innovation in Security
Critical Reflections
Edited by J. Peter Burgess, Genserik Reniers, Koen Ponnet, Wim Hardyns and Wim Smit

Visual Security Studies
Sights and Spectacles of Insecurity and War
Edited by Juha A. Vuori and Rune Saugmann Andersen

Privacy and Identity in a Networked Society
Refining Privacy Impact Assessment
Stefan Strauß

For more information about this series, please visit: www.routledge.com/Routledge-New-Security-Studies/book-series/RNSS

Privacy and Identity in a Networked Society

Refining Privacy Impact Assessment

Stefan Strauß

Routledge
Taylor & Francis Group

LONDON AND NEW YORK

First published 2019
by Routledge
2 Park Square, Milton Park, Abingdon, Oxon OX14 4RN

and by Routledge
605 Third Avenue, New York, NY 10017

First issued in paperback 2020

Routledge is an imprint of the Taylor & Francis Group, an informa business

© 2019 Stefan Strauß

British Library Cataloguing-in-Publication Data
A catalogue record for this book is available from the British Library

Library of Congress Cataloging-in-Publication Data
Names: Strauss, Stefan, author.
Title: Privacy and identity in a networked society : refining privacy impact assessment / Stefan Strauss.
Description: Abingdon, Oxon ; New York, NY : Routledge, 2019. | Series: Routledge new security studies | Includes bibliographical references and index.
Identifiers: LCCN 2018060076 (print) | LCCN 2019012895 (ebook) | ISBN 9780429836459 (Web PDF) | ISBN 9780429836442 (ePub) | ISBN 9780429836435 (Mobi) | ISBN 9781138323537 (hardback) | ISBN 9780429451355 (e-book)
Subjects: LCSH: Privacy, Right of– Social aspects. | Data protection. | Computer networks– Access control. | Computer security. | Online identities. | Identity (Philosophical concept)
Classification: LCC JC596 (ebook) | LCC JC596 .S78 2019 (print) | DDC 323.44/8– dc23
LC record available at https://lccn.loc.gov/2018060076

ISBN 13: 978-0-367-73013-0 (pbk)
ISBN 13: 978-1-138-32353-7 (hbk)

Typeset in Times New Roman
by Wearset Ltd, Boldon, Tyne and Wear

For Mathilda and a bright future.

Contents

Figures

Tables

Acknowledgements

Transformations are inextricably linked to the topic of this book which, as in every transformation process, would not have emerged without a few frictions. My thanks to all friends and colleagues who contributed to mind them within reasonable and constructive boundaries. Special thanks to Ingrid, Michael and Wolfgang for their support. I would also like to thank the publishing team around Routledge: Andrew Humphreys and Beth Lund-Yates, the editor of the new security series Peter Burgess, Karen O'Donnell and Pip Clubbs at Wearset, and the anonymous reviewers for their very valuable comments which helped to sharpen the focus of the chapters. Last not least my very special thanks to Angelika and Mathilda for their patience, inspiration and great support.

Abbreviations

API	Application programming interfaces
CCTV	Closed circuit television
CRM	Customer relationship management
DPA	Data protection authority
DPD	Data Protection Directive
DPI	Deep packet inspection
eID	Electronic identity
eIDMS	Electronic identity management system
EU	European Union
GCHQ	Government Communications Headquarters
GDPR	General Data Protection Regulation
ICT	Information and communications technologies
IDM	Identity management
IDMS	Identity management system
IMEI	International mobile equipment identity
ISD	Informational self-determination
ITU	International Telecommunication Union
LBS	Location-based service
MAC	Media access control
MST	Metasystem transition
NGIP	Next generation identification
NSA	National Security Agency
PbD	Privacy by design
PET	Privacy-enhancing technology
PGP	Pretty Good Privacy
PIA	Privacy impact assessment
PII	Personally identifiable information
RFID	Radio frequency identification
sCCTV	Smart CCTV
SIM	Subscriber identity module
SLT	Smartphone location tracking
SNS	Social networking sites
SOST	Surveillance-oriented technologies
SSO	Single sign on
TII	Technically identifiable information

1 Introduction

Is privacy suffering from a digital disease?

Privacy is a heavily threatened socio-technical concept and among the "endangered species" of our digitally networked society. The creation and use of information and communication technologies (ICTs) essentially transformed the organization and functioning of society which, their numerous benefits aside, enabled novel forms of privacy intrusion. As, e.g., Wright and De Hert (2012a: 3) put straight: "If privacy is a cornerstone of democracy, then democracy is in trouble." This critical appraisal addressed the numerous threats to privacy resulting from technology and surveillance practices, one year before whistleblower Edward Snowden informed the world about the yet unknown extent of mass surveillance. Since the Snowden revelations in 2013, there is hard evidence for surveillance programs at a global level exploiting personal information writ large (Greenwald 2014). Since then, the US National Security Agency (NSA) has become more or less synonymous with surveillance in public discourse. The case as such raised many serious questions which have yet been explored and addressed in only a rudimentary fashion: e.g., the legitimacy of surveillance practices and privacy intrusion for law enforcement, their effectiveness and threats to human rights, the accountability of security authorities and national intelligence and so forth. Irrespective of its explosive political impact, the Snowden case teaches the important lesson that contemporary technology provides numerous ways to intrude into privacy, which evidently serves various forms of surveillance. Apparently, though, privacy threats are not limited to the NSA or other security agencies mentioned in the Snowden files. In fact, privacy-intrusive practices exploiting digital technology were a critical issue long before the files were published. However, the revelations brought these issues to the wider public and intensified the societal demand to reinforce privacy protection as well as transparency and accountability of information processing. There is thus a certain "Snowden effect" observable as privacy awareness seems to have increased since then: for instance, privacy issues have gained importance in science and research: a simple search on the Web of Science[1] on privacy (conducted on September 17, 2018) leads to more than 28,600 results from 2000 to 2018. Nearly the half of these results (more than 14,200) concerns the years between 2013 and 2017. But among businesses as well as among the public, privacy issues increased in importance: companies started to invest more in protecting their data by, e.g., fostering encryption of online services (see, Finley 2014; Kuchler 2014) and several studies indicate increasing public concern about surveillance (see, Kerr 2015; Lyon 2014; Madden 2014). On the other hand, privacy and security experts observe a certain fade out of the Snowden effect (see, Weinger 2016) as surveillance practices continue and serious privacy threats are as-yet unsolved.

Hence, the Snowden case notwithstanding, protecting privacy is still often ineffective and increasingly challenging in our digitally networked society. Recent cases like the Facebook/Cambridge Analytica scandal, where more than 80 million personal user profiles were misused, leave no doubt that privacy is seriously threatened, which ultimately causes considerable damage to democratic processes (Hern and Pegg 2018; Nicols 2018). Despite the severity of this case it is just the tip of the iceberg or a symptom among many, indicating a serious "disease" that privacy protection suffers from in the digital age. But is there any chance for healing, at least in the longer run? Obviously, this question is far from being easy to answer and requires a closer look at the course of this "disease" of privacy and its consequences. Or is privacy trapped in a dead end? The short answer to this question is clearly NO. Privacy is neither dead and nor has it become a "walking dead", though, indeed, considerable action is needed to revitalize it. In other words: medication is not enough—there is need for intensive therapy and the will to recover, not least because ultimately nothing less is at stake than a free, democratic society. Imaginings of a post-privacy era without protection are thus rather illusive and fatal in this regard.

Basically, the recent data protection reform of the European Union (EU) is a strong indicator that society is trying to cope with privacy issues to ease this "disease". The newly created General Data Protection Regulation (GDPR), effective since May 2018, enforces private and public institutions to take data protection much more seriously. This paves the way for a reinforced privacy regime in Europe and may have stimulating effects on a global level to strengthen privacy as a fundamental human right. However, although updating legal frameworks is highly important, the effectiveness of regulation depends heavily on its practicability in socio-technical practices. Furthermore, even activities which do not violate data protection laws can be ethically problematic. A core problem of contemporary society is that the processing of personal information is often opaque and it is often unclear to what extent privacy is really affected. To improve the quality of protection measures thus essentially requires a deeper understanding of privacy impacts and of the very mechanisms inherent to socio-technical practices enabling privacy-intrusive activities. Today, digital information flows can include not merely one but various applications, often appearing as a conglomerate of multiple, interwoven technologies. Given the complexity of digital technology, there is a certain risk of getting lost in technological conflation when analyzing privacy impacts. Therefore, it can be very challenging to grasp the extent to which a technology, application or service bears privacy risks. As a consequence, it is equally difficult to implement effective protection mechanisms. Overall, privacy suffers from its generally abstract conceptualization and a broad range of socio-technical threats. A basic motivation of this book is thus to shed light on the theoretical understanding of privacy impacts. This can facilitate privacy impact assessment (PIA) as well as the implementation of privacy safeguards in the realm of privacy by design (PbD). Both issues are of utmost importance for the GDPR, and in particular the former—PIA—is an essential precondition for the latter. In accordance with the new regulation, new approaches are necessary to implement PIA and reinforce levels of privacy protection. This requires an analysis of the core functions of privacy and the main issues challenging their effectiveness. This book ties in here by putting emphasis on the interplay of privacy and (digital) identification, because privacy and identity are essentially linked, sharing a naturally close relationship. The extent to which this relationship is affected by ICTs and the related socio-technical practices is explored, to grasp the emergence of privacy impacts as well as approaches to improve corresponding safeguards. Based on the results, a novel framework for PIA is proposed to contribute to the theoretical understanding and practical implementation of privacy protection. This framework focuses on identifiability and includes a typology of the basic types of identifiable information. The typology supports the analysis and mapping of identifiable information flows. This can contribute to improving the quality of privacy protection and corresponding standards in the longer run.

Digital identification in a networked society

In the early days of the internet and the World Wide Web, a popular cartoon[2] from Peter Steiner, published in 1993, claimed that "on the Internet, nobody knows you're a dog". Today, this cartoon may be reworded to "on the Internet, everybody knows you and your dog, as well as why, when and how you got him". In fact, online anonymity, as the cartoon implicitly hints at, is far more complicated than it used to be during the 1990s. From a wider view, the popularity Steiner's cartoon gained is a good example of the powerful modalities of the internet and ICTs to spread information across multiple contexts, enriched with a vigorous self-dynamic. Today we would say that Steiner's cartoon got "viral" so to speak. While spreading a cartoon online differs significantly from distributing personal information, the very mechanisms are the same, resulting from the dynamics of ICTs: information is easily reproducible, more or less unbound from spatial and temporal limits. These dynamics accelerate, not least because today's technologies are nearly—if not already—ubiquitous. This has consequences for the ways our identities are represented and processed.

Cyberneticist Norbert Wiener once stated: "We are but whirlpools in a river of ever-flowing water. We are not stuff that abides, but patterns that perpetuate themselves. A pattern is a message, and may be transmitted as a message" (Wiener 1954: 96). In line with Wiener's notion of humans as self-perpetuating patterns, our identities may be perceived as unique patterns representable by information. This is not to be misunderstood as a reductionist approach (as partially suggested by classical cybernetics assuming analogies between human beings and machines). Apparently, identity is more than a unique pattern of (computable) information. Identity is a multifaceted phenomenon with various meanings and functions in society, hardly explainable by machine analogies or similar mechanistic views. But irrespective of its multiple functions, the peculiarities of an identity are representable by unique pieces of information enabling recognition that one entity differs from others. Against the background of an increasingly digitized, networked society, co-shaped by technology, the notion of identity as a pattern represented by information is of special relevance. ICTs created new ways of gathering and processing information about individuals serving a variety of social, economic and political purposes. Substantially, every use of ICTs may generate various forms of information suitable for identifying a particular person.

ICTs are not merely technical tools but integral parts of society serving various societal functions; they represent socio-technical systems which shape society and vice versa. With their rapid progress and widespread diffusion, ICTs deeply pervade a broad array of societal domains and everyday-life contexts. This pervasion entails what Moor (1998: 15) called "informational enrichment" (or informatization) of societal activities as well as their conceptions. This means that ICTs enabled new options to digitally represent and process information about societal entities such as organizations, domains, objects, or people and the activities involved. Consequently, ICT usage also affects the representation of identities, which today can be easily embedded in networking structures. This can reinforce identifiability because contemporary technology offers various methods of direct and indirect identification. In this regard, increasing identifiability is an important side-effect of the (digital) information age. In the "age of identification", as Hildebrandt (2008: 56) once stated, our personal identities are embedded in and exposed to a magnitude of digital environments. Technology alters the way identities are represented, organized and handled by individuals as well as groups and institutions (Whitley *et al.* 2014). These developments are phenomena of the "network society" as described by Manuel Castells (2000: 5) as a "social structure characteristic of the Information Age", triggered by globally networked ICTs. The structural setting of society changed with technology, adding a specific informational layer to the social structure. As "information processing is at the source of life, and of social action, every domain of our eco-social system is thereby transformed" (Castells 2000: 10). Castells realized early the deep structural shifts in society resulting from informatization. Today we may speak of a *networked* society as networking structures occur within and between offline and online environments in many respects, enabled and reinforced by ICTs. Hence, these shifts did not merely affect how information is structured and processed in digital environments. Society has increasingly entered a stage of convergence between analog and digital environments with information as a driving force in our whole ecosystem (Floridi 2010; Hofkirchner 2010). This ongoing socio-technical transformation proceeds quickly and is hard to grasp; or in other words: "Our technological tree has been growing much more widely, rapidly and chaotically than its conceptual, ethical and cultural roots" (Floridi 2010: 5). Floridi uses the term "infosphere" to describe this trans-formation embracing the (ontologically) powerful nature of information. The infosphere "denotes the whole informational environment constituted by all informational entities (thus including informational agents as well), their prop-erties, interactions, processes and mutual relations" (Floridi 2010: 6). This info-sphere constantly alters with ICTs and describes a highly dynamic environment comprising analog and digital settings,[3] linking online as well as offline domains. Hence, socio-technical change reaches a new quality including an incremental shift of the boundaries between society and technology, physical (or analog) and digital environments. As Verbeek (2011: 30ff.) pointed out, humans are "pro-foundly technologically mediated beings" and "technology is part of the human condition". Technologies basically represent socio-technical systems that affect the human condition and vice versa. ICTs highlight and enforce this interplay: their rapid diffusion and usage entails increasing connectivity and permanent availability of always-on computer devices, employed in various domains. There is an observable dramatic increase in digitally networked environments, reinfor-cing further growth in the amount of digital information. While in the year 2001 the number of global Internet users was about 500 million, today there are over 3.5 billion Internet users worldwide (ITU 2017). Network providers predict the amount of global internet traffic will soon exceed one zettabyte per year (10^{21} bytes and about one trillion gigabytes). Mobile computing in particular is on the rise. In 2016, about 50 percent of global Internet traffic resulted from wireless and mobile devices. By 2021, over 60 percent is expected. The number of net-worked devices is assumed to be three times higher than the world's population, i.e., more than 27 billion devices (Cisco 2017). Against this background, visions of a globally networked information society including classical notions of per-vasive or ubiquitous computing, ambient intelligence, etc. (Weiser 1991; ITU 2005) take more concrete shape with developments in the realm of "smart" tech-nologies, the Internet of Things and similar trends. The general boost in digital networks is accompanied by a further expansion of digital information process-ing. With these developments, individuals and thus their identities are increas-ingly interconnected and represented by their digital information, prominently highlighted by, but not limited to, Web 2.0 and social media platforms. Digital identities are already involved in a broad variety of interactions (e.g., informa-tion exchange, communication, collaboration, sharing and creating content), among others fulfilling (and stimulating) the societal need to communicate and exchange with others. But this also entails further growth in the amount of per-sonal information, personalization and uncontrolled information disclosure. Trends in the realm of big data, machine learning and so-called artificial "intelli-gence" (Mayer-Schönberger and Cukier 2013; Strauß 2015, 2018), aiming to exploit data from everyday life for novel services, further boost the processing of digital information in multiple application contexts.

Privacy versus (digital) identification?

Together, these developments amplify digital networking structures, which deeply affect society in general, including social practices, norms and values. Among the variety of societal impacts, serious threats and challenges concern the notion and protection of privacy. Various tensions result from the need "to fit the technological and socio-political evolutions", which generate "new threats for the individuals' capacity for 'self-development' of their personality" (Rouvroy and Poullet 2009: 55). Hence, threats to privacy ultimately affect identity-building (Hildebrandt 2006). In light of the proceeding socio-technical transformations, the need for "a radical re-interpretation of informational privacy, one that takes into account the essentially informational structure of human beings and of their operations as social agents" (Floridi 2013: 243) is more topical than ever. In other words, there is a certain demand to re-conceptualize privacy with respect to the informational nature of humans and the representation of their (digital) identities: on the one hand, because threats to privacy can threaten identity-building of the individual concerned as well; on the other hand, because ICTs also transformed the way identities are represented and processed, i.e., identification. In this regard, ICTs have impacted on the interplay of identification and privacy.

The dynamics of ICTs further intensify the challenge to effectively protect privacy and to adapt existing practices to the changed requirements. Digital information can flow across many different socio-technical contexts. As a consequence, the boundaries between personal and non-personal information, private and public spheres, can be strained. In between these boundaries, at the point of intersection, identity becomes a particular (informational) matter. An expansion of digital information processing affects the nexus between privacy and identity in manifold ways. Given the peculiarities of digital information, it can create a sort of permanent link to the identity of an individual person. This has effects on the privacy of this person as well: "one's informational sphere and one's personal identity are co-referential, or two sides of the same coin" (Floridi 2013: 245). Therefore, protecting privacy includes the protection of personal identity. Conversely, identification can be privacy-intrusive. Hence, to some extent, privacy and identification can be mutually exclusive, for instance, when identification is related to security and surveillance practices. There is a certain tension between privacy and security, which is mirrored in the discourse on digital identity (Halperin and Backhouse 2008; Strauß 2011). This tension can challenge the effectiveness of privacy protection as security considerations often dominate the implementation of identification processes. This is observable in the broad scope of digital identification processes being directly and indirectly involved in socio-technical systems and practices. Many technologies and online applications process different forms of personal (or identity) information. To ease the handling of this information, the field of identity management (IDM) emerged in research and development. The increasing relevance of IDM indi-cates a societal demand to deal with issues of identity in the information society

(Halperin and Backhouse 2008; Rannenberg *et al.* 2009; Aichholzer and Strauß 2010; Kubicek and Noack 2010; Strauß 2011; Whitley *et al.* 2014). The basic aim of IDM is to unify identification and authentication processes. Different technological artifacts such as digital devices (e.g., online profiles, electronic ID cards, smartcards, smartphones) can be used as carrier devices for managing individual identities. These artifacts can be seen as a sort of "strong tie" between analog and digital environments as they can support identification mechanisms in both: online and offline contexts. There are numerous application contexts where digital identification processes are involved ranging from transactions in e-government and e-commerce, multiple online services, and social media platforms. The implementation of IDM concepts or of digital identification systems primarily aims to foster efficiency and security of online services. In contrast to that, privacy protection plays a rather marginal or implicit role. Most IDM approaches provide unique identification without any features of anonymous and pseudonymous usage (Strauß 2011). This hampers the applicability of IDM for privacy protection. Besides explicit forms of identification, there are implicit forms of identification as well. Hence, identification is not merely a formal process (e.g., between citizens and the state, customers and businesses, etc.) but also occurs in the form of profiling activities, where information is gathered to create extensive profiles of the individuals concerned. Moreover, explicit and implicit identification may overlap. Overall, socio-technical identification practices affect not merely the handling of personal information but also the values and norms that information rests upon. In particular privacy and the individual's ability to control their information, i.e., informational self-determination (ISD), suffer from uncontrolled identification practices. The processing of identifiable information as well as the option to be identified (identifiability) can lead to an imbalance of control and information asymmetries at the cost of the individual concerned. Consequently, individuals have very limited options to effectively protect their privacy and to take action in cases of privacy abuse. This entails negative effects for society as a whole, which is fundamentally based upon free, informed individuals being able to actively engage in societal processes.

To tackle these problems, which are likely to worsen with further, ungoverned pervasion of ICTs, there is an increasing demand for novel approaches to detect and stem threats to privacy early. This demand refers to two crucial concepts: PIA and PbD. For many years, privacy advocates argued for making both concepts mandatory in order to raise the general level of protection (Wright and De Hert 2012b; EGE 2014). Finally, the new EU data protection framework fosters both concepts and foresees obligatory PIA under certain conditions. PbD aims to incorporate privacy protection in the very development processes of technologies (Cavoukian 2012; Klitou 2014). PIA is an instrument to explore privacy risks and the extent to which technologies are in accordance with privacy and data protection (Clarke 2009; Wright and De Hert 2012b; EGE 2014). Both approaches are interrelated and complement each other. Conducting a PIA is vital for the implementation of privacy safeguards and, in the longer run, it can facilitate the development of privacy-friendly technology. Conversely, when technologies have integrated PbD features, this can ease PIA. As the creation of privacy safeguards requires knowledge about the amount and processing of personal information, PIA is a precondition of PbD. PIA is not a new concept; early approaches date back to the 1990s. However, ICTs and their associated socio-technical transformations require a refinement of PIA conceptualizations. To come to enhanced approaches, it is crucial to gain deeper insights into the socio-technical transformation of privacy and how it is affected by technology.

Setting the scene—what is this book about?

The main focus of this book is on the interplay of privacy, identity and identification. Although this interplay seems apparent at first glance, it gained little conceptual attention for the assessment of privacy impacts. Making this relationship more explicit and revealing its dynamics in the realm of ICTs is thus considered important to allow for more effective privacy protection; particularly in an increasingly digitized, networked society. While there is broad scientific and societal consensus about privacy being threatened, there is a lack of common conceptual understanding of the way socio-technical systems enable privacy intrusions. As will be shown, (digital) identification and the processing of identity information play a very special role in this regard. However, this particular role has gained little attention in research and development, at least as regards the design and implementation of PIA and PbD. This book ties in here and sheds light on the interplay between privacy and (digital) identification to come toward a refined approach to PIA. The findings and elaborated concepts contribute to improving the theoretical understanding of privacy impacts as well as support institutions in the practical implementation of PIA and PbD processes.

Besides the various challenges resulting from technology and corresponding usage practices, the complexity of privacy as such also complicates its protection. Privacy has an abstract character and multidimensional scope on the one hand, and there are narrow conceptualizations on the other hand. Traditional notions of privacy frame it as the "right to be let alone" (Warren and Brandeis 1890). This notion is still popular and is mirrored in public discourse as well as in technology development. Partially similar is the view on privacy as data protection, which is dominant in the European privacy regime. Without doubt, these framings are relevant, particularly in a legal sense. However, as a crucial societal value, privacy protection is relevant beyond legal obligations. A narrow conceptual framing of privacy hampers the detection of impacts and creation of effective safeguards. Therefore, more differentiated views on privacy and on personal information are required. There are some promising conceptualizations in this regard such as Nissenbaum's (2010) theory of contextual integrity, which underlines the public and private value of privacy. Contextual integrity suggests that the contexts of personal information processing, i.e., informational norms, determine the extent to which privacy is affected. In the view of Nissenbaum (2010), a breach of informational norms results in a breach of privacy. However, in light of interconnected technologies and applications, the examination of norms as well as the detection of breaches can be demanding. It is thus important to gain a deeper conceptual understanding of the emergence of privacy impacts to come toward more effective protection. A general problem is that technology and usage practices impede the determination of what actually needs to be protected. Obviously, protecting personal information is essential. However, it can be very challenging to grasp the extent to which personal information is factually processed in a privacy-affecting manner. Conceptual approaches like the "seven types of privacy" suggested by Finn *et al.* (2013) or Solove's (2006) taxonomy of privacy-affecting activities can be useful to grasp the multiple dimensions of privacy. However, these approaches are also rather diverse and difficult to integrate in impact assessments. To ease this problem I argue for a stronger focus on issues of identifiability and identification. The basic assumption here is that a privacy impact is generally determined by the processing of information referring or relating to an individual, i.e., some form of identification. Identification is thus assumed to have a connecting role that enables interlinkage of different socio-technical systems. This book is an attempt to shed light on this connecting role from a wider, systemic perspective. Of particular interest are the emergence, functions and societal impacts of (digital) identification in relation to the protection of privacy.

There is indeed plenty of research about the general privacy impacts of new technologies and surveillance from sociological, political, economic, legal, ethical and technological perspectives (e.g., Haggerty and Ericson 2000; Lyon 2003; Clarke 2006; Hildebrandt 2006; Solove 2006; Nissenbaum 2010; Bennett 2011; Wright and De Hert 2012a; Finn *et al.* 2013; Lyon 2014; Wright *et al.* 2015). However, only a few studies explore socio-technical privacy impacts from different, interdisciplinary angles. Studies of privacy issues in the social sciences often neglect the peculiarities of technology, and studies in the realm of engineering or computer sciences focus on technical approaches while neglecting relevant social science perspectives on privacy. Hence, there is a certain research gap, particularly as regards the interplay between identity and privacy from a systemic perspective. This book contributes to narrowing this gap by applying an interdisciplinary approach. It is located in the research domains of technology assessment as well as science and technology studies, where multiple aspects, including socio-political, technological and ethical aspects, are taken into account. The book is guided by the following questions:

- What are the basic concepts and functions of identity, identification and privacy, and how are they interrelated?
- What are the relevant functions, drivers and dynamics of the emergence of digital identification?
- To what extent is digital identification related to security and surveillance practices and how does this affect the protection of privacy and ISD?
- What are the prospects and perils of privacy controls (PbD) and PIA? What are relevant conceptual approaches for overcoming existing barriers?

The issues outlined in this chapter build the foundation of this book, which is structured as follows: of particular interest are the implications of digital identification for the protection of privacy. As a starting point, Chapter 2 explores the general functions of privacy and identification through the lens of systems theory. This analytical perspective is relevant to grasp the complexity of socio-technical identification practices, and their impact on privacy protection, which are investigated in subsequent parts of the book. Chapter 3 investigates the interplay between identity, identification and privacy in depth. This includes a description of the basic concepts and socio-technical role of identity and identification, as well as a thorough discussion on the basic functions and meanings of privacy. The chapter also examines central controversies in the privacy discourse such as the assumed trade-off between privacy and security. This trade-off is deconstructed and its close relationship with security policy in the realm of securitization is discussed (this is also relevant for Chapter 5). In line with the notion of privacy as a control function, the interplay of privacy, autonomy and identity is presented and discussed. This control function essentially comprises the concept of ISD. The chapter ends with a brief discussion on the relationship between privacy and transparency as well as on informational norms and the limits of control over identity information, which is a central issue of contemporary privacy protection.

Chapter 4 sheds light on the emergence and transition paths of digital identification. A starting point is a brief overview on the main development stages of ICTs and the relevant socio-technical systems and practices through the lens of a metasystem transition. The timeframe for these stages is from about the 1990s until today, where the emergence of the internet and the World Wide Web (WWW) serves as a general point of reference. From these general transition paths, more emphasis is then put on digital identification. This begins with an examination of the major drivers, basic functions and technical approaches of digital IDM. Based on this, particular focus is set on social media platforms and social networking sites (SNS): these are prominent phenomena showcasing the networking structure of ICTs, their effects on interactive identity representation and its processing. The chapter finishes with a discussion on the transformation patterns of digital identification in the frame of a metasystem transition.

Chapter 5 analyses in depth to what extent the boundary control function of privacy is affected by ICTs and digital identification. The analysis involves theories and concepts from surveillance studies to explore the nexus between surveillance and identification as well as its political and economic drivers. The chapter argues that there is a privacy control dilemma of digital identification, which undermines effective protection. As shown, this dilemma is basically driven by a securitization and economization of identification. This is discussed around the question of how identification practices reinforce existing mechanisms of power and control, and what this implies for privacy protection. The chapter also presents empirical findings concerning the perceptions of European citizens on the interplay of privacy, security and surveillance. These results underline that information asymmetries between individuals and institutional entities conducting identification are increasingly problematic. Based on this, socio-technical identifiability is revealed as the core problem of contemporary privacy protection. This problem is highlighted by the concept of what I call "identity shadow", enabling the continuous proliferation of explicit and implicit identification beyond control. Then, relevant technological trends which contribute to a further expansion of individual identifiability are presented and discussed.

Based on the analysis conducted in the previous chapters, Chapter 6 explores concepts and approaches of PbD and PIA. This begins with an analysis of the prospects and perils of existing privacy control mechanisms in the realm of PbD. It is argued that individual control over identity information and thus over privacy has certain limits. This is particularly true against the background of trends of what I call a "privatization" of privacy. Therefore, more transparency and accountability of information processing is seen as crucial to improve privacy protection. PIA is a fundamental instrument in this regard, which is examined in detail following this discussion. This includes a general overview on the scope of PIA, its basic requirements and current limits in relation to the core problem of information asymmetries and identifiability (as presented in Chapter 5). The chapter also presents and discusses existing typologies of privacy types and privacy-affecting activities. It is argued that PIA is basically crucial to complement PbD, which, together, can raise the level of privacy protection in general. However, there are various barriers to existing approaches, which basically lie in their insufficient consideration of identity or identifiable information. On this basis, Chapter 7 elaborates a conceptual model which refines existing PIA approaches by integrating identifiability as a central privacy-affecting mechanism. This alternative PIA framework allows for a more systemic, process-oriented view on the emergence of privacy impacts. An enhanced PIA framework is particularly relevant in light of the new European data protection regulation, and the associated transformations of the privacy regime and of socio-technical practices. The regulation stimulates PIA on a general level but does not provide guidance on its implementation. There is thus demand for conceptual approaches to ease the practical implementation of PIA in institutions. The proposed framework can help in this regard but it is not limited to specific legal issues. It thus may be seen as a general, ethical PIA approach which ideally contributes to legally motivated assessments as well. A fundamental part of this proposed identifiability-based PIA framework is a typology of the basic types of identifiable information. This typology supports the analysis and mapping of identifiable information flows, which is a core task of every PIA process. Being a general typology, it may also contribute to improving the theoretical understanding of privacy impacts. The end of the chapter outlines how a PIA process may be carried out based on the proposed framework. Finally, Chapter 8 summarizes and discusses the main findings of this book. The concluding remarks highlight the most important aspects to come toward a more sustainable protection of privacy.

Notes

1 webofknowledge.com.
2 https://en.wikipedia.org/wiki/On_the_Internet,_nobody_knows_you%27re_a_dog.
3 It is thus conceptually broader than cyberspace, which primarily addresses online environments. The *Merriam Webster Dictionary* defines cyberspace as "the online world of computer networks and especially the Internet". www.merriam-webster.com/dictionary/cyberspace.

References

All URLs were checked last on October 23, 2018.

Aichholzer, G. and Strauß, S. (2010) Electronic Identity Management in e-Government 2.0: Exploring a system innovation exemplified by Austria. *Information Polity: An International Journal of Government and Democracy in the Information Age*, 15(1–2): 139–152.

Bennett, C. J. (2011) In Defence of Privacy: The concept and the regime. *Surveillance and Society*, 8(4): 485–496.

Castells, M. (2000) Materials for an Exploratory Theory of the Network Society. *British Journal of Sociology*, 51(1): 5–24.

Cavoukian, A. (2012) *Privacy by Design and the Emerging Personal Data Ecosystem*. Information and Privacy Commissioner, Ontario, Canada. www.ipc.on.ca/wp-content/uploads/Resources/pbd-pde.pdf.

Cisco (2017) The Zettabyte Era: Trends and analysis, white paper. www.cisco.com/c/en/us/solutions/collateral/service-provider/visual-networking-index-vni/vni-hyper connectivity-wp.html.

Clarke, R. (2006) *What's "Privacy"?* www.rogerclarke.com/DV/Privacy.html.

Clarke, R. (2009) Privacy Impact Assessment: Its origins and development. *Computer Law and Security Review*, 25(2): 123–135. http://rogerclarke.com/DV/PIAHist-08.html.

EGE—European Group on Ethics in Science and New Technologies (2014) *Ethics of Security and Surveillance Technologies*. Opinion No. 28 of the European Groups on Ethics in Science and New Technologies. Brussels, May 20.

Finley, K. (2014) Encrypted Web Traffic More Than Doubles after NSA Revelations. *Wired*, May 16, www.wired.com/2014/05/sandvine-report/.

Finn, R. L., Wright, D. and Friedewald, M. (2013) Seven Types of Privacy. In Gutwirth, S., Leenes, R., De Hert, P. and Poullet, Y. (eds.), *European Data Protection: Coming of age*. Dordrecht: Springer, 3–32.

Floridi, L. (2010) Ethics after the Information Revolution. In Floridi, L. (ed.), *The Cambridge Handbook of Information and Computer Ethics*. Cambridge/UK: Cambridge University Press, 3–19.

Floridi, L. (2013) *The Ethics of Information*. Oxford: Oxford University Press.

GDPR—General Data Protection Regulation (2016) Regulation (EU) 2016/679 of the European Parliament and of the Council of 27 April 2016 on the Protection of Natural Persons with Regard to the Processing of Personal Data and on the Free Movement of Such Data, and Repealing Directive 95/46/EC (General Data Protection Regulation). http://eur-lex.europa.eu/legal-content/EN/TXT/HTML/?uri=CELEX:32016R0679&qid=1485427623759&from=en.

Greenwald, G. (2014) *No Place to Hide: Edward Snowden, the NSA and the surveillance state*. London: Hamish Hamilton/Penguin Books.

Haggerty, K. D. and Ericson, R. V. (2000) The Surveillant Assemblage. *British Journal of Sociology*, 51(4): 605–622.

Halperin, R. and Backhouse, J. (2008) A Roadmap for Research on Identity in the Information Society. *Identity in the Information Society*, 1(1): 71–87.

Hern, A. and Pegg, D. (2018) Facebook Fined for Data Breaches in Cambridge Analytica Scandal. *Guardian*, July 11, www.theguardian.com/technology/2018/jul/11/facebook-fined-for-data-breaches-in-cambridge-analytica-scandal.

Hildebrandt, M. (2006) Privacy and Identity. In Claes, E., Duff, A. and Gutwirth, S. (eds.), *Privacy and the Criminal Law*. Antwerpen/Oxford: Intersentia, 43–57.

Hildebrandt, M. (2008) Profiling and the Rule of Law. *Identity in the Information Society (IDIS)*, 1(1): 55–70. http://link.springer.com/article/10.1007/s12394-008-0003-1#Fn1.

Hofkirchner, W. (2010) How to Design the Infosphere: The fourth revolution, the management of the life cycle of information, and information ethics as a macroethics. *Knowledge, Technology and Policy*, 23(1–2): 177–192.

ITU—International Telecommunication Union (2005) *Privacy and Ubiquitous Network Societies*. Background paper, ITU workshop on ubiquitous network societies, ITU new initiatives programme April 6–8. UNS/05. www.itu.int/osg/spu/ni/ubiquitous/Papers/Privacy%20background%20paper.pdf.

ITU—International Telecommunication Union (2017) *ICT Facts and Figures 2017*. www.itu.int/en/ITU-D/Statistics/Pages/facts/default.aspx.

Kerr, O. (2015) Edward Snowden's Impact. *Washington Post*, April 9, www.washingtonpost.com/news/volokh-conspiracy/wp/2015/04/09/edward-snowdens-impact/.

Klitou, D. (2014) Privacy, Liberty and Security. In *Privacy-Invading Technologies and Privacy by Design: Safeguarding privacy, liberty and security in the 21st century*. Information Technology and Law Series. The Hague: Springer/TMC Asser Press, 13–25.

Kubicek, H. and Noack, T. (2010) Different Countries—Different Extended Comparison of the Introduction of eIDs in Eight European Countries. *Identity in the Information Society (IDIS)*, 3(1): 235–245.

Kuchler, H. (2014) Tech Companies Step Up Encryption in Wake of Snowden. *Financial Times*, November 4, www.ft.com/content/3c1553a6-6429-11e4-bac8-00144feabdc0.

Lyon, D. (2003) *Surveillance as Social Sorting: Privacy, risk and automated discrimination*. London: Routledge.

Lyon, D. (2014) Surveillance, Snowden, and Big Data: Capacities, consequences, critique. *Big Data and Society*, July–December: 1–13. http://journals.sagepub.com/doi/abs/10.1177/2053951714541861.

Madden, M. (2014) Public Perceptions of Privacy and Security in the Post-Snowden Era. Report. *Pew Research Center Internet and Technology*. www.pewinternet.org/2014/11/12/public-privacy-perceptions/.

Mayer-Schönberger, V. and Cukier, K. (2013) *Big Data: A revolution that will transform how we live, work and think*. New York: Houghton Mifflin Harcourt.

Moor, J. H. (1998) Reason, Relativity and Responsibility in Computer Ethics. *Computers and Society*, 28(1): 14–21.

Nicols, S. (2018) Cambridge Analytica Dismantled for Good? Nope: It just changed its name to Emerdata. *The Register*, May 2, www.theregister.co.uk/2018/05/02/cambridge_analytica_shutdown/.

Nissenbaum, H. (2010) *Privacy in Context: Technology, policy, and the integrity of social life*. Stanford: Stanford University Press.

Rannenberg, K., Royer, D. and Deuker, A. (eds.) (2009) *The Future of Identity in the Information Society: Challenges and opportunities*. Berlin: Springer.

Rouvroy, A. and Poullet, Y. (2009) The Right to Informational Self-Determination and the Value of Self-Development: Reassessing the importance of privacy for democracy. In Gutwirth, S., Poullet, Y., de Hert, P., de Terwangne, C., Nouwt, S. (eds.), *Reinventing Data Protection?* Dordrecht: Springer, 45–76.

Solove, D. J. (2006) A Taxonomy of Privacy. *University of Pennsylvania Law Review*, 154(3): 477–560.

Strauß, S. (2011) The Limits of Control: (Governmental) identity management from a privacy perspective. In Fischer-Hübner, S., Duquenoy, P., Hansen, M., Leenes, R. and Zhang, G. (eds.), *Privacy and Identity Management for Life, 6th IFIP/PrimeLife International Summer School, Helsingborg, Sweden, August 2–6 2010, Revised Selected Papers*. Dordrecht: Springer, 206–218.

Strauß, S. (2015) Datafication and the Seductive Power of Uncertainty: A critical exploration of big data enthusiasm. *Information*, 6: 836–847. www.mdpi.com/2078-2489/6/4/836/pdf.

Strauß, S. (2018) From Big Data to Deep Learning: A leap towards strong AI or "*intelligentia obscura*"? *Big Data and Cognitive Computing*, 2(3): 16. www.mdpi.com/2504-2289/2/3/16.

Verbeek, P. (2011) Subject to Technology: On autonomic computing and human autonomy. In Hildebrandt, M. and Rouvroy, A. (eds.), *Law, Human Agency and Autonomic Computing*. London/New York: Routledge, 27–45.

Warren, S. D. and Brandeis, L. D. (1890) The Right to Privacy. *Harvard Law Review*, 193, IV, December 15, 1890, No. 5. http://faculty.uml.edu/sgallagher/Brandeisprivacy.htm.

Weinger, M. (2016) Snowden's Impact Fades After Three Years. *The Cypher Brief*, June 5, www.thecipherbrief.com/article/exclusive/north-america/snowden%E2%80%99s-impact-fades-after-three-years-1089.

Weiser, M. (1991) The Computer of the 21st Century. *Scientific American*, 265(3): 94–104. www.lri.fr/~mbl/Stanford/CS477/papers/Weiser-SciAm.pdf.

Whitley, E. A., Gal, U. and Kjaergaard, A. (2014) Who Do You Think You Are? A review of the complex interplay between information systems, identification and identity. *European Journal of Information Systems*, 23(1): 17–35.

Wiener, N. (1954) *The Human Use of Human Beings: Cybernetics and society*. (First published 1950, reprint of revised edition of 1954). Boston: Da Capo Press.

Wright, D. and De Hert, P. (eds.) (2012a) *Privacy Impact Assessment*. Law, Governance and Technology Series 6. Dordrecht: Springer.

Wright, D. and De Hert (2012b) Introduction to Privacy Impact Assessment. In Wright, D. and De Hert, P. (eds.), *Privacy Impact Assessment*. Law, Governance and Technology Series 6. Dordrecht: Springer, 3–32.

Wright, D., Rodrigues, R., Raab, C., Jones, R., Székely, I., Ball, K., Bellanova, R. and Bergersen, S. (2015) Questioning Surveillance. *Computer Law and Security Review*, 31(2): 280–292.

2 A systemic perspective on privacy and identification

What are the general functions of privacy and (digital) identification? To answer this question a systemic approach is used as a conceptual frame. This frame is important for understanding the subsequent parts of this book, which elaborate on the interplay of privacy and identification in light of our increasingly digitized, networked society. The following sections briefly outline the basic idea and concepts of systems theory and explain what is meant by "system" in the context of this book. Then focus is put on the systemic interplay between privacy and identification and how it alters through technology.

What's in a system?

In the broadest sense, a system is a specific organizational entity constituted by a set of related elements with particular characteristics. The "identity" of a system is shaped by its elements, which are related to each other as well as to the system's environment. The roots of systems theory can be traced back to Aristotle's statement: "The whole is more than the sum of its parts." This means that a system is not just determined by a quantity of elements but it is dynamically constituted by the interplay of its elements and their interactions. A system is thus not merely explainable by an isolated view on (nor is it reducible to) the number of its elements, which together build a common structural setting; because this setting affects the properties and dynamics of a system as a whole (Bertalanffy 1969, 1972; Laszlo and Krippner 1998; Hofkirchner 2013). As scientific paradigm, systems thinking emerged in the 1950s and 1960s coined mainly by biologist Ludwig von Bertalanffy (1950). He began to discuss the approach of a general systems theory, which he later described as "a model of certain general aspects of reality" (Bertalanffy 1972: 424). It includes "a methodological maxim" of taking aspects into account "which were previously overlooked or bypassed … and tries to give its answer to perennial problems of philosophy" (ibid.). In this sense, a systemic perspective enables looking beyond the limits of mechanistic views on complex phenomena to analyze theoretical problems as well as issues related to modern technology (Bertalanffy 1969/1972). This general understanding is the basic idea of systems thinking, which entered several disciplines such as mathematics, physics, biology, sociology, philosophy, cybernetics, organization and management theory, psychology, engineering, computer science, up to innovation and transition management (Wiener 1954; Bertalanffy 1969; Ackoff 1971; Varela *et al.* 1974; Giddens 1984; Luhmann 1991; Parsons 1991; Laszlo and Krippner 1998; Geels 2004; Fuchs and Hofkirchner 2005; Hofkirchner and Schafranek 2011; Hofkirchner 2013). Although in each of these domains a system means different things specifically, there are some general features of a system irrespective of the domain. Figure 2.1 sketches the basic characteristics of a system.

As illustrated, a system consists of different elements. These elements are interconnected, have relations and shape the dynamics of the system. Elements with relatively stable relations may together be seen as a sub-system of a larger system.[1] A system is embedded in an environment, which implies that there are external systems, components, etc. beyond its boundary. The boundary of a system is the edge that makes the elements and relationships of a system distinguishable from the external environment outside the system. External relations can occur, e.g., through interfaces. Finally, an interaction of a system with others can be described as a process with an input and an output, meaning that things flow into the system (e.g., matter, energy, goods, information, etc.) as well as out of it into its environment (e.g., into another system or its components). Input and output can be accompanied by feedback loops, meaning that the processes triggered by a system or its elements may loop back. Or in other words: a system is dynamically interrelated with its environment (Bertalanffy 1969, 1972; Laszlo and Krippner 1998; Hofkirchner 2013).

A general asset of a system-theoretical approach is the meta-perspective it provides through abstraction, enabling an analytical view from multiple angles. This allows for cross-disciplinary investigation of socio-technical phenomena

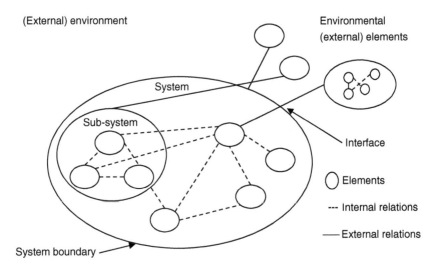

Figure 2.1 Basic system characteristics.

which are accompanied by high (and increasing) complexity. Systems theory provides a methodological approach to cope with this complexity through different layers of abstraction and thus allows the bigger picture of socio-technical change to be grasped (Bertalanffy 1972; Hofkirchner 2013). On the one hand, conceptualizing a phenomenon as a system allows focusing on the interplay of its interrelated components including their dynamics. On the other hand, it also supports investigation of how a system is related to external factors in its environment (e.g., how a technology pervades and transforms specific domains of society). This supports the analysis of transformation patterns of socio-technical phenomena and the assessment of societal impacts resulting from them, such as those represented by ICTs.

Naturally, as in every methodology, systems theory is not without controversy and certainly has limits, especially the high degree of abstraction it offers, which suggests it should be combined with other approaches. Otherwise, it might be misinterpreted as a supposedly holistic or universal approach as critics used to argue. Major points of criticism include an implied tendency of systemic approaches to mechanical explanations, excessive abstraction, and a distinct lack of historical or political contextualization. Consequently, the complexity of reality would be oversimplified for the sake of explicability, including deterministic views on societal phenomena conveying technocratic ideology (Hoos 1972; Hughes and Hughes 2000; Featherston and Doolan 2012). Obviously, every notion of systems theory as a universal approach is doomed to fail. In particular, social phenomena are hardly explainable without taking other methods into account. From the 1950s to the 1970s, when systems thinking bloomed, there were indeed some misleading notions of systems theory as a means toward a universal model of reality. Cybernetics in particular, which had some influence on systems thinking, conveyed rather mechanistic and deterministic views of real-world phenomena during that period. This is a main reason for the criticism of systems theory. However, its main benefit, i.e., gaining a meta-perspective on complex phenomena through abstraction, does not necessarily imply a deterministic view on reality. Furthermore, the basic idea of general systems theory is inter- and transdisciplinary by nature. Hence, ultimately, it implies that a cross-disciplinary combination of different research approaches is vital to explore real-world phenomena. Therefore, in contrast to the major points of criticism, systemic approaches applied in this way can help in avoiding deterministic perspectives by allowing for explicit focus on socio-technical interrelations. But this of course requires being realistic about the scope of systems theory. Its scope depends not least on analytical decisions that need to be taken such as where to draw the boundary of a system and which elements are seen as internal and external system components. Hence, to avoid an eventual deterministic "trap", a systemic perspective is to be seen instead as a research heuristic which is useful in combination with other methods and especially empirical research. As it allows abstracting from technological details and focusing on information processes, it is very suitable for combining computer and social sciences perspectives. This combination is particularly important in the context of this book.

As yet, the privacy discourse is mainly dominated by empirical investigations from either the social or technical sciences discussing privacy risks and societal impacts due to ICTs in many variations. However, there is a lack of combined approaches dealing with information processing practices, and more precisely with identification practices, which (as this book argues in depth) essentially trigger the occurrence of privacy impacts in socio-technical systems. These practices can be explained neither by social sciences nor by technical sciences alone. So, both perspectives are needed to understand the interplay of privacy and identification particularly against the background of the digital transformation of our society. A systemic approach is thus used in this book as an analytical umbrella taking both research perspectives (social and technical sciences) into account.

Throughout this book, the term "system" primarily means a socio-technical system, i.e., a technology or a set of technologies and their interplay with societal entities, structures, functions and practices. The main focus is on ICTs, understood as an information processing metasystem. The basic rationale here is that in order to understand what privacy and identification really mean in a digitally networked society initially requires understanding of the dynamics of socio-technical systems. ICTs co-shape our society and thus also affect fundamental societal functions such as privacy and identification. This co-shaping process is mutual and highly dynamic, continuously entailing socio-technical transformations or transitions. As a systemic perspective enables abstraction, it helps to avoid getting lost in technological complexity and conflation. My argument is that in order to understand the wider societal implications of ICTs on privacy we need better conceptual knowledge about the basic functions of privacy as well as of the very mechanisms of information processing inherent to technology. While ICTs comprise numerous different technologies and applications, the mechanisms of information processing, and more precisely of identification, are largely similar in each case. Moreover, systems thinking plays an important role in ICT development, though in a rather technology-centered manner. Understanding these mechanisms and their implications on societal functions and processes is thus crucial in coming toward better ways of protecting privacy.

Self-organization and metasystem transition

As outlined previously, a system is mostly not static or mechanical but dynamic by nature and has emergent properties. Given these dynamics, a system and its properties can alter as it features a transformative capacity due to its relations and interactions. This transformative capacity is closely related to processes of self-organization,[2] i.e., transformation processes emerging within the system altering its structure and form of organization. Self-organization processes affect "the way evolutionary systems come into existence or change their structure, state or behaviour and the way they maintain themselves" (Hofkirchner 2013: 115). A system thus has no strictly determined, immutable order or organization but alters and transforms. These transformation patterns may have effects on the system itself as well as on its environment. For example, the introduction of a new technology affects existing user practices. The way users interact with the technology may have further societal impact, which then can affect the technology, e.g., by necessitating adaptations in design.

Considering its dynamics, a system can be seen as an evolutionary system, where relations between elements emerge which enable interactions that provide synergetic effects. This can lead to a self-reinforcing dynamic as certain relations begin to dominate their interaction (Hofkirchner 2013). This dynamic process thus has two basic properties: emergence and dominance, i.e., elements and interactions between these elements emerge, which then have effects on the state of the system. The interactions and processes within a system are not strictly deterministic but dynamic. Consequently, relations can emerge and also dominate an interaction process that may cause multiple effects (Fuchs and Hofkirchner 2005; Hofkirchner 2013). Similar dynamics exist in societal structures which emerge from the actions of individual actors (societal agents) but also affect them at the same time. In short, in social systems the individuals, who represent interacting agents at the micro level, generate social, cultural, economic and political structures, values, norms, organizations, institutions, technologies, processes, practices, etc., which then emerge at the macro level. These generated items can be subsumed under the term "socio-technical regime" (Kemp *et al.* 2001; Smith *et al.* 2005). The interactions between elements at the macro level can loop back to the micro level (Fuchs and Hofkirchner 2005). Figure 2.2 illustrates this interplay (inspired by Hofkirchner 2013).

This setting partially refers to Giddens' (1984) structuration theory, which assumes a dialectical interplay of agency and structure: social structures emerge from as well as result in social actions. Societal structures entail enabling and constraining effects which may have some influence on individual action, though not in a direct, causal sense.[3] Or in other words: there are governance structures resulting from regimes, which enable and constrain societal functions, policies, processes, practices, etc. Similar dynamics can be found in socio-technical

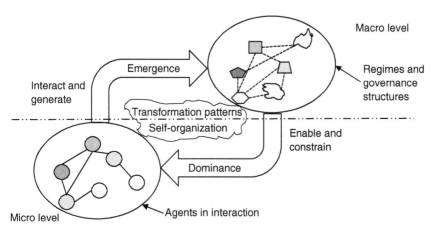

Figure 2.2 Model of systemic interplay between micro and macro level.

systems as the creation and use of a technology, e.g., involve organizations, structures, policies, formal and informal norms, individual practices, etc., which influence each other.

Self-organization processes and transformation patterns of an evolutionary system can be generally grasped by the concept of metasystem transition (MST) (Hofkirchner 2013). Physicist and cyberneticist Valentin Turchin (1977: 98) described MST as the "quantum of development", i.e., a common feature of development processes where incremental progress takes place resulting in more complex forms of organization. It leads to "a higher level of organization, the meta-level in relation to the level of subsystems being integrated" (Turchin 1977: 56). A simple example is the following:

> When a human being applies tool B to objects of a certain class A, this tool, together with objects A, forms a metasystem, in relation to subsystems A.... Thus, the appearance of a tool for working on certain objects that had not previously been worked on is a metasystem transition within the production system.
>
> (Turchin 1977: 93)

Processes akin to MST are observable in many different real-world phenomena. Besides evolutionary processes, such as the emergence of multicellular organisms, biological processes in animal and human development etc., Turchin (1977) outlined a number of examples such as the creation of language, cultural achievements as the production of metal tools, community building and social integration, the division of labor, and other economic and technological developments perceivable as metasystem transitions (Turchin 1977; Heylighen and Campbell 1995). His original approach is not without controversy because of its assumed higher order control system, which gives the misleading impression that a centralized metasystem would emerge with the ability to control other subsystems. However, this notion of control is not to be misinterpreted in that way but is meant instead in the sense of a more complex form of organization emerging where different (formerly less structured) elements build an integrative, structural or functional entity. Hence, MST addresses the emergence of new systemic properties with a more complex form of organization inherent to the dynamics of evolutionary systems (Hofkirchner 2013). It describes a process of three main stages (individuation, interaction, integration), where a higher level of organization, perceivable as a metasystem, occurs through increasing interactions between homogenous sub-systems (Turchin 1977; Heylighen and Campbell 1995; Fuchs and Hofkirchner 2005; Hofkirchner 2013). Figure 2.3 below illustrates the different transition stages of MST (author's representation, adapted from Hofkirchner 2013: 116ff.).

(1) The individual phase is characterized by various entities (or isolated, unrelated elements) that have no connections yet. In other words: there are different systems that are rather isolated from each other. Internal information processes within these systems are dominating this stage. (2) In the interaction phase,

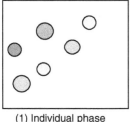 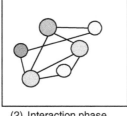 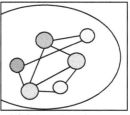

(1) Individual phase   (2) Interaction phase   (3) Integration phase

Figure 2.3 Main phases of a metasystem transition.

occasional relations between the different entities emerge as they interact with each other. Hence, individual systems are increasingly connected and in inter-action. These interactions are not stable and can change or diminish. Processes in this phase are less affected by path dependencies and are reversible. (3) In the third phase of integration, the interactions among the entities expand further, become more stable and the entities (sub-systems) become elements of the emerging system. Specialization occurs as a sub-system becomes adapted to the new structure, which alters its functionality. The changes taking place in this phase are not easily reversed as the established structure and organization of the system are stable and thus do not easily change. This does not mean, though, that the relations between the elements are not changeable at all. To the contrary, the system as a whole and its interactions remain highly dynamic (Hofkirchner 2013). Therefore, the integration phase is not to be misunderstood as the final development but rather as the occurrence of significant changes in the quality and organization of a system. Furthermore, these transition phases can recur at different organizational levels. Turchin (1977) called this the "stairway effect", where small transitions may induce larger transitions, such as the production of tools serving the production of further, more complex tools (ibid.: 89ff.).

Another example is a technology scaling up from its originating market niche and entering the regime level, e.g., becoming a product of widespread diffusion. This effect is thus related to economies of scale. In science and technology studies, a transition is often categorized by three interrelated levels, i.e., socio-technical niche, regime and landscape (Kemp *et al.* 2001; Geels 2004; Smith *et al.* 2005; Geels and Schot 2007). These levels can be seen as equivalents to micro level, macro level and system environment. Novel technologies, applica-tions, functions, etc. emerge in niches, which are limited domains, serving as sort of "incubation chambers" for novelties supported by a small group of actors to gain internal momentum. Niche developments are influenced by regimes, i.e., the cluster of existing technologies, organizations, knowledge, rules and norms, socio-technical practices, etc. The landscape represents the exogenous environ-ment where niches and regimes have no direct influence (Geels 2004; Geels and Schot 2007). Niches are rather isolated and have little or no interactions with other entities at the regime level. When a niche development gains momentum, its relations and interactions increase and it may become an integral part of the regime level. There, it may gain further momentum and have wider impacts on society, i.e., the landscape level. These dynamics at multiple levels are akin to an MST. Indeed, a three-stage model alone cannot fully grasp the vast complexity of real-world phenomena. Apparently, their settings and characteristics are not always easy to define, particularly if social systems are involved. Nevertheless, the MST perspective facilitates abstracting this complexity and allows the dynamics of systemic change along its three basic transition phases to be grasped. This is very useful to heuristically gain a simplified view on the dynamics of real-world phenomena from a wider perspective. On this basis, further, more detailed explorations can be conducted. In this respect, the analytical lens MST provides is particularly helpful in exploring socio-technical change, trends or transition paths.

Socio-technical transitions are transformation processes entailing wider changes in society or a societal sub-system. They are co-evolutionary, unfold within long timescales, involve multiple actors and include changes that encroach upon existing technology and user practices (Kemp *et al.* 2001; Geels 2004; Geels and Schot 2007). A system transition is thus not an isolated or deterministic process. It involves several transformation processes resulting from a complex interplay of actors, organizational and institutional contexts, markets, technologies and infrastructures (Kemp *et al.* 2001). Hence it has inherent systemic dynamics shaped by interactions between its different components, which entail network effects (Katz and Shapiro 1994). At the same time, path dependencies and technological lock-ins emerge (Arthur 1989). This benefits further diffusion of a technology but also exacerbates the emergence of alternatives to the prevailing socio-technical system and its related usage practices. The diffusion and usage of a technology thus have consequences for society: with increases in this, social practices and thus societal functions, processes and structures incrementally adapt to the technology. This is often not without friction and tensions between technology usage and social practices, societal functions, etc. can occur. Privacy issues are prominent examples of this. The next section explains how the interplay of privacy and identification alters with technology.

Why technology makes a difference

The outlined characteristics of a system underline that it is more than a set of elements triggering particular mechanisms with specific (determinable) effects. A system can serve multiple purposes also with multiple unintended side-effects. For instance, if an element of a system changes (e.g., due to an environmental impact), this can have effects on the system as a whole as well as on its environment.[4] When a socio-technical system emerges it becomes a (contextually embedded) part of societal reality which consequently has an impact on society. As a socio-technical system (and thus every technology) is a sub-system of society, the way it is implemented and used has effects on those societal processes, functions, practices, etc. that the system relates to and vice versa. There is thus a mutual process of co-shaping at different levels entailing transformation patterns. In general, a new technology can enable innovation, new strategies to solve existing problems and improvements of socio-technical settings, processes, functions, applications, practices, etc. But it can also constrain those existing items and practices, which can induce transformation patterns as societal actors try to cope with these challenges. For instance, mobile phones enabled mobile communications and permanent accessibility but constrained possibilities of solitude and being unavailable. The same dynamics occur in other socio-technical systems as well. In our case, the focus is on two vital societal concepts and functions and their very dynamics in relation to ICTs: privacy and (digital) identification. Put simply, ICTs enabled and reinforced the latter but led to constraints on the former.

To understand this more thoroughly, ICTs can be framed as socio-technical metasystem through the lens of an MST. This is vital to grasp the main socio-technical transition paths of ICTs and how they affect the interplay between privacy and identification. As will be shown, identification processes of various kinds are an integral part of ICTs. They altered with particular driving forces which affected technology design and usage practices (see Chapter 4). These developments and the identification mechanisms and practices involved constrain the effectiveness of privacy protection in many respects. A core argument of this book is that the processing of information related to an individual's identity is the main determinant of a (informational) privacy-affecting activity concerning this individual. In other words: the processing of identity information has an enabling effect for a privacy impact to emerge. This does not necessarily imply that privacy is permanently violated. But deeper understanding of this nexus between identity information and privacy is crucial for the assessment of the associated impacts.

From a systemic perspective, the interplay between privacy and identity in relation to ICTs can be grasped as follows: information processing is generally essential for the dynamics of a socio-technical system, which depends on the relations and interactions between its different elements (Fuchs and Hofkirchner 2005; Hofkirchner 2013). An evolutionary system has three (hierarchically) interrelated information-generating functions (Hofkirchner 2013: 184ff.): cognition, communication and cooperation. Cognition is "the individual, (internal) generation (and utilisation) of information by a system". Communication is "the interactional, interfacial generation (and utilisation) of information by (co-) systems". Cooperation is "the collective, external generation (and utilisation) of information by (co-)systems in conjunction" (ibid.). An interaction between two entities (or systems) requires initial processing of information (enabling the interaction). Information thus allows links between different systems to be established. Interaction may stimulate the generation of further information. Hence, an increasing degree of interactions and networking stimulates a growth in information processing. ICTs represent a multifunctional conglomerate of different socio-technical sub-systems, which is perceivable as an informational metasystem. The essence of the interactions and dynamics of this metasystem is the processing of (digital) information. The way information is processed (among various other societal impacts) affects the digital representation and availability of individual identities as well as identification practices. This has consequences for the functionality of privacy and data protection. In the scope of this book, identification is basically seen as form of (re-)cognition which enables further information generation and processing. Identity is framed as the informational representation of an individual (human) entity (A). Identification involves the processing of identity-related information by another entity (an individual or institution—system B). In its simplest form, there is a relation between the systems A and B, where B processes identity information representing A. As soon as a technology is involved, an additional entity C as an intermediary occurs, which creates additional relations and interactions. Figure 2.4 provides a simple illustration of this setting, which may be seen as an identification system where A, B and C are sub-systems.

Depending on the form of identification, the identity may be represented implicitly by the presence or actions of the individual person, or explicitly by some technological artifact (e.g., an ID card or an online user profile).[5] This simple illustration highlights the influence of technology on this setting: it transforms the relations and interactions in the system, which then alters its structure. It thus has an effect on the identification system as a whole. This is a standard setting in contexts of everyday life where identification occurs, and it is basically alike in analog and in digital contexts. However, given the peculiarities of ICTs, the consequences of digital identification are different than in analog (or offline) settings. ICTs enable digital identification partially decoupled from spatial and temporal limits: the additional, technical system (e.g., an online service) involved in the processing of an individual's identity information may have networking capabilities. Hence, the input to this system is the (digitized) identity information. To some extent, this information then represents the individual's digital identity. As this technical system is networked, this digital identity or parts of the information can be passed on to further socio-technical systems. Identity is naturally a relational concept, affected by relations and interactions with others. Hence, in this regard, the relations and interactions of the individual identity increase with the use of ICTs. To some

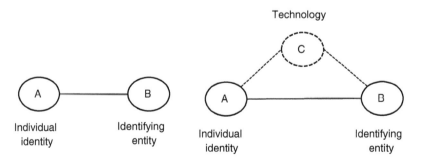

Figure 2.4 Simple identification system without and including a technical system.

extent, the digital identity gains a dynamic of its own as it can also be used decoupled from the individual it represents. A person can be identified by her digital information without being directly involved. Considering that ICTs incorporate manifold socio-technical systems and application contexts to process digital identity information, this network effect on digital identity is likely to amplify. Basically, all socio-technical systems (e.g., devices, applications, etc.) a person uses or interacts with, may involve the processing of information about her. This implies that some relations between those systems and the identity of this person exist. Although these relations are mostly context-dependent and not persistent, the generated information can be available for other purposes, decoupled from the original processing context. This has manifold societal implications and particularly on the individual's privacy as her information is being processed.

A further, related issue concerns the inherent connecting function of identification which enables a link between different entities to be established. The processing of identity-related information is assumed to be an essential process that contributes to the emergence of connections between socio-technical (sub-) systems. In social contexts, identification is commonly understood as revealing an individual's identity. This occurs in a formal sense where a person is prompted to show her passport etc. or in less formal contexts where a person introduces herself to others. However, understood in a broader sense, we can already speak of identification when particular information is being processed which refers or relates to an individual entity. In this regard, identification is a form of (re-)cognition. A basic premise here is that in order to establish a connection and/or relation between different entities, some form of (re-)cognition process, i.e., an exchange of information *about* the involved entities, is needed. This does not necessarily imply that the factual identity of an individual is completely revealed. For example, the process of recognizing a person passing by so that they are perceived as distinct from another involves some form of identifiable information (such as facial features or other bodily characteristics). In situations in the physical (or analog) world, where identification does not happen on purpose, and therefore no interaction emerges, this is mostly an unconscious process with limited impacts on privacy as this information diminishes and is not recorded (or made available by other means). In the digital world, though, the implications are different as identity information can be gathered and processed more easily. Furthermore, identification is often involved when different digital systems (or elements thereof) establish a connection and interact with each other. If one system (sender) interacts with, or transmits information to, a particular other, it initially needs some piece of specific information (such as an identifier) about this particular system. Otherwise, there is no defined receiver of this information.[6] This is in line with the classic sender–receiver model, as introduced by Shannon (1948), which had a significant impact on the development of information systems. The emergence of information as such, though, is far more complex than this classical reductionist notion suggests (Hofkirchner 2013). When human entities are (directly or indirectly) involved in an interaction between two or more information systems, the different forms of identification inherent to technology can have privacy consequences.

Also, privacy can be explained in systemic terms: (informational) privacy is seen here as a concept with an inherent boundary control function, which enables the individual to regulate her relations to and interactions with others. This implies informational self-determination (ISD) and individual control over her information (concerning her identity). From a wider perspective, ISD implies some autonomy and may be seen as a concept related to the self-organization of an individual (for more details see Chapter 3). Put simply, the boundary that is determined by privacy is the threshold between the private sphere of an individual identity and its (socio-technical) environment or public sphere. The basic function of privacy is to enable an individual person in regulating the extent to which her information crosses the boundaries of her private sphere. ICTs complicate this function as they enable and reinforce the processing of identity information and thus identification beyond the individual's control. But the transformations of identification and privacy are obviously not reducible to technological progress but result from a complex interplay of societal factors. Hence, ICTs amplified identification processes, but the usage contexts of these processes emerge from and are driven by the dynamics of societal practices.

Identification is basically a vital process for the functioning of society, serving various social, political and economic purposes. ICTs created new possibilities to implement and employ this process in various domains. ICTs inter alia stimulated a growth in electronic transactions and personalized online services in the public as well as private sectors. This amplified the processing of personal information. Consequently, identity management systems as well as the integration of identification mechanisms into online services increased, as prominently exemplified by Web 2.0 and social media. These developments led to a paradigm shift in the handling of personal information with an extension of identification in many respects (see Chapter 4). The enormous diffusion of ICTs with an associated broad availability of information about individuals stimulated a broad range of business models based on the commercialization of this information. This affected ISD as well as security and surveillance practices. Hence, in brief, the emergence of digital identification results from and is driven by technological development, and several political and economic interests located in regimes of the digital economy as well as of security and surveillance actors. Digital identification has an ambiguous function in relation to privacy: it can contribute to improving the security and efficiency of identity verifications, e.g., in electronic transactions or online services. In this regard, it contributes to regaining control over digital information. However, identification itself can be used as a mechanism to control the individual for economic as well as security purposes, which can lead to limitations of privacy.

These developments affect the privacy regime, which is constituted by governance practices, legal frameworks and policies with incorporated values and norms, social, political and economic practices, etc., as well as the conglomerate of public and private institutions, organizations and other entities processing personal information. To some extent, there are tensions between the privacy regime and those domains where identification is reinforced. This is particularly the case when identification is employed as a control mechanism at the cost of individual privacy. In this regard, there is an assumed control dilemma of digital identification as it attempts to regain control over digital information, which can lead to a further loss of control for the individual concerned (discussed in depth in Chapter 5). Or in other words: the socio-technical transition paths (of ICTs and digital identification) alter the requirements for privacy protection and reinforce the pressure on society to adapt to technology. To compensate for this loss of control and foster effectiveness of privacy protection requires additional control mechanisms for the individual as well as for the information processing institutions as part of the privacy regime. This includes demand for enhanced approaches for PIA (as discussed and presented in Chapters 6 and 7), which can also be vital for coming toward more effective PbD. As will be shown in subsequent parts of this book, identifiability, increasing through technology, is the core problem of contemporary privacy protection. Accordingly, there is need to develop appropriate strategies, concepts and measures to effectively tackle this risk. But this requires thorough knowledge about the basic concepts, meanings, roles and interplay of identity, identification and privacy. The next chapter examines these issues in depth, and highlights and discusses controversies which are central in the privacy discourse.

Notes

1 For example, an organizational unit may be seen as a sub-system of an enterprise. The departments of this unit may be seen as sub-systems thereof, determined and affected by the individuals working in these departments, etc. A simple technological example is a web browser, which may be seen as a (software) sub-system of a computer system.

2 Self-organization is the broader term of what Varela *et al.* (1974) termed "autopoiesis", i.e., the ability of all living systems to reorganize and reproduce.

3 For example, the organization of a company has formal and informal rules and structures, which have some impact on the behavior and actions of employees.

4 A drastic example is the nuclear disaster of Fukushima in 2011: an earth quake triggered a series of destructive effects on components of the power plant which led to a nuclear meltdown with accordingly critical environmental and societal consequences. Positive examples can be found, e.g., related to the emergence of the internet such as fostering free access to information worldwide at the individual as well as organizational and societal level.

5 For more details about the notions and functions of identity and identification see Chapter 3.

6 An exception is broadcasting, where information is distributed to a dispersed mass of entities. Even in this case, though, some kind of identifiable information related to the sender is involved (such as a unique frequency of a radio station or a TV channel, etc.).

References

All URLs were checked last on October 23, 2018.

Ackoff, R. L. (1971) Towards a System of Systems Concept. *Management Science*, 17(11): 661–671.

28 *A systemic perspective*

Arthur, B. W. (1989) Competing Technologies, Increasing Returns, and Lock-in by Historical Events. *Economic Journal*, 99: 116–131.

Bertalanffy, L. (1950) An Outline of General System Theory. *The British Journal for the Philosophy of Science*, 1(2): 134–165.

Bertalanffy, L. (1969) *General System Theory: Foundations, development, applications.* Revised edition, New York: George Braziller. 18th Paperback Printing 2015.

Bertalanffy, L. (1972) The History and Status of General Systems Theory. In Klir, G. (ed.), *Trends in General Systems Theory.* New York: Wiley, 21–41; reprinted in *Academy of Management Journal*, 15(4): 407–426.

Featherston, C. R. and Doolan, M. (2012) A Critical Review of the Criticisms of System Dynamics. In Husemann, E. and Lane, D. (eds.), *Proceedings of the 30th International Conference of the System Dynamics Society*, July 22–26, 2012, St Gallen, Switzerland, 1–13.

Fuchs, C. and Hofkirchner, W. (2005) The Dialectic of Bottom-up and Top-down Emergence in Social Systems. *TripleC*, 3(2): 28–50.

Geels, F. W. (2004) Understanding System Innovations: A critical literature review and a conceptual synthesis. In Elzen, B., Geels, F. W. and Green, K. (eds.), *System Innovation and the Transition to Sustainability: Theory, evidence and policy.* Cheltenham, UK/Northampton: Edward Elgar, 19–47.

Geels, F. W. and Schot, J. (2007) Typology of Sociotechnical Transition Pathways. *Research Policy*, 36: 399–417.

Giddens, A. (1984) *The Constitution of Society. Outline of the theory of structuration.* Cambridge: Polity Press.

Heylighen, F. and Campbell, D. (1995) Selection of Organization at the Social Level: Obstacles and facilitators of metasystem transitions. *World Futures: The Journal of General Evolution*, 45(1–4): 181–212.

Hofkirchner, W. (2013) *Emergent Information: A unified theory of information framework.* World Scientific Series in Information Studies: Vol. 3. London: World Scientific Publishing Co.

Hofkirchner, W. and Schafranek, M. (2011) General System Theory. In Hooker, C. (ed.), *The Philosophy of Complex Systems.* Series: Handbook of the Philosophy of Science Vol. 10. North Holland, Oxford: Elsevier, 177–194.

Hoos, I. (1972) *Systems Analysis in Public Policy: A critique.* Berkeley: University of California Press.

Hughes, A. C. and Hughes, T. P. (2000) *Systems, Experts, and Computers: The systems approach in management and engineering, World War II and after.* Cambridge MA: MIT Press.

Katz, M. L. and Shapiro, C. (1994) Systems Competition and Network Effects. *Journal of Economic Perspectives*, 8(2): 93–115. http://socrates.berkeley.edu/~scotch/katz_shapiro.pdf.

Kemp, R., Rip, A. and Schot, J. (2001) Constructing Transition Paths through the Management of Niches. In Garud, R. and Karnoe, P. (eds.), *Path Dependence and Creation.* Mahwa/London: Lawrence Erlbaum, 269–299.

Laszlo, A. and Krippner, S. (1998) Systems Theories: Their origins, foundations, and development. In Jordan, J. S. (ed.), *Systems Theories and a Priori Aspects of Perception. Advances in psychology 126.* Amsterdam: Elsevier Science, 47–74. doi.org/10.1016/S0166-4115(98)80017-4.

Luhmann, N. (1991) *Soziale Systeme. Grundriß einer allgemeinen Theorie.* 4. Auflage (Erste Auflage 1984). Frankfurt: Suhrkamp Taschenbuch Wissenschaft.

Parsons, T. (1991) *The Social System.* New edition (2005), first published 1991 (first edition 1951), Sociology Classics. London: Routledge.

Shannon, C. E. (1948) A Mathematical Theory of Communication. *The Bell System Technical Journal*, 27(4): 623–656. http://math.harvard.edu/~ctm/home/text/others/shannon/entropy/entropy.pdf.

Smith, A., Sterling, A. and Berkhout, F. (2005) The Governance of Sustainable Sociotechnical Transitions. *Research Policy*, 34(10): 1491–1510.

Turchin, V. F. (1977) *The Phenomenon of Science: A cybernetic approach to human evolution.* New York: Columbia University Press.

Varela, F., Maturana, H. and Uribe, R. (1974) Autopoiesis: The organization of living systems, its characterization, and a model. *Biosystems*, 5(4): 187–196.

Wiener, N. (1954) *The Human Use of Human Beings: Cybernetics and society.* (First published 1950, reprint of revised edition of 1954). Boston: Da Capo Press.

3   The interplay between identity, identification and privacy

Privacy and identity are intrinsically related concepts. In general, this interplay is rather obvious because privacy concerns the private life of the individual. Intrusions into an individual's privacy affect her identity and, consequently, protecting privacy embraces the protection of an individual's identity. Therefore, privacy and data protection laws address personal data in particular, mostly understood as information related to the identity of a person. The processing of this information is a form of identification. Identification is commonly known as the process of determining who a particular person is. It is an important societal process ranging from personal and professional relationships, service provision in public and private sectors (e.g., citizen–government as well as business–customer relationships) and so forth. But forms of identification are also involved in profiling, security and surveillance practices. Irrespective of the function it fulfills, identification is an information process. This is particularly important because ICTs affect identification in many respects and basically transform the modalities of this information process. Today, ICTs are nearly ubiquitous technical tools which informationally enrich our identities so that they are digitally available. Digital (or electronic) identification has become a standard procedure in many domains.[1] This has serious implications for the protection of privacy. In order to explore these implications, it is necessary to first shed light on the interplay between identity and privacy. Thus, initially, this chapter presents and discusses the basic notions and functions of identity and identification. Then, the role and meaning of privacy are outlined; including a brief overview on legal issues and data protection principles. This is followed by a presentation of a core function of privacy, i.e., to control and regulate the boundary between the private and the public spheres. This includes an exploration of the interrelations between identity, privacy and autonomy with a focus on the crucial concept of informational self-determination (ISD). Finally, relevant controversies of the privacy discourse are discussed, in particular between privacy and the concepts of security and transparency.

What is identity?

Identity and identification are multifaceted phenomena. A number of philosophers have dealt with personal identity as the substance matter of existence, literally ranging from birth to death (Korfmacher 2006). The question "What is identity?" is not a trivial one and is an issue of concern for many disciplines (ranging from anthropology, computer and information sciences, gender studies, history, legal studies, neurology, philosophy, psychology, sociology, etc.). Hence, obviously, there is no simple, meaningful answer to this question as identity means different things in different disciplines and taking all these issues into consideration is far beyond the scope of this book. Nevertheless, there are some important common features across all disciplines. Above all, identity comprises information representing a particular individual entity. Throughout this book, identity primarily means personal or individual identity, hence, the identity of an individual person. Identity is basically understood as the very concept describing and representing the specific characteristics of an individual. The exact nature of identity is of less concern here, but more relevant is how identity is represented by (digital) information in socio-technical contexts.

At a general level, identity is represented by a number of individual characteristics that refer to a person. In social interactions of everyday life, the most common identity attribute is the name of a person. Identity is unique in the way that it allows one person or entity to be distinguished from another. In this respect, identity is the construct of a set of properties that determines the uniqueness of a particular entity in relation to others.[2] Personal identity may be seen as "sameness of a same person in different moments in time" (Rundle *et al.* 2008: 7). For Wiener (1954: 96) homeostasis (i.e., the self-regulatory capacity of a biological system) is "the touchstone of our personal identity", which implies a permanent interaction with its environment. In a similar vein, Varela (1997: 76ff.) described the identity of living systems as an "autopoietic unity" with the capability to maintain itself, making it distinct from its environment. At the same time, it maintains its relations with its environment, which are vital for its existence. In this regard, identity can be seen as a construct that maintains itself, distinct from others, but at the same time it is shaped by every interaction with its surroundings. Thus, identity is continually progressing, based on the dynamics of its relations and interactions. This process is also a physical feature of biological systems: for Varela (1997: 73), "living identities are produced by some manner of closure, but what is produced is an emerging interactive level." This dynamic is observed in societal contexts as well: Giddens (1991) argues that a person's identity is coupled with her biography, which continually evolves. Hence:

> [I]dentity is not to be found in behaviour, nor—important though this is—in the reactions of others, but in the capacity to keep a particular narrative going. The individual's biography, if she is to maintain regular interaction with others in the day-to-day world, cannot be wholly fictive. It must continually integrate events which occur in the external world, and sort them into the ongoing "story" about the self.

> (Giddens 1991: 54)

Similarly, Paul Ricoeur (1992) highlights aspects of continuity and change whereby he distinguishes between two meanings of identity: *idem* and *ipse*. The Latin word "*idem*" means "same" and refers to the physical characteristics for which "permanence in time constitutes the highest order" (Ricoeur 1992: 2). With "*ipse*" or "selfhood", Ricoeur means the part of identity that is dynamic and changeable through one's lifetime. In this regard, identity is dialectical as it comprises both sameness and selfhood. Similarly to Giddens, he also pointed out that identity is narrative (Ricoeur 1992: 147f.), i.e., that identity is partially constructed and determined by the relations to its environments it interacts with. Hence, the different notions of identity share an important commonality: identity is understood as a concept with permanent or stable as well as dynamic features. Or in other words: identity is a permanent as well as a dynamic concept. Given its dynamic character, identity is thus not reducible to the sum of its (informational) parts. Nevertheless, a certain set of attributes can be sufficient to uniquely identify an individual in a particular context. In this regard, identity entails unique information to allow for recognition of an entity at a certain point in space and time.

Identity features a number of different, intertwined properties (Rundle *et al.* 2008; Pfitzmann and Hansen 2010; Whitley *et al.* 2014), which can be briefly summarized as follows. Identity is:

- social: humans are social beings; and for their interactions, they need a certain foundation for the recognition of a person, referring to an identity
- subjective: the notion of identity differs from person to person and is thus subjective as is the interpretation of the attributes linked to a person. One (partial) identity can have different (subjective) meanings in different contexts
- valuable: identity offers some certainty and confidence between interacting individuals, enables the creation of relationships, and can be functional in enabling transactions
- referential: the items, artifacts and/or the information used for identification links back to an individual (or more generally an entity). An "identity is not a person" but "a reference to a person" (Rundle *et al.* 2008: 26)
- composite: identity information can consist of many different sources also without the involvement of the individual concerned
- consequential: identity information provides manifold insights into personal details, actions and behavior. Unintended or unaware provision as well as disclosure of this information thus have consequences and can be harmful
- dynamic: identity is not a static concept but changes over time
- contextual: identity is not universal but is context-dependent. A person can have different identities in different contexts and separating them contributes to privacy and autonomy
- equivocal: "The process of identification is inherently error-prone" (Rundle *et al.* 2008: 26), because there can be, e.g., duplicate identity information; the information can be wrong or incorrect; or this information can be misused in different contexts etc.

The role identity plays in society results from many different but intertwined dimensions (such as cultural, economic, legal, organizational, political, psychological, social, technological, etc.). Individual people have various functions in social, economic and political domains with roles such as citizens, employees, customers and consumers, partners, members, etc. (Raab 2009). Judith Butler (2006) speaks of "identity performance" and deals with the dynamics of identity by understanding it as a performative concept, meaning that identity is socially constructed. For Whitley *et al.* (2014: 19) personal identity is a "practice-based, relational and dynamic" concept. They further state that "identity is produced and reproduced through ongoing communicative activities that take place within and across people and organisations" (ibid.). David Lyon (2009: 10) argues that identity is "a composite and malleable entity, with some elements derived from the corporeal person and others from categories or collectivities in which they fit". These categories are created and vary from the broad range of usage contexts in which identity is embedded such as social and organizational practices, political systems, commercial applications, etc. Depending on the usage and implementation of technological identity artifacts, identity may convey particular values and is related to policy and regulation (such as privacy and data protection). Hence, in a broader sense, identity can be seen as a socio-technical co-construct, shaped by a number of interrelated factors such as social, economic, political and technological dimensions and embedded issues (e.g., artifacts, cultural meaning, infrastructure, knowledge, markets, policy and regulation) as Figure 3.1 below illustrates.

During her lifetime, a person is represented by a magnitude of information in multiple different socio-technical contexts in which this information is gathered, collected, processed, stored, etc. Although there are basic types of information representing an identity (such as a name), identity is not merely composed of a

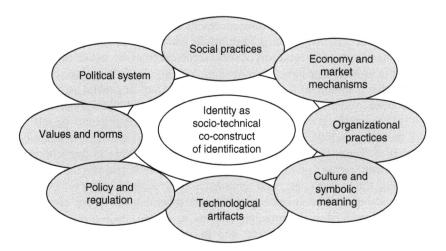

Figure 3.1 Socio-technical determinants of identity construction.

core set of information. Given its dynamics, identity emerges and develops further, depending of the interactions with its (e.g., social, economic, political, technical) environment. Referring to Varela, Hildebrandt (2006: 54) states that "the most interesting thing about human nature is its indeterminacy and the vast possibilities this implies: our non-essentialist essence is that we are correlatable humans before being correlated data subjects". Therefore, "[w]hatever our profile predicts about our future, a radical unpredictability remains that constitutes the core of our identity" (ibid.). This core of identity consists of continuity as well as change and is a basic building block of individual freedom. As essentially a dynamic concept, "there is no such thing as 'the identity'" (Pfitzmann and Hansen 2010: 30). This means that an individual is not represented by a universal identity but can have multiple, partial identities (or roles) in different contexts. Identity is thus context-sensitive as it is a "representation of an entity in the form of one or more attributes that allow the entity or entities to be sufficiently distinguished within context" (ITU 2010: 4).

What is identification?

As shown, identity is a complex, dynamic concept with multiple features and dimensions. A central function of identity in society is to provide a means to determine or ascertain who a particular person is. Knowledge about a person's identity contributes, e.g., to the building of trust and security among interaction partners in social, political or economic contexts (such as commercial transactions). This process of determining or recognizing an individual by her contextual characteristics is identification (ITU 2010: 3). An individual human person can be subject to identification, but so can basically every object or any kind of entity.

Identification has an essential feature which determines its significance: it has an inherent connecting function as it enables a link between different entities to be established. This connecting function results from the ability of identities to "build and articulate ties to other identities in network-domains" (White 2008: 2). Identification is an integral part of socio-technical contexts, which can be categorized in at least four basic (overlapping) domains. (1) In the social domain, identification is important for interpersonal relationships in general as it fits the societal need to communicate and interact with each other, building relationships etc. (2) In the political domain, identification enables citizenship and the related rights that allow individuals to engage in the political system. But it is also used to govern or control the rights and duties of individuals. (3) In the economic domain, identification is related to the provision of public and private services, conducting transactions, etc. and contributes to procedural security. (4) The technological domain serves as a vehicle for the other domains. Here, identification is implemented in information systems to enable socio-technical interactions, information exchange, etc. and to support the other domains with technological means. These domains are basically included when speaking of socio-technical contexts in this book.

Hence, identification of individuals is a practice of everyday life and a basic instrument of governance, serving a variety of functions across all societal domains with a long history and obvious relevance for the functioning of society, polity and the economy (Clarke 1994a/1994b; Bennett and Lyon 2008; Lyon 2009; Whitley *et al.* 2014). Besides ancient forms of identification, the genesis of the modern state in Europe paved the way for the identification of citizens (such as in contact with public administration, at national borders, etc.). Among other scholars, David Lyon (2009) provides an overview on historical developments of identification. Early approaches of administrative schemes for purposes of authentication and identification of individuals date back to the mid-1500s. Some people had to wear special badges or insignia to prove legitimacy of their activities, such as pilgrims, couriers or diplomats. For example, couriers carried particular signs when submitting a message. Identity badges were also used to mark minority groups such as homeless people, ethnic minorities or immigrants. The emergence of citizenship and citizen registration after the French Revolution contributed to the employment of identity documents such as passports, which became increasingly common in many countries by the twentieth century (Lyon 2009: 20ff.). Hence the identification and registration of people have a long tradition and are core functions of government and public administration worldwide. Governments have complex administrative infrastructures to provide official identity devices to their citizens (such as birth certificates, passports, driving licenses, social security cards, particular citizen ID card schemes, etc.). In most national states, citizens are initially equipped with a legal identity, which begins with the enrolment of a birth certificate. This then serves as a basic credential to receive further identity documents. ID documents prove one's legal identity and enable citizenship, including the associated rights and responsibilities to be involved in the functioning of society. Besides its relevance for administrative procedures, identification is also an important means of criminal investigation, law enforcement, and national and international security. Basically, individuals become identified in many socio-technical domains and contexts: identification serves as a mechanism to establish a certain amount of trust in social interactions between individuals, groups or institutions, among interacting business partners, customers and vendors in commercial transactions, customer relationship management, etc. Different forms of identification enable access to a broad scope of services in public and private sectors (e.g., in the fields of e-government, e-health, e-commerce and e-business, etc.), implemented and amplified by the use of ICTs (Lyon 2003, 2009; Raab 2006; Bennett and Lyon 2008; Hildebrandt and Gutwirth 2008; Aichholzer and Strauß 2010; Kubicek and Noack 2010; Whitley *et al.* 2014).

In general, a crucial aim of identification in socio-technical contexts is to reduce uncertainty and to improve security, e.g., of applications, individuals, organizations, processes, systems, etc. (Clarke 1994a; Bennett and Lyon 2008; White 2008; Lyon 2009; Raab 2009; Kubicek and Noack 2010; Strauß 2011; Whitley *et al.* 2014). In this regard, identity is also linked to control efforts, as White (2008: 1) points out:

An identity emerges for each of us only out of efforts at control amid contingencies and contentions in interaction. These control efforts need not have anything to do with domination over other identities. Before anything else, control is about finding footings among other identities. Such footing is a position that entails a stance, which brings orientation in relation to other identities.

With footing, White means that identity has a certain foundation which makes it unique, tangible and controllable. More precisely, this foundation consists of a certain piece of (identifiable) information that allows recognizing an individual based on its characteristics, distinct from others. This identity (or identifiable) information represents an individual entity in a particular context. Thus, a necessary condition of identification is the existence of a certain amount of information serving as (informational) representation of an identity.

As information is a necessary condition for this recognition process, identification can be defined as the processing of information related or referring to the identity of a particular individual. As Figure 3.2 illustrates, in its broadest sense, identification implies that (at least) two entities interact, where identity information is exchanged: the to-be-identified entity (A) interacts with the identifying entity (B), which processes the identity information representing entity A. In social interactions between two human entities, this process is usually bidirectional, meaning that entities A and B switch roles as B also becomes identified. In socio-technical systems, though, individuals often become identified in a unidirectional way by, e.g., institutional or organizational entities during usage of a technology.

As identification is a mechanism with at least two entities involved, the technical processing of identity information links at least two systems. Consequently, the control over the identification process and, therefore, over the identity information is not merely a matter of a single entity but of multiple entities. As will be shown, this has an impact on the protection of this information and thus on the privacy of the identified individual. It also makes a difference whether a person proactively reveals her identity, or is identified without being directly involved in the identification process.

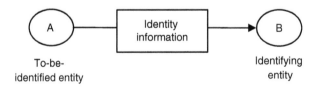

Figure 3.2 Simple unidirectional identification process.

Various approaches and modalities of identification

There are several types of identity information being used for identification with various approaches to categorize them. Clarke (1994a) described the following basic categories of identification:

- names
- biometrics, including appearance, i.e., how the person looks (e.g., gender, height, weight, color of eyes, hair color etc.), including bodily and physical characteristics; what the person is (e.g., biometric features such as finger-print, iris pattern, DNA, etc.); what the person has (such as glasses, tattoos, piercings, or any other additional bodily feature); and bio-dynamics and behavior, i.e., what the person does or how she interacts (e.g., pattern of handwritten signature, voice pattern, movement patterns, style of speech etc.)
- codes and schemes—how the person is represented (e.g., by an identification number such as a passport no., social security no. and so on)
- knowledge—what the person knows (e.g., a password or a PIN code, i.e., a personal identification number etc.)
- tokens—what the person has (e.g., an ID document such as a birth certificate, passport, or any other identity device).

Gary Marx (2001) suggests a partially different categorization and speaks of different types of information usable for identification as "identity knowledge". This is, for instance: legal name; information about temporal and spatial location ("locatability") such as address; pseudonyms used in combination with the other two, i.e., an identifier such as phone number, social security number, etc.; pseudonyms not relatable to other types and thus providing anonymity; and pattern knowledge, i.e., information referring to the distinctive appearance or behavioral patterns of a person (Marx 2001). Moreover, identification usually involves social categorization with categories such as activities, age, class, employment status, gender, health status, memberships, nationality, profession, relationships, religion, sexual orientation, etc. Additional categories may comprise consumer habits, credit scores, financial status, individual preferences, life-style and so on (Marx 2001; Raab 2009). In privacy contexts and standards for information security, identity information is labeled personal data or personally identifiable information (PII) (for a detailed discussion on identity information and a general typology see Chapter 7).

The various categorizations suggest that there is no clear-cut answer to the question of exactly what types of attributes refer to an identity, neither can there be an exhaustive, comprehensive list of such attributes. This has several reasons and a specific reason lies in the complex relation between identity and time. On the one hand, identity is permanent and uniquely represents an entity in contrast to others. On the other hand, identity is constructed and context-specific with a highly dynamic momentum. In other words: identity is not static but it evolves over time (Abelson and Lessig 1998; Pfitzmann and Borcea-Pfitzmann 2010).

Thus, the representation of an "identity as a set of attribute values valid at a particular time can stay the same or grow, but never shrink" (Pfitzmann and Borcea-Pfitzmann 2010: 3). While some attributes may remain steady (such as birth name, date of birth); others may change over time (e.g., weight, hair color, address, etc.). Therefore, attributes remaining relatively constant over a longer period of time are basically more suitable for identification than dynamic ones. Hence, generally speaking, it is neither possible nor necessary for identification to have a large, complete set of identity attributes: depending on the application context, it is sufficient to have a certain amount of information that represents the uniqueness of a person in a certain context. The uniqueness of one or more attributes must not be without limits but be context-sensitive and only valid in a certain time frame. Therefore, different identity information is mostly combined, depending on the purpose of identification and the corresponding security requirements. A combined set of identity attributes can lower the risk of errors or insufficient identification, e.g., resulting from duplicates. For instance, typical attributes like name or date of birth alone cannot be expected to be unique because there can be more people with the same attributes. But a combination with additional information such as the home address, representing the location of an individual, is often sufficient for unique identification. In general, whether a person is uniquely identifiable (without ambiguity) or not depends on the environment of that person. In a crowd of 100 people, for example, hair color is very likely to be insufficient for identification. In combination with eye color and name, the likelihood for identification increases as ambiguity is likely to decrease with the number of attributes.[3] Or in other words: a combined set of identity attributes enables a distinct pattern related to a particular person to be drawn. Thus, basically, identification implies the recognition of a unique pattern that allows one entity to be distinguished from another (Rundle *et al.* 2008; ITU 2010). Once an applicable pattern is found it can be represented by or transformed into a code (e.g., digits, characters or both)—typically an identifier—which then can be used to link to a set of different identity attributes. An identifier facilitates identification (as it refers to a collection of attributes) and it also allows cross-linking of data over different contexts. In practice, code schemes are commonly used as an implicit component of most forms of identification.

As regards the modality of identification, there are two basic approaches. (1) Knowledge-based identification makes use of information that a person is expected to know for identity verification. This type is widespread and most common as a combination of username and password, or PIN codes. (2) Token-based identification is based on an ID device as identity proof and is well known in everyday life in the form of ATM[4] cards, debit cards, passports, social security cards, etc. as well as of mobile phones. In general, the combination of knowledge and possession of a token usually provides a higher level of security than approaches without a physical device (though obviously depending on the quality of the implementation). These general approaches are also known as multi-factor authentication, which is often used as a method for (computerized) access control or as a security measure for transactions (such as in e-banking systems). Another common distinction is between the categories of knowledge (what one knows; e.g., a password), possession (what one has; e.g., an identity document), and inherence (what one is; e.g., biometric information such as a fingerprint) (Clarke 1994a; De Cristofaro *et al.* 2014).

Different qualities of identification

Irrespective of these categories, identification requires the representation of identity information, either directly by the person or by some kind of object. In social, interpersonal relationships, identification is often an implicit process. For instance, a person that is already known does not need to be explicitly identified because her physical presence alone may be sufficient as well as the knowledge of her name (frequently used as a typical identifier). But besides that, identification mostly requires some kind of artifact (such as an identity token, device, scheme or credential), which determines the form of identity representation. An ID artifact serves as a means to recognize a person and/or entity by providing information to ascertain who one is, i.e., as tool of identification.

Depending on the application context, an ID device can be formal or informal. Typical formal identity artifacts (or schemes) are, e.g., identity documents like a passport, driver's license, social security card, etc.; less formal are typical user profiles based on credentials (e.g., username and password) such as in computer applications or information systems. Therefore, technical definitions often describe identity as a "collection of attributes", "collection of claims" (Cameron 2005; Rundle *et al.* 2008) or "a set of attribute values related to one and the same data subject" (e.g., Pfitzmann and Borcea-Pfitzmann 2010: 3). Identity attributes and/or identity information can serve as identifiers. In information systems, identity information is mostly associated with one or more (unique) identifiers. An identifier is information referring to a certain identity's collection of attributes or claims (Rundle *et al.* 2008; ITU 2010). A unique identifier allows distinguishing one set of identity attributes from another, at least in a particular context (such as a telephone, passport or a user-ID number, etc.). If identity information is represented by digital means, we can speak of *digital identity*. Thus, identity can be understood as a concept of the "real world" as well as a (digital) artifact representing an individual entity.[5] Technical definitions see it as "a digital representation of a set of claims made by one party about itself or another data subject" (Rundle *et al.* 2008: 7). Similar is Cameron (2005), who notes that claims are expressions of identity attributes. Claims typically include information referring to the identity of an individual (e.g., "My name is John Doe"), but it can be sufficient to have information that qualifies a person for a specific action, such as a certain age ("I am over 18 years old") which may allow casting a vote in official elections, or driving a car, etc. In practice, identity verification and authentication are often combined. For example, border control verifies the identity of person as well as the (implicit) claim to have a certain nationality etc. This process of verifying a claim, i.e., that particular information referring to an entity is valid in a particular context, is understood as authentication (Rundle *et al.* 2008; ITU 2010).

Identification can have different qualities and a basic distinction can be made between "hard" and "soft" identification: the former means the explicit processing of identity information to prove the identity of a particular person and know exactly who that person is (e.g., by providing an ID document, ID card etc.). The latter means that a person provides some information related to her but she is not requested to prove her real identity. Hard identification is usually requested for transactions with a legal relevance where a public or private authority (e.g., a company, a government institution) is involved. This form is the main issue, e.g., in official procedures of government and public administration as well as commercial transactions (such as requesting a public service or conducting a financial transaction). Soft identification occurs, for example, in online services, social media and similar applications that typically require a registered user account or profile but not necessarily proof of one's real identity. In practice, the boundary between these types is mostly fluid. Given the growing amount of identifiable information being processed in digital environments and sociotechnical systems, possibilities for hard identification are likely to expand (the emergence of digital identification is explored in Chapter 4). In the same application context, many different forms of identifiable information can be processed (e.g., in social media platforms). Furthermore, soft identification can easily become hard identification due to the aggregation or linkage of different information sets related to a person (e.g., by linking a person's username with her date of birth and address, or further information). A further aspect concerns the modality of identification. In general, an individual can be confronted with identification in different ways:

1   as a voluntary act based on an informed decision or as an act of an accepted social norm, i.e., the person reveals her identity or provides personal information (e.g., in a social interaction) because she wants to or finds it appropriate
2   as a mandatory, intentional act based on a legal requirement (e.g., providing a passport at a national border, requesting a public service, agreeing a contract etc.)
3   as a mandatory act without choice or with negative consequences, e.g., a person is enforced to reveal her identity or becomes identified by law enforcement or other authorities
4   as a non-mandatory act but with limited choice, i.e., a quasi-obligation, e.g., the provision of personal information is requested to access a service
5   as an involuntary and unknown process that happens without the consent and knowledge of the individual concerned, such as an illegal action or the further processing of identity information by third parties.

Each mode can be problematic in terms of privacy protection but the latter, i.e., being identified without even noticing it, is particularly critical as it precludes the individual concerned from taking action against unwanted identification. Moreover, technology can lead to various overlaps between these modes. Indeed, there are numerous legitimate purposes of identification where the individual is aware of being identified in a particular context for a particular purpose (for example, a traveler crossing a border proves her identity with a passport, an applicant provides personal information to gain entitlement to benefits, or a driver's license is requested when buying a car). However, identification is neither adequate nor necessary in every context. As revealing one's identity can be a sensitive process, anonymity used to be the standard case in most contexts of everyday life. Technology usage, though, challenges anonymity in many respects.

Identification is commonly expected to involve particular, aware action of the individual concerned (such as showing an ID or providing identity information). However, as outlined, this is not necessarily the case as a person can also become identified without her direct involvement. An example of direct identification is a situation where a person is requested to enter her username and password; an example of indirect identification is where identity information is gathered and processed automatically (e.g., by being observed through a video camera, or being identified based on technology usage, such as via an internet protocol (IP) address in a computer network). Thus, as regards the knowledge or awareness of the identified individual, a further distinction can be made between explicit and implicit identification: in cases of the former, a person is, e.g., prompted to provide identifiable information and is aware of that; in cases of the latter, a person is not aware of being identified or identifiable from information concerning her. Profiling and surveillance activities are particular examples of the latter, and these are discussed in Chapter 5.

Anonymity, pseudonymity and identifiability

Today, identification procedures are widespread in many different contexts; and, as will be shown, there are several tendencies for further growth in different forms of identification. Reasons for this growth are manifold. For instance, Clarke (1994a) claims that institutions growing in size and structure, decreasing trust between individuals and organizations, as well as increasing forms of long-term economic relationships (i.e., customer loyalty and/or customer relationship management) contribute to increasing identification. Clarke argues that these developments stimulated a widespread presumption among many organizations: that identifying a person would be necessary in most cases to conduct transactions (ibid.). From a wider perspective, in line with the connecting function of identification, a further explanation is that globalization and increasing networking structures are likely to foster identification as an increasing number of entities interact with each other. Particularly in distant communications and interactions, a certain demand to identify individuals as well as institutions is plausible, which is one reason for the expansion of digital identification (as explored further in Chapter 4).

Nevertheless, there are a many contexts in everyday life where identification and knowledge about an individual's real identity is not needed at all. Therefore, being anonymous (and thus not identified) used to be a standard mode in many societal contexts. Anonymity is particularly crucial for the protection of privacy and other fundamental human rights such as freedom of expression. Put simply, anonymity means to be not identifiable. Or in other words: anonymity is the absence of identifiability. It is a common part of everyday life and, in many cases, individuals usually remain anonymous in pursuing their activities in their private sphere as well as in the public sphere. Anonymity is an essential concept for the functioning of democracy: secrecy of the ballot and anonymous elections ensure that citizens can freely and anonymously decide to whom they give their vote; sensitive professional groups such as diplomats, journalists, lawyers, medical doctors, police officers, politicians, researchers, security agents, etc. all have certain situations where anonymity is crucial for exercising their professions; insiders, informants and whistleblowers need some degree of anonymity to inform the public about eventual scandals, human rights abuses, illegal actions, etc.; and without anonymity, individuals living in authoritarian regimes are in permanent danger of being persecuted.

In the case of criminal activity, anonymity can also be problematic, which is one reason why law enforcement and security authorities aim to extend privacy-intrusive security and surveillance measures. Indeed, in various contexts, there are many plausible reasons for hard or formal identification. But this does not imply that anonymity is problematic. On the contrary, anonymity is fundamental for privacy and for democracy. Moreover, anonymity does not necessarily imply the absence of any form of authentication. In fact, authentication is basically possible without identification, in digital environments, too (Chaum 1985; Clarke 1994a; Pfitzmann and Hansen 2010). In many transactions it is sufficient to (implicitly or explicitly) have plausibility about the individual's qualification or ability to, e.g., conduct a transaction, request a service, etc. without the need to reveal one's real identity. For instance, simple commercial transactions such as the buying of a good or service may not require any knowledge about an individual as long as a good is delivered and paid for in exchange. Therefore, anonymity in typical commercial transactions with cash payment is usually unproblematic. Some transactions may require age verification but also in these cases it is not per se necessary to know exactly who a person is. Depending on the context, it may be sufficient to know, e.g., their state of solvency or whether a person is underage or not.

Basically, the real identity of a person is often less relevant than a specific attribute in a transaction or interaction. In practice, though, identification and authentication are mostly combined or mixed up and are often difficult to distinguish. As a consequence, more identity information than may be necessary in a particular context is often being processed (Chaum 1985; Nauman and Hobgen 2009; Pfitzmann and Hansen 2010; Strauß 2011; De Andrade *et al.* 2013; Danezis *et al.* 2014). This can have many different (intended as well as unintended) reasons. Leaving reasons aside here, an important factor why face-to-face transactions may be easier to conduct anonymously than digital transactions concerns uncertainty.

As outlined, identification and authentication are used mostly to reduce a certain degree of uncertainty. In economic terms this is particularly relevant to reducing eventual risks when, e.g., a transaction does not succeed as intended (for example when a client does not pay etc.). This is also a matter of trust and confidence among the interacting parties. Not knowing a transaction partner can trigger uncertainty, e.g., about who is responsible in case of failure, fraud etc. Transactions, where the exchange of goods or services and payment are conducted instantly (e.g., paying cash in a store), may not require identification as there is usually no uncertainty in this regard. Put simply, without payment, the good is not handed over. The instant character of a transaction can be help in reducing uncertainty about its successful operation. Hence, the space and time of a transaction (or more generally of an interaction) may affect the need for identification among the interacting parties. In face-to-face transactions, for example, identification happens implicitly (e.g., by recognizing a person's appearance) and (if not recorded) identifiable information diminishes at the end of the transaction. A further aspect is that this setting is usually less complex in analog environments, where no technology is involved, compared to digital environments, where one or more additional entities are included.

In digital environments, the achievement of anonymity is not trivial. In a technical sense, anonymity can be seen as a "situation where an entity cannot be identified within a set of entities" (ITU 2010: 2). To enable anonymity of an individual entity compared to others requires that the identity attributes of this entity are non-distinct from others (Pfitzmann and Hansen 2010). Information is anonymous when all items are removed which could identify the person concerned and none of the remaining information is sufficient to re-identity that person (Pfitzmann and Hansen 2010; FRA 2014). Anonymous information is not equivalent to pseudonymous information, which merely means that an identifiable part of an information set is replaced by another type of information (e.g., a name being replaced by an alias, a number, text string or similar). For the provision of anonymity, the concepts of unlinkability and pseudonymity are highly relevant. Unlinkability means that "the exchange of identity information should not allow a linking of information from different transactions, unless a user specifically wishes to do so" (Rundle *et al.* 2008: 34). It is a crucial requirement to avoid that identity information is linked and aggregated across different contexts (Strauß 2011). Pseudonymity means that a piece of information that does not directly link to one's identity is used for identification (e.g., an alias or a number that changes in every usage context) (Chaum 1985; Pfitzmann and Hansen 2010). Pfitzmann and Hansen (2010) distinguish five forms of pseudonymity: transaction pseudonyms enable the highest level of unlinkability and thus strong anonymity. Each transaction uses a new pseudonym, which is only applied for a specific context. A common example is the use of transaction authentication numbers in online banking. A person pseudonym, i.e., a substitute for the identity of the holder (e.g., a unique number of an ID card, phone number or nickname) provides the lowest anonymity level. Moderate linkability is given by role and relationship pseudonyms, which are either limited to specific roles (e.g., client) or differ for each communication partner. Figure 3.3 illustrates these different types as suggested by Pfitzmann and Hansen (2010: 27).

The use of pseudonyms in different contexts is a means to establish an intended degree of (un)linkability. This also implies the avoidance of (global) unique identifiers that are valid in multiple contexts. Avoiding unique identifiers is highly important because they can be used to link and aggregate data across different contexts. This facilitates intrusions into privacy and corresponding activities like data mining and profiling (Hildebrandt and Gutwirth 2008; Hildebrandt and Rouvroy 2011).

Hence, unlinkability is a fundamental principle to protect identity information and thus privacy (for an overview on technical examples in the field of PbD see Chapter 6). More precisely, it contributes to the boundary control function of privacy and ISD (as described in the following sections). Unlinkability supports to avoiding a concentration of informational power by avoiding information aggregation across separated domains. The mechanism is partially comparable to the separation of powers in democratic states, i.e., keeping different administrative domains detached from each other in order to inhibit a concentration of power and prevent totalitarianism. For instance, domains such as education, health, social security, tax, etc. have different data repositories so that information about the population is not stored by or accessible to a centralized control unit. These domains are mostly not allowed to link their records with those of other domains in order to reduce the risk of mass surveillance and population control. However, unlinkability is not easy to achieve and is undermined by the

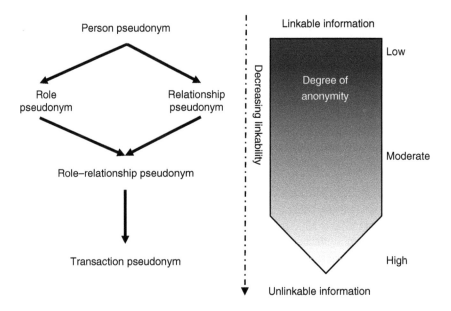

Figure 3.3 Interplay between pseudonyms, unlinkability and anonymity.
Source: author's representation, adapted from Pfitzmann and Hansen (2010: 27).

widespread and continuing pervasion of society with ICTs. Digital technology has enabled a multitude of possibilities to collect and store information about individuals in numerous contexts. This entails expanding, networked representations of digital identities, and increasing digital identification practices (see Chapters 4 and 5). There is thus an observable general increase in identifiability, resulting from the extensive amounts of identity information available. Digitally networked environments bear multiple application contexts, which foster the aggregation and cross-linkage of identity information, collected and processed by various institutions in the public as well as the private sector. This has serious implications for privacy (as explored more thoroughly in Chapter 5). The next section deals with the basic meaning and function of privacy, which builds the foundation for further analysis.

The societal role and meaning of privacy

Privacy is a more than fundamental human right. It is a *sine qua non* for individual well-being as well as for the functioning of society. Although regulations on privacy and data protection are an achievement of modernity, privacy's basic role and meaning can be found in ancient societies and in nature. Seclusion and differentiation from the individual in and between communities is important among humans and is even observable among animals. Cultural and anthropological studies show that different aspects of privacy are and were part of different societies worldwide (Westin 1967; Moore 1984). Eventual conflicts and balancing acts between one's private sphere and the public sphere can be described by Arthur Schopenhauer's metaphoric porcupine's (or hedgehog's) dilemma: porcupines (as well as hedgehogs) are reliant on their fellows sharing warmth and affection. However, as they have spikes on their backs, they can hurt each other if they do not keep an adequate distance from each other. This metaphor fits well to human society and the complex interrelations between social proximity and distance[6] that privacy is involved in. Indeed, several scholars assume that privacy also has a biological meaning: even in the life of animals, e.g., in the form of seclusion or intimacy in small groups, privacy seems to play an important role (Westin 1967; Klopfer and Rubenstein 1977). Thus, privacy is not "just" an invention of modernity but can be seen as a cultural universal (Westin 1967). As a multidimensional concept, privacy comprises different types and functions. Westin (1967: 31f.) identified four basic states of individual privacy: (1) solitude, meaning the physical separation of an individual from others; (2) intimacy, i.e., private relationships between two or more people or distinct groups; (3) anonymity, understood as the state of being unknown; and (4) reserve, i.e., the individual's psychological barrier that protects her personality from unwanted intrusion. Clarke (2006) distinguishes between privacy of the person, of personal behavior, of social communications and of personal data. Finn *et al.* (2013) suggest seven types of privacy based on Clarke's typology, adding privacy of thoughts and feelings, location and space as well as association (for a more detailed discussion on different privacy types see Chapter 6).

Basically, privacy encompasses all domains of an individual's life (e.g., cultural, economic, personal, political, psychological, social, etc.) including her actions, associations and relationships with others, behavior, beliefs, characteristics, communications, desires, health, opinions, preferences, racial or ethnic origins, religion, thoughts, etc. (Westin 1967; Clarke 2006; Hildebrandt 2006; Solove 2006; Rouvroy and Poullet 2009; Nissenbaum 2010; Finn *et al.* 2013). Or in other words: privacy enfolds identity.

Protecting privacy involves safeguarding corresponding types of information from being processed without a legal basis or beyond the intention of the individuals concerned. The relationship between identity and privacy is also part of legal frameworks. The GDPR of the EU defines personal data as "any information relating to an identified or identifiable natural person",[7] i.e., an individual

> who can be identified, directly or indirectly, in particular by reference to an identifier such as a name, an identification number, location data, an online identifier or to one or more factors specific to the physical, physiological, genetic, mental, economic, cultural or social identity of that natural person.
>
> (Article 4 (1) GDPR)

Another term for personal data is so-called "personally identifiable information" (PII), i.e., any information that is related to, or directly or indirectly linked to, a natural person and that can be used to identify that person (ISO 2011: 2). PII is a common term in technical privacy frameworks and basically means all kinds of data or information linked to the identity of a person. The preferred term in this book is identity or identifiable information because it is broader and allows considering technical information related to a personal identity as well. As will be shown (particularly in Chapters 5, 6 and 7), this makes an important difference for the protection of privacy. Hence, put simply, personal data is information related to an identified or identifiable person. This implies that direct as well as indirect identification affects privacy, in a legal but also in a broader socio-technical sense.

Fundamental legal issues and protection principles

As privacy affects all domains of an individual's life, its significance as a fundamental human right is obvious. Thus, most countries worldwide have specific laws for privacy and data protection. Irrespective of national peculiarities, privacy has been a fundamental human right since 1948: Article 12 of the Universal Declaration of Human Rights states that

> [n]o one shall be subjected to arbitrary interference with his privacy, family, home or correspondence, nor to attacks upon his honour and reputation. Everyone has the right to the protection of the law against such interference or attacks.

The same is declared in Article 17 of the International Covenant on Civil and Political Rights.[8] Similarly, Article 8 of the European Convention on Human Rights (ECHR) is dedicated to privacy:

> 1. Everyone has the right to respect for his private and family life, his home and his correspondence. 2. There shall be no interference by a public authority with the exercise of this right except such as is in accordance with the law and is necessary in a democratic society in the interests of national security, public safety or the economic well-being of the country, for the prevention of disorder or crime, for the protection of health or morals, or for the protection of the rights and freedoms of others.

In a similar vein, the Charter of Fundamental Rights of the European Union (EUCFR) includes the right to privacy and the protection of personal data (in Articles 7 and 8) (CFREU 2000). Democracies worldwide have directly or indirectly incorporated similar regulations in their rules of law. In Europe, the ECHR and the EUCFR represent general reference points which are incorporated in the legal frameworks at EU as well as national levels. In legal contexts, the protection of privacy is mostly described as data protection in Europe. However, from an individual human rights perspective, essentially, both strands address the same issues.[9] Therefore, privacy is the preferred term here as it is broader, includes data protection and implies that protection is not limited to data.

The prevalence of the term "data protection" has some historical reasons: the necessity to create particular legal frameworks emerged from the growing importance of electronic data processing in the 1960s and 1970s. Many privacy frameworks emerged during the 1970s and 1980s. The first countries worldwide to create privacy laws were Germany (initially in the state of Hessen), Sweden and France during in the early 1970s. In the US, the first legal framework was the Privacy Act of 1974. Germany is particularly relevant as its privacy regime enjoys a good international reputation and had an impact on the emergence of the European privacy framework as well (González-Fuster 2014). In 1980, the Organization for Economic Cooperation and Development published guidelines "on the Protection of Privacy and Transborder Flows of Personal Data" (last updated in 2013), which are still today of international relevance (OECD 2013). One year later, with the so-called Convention 108 of the Council of Europe, the first international privacy treaty, currently ratified by over 40 countries worldwide, was created. Convention 108, entitled "Convention for the protection of individuals with regard to automatic processing of personal data", contains general principles for the proper processing of personal data with respect for the rights of individuals. Being a treaty with multiple nations involved, it is as yet the only international data protection instrument with a legally binding effect (FRA 2014). In 1983, the right to ISD was created in Germany, which represented a landmark ruling for the European privacy regime (for more details about its relevance see the discussion on autonomy in the following sections). Until

2018, the central regulation of the EU was the Data Protection Directive 95/46/ EC (DPD 1995). It was adopted in 1995 as the first privacy regulation valid for all member states aiming to create a common legal baseline for privacy laws in Europe. It also substantiated and expanded some of the norms of Convention 108 (FRA 2014; González-Fuster 2014). The DPD used to be the main instrument of the EU data protection framework until May 2018, when the new general regulation became effective (see below). It contained mandatory minimum standards for all member states, who had to implement the regulation into their national laws. In addition to the DPD, there are some further laws such as the ePrivacy Directive 2002/58/EC complementing the DPD. It, inter alia, regulates data processing in the context of publicly available electronic communications networks (FRA 2014). The ePrivacy Directive was controversial from its beginnings among privacy experts due to its relatively narrow scope and insufficient regulation of transborder data flows. Given the widespread use of global communications networks, developments such as pervasive computing and the Internet of Things, etc., its applicability is limited. Therefore, significant updates were highly recommended (e.g., recently by the European Data Protection Supervisor, EDPS 2016). This law is currently under revision with respect to the EU privacy reform.[10] In May 2018, the GDPR, which replaced the DPD, became effective. The implementation of the GDPR is a crucial milestone of privacy reform. It aims to further harmonize and strengthen the privacy regime in Europe to cope with the technological challenges of globally available personal information. The GDPR is partially based on the DPD. However, there are several changes and novelties such as high penalties for illegal data processing for enterprises, a stimulation of PbD, as well as the introduction of obligatory PIAs under certain conditions (for more details see Chapters 6 and 7, which are dedicated to these instruments). The creation of the GDPR is a crucial part of the still-ongoing privacy reform in Europe, which has an international impact, particularly on the political and economic affairs between the EU and the US. For several years, there have been attempts to create an international standard for privacy and data protection on the basis of Convention 108 (FRA 2014). Since 2016, there has been an corresponding revision in progress (Greenleaf 2017). A further regulation regarding the transborder flow of personal information between the EU and the US is the so-called "Privacy Shield" adopted in 2016. This agreement is based on self-commitment and replaced its predecessor, the "Safe Harbour decision", which was declared as invalid by the European Court of Justice in 2015. However, privacy experts criticized this regulation for being insufficient (WP29 2016). Moreover, according to media reports, current US president, Donald Trump, could revoke the privacy shield, which makes its efficacy as-yet generally uncertain (McCarthy 2017).

Besides particular legal regulations, there are some commonly accepted principles (also referred to as fair information practices, particularly in the US) which represent the backbone of most privacy and data protection laws worldwide. Key principles are especially (De Hert 2012; OECD 2013; Danezis *et al.* 2014; FRA 2014):

1   *legality and lawful processing*: i.e., personal data is processed in accordance with the law, for a legitimate purpose, and the processing is necessary in a democratic society
2   *purpose specification and purpose binding/limitation*: i.e., the purpose needs to be specified in advance of the processing and the use of personal data for other purposes requires a legal basis as well. Another purpose is particularly true in the case of data transfer to third parties
3   *data minimization*: only those data necessary for a particular purpose should be processed and deleted when the purpose of processing ceases to exist
4   *data quality*: data needs to be adequate, relevant and not excessively collected in relation to the purpose of processing, data should be accurate and kept up to date, limited use/retention so that data is not kept longer than needed
5   *transparency and fair processing*: so that the individuals concerned can comprehend how their data is being processed, by whom and for what purposes
6   *accountability*: i.e., the data processing entity has to act in compliance with the law and safeguard personal data in their activities.

These principles build a basic foundation of privacy regulation. They were already part of the former regulation (the DPD) as they are now in the GDPR. For instance, according to Article 5 of the GDPR, personal data must be:

> (a) processed lawfully, fairly and in a transparent manner in relation to the data subject ("lawfulness, fairness and transparency"); (b) collected for specified, explicit and legitimate purposes and not further processed in a manner that is incompatible with those purposes[11]; (c) adequate, relevant and limited to what is necessary in relation to the purposes for which they are processed ("data minimization"); (d) accurate and, where necessary, kept up to date; every reasonable step must be taken to ensure that personal data that are inaccurate, having regard to the purposes for which they are processed, are erased or rectified without delay ("accuracy"); (e) kept in a form which permits identification of data subjects for no longer than is necessary for the purposes for which the personal data are processed ("storage limitation"); (f) processed in a manner that ensures appropriate security of the personal data, including protection against unauthorized or unlawful processing and against accidental loss, destruction or damage, using appropriate technical or organizational measures ("integrity and confidentiality").

For technical implementation of safeguards, particularly as regards (2) and (3), the concept of unlinkability (as outlined previously) is important. The ISO/IEC 29100:2011 privacy framework provides relevant specifications and guidelines, particularly as regards the handling of personal information (for more details on technical privacy protection and impact assessment, see Chapters 5, 6 and 7).

The boundary control function of privacy

Basically, privacy is located at the boundary between the public and the private spheres. Privacy constitutes the private sphere of an individual. However, it is not to be misinterpreted as a means where the individual protects her privacy by decoupling from the public. The framing of privacy as a means of decoupling and a concept of seclusion is a general issue which complicates understanding what the claim that privacy needs to be protected precisely means (Solove 2006). For instance, confidentiality and protection of information from being unintentionally disclosed are indeed relevant issues of privacy. However, this does not imply that privacy is equivalent to secrecy or hiding something, although often misinterpreted in this regard (Agre and Rotenberg 1998; Solove 2004/2006; Strauß 2017). The framing as a concept of seclusion is particularly true in the common, classical notion of privacy (or data protection) as "the right to be let alone" (Warren and Brandeis 1890). As will be shown, this notion is too narrow and misleadingly reduces privacy to a concept of seclusion and separation from others. In fact, privacy serves as a substantial enabler of both personal development of an individual and individual involvement in community and society. Metaphorically speaking, the previously mentioned distance hedgehogs keep to each other does not imply that they are unsocial and lack in community. In contrast to its common classical notion, privacy is not to be misunderstood as an individual's claim and right to decouple from society. To the contrary, it is a societal achievement that relieves different kinds of social frictions and "enables people to engage in worthwhile activities that they would otherwise find difficult or impossible" (Solove 2006: 484). Privacy is thus not an isolated concept but it empowers other fundamental rights, values and freedoms such as association, expression, movement, thought, etc. As such it is a vital prerequisite for democracy and political participation (Westin 1967; ibid.; Hildebrandt 2006; Nissenbaum 2010). Therefore, privacy can be located "in its functional relationship to valued ends, including human well-being and development, creativity, autonomy, mental health, and liberty" (Nissenbaum 2010: 74f.). Privacy is a *sine qua non* for human well-being and development: in order to freely develop thoughts, ideas, intellectual capacity, creativity, artistic expressions, ethical and political judgments etc., individuals need spheres free from permanent scrutiny and "leeway to experiment without the distraction of being watched … free from pressure to conform to popular conventional standards" (ibid.). Protecting privacy involves protection of the process of "becoming, being and remaining a person" (Reiman 1976: 44). Thus, privacy essentially preserves human dignity and individual identity development (Kahn 2003; Rouvroy and Poullet 2009; Nissenbaum 2010). In this regard, privacy is "a unifying principle that is itself the means for creating the notions of dignity and identity" (Kahn 2003: 410). Harms to privacy thus have a negative impact on individual dignity and identity-building. This also has wider societal effects as privacy impairments "impede individual activities that contribute to the greater social good" (Solove 2006: 488). To protect this fundamental right is thus essential for the well-being of the individual as well as of society.

Hence, although occasionally presented as contradictory, the private sphere is not the opposite of the public sphere. To the contrary, both are intrinsically linked and a prerequisite for each other. Several scholars underline that privacy is not merely a private but also a public value, vital for democratic processes (e.g., Habermas 1989; Kahn 2003; Hildebrandt 2006; Rouvroy and Poullet 2009; Nissenbaum 2010; Cohen 2012). Although privacy serves the individual directly, its functions and benefits are wider and translate into societal good (Nissenbaum 2010). Hence there is a close connection to the public sphere. The public sphere is an essential element of deliberative democracy that serves to mediate between citizens and political decision-makers (Habermas 1989). With its inherently deliberative character and quality it also provides a domain where public communication transforms into public opinion (ibid.; Frazer 2007; Trenz 2008). But the public sphere is not to be (mis-)understood as a single, universal space of public deliberation and discourse. It is a "communicative network where different publics partially overlap" (Nanz 2007: 19). The formation of the public sphere and its deliberative quality are closely linked to private sphere(s), i.e., those domains and spaces where individuals enjoy their privacy and have the ability to be and act freely without interference from others. Thus, to some extent, the relationship between the private and the public sphere is complementary. In this regard, privacy also contributes to societal diversity as individuals are enabled in their specific personal development, which can benefit the well-being of society. In the private sphere, individuals build their very opinions; as these opinions are communicated, shared, discussed, shaped etc. with others, the public sphere emerges and takes shape (Habermas 1989). Therefore, both spheres are intrinsically linked and together are vital for democratic will-formation. Both need physical and virtual space to emerge and develop where individuals can interact, meet, exchange ideas and thoughts, etc. freely without fear of intrusion, impairment or repression. Thus, limitations to privacy can also put the deliberative quality of the public sphere at stake.

In short, "privacy defines a state where an individual is free from interference" (Strauß 2017: 260). This means that privacy enables the individual's being, actions, behavior, relationships, etc. to be free and without haphazard, uncontrollable intrusion or observation from external entities such as the state, public and private institutions or other individuals. But as outlined, enjoying privacy does imply that individuals seclude from others, or decouple from society and public engagement. Essentially, privacy has an inherent boundary control function. This function allows the individual to open as well as to close herself to others (Altman 1975; Hildebrandt 2006). For Westin (1967: 7), privacy is the result of a recurring process of negotiation and enforcement as:

> each individual is continually engaged in a personal adjustment process in which he balances the desire for privacy with the desire of disclosure and communication of himself to others, in light of the environmental and social norms set by the society in which he lives.

As societal contexts are dynamic, this boundary control is a continuous process, where the individual shifts her boundaries in relation to her environment and the entities which may access information about her (Hildebrandt 2006). In this regard, "privacy can best be understood as the virtual and actual space needed to continuously reconstruct the self in the face of ever changing contexts" (ibid.: 44). Hence, the boundary control function of privacy is naturally dynamic as the individual is in permanent interaction with her environment. The subject of control mainly concerns information about the individual where (in an ideal case) she selectively controls whom to provide with personal insights. This is in accordance with Westin's (1967: 7) definition of privacy as "the claim of individuals, groups or institutions to determine for themselves when, how, and to what extent information is communicated to others". Hence, information plays an essential role for privacy protection and is the major determinant of the boundary control function of privacy. Accordingly, Agre and Rotenberg (1998: 7) highlight the relationship of privacy with identity and state that "control over personal information is control over an aspect of the identity one projects to the world, and the right to privacy is the freedom from unreasonable constraints on the construction of one's own identity". Comprehending the interrelations between privacy and identity is also important to overcome the misleading reductionist view on privacy as a means of seclusion or secrecy (see also the discussion on privacy controversies in the subsequent sections). Correspondingly, Hildebrandt (2006: 50) points out "the core of privacy is to be found in the idea of identity ... because the process of identity-building is what is at stake in privacy." Floridi (2013: 243) even speaks of privacy breaches as "a form of aggression towards one's personal identity". Kahn (2003) points out that privacy invasion can cause harm to dignity and destabilize the integrity of an individual's identity.

The interplay between privacy, identity and autonomy

The presented boundary control function is intrinsically linked to the complex interplay of privacy, identity and autonomy. As shown, privacy is an intermediate value for other human rights and an essential means for identity-building, which fosters liberty, autonomy and self-determination (Rouvroy and Poullet 2009; Nissenbaum 2010; Cohen 2012). Privacy enables the formation of a particular space or sphere, i.e., the individual's private sphere, in which identity development, autonomy and self-determined living are enabled free from interference. This private sphere is linked to but different from the public sphere. In this respect, privacy, identity and autonomy build a triad of intrinsically interrelated concepts. As illustrated in Figure 3.4 autonomy presupposes identity, because without identity there is no entity that can act autonomously, and privacy can be seen as a constitutive framework for autonomy and identity development.

As outlined, the identity of an individual person represents her as distinct from others. At the same time, identity is continually shaped by its interactions

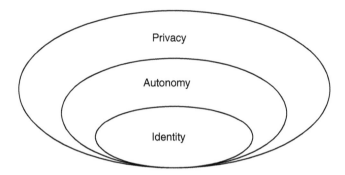

Figure 3.4 Privacy enables autonomy and identity development.

with other entities and society. In this regard, identity can be seen as a construct which enables linkage between the private and the public sphere. In line with Ricoeur's notion of enduring as well as dynamic features of identity (*idem* and *ipse*), privacy "allows a person to hold together while changing; it presumes some measure of autonomy, … intimacy and some space to rebuild the self in accordance with one's past while anticipating one's future" (Hildebrandt 2006: 52). Hence, identity-building is dynamic and does follow a particular order. Consequently, the "construction of the identity of the self implies indeterminacy, and privacy therefore implies the recognition of this indeterminacy" (ibid.). This recognition refers to autonomy and self-determination, which are essential for privacy and vice versa. Autonomy requires some domain in which it is factual, and where individuals can act as self-determined and free from interference. This domain is represented by one's private sphere, in a virtual as well as in a spatial sense. Hence, the protection of privacy implies protecting autonomy and its function to act on free will. Consequently, intrusion into the privacy of an individual also affects her ability to exercise autonomy (e.g., Treiger-Bar-Am 2008; Rouvroy and Poullet 2009; Nissenbaum 2010). As a form of autonomy, Nissenbaum (2010: 81) describes privacy as "self-determination with respect to information about oneself".

Autonomy as freedom to self-govern

Put simply, autonomy means self-rule. The term consists of the Greek words for "self" (autos) and "rule" or law (nomos) and thus literally means to have or make one's own (moral) laws. Autonomy may be seen in relation to processes of self-organization inherent to autopoietic systems, as human beings represent. Being autonomous implies being able to take free decisions. Autonomy is an essential concept in moral and political philosophy that plays a crucial role in law and culture, strongly advocated by Immanuel Kant or John Stuart Mill (Treiger-Bar-Am 2008; Christman 2015). According to Kant, autonomy is the ability to freely and self-determinedly establish moral laws and act upon them, closely linked to the freedom of the will to choose (Kant 1785/1997). In this regard, autonomy is the capacity to self-govern with a state of self-determination that empowers the individual to act freely without external intervention. Hence, it is a core element of personal well-being. But it is also the source of (moral and non-moral) obligations as it is "the capacity to impose upon ourselves, by virtue of our practical identities" (Christman 2015). Hence, autonomy is also a condition for reason, a condition for humans to act reasonably "on rational principles and freely to exercise the moral reasoning will, through the freedom of choice" (Treiger-Bar-Am 2008: 555). Being autonomous means being a self-determined person, governed by personal intrinsic values, beliefs, desires, reflections, conditions, characteristics etc., which are not purely imposed upon a person from external sources and thus can be seen as part of her authentic self (Christman 2015). Certainly, autonomy is an ideal and as such is not always completely obtainable in every societal context as regulated by the rule of law. Citizens enjoy rights but are also obliged with certain duties. Hence, in socio-political contexts, autonomy is often provided only to a certain degree under specific conditions. However, irrespective of eventual limiting conditions, the provision of liberty and autonomy is a *sine qua non* for a democratic society. Democratic processes require autonomy, may it be to freely express one's opinion, cast a vote without being enforced or constrained, or counteract oppression and eventual injustices in society (e.g., by the rights of civil disobedience, demonstrations, freedom of expression, etc.). Though closely related, autonomy is not equal to, but is a consequence of, freedom (and vice versa). Liberty, i.e., political freedom, is "a prerequisite to the exercise of autonomy" (Treiger-Bar-Am 2008: 557). The idea of autonomy articulates freedom and obligation in one haul: through the form of self-legislated laws (Khurana 2013). Autonomy overlaps with positive freedom, i.e., the ability to act on free will (Christman 2015). An intrinsic part of autonomy is also the ability to self-reflect, i.e., (re-) assessing one's desires, reasons, actions, etc. in relation to universal duties and obligation. Briefly speaking, autonomy concerns an individual's ability to rethink and reflect upon her moral identity. Thus, autonomy also plays a crucial role for justice:

> [I]t serves as the model of the person whose perspective is used to formulate and justify political principles, as in social contract models of principles of justice.... [C]orrespondingly, it serves as the model of the citizen whose basic interests are reflected in those principles, such as in the claim that basic liberties, opportunities, and other primary goods are fundamental to flourishing lives no matter what moral commitments, life plans, or other particulars of the person might obtain.
>
> (Christman 2015)

Autonomy implies freedom from interference, but it is also relational as being autonomous requires a point of reference. This implies recognition or acceptance of autonomous actions by others, which is a necessary but not sufficient condition of autonomy as well as of personal identity. Both autonomy and identity are based on mutual recognition and acceptance between different individuals: as freedom implies being free from something, a person cannot be free in her actions, i.e., act autonomously merely by herself without a referent object; the same is true for a personal identity being distinct from others, who are its referent objects. Personal identity is based on autonomy and its capacity to constitute for oneself a type of action that is recognizable to others (Treiger-Bar-Am 2008; Christman 2015).

As shown in the previous section, privacy does not imply that the individual is completely decoupled from the environment in her private sphere. Private and public spheres complement each other and privacy has an inherent boundary control function to regulate the interactions between individual identities and society (perceivable as a multi-agent system). Identity here serves multiple functions: as its fundamental core, it constitutes the private sphere of a particular individual, because individual privacy has no meaning without her identity as a prerequisite determinant. In this regard, it also predetermines the boundary between the private and the public spheres, even though this boundary is dynamic and changeable. At the same time, identity enables interactions through these spheres as individuals (represented by their identities) interact with other entities in their societal environment. The boundary privacy enables regulation of can be understood as an informational one. According to Floridi (2013: 232), privacy fulfills "the function of the ontological friction in the infosphere". This means that privacy provides an environment for the free flow of personal information, where this information flow is (ideally) not disclosed or accessible to other entities unless intended to be by the individual concerned. Thus, privacy supports the individual in preventing her information from flowing seamlessly from one context to another without her allowing information disclosure. Hence, privacy facilitates autonomy, which here refers to ISD. This includes determining what kind of information about one's private life and parts of one's identity are disclosed or shared with others. In this regard, privacy allows the individual to partially regulate social interactions and the level of transparency in relation to her societal environment. Without privacy, this capability for self-regulation and self-determination would be significantly constrained if not nullified.

Informational self-determination

The form of autonomy intrinsic to privacy is ISD, which is thus a core concept of privacy protection. It involves "connections between privacy and self-representation, and ... identity formation" (Nissenbaum 2010: 81). Or in other words: privacy also concerns the individual's self-determined maintenance and performance of her personal identity. ISD defines a state in which the individual that is affected by the processing of her information is aware of this process and enabled in controlling how and what personal information is involved. There are two major aspects of ISD: *knowledge* about the context of information processing and *control* over that context, i.e., over the personal information flows (Strauß and Nentwich 2013). Thus, in order to make an informed decision about the disclosure and use of her personal information, the individual needs to know, e.g., what personal information is collected, stored and processed for what purpose, and by whom. This adds the issue of *transparency* of information processing as an intrinsic requirement for ISD.

Basically, ISD is an integrative part of the European privacy and data protection regime. This role was developed by the legal discourse in Germany on ISD, although there is no explicit right to ISD in EU legal frameworks. In German law, ISD has been explicitly defined as a legal right since 1983. In its famous decision on the population census, the German Federal Constitutional Court[12] ("Bundesverfassungsgericht") highlighted that the individual needs to "be protected from unlimited collection, storage, use, and transmission of personal data as a condition of development of his or her free personality under the modern conditions of data processing" (BVerfGE 65 E 40, cited from De Hert 2008: 74; see also, De Hert 2008; Rouvroy and Poullet 2009). The major reason for the Court's fundamental decision[13] was a census of the whole German population planned for 1983 which triggered a number of protests and constitutional complaints which enabled the Court to examine the law regulating the census ("Volkszählungsgesetz"). The Court found that the law was not in accordance with the German constitution and created the right to ISD (Hornung and Schnabel 2009). This right to ISD was articulated by the Court as "the authority of the individual to decide himself, on the basis of the idea of self-determination, when and within what limits information about his private life should be communicated to others" (Rouvroy and Poullet 2009: 45). This is similar to Westin's (1967) definition of privacy as outlined in the previous section. The intention of the right to ISD is to "enable citizens to freely develop their personality" (Hornung and Schnabel 2009: 86). Following De Hert's (2008: 75) interpretation, the Court explained with precision "the shift of power that takes places whenever the state or private actors interact with an individual through ICTs". The reasoning of the Court highlighted that "a person's knowledge that his or her actions are being watched inevitably curtails his or her freedom to act" (ibid.). Indeed, the decision points out that against the background of technical means that allow unlimited collection, storage and processing of information concerning individual people, ISD needs particular protection; especially in light of advances in autonomic data processing (Hildebrandt and Rouvroy 2011).

Furthermore, the Court also explained that with the possibility to create "a partial or virtually complete personality profile" by aggregating or linking data from different sources, the people concerned have "no sufficient means of controlling its truth and application" (ibid.: 53). The Court argued further that technological means reinforce the possibilities of influencing individuals' behavior to an unknown degree so that public interests can exert psychological pressure on individuals. Irrespective of the "certain conditions of modern information processing technology", an essential precondition of ISD is thus that the individuals have the freedom to decide about actions or omissions "including the possibility to follow that decision in practice" (ibid.). Hence this implies that some certainty is needed for the individual to act freely and make informed decisions in this regard. Otherwise, the individual is hampered in this freedom and thus his or her ISD:

> If someone is uncertain whether deviant behaviour is noted down and stored permanent[ly] as information, or is applied or passed, he will try not to attract attention by such behaviour. If he reckons that participation in an assembly or a citizens' initiative will be registered officially and that personal risks might result from it, he may possibly renounce the exercise of his respective rights. This would not only impact his chances of development but would also impact the common good ("Gemeinwohl"), because self-determination is an elementary functional condition of a free democratic society based on its citizens' capacity to act and to cooperate.
> (Excerpt from the Court's decision; cited from Rouvroy and Poullet 2009: 53)

In order to reduce the risk of profiling and compilation of all personal information of an individual, the Court's ruling also included the prohibition of "the introduction of a unique personal identifier for every citizen" (Hornung and Schnabel 2009: 87). This is particularly crucial as the creation of "a complete personality profile would violate the guarantee to have one's dignity recognised" (ibid.).

The Court's decision and the introduction of the right to ISD was a milestone for privacy protection. It had a significant impact on data protection legislation in Europe and represents a cornerstone of contemporary privacy protection frameworks (De Hert 2008; Hornung and Schnabel 2009; Rouvroy and Poullet 2009). According to Hornung and Schnabel (2009: 85), the reasoning of the Constitutional Court is partially based on social systems theory, where fundamental rights "have the function of guarding the differentiation of society into sub-systems". Privacy and ISD play an essential role: "to protect the consistency of the individuality of the individual, and consistent self-expressions rely heavily on the separation of societal sub-systems" (ibid.). This separation means that individuals can enjoy a free and self-determined life, which is essential for the functioning of a free and democratic society. In this regard, ISD relates to the boundary control function of privacy and its double effect: "[t]he individual is shielded from interference in personal matters, thus creating a sphere in which he or she can feel safe from any interference. At the same time, data protection is also a precondition for citizens' unbiased participation" in political processes (ibid.: 86).

A further legal issue related to ISD in German privacy law is the basic right to confidentiality and integrity of information systems (basic IT right "IT-Grundrecht") that complements the right to privacy and ISD. It aims to specify the "Volkszählungsurteil" as it also explicitly addresses personal use of ICTs that are to be protected from privacy infringement. This new right was created in

2008 because of a broader societal debate in Germany during that time about the use of online surveillance tools by security authorities to monitor personal computers (so-called "Online-Durchsuchungen"). The Court argued that information systems of whatever kind (laptops, mobile phones, etc.) enable the gathering of insight into significant parts of the life of a person or even the drawing of a detailed picture of one's personality (De Hert 2008; Wehage 2013). For De Hert (2008: 75) this new fundamental law represents a "landmark ruling, that recognises a citizen's right to the integrity of their information-technology systems and introduces elements of user-centric identity management". Interestingly, this new regulation seems to play a marginal role in socio-technical practices so far. Reasons for this may lie in the relative novelty of the regulation and lack of reference points about its practical applicability (Baum *et al.* 2013; Wehage 2013). Irrespective of its legal meaning, the pervasiveness of ICTs and their associated socio-technical transformations essentially strain and undermine ISD: in digital environments, personal information is often processed without the knowledge and control of the individual concerned. While the processing of her information is opaque to the individual, her identity being digitally represented can be highly transparent beyond her control. To some extent, ISD is exposed to controversial issues which are seemingly contradictory to privacy protection, as discussed in the following.

General privacy controversies

As discussed in the previous sections, the emergence of national and international privacy regimes is strongly influenced by technological progress. Basically, novel technologies and their usage practices frequently put privacy protection under pressure. The growing importance of electronic data processing during the 1960s and 1970s had some ignition effect for the creation of privacy regulation on a global level. Since then, the rapid diffusion of ICTs (particularly from the 1990s until today) significantly boosted privacy challenges. To cope with the changed socio-technical requirements for privacy protection, law and policy makers try to adopt regulation accordingly. The European privacy reform is an important development in this regard. Nevertheless, several privacy problems are aggravated with altering socio-technical practices beyond the scope of the law. The enormous complexity of international policies and regulations hampers the development and enforcement of international standards. A general crux of privacy and data protection is the highly complex legal situation. Besides issues resulting from privacy intrusions serving various indefinite security purposes, a complicated aspect is, for instance, the so-called "informed consent" of the person concerned for data processing: when a person accepts the processing by giving consent, processing mostly receives a legal basis. The GDPR regulates informed consent basically in this manner, where processing is lawful if "the data subject has given consent to the processing of his or her personal data" (Article 6 GDPR). This consent is valid under certain conditions such as it needs to be comprehensible and can be withdrawn (Article 7 GDPR). Indeed, consent is an important requirement for personal data processing with the aim to protect from abuse. Hence, the idea is that information should not be processed against the will of the individual concerned. However, in practice, there are several difficulties. Giving consent can be especially problematic when an individual wants or needs to use a particular service, has no other option than to accept the processing of their data and cannot control its usage (Nissenbaum 2010; De Andrade *et al.* 2013; EGE 2014). Informed consent is mostly a necessary condition for using an online service, application or a technology, e.g., by accepting the terms of use. This is in most cases sufficient to allow for, e.g., commercial exploitation of personal information, including third-party access to the data. As digital data processing mostly includes data flows between multiple entities beyond national borders and legal frameworks, appropriate regulation and privacy protection is increasingly challenging. Consequently, individuals lack control over their information and thus have limited options for ISD, as will be shown in subsequent chapters.

Given the strong link between technology, personal identity and identification (see Chapter 4), privacy protection and ISD are increasingly hampered. Digital identities are often free-floating in socio-technical contexts and consequently their holders are exposed to risks of misuse without knowledge or control thereof. This is aggravated by the fact that threats to privacy do not necessarily result from abuse of legal rights. For instance, profiling activities of various kinds can gather information related to individual identities from various sources. This may be acceptable in a strict legal sense as individual users have accepted the terms of use, e.g., of an online service where third-party access to data, such as for further commercial purposes, is included. However, although this is not privacy abuse by law, profiling activities intrude into privacy and affect identity-building (Hildebrandt 2006; Hildebrandt and Gutwirth 2008). A further issue concerns security and surveillance practices based on the exploitation of personal information for purposes of law enforcement and national security. Interfering with privacy is foreseen by the law under certain conditions: i.e., to fulfill public interest in accordance with the law and the protection of the foundations of a democratic society (EGE 2014; FRA 2014; Strauß 2017). As security is also a basic human right and the state aims to protect its integrity, privacy intrusions and surveillance activities are frequently justified by security purposes. Hence, also in these cases, privacy may not be violated in a legal sense. Nevertheless, in many cases, profiling and surveillance are privacy-intrusive activities, entailing serious risks to privacy. Or as De Hert (2008: 73) put it: "Lawful collection and processing of personal data does not prevent per se unethical practices deployed in the name of security, or unjust decisions made on them." Similar is true for ICT usage: to some extent, it enables new forms of privacy intrusion. But ICTs particularly reinforce the privacy impact of pre-existing practices, when the technology is applied in a manner that is privacy-intrusive (Chapter 5 explores these issues in more depth). This is closely connected to concepts that are partially in conflict with privacy. In the following, two important issues in this regard are discussed: the relation between privacy and security as well as between privacy and transparency. The former is frequently framed as the main reason to justify privacy intrusion and surveillance practices. The latter is linked to notions of post-privacy.

Privacy and security—a contradiction in terms?

In the public discourse, privacy is often presented as a sort of counterpart to security, especially when political interests strive for an extension of security measures. Indeed, privacy intrusions are foreseen by the law under certain conditions, i.e., for law enforcement to protect the interests of the public under the premise of protecting issues vital for a democratic society. However, this does not imply that there is a state of permanent conflict between privacy and security. Above all, these limitations are the exception to the rule while human rights catalogs and legal frameworks suggest that privacy protection is the standard mode (Strauß 2017). However, this quasi-standard setting is strained by a number of issues, reinforced by the assumption of a permanent trade-off with an inherent conflict between privacy and security.

In general, the term "security" stems from the Latin word *securus* which consists of *sine* (without) and *cura* (concern, worry or problem). Hence, generally speaking, security describes a state without the need to worry or be cautious. This already indicates that security has a subjective meaning as the perception of what is a security threat may differ from individual to individual. Thus, security is subjective and relative. Consequently, objective and subjective notions of security are most often not equal. The former instead "refers to the low probability of damage" and the latter is "the feeling of security, or the absence of fear that acquired values are threatened" (Chandler 2009: 123). However, both are closely related and can influence each other. Security is not an absolute concept that can be permanently assured but depends on its environmental conditions, which cannot be fully controlled. In other words: there is no state of absolute, 100 percent security achievable as security is naturally limited and dependent on the conditions of its referent object. Many security scholars therefore point out that security is an ambiguous and contested concept (Buzan *et al.* 1998; Balzacq 2005; Guild *et al.* 2008; Bigo 2008; Watson 2011). The relationship between the individual and the state plays an important role in the security discourse. Since the eighteenth century, there has been a long tradition, inter alia, based on Hobbes' contribution to state philosophy,[14] where security is seen as a responsibility of the sovereign (UN 1994; Owen 2004). Security is also part of human rights catalogs. The Universal Declaration of Human Rights (resolved in 1948) states in Article 3: "Everyone has the right to life, liberty and security of person." Social security is addressed in Article 22:

> Everyone, as a member of society, has the right to social security and is entitled to realization, through national effort and international cooperation and in accordance with the organization and resources of each state, of the economic, social and cultural rights indispensable for his dignity and the free development of his personality.

These legal terms already indicate that liberty, security and personality development or identity are interwoven and on the same side of the coin.

The dynamics of human-centered security

While the provision of public or national security was in the main the responsibility of the state, the traditional framing of security also put the main focus on protecting the integrity of the state from different kinds of threats (such as conflicts, wars, nuclear proliferation). International tensions contributed to strengthening this focus also as regards military force. Traditional state-centered security was the dominating concept that reached a peak during the Cold War, as Owen (2004: 16) points out:

> This type of security relied primarily on an anarchistic balance of power (power as the sole controlling mechanism), the military build-up of two superpowers, and on the absolute sovereignty of the nation-state.... Security was seen as protection from invading armies; protection was provided by technical and military capabilities; and wars were never to be fought on home soil—rather, proxy wars were used if direct combat were necessary.

This traditional, state-centered security concept was predominating for many decades. However, after the end of the Cold War during the 1990s, a new approach emerged which put more emphasis on the protection of the individual rather than on the national state. In 1994 the United Nations Development Programme introduced the new concept of human security with two main aspects: the freedom from chronic threats such as hunger, disease and repression, linked with protection from sudden calamities (UN 1994; Owen 2004; Jolly and Ray 2006). In a speech in 2000, former general-secretary of the UN, Kofi Annan, highlighted human security as a concept that

> in its broadest sense, embraces far more than the absence of violent conflict. It encompasses human rights, good governance, access to education and health care.... Every step in this direction is also a step towards reducing poverty, achieving economic growth and preventing conflict. Freedom from want, freedom from fear, and the freedom of future generations to inherit a healthy natural environment—these are the interrelated building blocks of human—and therefore national—security.
>
> (Annan 2000)

This human-centered security concept initially aimed to reduce insecurities in order to ensure that human development is in accordance with freedom and health. Owen (2004: 19) defines human security as "the protection of the vital core of all human lives from critical and pervasive environmental, economic, food, health, personal and political threats". However, increasingly complex security challenges reinforced surveillance and security measures on a global scale and also led to an extended conceptualization of security. These developments had already emerged before the terrorist attacks on September 11, 2001 in the US. However, the tragedy of 9/11 amplified the shift in security policy at a global level. Many governments worldwide significantly intensified their security and surveillance efforts (Ball and Webster 2003; Haggerty and Samatas 2010). Increasing claims for a holistic security approach played an important role in the transformation of security policy, which also complicated the concept of human security. This development includes a tendency to frame security threats as a form of physical attack or violence from external sources (such as terrorism, organized crime, etc.). While there are without doubt many external security threats, there are also internal ones that do not necessarily involve physical violations. Threats to economic stability or human rights are also security threats. This circumstance was initially addressed by the human security concept. Originally, human security focused on protecting the integrity of the individual from different kinds of threats such as conflicts, diseases, human rights violations, hunger or natural disasters (Owen 2004). However, to some extent, it created a life of its own (Jolly and Ray 2006; Watson 2011). The extension of security measures with an inherent logic of increasing pre-emptive and preventive approaches (to detect and combat potential threats early) also fostered surveillance. In this regard, individuals are not merely objects of protection but are, to some extent, also framed as potential threats. Thus, there is an observable partial inversion of the human security concept. This changed framing in security policy also stimulated surveillance activities and further complicates the relationship between privacy and security (Strauß 2017).

Securitization: a dominant but controversial trend

From a theoretical stance, this paradigm shift and the transformations in security policy refer to so-called "securitization", which frames security as a permanent process and seduces with a seemingly predictive view on threats to foster the effectivity of security measures (Buzan *et al.* 1998; Bigo 2000/2008; Balzacq 2005; Guild *et al.* 2008; Watson 2011). In the sense of Foucault, securitization is a technique of government, "a mode of governmentality, drawing the lines of fear and unease at both the individual and the collective level" (CASE 2006: 457). It includes a rhetorical technique that makes strategic use of the term "security" to foster political objectives by rephrasing problems into existential security threats (Buzan *et al.* 1998). In this regard, securitization benefits self-fulfilling prophecy in the security discourse, and is thus also "a capacity to manage (and create) insecurity" (Bigo 2000: 174). Consequently, this can create a security dilemma where "the more one tries to securitize social phenomena … to ensure 'security' … the more one creates (intentionally or non-intentionally) a feeling of insecurity" (CASE 2006: 461). Hence, security here becomes an indeterminate, continuing process that is "marked by the intersubjective establishment of an existential threat with sufficient saliency to have political effects" (Watson 2011: 3). In this process, security is not framed as an objective condition but is linked and exposed to the political discourse (Balzacq 2005). Herein entailed is the risk that securitization seeks and creates legitimacy for exceptional security measures that are "outside the normal bounds of political procedure" (Buzan *et al.* 1998: 28f.). Due to its own particular dynamics, the process of securitization can lead to a "security continuum" in a problematic sense where the designation of "certain persons and practices as 'threats'" happens in a rather arbitrary manner (Guild *et al.* 2008: 2). Several scholars highlight that the linking of security and (im)migration is a prominent example of the dangerous effects of securitization (e.g., CASE 2006; ibid.; Watson 2011). Securitization becomes particularly problematic if security is presented as a dominant issue of societal concern deserving higher priority than other state functions, and the protection of fundamental rights such as the right to privacy. In this regard, it justifies privacy intrusions and surveillance as necessary for a security purpose.

There is obviously no state of permanent security in the sense of an effective protection from all possible threats. However, security policy affected by the logic of securitization gives the impression that permanent security would be achievable. In fact, an overwhelming focus on security framed as the predomi-nating issue can undermine the effectiveness of security measures at the cost of fundamental human rights, above all of the right to privacy (Schneier 2003/2006; Chandler 2009; Nissenbaum 2010; Solove 2011; EGE 2014). More precisely, a central issue that complicates the relationship between privacy and security is its framing as contradictory in terms of a trade-off in the public discourse. Securiti-zation reinforces this framing. The employment of security and surveillance measures is predominantly based on this trade-off, which assumes a necessity to trade privacy for security. Privacy intrusions are then simply presented as a basic requirement in order to improve security. Two basic arguments that are often brought into the debate are that personal information needs to be gathered to improve security and that citizens accept this trade-off as they require more security. However, a number of scholars have criticized this trade-off model as being too simplistic as it reduces the complex interplay between privacy and security to a permanent contradiction in terms (e.g., Schneier 2006; Nissenbaum 2010; Solove 2011; Pavone and Degli Esposti 2012; Friedewald *et al.* 2015; Valkenburg 2015; Strauß 2017). Among others, Friedewald *et al.* (2015) explored the validity of this trade-off with a survey about individual attitudes on privacy and security. The logic of a trade-off suggests that those people with high security concerns care less about privacy. However, research results refute this assumption as no correlation between security concerns and privacy in the sense of a trade-off has been found. Hence, this statistical evidence against the validity of this trade-off model at the individual level shows that security is not weighed as more important than privacy. Similar findings result from the Sur-PRISE project the author was involved in (for empirical results concerning the perceptions of citizens see Chapter 5). Altogether, there is empirical evidence pointing out that the relationship between privacy and security is not as simple as the trade-off model suggests. Furthermore, and even more important: there are serious conceptual arguments against a trade-off framing. Beginning with the term as such, the wording "trade-off" already implies that there are contradictory items where one wins at the cost of the other and vice versa. This trade-off operates at a political as well as at an individual level. At the political level, privacy is framed as a burden to effective security measures; hence, privacy intrusions here are quasi-justified as a precondition to improving security. At the individual level, the trade-off conveys that more security is possible but only if individuals accept privacy intrusions (EGE 2014). Thus, the assumption of a trade-off is an "all-or-nothing fallacy" (Solove 2011) where privacy and security are misleadingly presented as concepts being in a "natural" conflict. This assumption attempts to neglect privacy and data protection because they are framed as obstacles to security. Consequently, it inhibits comprehension that the relationship between privacy and security is to some extent complementary and not contradictory per se. This complementarity is undermined by the assumed (and constructed) permanent demand to make a mutually exclusive choice between these values. Furthermore, security measures that do not self-evidently entail privacy intrusion are neglected in this logic. This also hampers gaining a view on security which does not require privacy intrusion. Hence alternative and less intrusive security options are now barely conceivable (Strauß 2017).

The trade-off model with privacy as antagonist to security is ethically problematic as it ultimately jeopardizes liberty, which essentially is the defining value for both concepts: privacy and security. Guild *et al.* (2008: 9) thus highlight that

> democracy, the rule of law and fundamental rights are designed to protect the liberty of the individual within the society.... The precedence of liberty as a value that must be protected by all states ... is key to ensuring that security in its coercive form is used only as a tool to support freedom and is subject to its priority. Hence, the individual is entitled to freedom and any interference with that freedom must be justified by the state on limited grounds and be subject to the important procedural requirements set out in ... human rights instruments.
>
> (Guild *et al.* 2008: 9)

This means that security is not a prior value as often presented in political discourse. To the contrary, liberty is the superior value that connects privacy and security (Hildebrandt 2006; Lever 2006; Nissenbaum 2010; EGE 2014; Klitou 2014). The essential role of liberty and freedom in fundamental rights frameworks highlights this fact. Privacy as well as security represent a human right being part of these legal frameworks. Hence, neither privacy nor security is an absolute right but each are always legally linked to broader public interest and the well-being of the general public. It is the task of jurisdiction to clarify eventual conflicts. Here, the principle of proportionality is crucial, which aims to come to a fair balance between the general interests of the public and the fundamental rights of individuals and their basic needs (De Hert 2012). The negotiation of this fair balance to ensure proportionality is the role of jurisdiction in the case of conflicts. However, this does not imply the existence of a permanent conflict. In brief, the right to privacy means that an individual has the general right to live freely without being exposed to interference into her private life. Thus, in legal norms (such as Article 8 ECHR, Article 8 and Article 52 CFREU or Article 12 UDHR) privacy intrusions are only allowed as exceptions under certain conditions. Such conditions have to be generally in compliance with the public interest and have to be in accordance with the law and the protection of the foundations of democracy. Although interference with privacy is foreseen by the law under certain conditions, this mode is always the exception to the rule and by no means a permanent choice.

As described in the previous sections, privacy is an enabler of other fundamental rights and represents a form of liberty, namely autonomy. Hence, the trade-off model that frames privacy intrusions as *sine qua non* for security neglects this and detracts from the function of privacy as enabler for other fundamental rights such as freedom of expression, information, assembly and movement (Lever 2006; EGE 2014; Klitou 2014). Finally, such a setting of inevitable privacy intrusions would reverse this as the exception and falsely present privacy intrusions as the norm. Furthermore, a security approach entailing a permanent conflict with privacy also undermines its very aim, to improve security: because intrusions into privacy can also create more insecurity by reducing the subjective, individual perception of security. For instance, a citizen may feel rather insecure and endangered in a political system that employs mass surveillance and exercises extensive power over public deliberation (for more details on this issue, see Chapter 5). Considering the intrinsic relationship between privacy, autonomy and identity, protecting privacy implies the protection of identity, which is an important condition for individual security. Surely, balancing privacy and security is necessary as neither the former nor the latter is an absolute right. However, as shown, this does not imply that there is a permanent conflict in the sense of a trade-off given. Nevertheless, this trade-off rather dominates security and surveillance practices, entailing a self-reinforcing dynamic as regards the security continuum of securitization.

Notions of post-privacy and transparency

Besides security controversies, another controversy related to ICTs concerns the tensions in the relationship between privacy and transparency. On the one hand, ICT-related societal transformations underline the need for re-conceptualizations of privacy. Enhancing transparency of information processing and of the involved (institutional) entities is a crucial part in this regard. On the other hand, society overall is assumed to become more transparent due to an extensive growth in personal data being processed. Consequently, the role of privacy and its protection is also increasingly questioned. Proponents of a so-called "post-privacy" era occasionally proclaim the end of privacy due to the lack of individual control over information flows. However, as networked data and free information flows would entail a more open society without discrimination, there would also be no need for privacy anymore (e.g., Brin 1998; Heller 2011). This notion of post-privacy received some attention after science fiction author David Brin (1998) published the non-fiction book *The Transparent Society*. The main argument of the book is that societal transparency would constantly increase due to informatization and electronic surveillance, which leads to an erosion of privacy. Similar arguments were brought after the Snowden revelations (e.g., by Spivack 2013). Brin also argued that surveillance practices would benefit society bottom-up if citizens employ these practices to observe the observers. This line of argument partially corresponds with a statement by former CEO of Sun Microsystems Scott McNealy, who claimed in 1999 "you have zero privacy anyway.... Get over it." Interestingly, McNealy revised his statement a few years later and referred to the vast importance of appropriate privacy protection: "It's going to get scarier if we don't come up with technology and rules to protect appropriately privacy and secure the data, and the most important asset we have is obviously the data on people" (cited from Lemos 2006). Several years later, similar pro-privacy statements came from other tech companies, e.g., Google. In 2013, executive chairman Eric Schmidt stated in an interview: "You have to fight for your privacy, or you will lose it" (cited from Colvile 2013). However, at the same time, Schmidt denied any responsibility of Google or other tech companies for privacy issues as they would just provide innovative services. In Schmidt's view, privacy protection is mainly the task of individuals.

In fact, though, Google, Facebook and other big technology companies contribute in many respects to contemporary privacy problems. Hence, such statements can be seen as part of their public-relations strategy (such as Google's motto "don't be evil"). Moreover, the entrepreneurship spirit of Internet companies seems to be relatively similar to a post-privacy notion. Among others, Schmidt also stated that "Google is a belief system. And we believe passionately in the open internet model. So, all of the answers to the questions that we give are, at the core, about the benefits of a free and open internet" (ibid.). Put simply, the main entrepreneurial attitude here seems to be that "privacy is important but not part of our business model". Furthermore, being asked about his opinion on the surveillance programs revealed by Edward Snowden, Schmidt[15] also said that state surveillance is "the nature of our society" (ibid.; Holpuch 2013). Similar statements can be found from Facebook founder Mark Zuckerberg, who, among other things, once said that privacy would no longer be a social norm as people today were more open and comfortable with sharing information (Johnson 2010). Being confronted with Facebook's privacy issues he stated: "What people want isn't complete privacy. It isn't that they want secrecy. It's that they want control over what they share and what they don't" (cited from Zimmer 2014).

These views suggest that privacy is not a main concern of major players in the online business but rather is seen as an obstacle to a flourishing post-privacy age. With this logic, privacy protection is then framed as the responsibility of the individual alone (for a discussion on this aspect see Chapter 6). Indeed, companies like those mentioned provide many innovative technologies and services which contribute to an open society in many respects, ranging from fostering free access to information, distant communications, interactions, etc. However, it is also a fact that there are privacy-intrusive practices related to these services. A notion of post-privacy with the complete disregard of corporate social responsibility undermines the societal function of privacy and, as a consequence, the vision of a more open society fostered by the responsible use of ICTs.

Considering the complexity of institutional power structures, agency problems, information asymmetries, imbalanced control over personal information etc., the elusiveness of the utopian post-privacy vision is nearly self-explanatory (these issues are discussed thoroughly in Chapter 5). For instance, the Snowden revelations (Greenwald 2014; Lyon 2014) prominently highlight that in our digitized, networked society surveillance practices of whatever kind basically result from the exercise of institutional power. Furthermore, surveillance mostly leads to a certain disparity and thus creates or reinforces power imbalances at the cost of the observed. Hence, although bottom-up surveillance can contribute to relativizing institutional power exercised top-down, it cannot negate it and, more importantly, it cannot emerge effectively without privacy: institutional power has the "starting advantage" of having already established control structures and corresponding organizations. In a fictive scenario without privacy being protected, individuals would not be able to organize themselves in an undetected and uncontrolled manner beyond this institutional power. Consequently, bottom-up surveillance would be hampered from its very beginning.

Multiple meanings of transparency

While the post-privacy notion itself is delusive, the debate is interesting as it mirrors the interplay of transparency and privacy, which alters with ICTs. Transparency has multiple, though interrelated, meanings: in common parlance, transparency relates to comprehensibility. This common notion conveys that information is transparent and broadly available (although with different implications top-down and bottom-up). This broad availability results from technology usage which increases transparency of information. Consequently, individuals are increasingly observable and the protection of privacy is hampered. At the same time, the function of transparency transforms bottom-up with ICTs, enabling individuals and civil society to scrutinize organizations, thus fostering institutional accountability. This form of transparency is inter alia enforced by novel forms of activism and civil disobedience (e.g., visible in contemporary phenomena such as Wikileaks, the Anonymous collective, the Occupy movement, online activism, etc.) as a certain counterweight to institutional power regimes in the public as well as in the private domains. Also, whistleblower Edward Snowden argued that reinforcing transparency and accountability of security agencies was a basic motivation for him to reveal secret surveillance programs (Gellman and Makron 2013). Leaving a discussion about eventual controversies of these examples aside, they (and many others) have an important commonality: they indicate that extensive ICT diffusion, informatization and digitization of society driven by institutional power regimes boost the societal demand for more transparency and accountability. In this regard, transparency is not a counterpart to privacy, but is instead a complementary concept as regards the aim to foster accountability of (public and private) power regimes. In contrast to the common notion of comprehensibility, there is another, rather technical, meaning of transparency in the sense of hiding or masking information. This form of transparency is inter alia relevant in human–computer interaction and the development of distributed computer systems, where the design of transparent user interfaces helps to avoid information overload of users. Information, or parts of it, which are not necessary for a particular usage context, are hidden from the user in order to reduce complexity and improve usability (e.g., of a technology, or application, etc.).[16] At first glance, this meaning of transparency is contradictory to a notion of comprehensibility. However, the aim is similar, i.e., to foster user comprehension of, e.g., information processes relevant for an interaction. The crux is that maximum information is difficult if not impossible to scrutinize. Hence, there is need for approaches to reduce the complexity of information processing in order to support scrutiny. This rather technical notion of transparency includes this by restructuring information in layers so that information is easier to understand in different usage contexts for an individual user. A similar demand for restructuring information exists for the broader, socio-political dimension of transparency because, otherwise, individuals and civil society in general may be overburdened with masses of information which is neither comprehensible nor controllable. Therefore, intermediary entities are required, such as interest groups, the media, data protection authorities or similar, who, e.g., scrutinize information processing of technologies and applications on behalf of individual citizens. Generally speaking, individuals alone can hardly comprehend the full complexity of societal processes. The same is true for all types of processes and systems in which personal information is involved, which are hardly controllable by a single individual. The line of argument of the post-privacy proponents is thus misleading as it neglects these aspects. This meaning of transparency is particularly relevant for visions of ubiquitous or pervasive computing with the aim to deeply integrate technology in society so that it is permanently available in a transparent, i.e., invisible way (Weiser 1991; Zhang and Zhou 2006). Indeed, though, this vision entails serious conflicts with privacy, when information flows seamlessly from one socio-technical context to another so that there is no (informational) boundary anymore between the individual and technology (this aspect is discussed in more depth in Chapter 4 and subsequent chapters).

Privacy is not a secret

The different shades and meanings of transparency are also mirrored in the privacy discourse. Traditional conceptualizations of privacy frame it as a form of secrecy (which partially overlaps with the latter form of transparency in the sense of hiding information). Solove (2004: 42) called this the "secrecy paradigm", which "is so embedded in our privacy discourse that privacy is often represented visually by a roving eye, an open keyhole, or a person peeking through Venetian blinds". The problem Solove addresses is that a reductionist view on privacy as a form of secrecy neglects its vital functions for democracy and further complicates effective protection. Indeed, confidentiality and the way information is disclosed are important privacy issues. But privacy problems do not merely concern breaches of secrecy or confidentiality of information, and privacy is not just about hiding information or avoiding disclosure. Every individual has some things kept private and some selectively disclosed to others. However, this does not imply that "avoiding disclosure is the sum and substance of our interest in privacy" (Solove 2004: 43). For example, a person (call her Alice) with cancer may tell her closest friends and some colleagues about her disease; but this does not mean that she wants everyone in her workplace to know about her disease. Hence, in this case, a privacy breach would occur when, e.g., a trusted colleague breaks confidentiality and tells another colleague. In the logic of privacy as secrecy, Alice would be better off not telling anyone and mistrust all of her colleagues. However, as privacy is more than secrecy, i.e.

> a right to context-appropriate flows [of information] … there is no paradox in caring deeply about privacy, and, at the same time, eagerly sharing information as long as the sharing and withholding conforms with the principled conditions prescribed by governing contextual norms.
>
> (Nissenbaum 2010: 189)

Thus, equally important as confidentiality is that the processing entities, as well as the purposes and contexts personal information is used for, are trustworthy and transparent, i.e., comprehensible and accountable. Similar to the logic of a false trade-off between privacy and security (as discussed in the previous section), a notion of post-privacy implicitly embraces this secrecy paradigm, where privacy is reduced to a concept of hiding information. This view falsely frames privacy as a concept contradictory to transparency. At the same time, privacy is framed as irrelevant because, in this logic, keeping information secret is hardly applicable when digital environments boost the availability of information.

This framing of privacy as a form of secrecy misses its public value. Most individuals normally and legitimately expect their privacy to be respected not just in their private homes but also in the public. Privacy is thus not merely about avoiding information disclosure but also about ensuring that information is only available to selected people and used for particular, legitimate purposes (Solove 2004; Nissenbaum 2010). This issue is observable in social media and ICT usage in general. These technological means offer a large variety of options to share, link and exchange personal and non-personal information. The fact that these options are enjoyed by a vast range of users does not necessarily imply that these people care less about their privacy or accept permanent disclosure and use of their personal information. Several studies (e.g., Hazari and Brown 2013;

Leimbach *et al.* 2014; EB 2015) challenge the assumption of lacking privacy awareness among social media or Internet users. As will be shown in Chapter 5, similar is true as regards the perceptions of citizens on surveillance technology. Chapter 5 takes a closer look at the various privacy issues related to ICTs and the associated usage practices in security and surveillance contexts.

The significance of controlled information processing

Unintended disclosure of information is one among many important aspects. Another essential issue is the purpose and use of information beyond the control of the individual concerned. Transparency of information processing is also an important criterion for ISD, though in the sense of the individual concerned being enabled to comprehend and control her personal information flows, i.e., the contexts in which her information is being processed. The issues concerning ISD (as presented in previous sections) are clear indications for how technology fundamentally altered the notion of privacy. The German Constitutional Court's line of argument impressively highlights several of today's core problems of privacy protection, which have grown significantly since then, especially as regards the creation of personality profiles and how this undermines privacy. This refers to the problems of data mining and profiling, i.e., the use of technological means and algorithms to explore patterns in large data sets for the gathering and storage of information about individual people (Hildebrandt and Gutwirth 2008). ICTs provide manifold options for sophisticated profiling techniques, facilitated by the transformed relationship between public and private spheres, accompanied by increasing transparency of digital identities. This is prominently exemplified by social media platforms such as social networking site Facebook and others, which, at first glance, appear as sort of technology-mediated public spaces (Boyd and Ellison 2007). However, in fact, social media platforms significantly differ from traditional public spaces as their accessibility and availability have other implications compared to the physical world: as a result of their technical design, in social media environments user profiles—including personal details, interactions, social relationships to personal entities (contacts, friends, etc.) and non-personal entities (content used, produced, linked, shared, liked, etc.) as well as the content of communications—are commonly disclosed and thus explicitly observable (Strauß and Nentwich 2013). Hence, there is an explicit transparency of individual identity representations given, their preferences, relationships and interactions, etc., which did not exist in a similar form in physical public domains. In the analog world, there is usually no systematic monitoring of this kind. Similar issues are true in the case of other ICTs which foster connectivity, interactivity and transparency of their individual users. Substantially, ICTs enable numerous means to represent individual identities online or in other digital environments and thus facilitate digital identification (these developments are explored in Chapter 4). Associated with this development are additional options for privacy intrusion, profiling and surveillance (as analyzed in Chapter 5). These issues highlight that ICTs transformed the relationship between the public and the private, with a certain process of renegotiation. With their informational connectivity and interactivity, digital environments represent a blurry hybrid between private and public spheres with diminishing boundaries in between. This has consequences for the representation and availability of individual identities and thus for privacy. Nissenbaum (2010) argues that privacy intrusions in general affect what she calls contextual integrity, as information concerning an individual is misused beyond the original context of information processing the individual may have agreed upon. In her view, informational norms determine the integrity of a particular context in which personal information is being processed. Otherwise, if these norms are breached then privacy is violated (ibid.). Within context she means "structured social settings characterized by canonical activities, roles, relationships, power structures, norms (or rules), and internal values (goals, ends, purposes)" (ibid.: 132). Hence, for Nissenbaum, social contexts and context-relative informational norms are the central building blocks of contextual integrity, which she proposes as a benchmark for privacy. She argues that the transgression of context-relative norms is among the core problems of privacy protection: "The norms, which prescribe the flow of personal information in a given context, are a function of the types of information in question.... When these norms are contravened, we experience this as a violation of privacy ..." (Nissenbaum 2010: 127). Hence, put simply, the context of information processing is of utmost importance for privacy protection. Contextual integrity embraces ISD and the privacy principle of purpose binding. Each is heavily strained as ICT usage entails multiple contexts of information processing fostered by the blurry boundaries between private and public spheres. The crux is that socio-technical systems are increasingly networked so that information processing can span across multiple contexts and domains (see Chapter 5). The multitude of socio-technical systems and practices may intentionally or unintentionally breach contextual integrity. Thus, individuals can hardly comprehend and control the processing of their information as these contexts often remain unknown or hidden to them. Therefore, a lack of accountability and transparency of information processing in socio-technical systems is a critical privacy problem. Or in other words: privacy protection is hampered when information asymmetries exist between the individual and the information processing entities, at the cost of the individual's ISD. Furthermore, even in known contexts, personal information may not be controllable for the individual. Consequently, simply enacting individual control over personal information alone may not be enough to ease this problem (these issues are discussed thoroughly in Chapters 5 and 6).

Therefore, the boundary control function of privacy is not merely a matter for the individual concerned but also for the entities that process her information. Although privacy protection apparently involves individual responsibility, privacy also needs to be a predetermined, institutionalized concept inherent to societal values, norms and practices, etc., provided and protected by all societal actors. Otherwise, the individual is literally left alone in protecting her privacy. The fact that privacy is intrinsically linked to autonomy and ISD does not imply that the individual is solely responsible for its protection. Self-controlled hand-ling and provision of personal information is an important aspect of privacy, but it is by no means the only relevant one. As outlined in the previous sections, privacy is not merely a private value but is also a public one. Basically, the insti-tutionalization of privacy and data protection (at least in Europe) is an expres-sion of this public value, including legal frameworks based on common privacy principles and their consideration in socio-technical practices. However, ICTs have significantly challenged the applicability of regulation and the privacy regime is considerably hampered in its effectiveness. One aspect is the lack of effective legal protection as technology usage partially involves legal gray areas (such as issues regarding consent). A general problem is that, to some extent, the law lags behind technological development. However, this is a matter less of insufficient laws and more of their implementation and enforcement. The effec-tiveness of legal regulations and international privacy protection standards also suffers from insufficient knowledge about the emergence of privacy impacts. Ambiguity about the mechanisms and forms of information processing that affect privacy also complicates the implementation of appropriate protection mechanisms. This is also mirrored in socio-technical practices with digital iden-tification playing an important role in this regard, as will be shown in subsequent chapters. As discussed in this chapter, intrusions into privacy and insufficient protection thereof can also have a negative impact on individual identity-building. But also, conversely, the way identity information is represented, accessed and processed can significantly affect individual privacy. Before privacy impacts and issues of lacking control over identity information are explored in depth (in Chapter 5), the next chapter sheds light on the emergence of digital identification resulting from ICTs. This is particularly important because of the strong interplay between privacy and identity: both concepts are mutually dependent and, con-sequently, transformations of socio-technical identification practices affect privacy and vice versa. As will be shown, ICTs entail and foster novel forms of digital identity representation and identification. As a consequence, identity information becomes more networked, available and transparent.

Notes

1 The terms "digital" and "electronic" identification are used synonymously here.
2 For instance: a tree is an entity. There are many different trees in a forest. Without additional information about its properties, one tree is not distinguishable from others. Information about the "identity" of a tree, such as shape, location, type of tree (e.g., apple tree), age (number of its annual rings), height, etc., allows one tree to be distin-guished from others. Hence, information about its properties gives identity to an entity.
3 This is an issue of mathematics and statistics, which is not discussed in more depth in this book.
4 Automated Teller Machine.
5 The field of IDM deals with peculiarities of digital identification. See Chapter 4.
6 This is a common issue of psychoanalysis, also known as the porcupine problem; e.g., Luepnitz (2003).

7 This definition is widely similar to that in the former Data Protection Directive 95/46/EC Article 2 (DPD 1995).
8 The United Nations International Covenant on Civil and Political Rights: www.hrweb.org/legal/cpr.html.
9 Eventual differences may be more relevant in specific national laws, which are not considered here.
10 European Commission: Proposal for an ePrivacy Regulation, January 2017, https://ec.europa.eu/digital-single-market/en/proposal-eprivacy-regulation.
11 Provided that member states ensure appropriate safeguards, the processing of data "for historical, statistical or scientific purposes shall, in accordance with Article 89(1), not be considered to be incompatible with the initial purposes ('purpose limitation')" (Article 5 (1) (b) GDPR).
12 Judgment of the First Senate from 15 December 1983, 1 BvR 209/83 *et al.*—Population Census, BVerfGE 65, 1.
13 In Germany known as the so-called "Volkszählungsurteil".
14 Referring to Thomas Hobbes' major work *The Leviathan* first published in 1651.
15 Google also cultivates some contacts with security authorities. CEO Schmidt, for instance, is also the chair of a think tank of the US pentagon, the Defense Innovation Advisory Board; e.g., Alba (2016).
16 For instance, a standard e-mail program would be less usable with a text-based command line and without a graphical user interface, which provides simple mechanisms to send and receive e-mails.

References

All URLs were checked last on October 23, 2018.

Abelson, H. and Lessig, L. (1998) Digital Identity in Cyberspace. White paper Submitted for 6.805/Law of Cyberspace: Social Protocols. http://groups.csail.mit.edu/mac/classes/6.805/student-papers/fall98-papers/identity/linked-white-paper.html.

Agre, P. E. and Rotenberg, M. (eds.) (1998) *Technology and Privacy: The new landscape.* Cambridge: MIT Press.

Aichholzer, G. and Strauß, S. (2010) The Austrian Case: Multi-card concept and the relationship between citizen ID and social security cards. *Identity in the Information Society (IDIS)*, 3(1): 65–85.

Alba, D. (2016) Pentagon Taps Eric Schmidt to Make Itself More Google-ish. *Wired*, February 3, www.wired.com/2016/03/ex-google-ceo-eric-schmidt-head-pentagon-innovation-board/.

Altman, I. (1975) *The Environment and Social Behavior: Privacy, personal space, territory, crowding.* Montery: Brooks/Cole.

Annan, Kofi (2000) Secretary-General Salutes. *International Workshop on Human Security in Mongolia. Two-Day Session in Ulaanbaatar, May 8–10*, Press Release SG/SM/7382. www.gdrc.org/sustdev/husec/Definitions.pdf.

Ball, K. and Webster, F. (2003) *The Intensification of Surveillance: Crime, terrorism and warfare in the information age.* London: Pluto.

Balzacq, T. (2005) The Three Faces of Securitization: Political agency, audience and context. *European Journal of International Relations*, 11(2): 171–201.

Baum, G. R., Kurz, C. and Schantz, P. (2013) Das vergessene Grundrecht. *Frankfurter Allgemein Zeitung*, 27. Februar, www.faz.net/aktuell/feuilleton/debatten/datenschutz-das-vergessene-grundrecht-12095331.html.

Bennett, C. J. and Lyon, D. (2008) *Playing the Identity Card: Surveillance, security and identification in global perspective.* London/New York: Routledge.

Bigo, D. (2000) When Two Become One: Internal and external securitisations in Europe. In Kelstrup, M. and Williams, M. (eds.), *International Relations Theory and the Politics of European Integration. Power, security and community*. London: Routledge, 171–204.

Bigo, D. (2008) Globalized (In)Security: The field and the Ban-Opticon. In Bigo, D. and Tsoukala, A. (eds.), *Terror, Insecurity and Liberty. Illiberal practices of liberal regimes after 9/11*. Oxon/New York: Routledge, 10–48.

Boyd, D. M. and Ellison, N. B. (2007) Social Network Sites: Definition, history, and scholarship. *Journal of Computer-Mediated Communication*, 13(1): 210–230.

Brin, D. (1998) *The Transparent Society. Will technology force us to choose between privacy and freedom?* Reading, MA: Perseus Publishing.

Butler, J. (2006) *Gender Trouble: Feminism and the subversion of identity*. New York: Routledge.

Buzan, B., Weaver, O. and de Wilde, J. (1998) *Security: A new framework for analysis*. Boulder: Lynne Rienner.

Cameron, K. (2005) The Laws of Identity. *Identityblog*, November 5, www.identityblog. com/stories/2005/05/13/TheLawsOfIdentity.pdf.

CASE Collective (2006) Critical Approaches to Security in Europe: A networked manifesto. *Security Dialogue*, 37(4): 443–487.

CFREU (2000) *Charter of Fundamental Rights of the European Union*. www.europarl. europa.eu/charter/pdf/text_en.pdf.

Chandler, J. (2009) Privacy Versus National Security: Clarifying the trade-off. In Kerr, I., Steeves, V. and Lucock, C. (eds.), *Lessons from the Identity Trail: Anonymity, privacy and identity in a networked society*. Oxford: Oxford University Press, 121–138.

Chaum, D. (1985) Security Without Identification: Transaction systems to make big brother obsolete. *Communications of the ACM*, 28(10): 1030–1044. Available at: https://gnunet.org/sites/default/files/10.1.1.48.4680.pdf.

Christman, J. (2015) Autonomy in Moral and Political Philosophy. In *Stanford Encyclopedia of Philosophy*. First published 2003, updated 2015. http://plato.stanford.edu/entries/autonomy-moral/.

Clarke, R. (1994a) Human Identification in Information Systems: Management challenges and public policy issues. *Information Technology and People*, 7(4): 6–37. www.roger clarke.com/DV/HumanID.html.

Clarke, R. (1994b) The Digital Persona and its Application to Data Surveillance. *The Information Society*, 10(2): 77–92. www.rogerclarke.com/DV/DigPersona.html#DP.

Clarke, R. (2006) *What's "Privacy"?* www.rogerclarke.com/DV/Privacy.html.

Cohen, J. E. (2012) *Configuring the Networked Self: Law, code, and the play of everyday practice*. Yale: Yale University Press.

Colvile, R. (2013) Eric Schmidt interview: "You have to fight for your privacy or you will lose it". *Telegraph*, May 25, www.telegraph.co.uk/technology/eric-schmidt/1007 6175/Eric-Schmidt-interview-You-have-to-fight-for-your-privacy-or-you-will-lose-it. html.

Danezis, G., Domingo-Ferrer, J., Hansen, M., Hoepman, J., Le Métayer, D., Tirtea, R. and Schiffner, S. (2014) *Privacy and Data Protection by Design: From policy to engineering*. European Union Agency for Network and Information Security (ENISA), December 2014.

De Andrade, N. N. G., Monteleone, S. and Martin, A. (2013) *Electronic Identity in Europe: Legal challenges and future perspectives (e-ID 2020)*. JRC Scientific and Policy Reports. Joint Research Centre, European Commission.

De Cristofaro, E., Du, H., Freudiger, J. and Norcie, G. (2014) A Comparative Usability Study of Two-Factor Authentication. *8th NDSS Workshop on Usable Security (USEC 2014)*, briefing paper, Internet Society. www.internetsociety.org/sites/default/files/01_5-paper.pdf.

De Hert, P. (2008) Identity Management of e-ID, Privacy and Security in Europe. A human rights view. *Information Security Technical Report*, 13: 71–75.

De Hert P. (2012) A Human Rights Perspective on Privacy and Data Protection Impact Assessments. In Wright, D. and De Hert, P. (eds.). *Privacy Impact Assessment. Law, Governance and Technology Series*, Vol. 6. Dordrecht: Springer, 33–76.

DPD—Data Protection Directive (1995) EU Directive 95/46/EC of the European Parliament and of the Council of 24 October 1995 on the Protection of Individuals with Regard to the Processing of Personal Data and On the Free Movement of Such Data. http://eur-lex. europa.eu/legal-content/EN/TXT/PDF/?uri=CELEX:31995L0046&from=DE.

EB—Eurobarometer (2015) *Special Eurobarometer 431: Data protection*. EU. http://ec. europa.eu/commfrontoffice/publicopinion/archives/ebs/ebs_431_en.pdf.

EDPS—European Data Protection Supervisor (2016) *Opinion 5/2016—Preliminary EDPS Opinion on the Review of the ePrivacy Directive (2002/58/EC)*. https://edps.europa.eu/ sites/edp/files/publication/16-07-22_opinion_eprivacy_en.pdf.

EGE—European Group on Ethics in Science and New Technologies (2014) *Ethics of Security and Surveillance Technologies*. Opinion No. 28 of the European Groups on Ethics in Science and New Technologies. Brussels, May 20.

Finn, R. L., Wright, D. and Friedewald, M. (2013) Seven Types of Privacy. In Gutwirth, S., Leenes, R., De Hert, P. and Poullet, Y. (eds.), *European Data Protection: Coming of age*. Dordrecht: Springer, 3–32.

Floridi, L. (2013) *The Ethics of Information*. Oxford: Oxford University Press.

FRA—European Union Agency for Fundamental Rights (2014) *Handbook on European Data Protection Law*. Luxembourg: Publications Office of the EU.

Frazer, N. (2007) Transnationalising the Public Sphere: On the legitimacy and efficacy of public opinion in a post-Westphalian world. *Theory, Culture and Society*, 24: 7–30.

Friedewald, M., van Lieshout, M., Rung, S., Ooms, M. and Ypma, J. (2015) Privacy and Security Perceptions of European Citizens: A test of the trade-off model. In Camenisch, J., Fischer-Hübner, S. and Hansen, M. (eds.), *Privacy and Identity for the Future Internet in the Age of Globalization*, series IFIP AICT Vol. 457. Heidelberg: Springer, 39–53.

GDPR—General Data Protection Regulation (2016) Regulation (EU) 2016/679 of the European Parliament and of the Council of 27 April 2016 on the Protection of Natural Persons with Regard to the Processing of Personal Data and On the Free Movement of Such Data, and Repealing Directive 95/46/EC (General Data Protection Regulation). http://eur-lex.europa.eu/legal-content/EN/TXT/HTML/?uri=CELEX:32016R0679&qid =1485427623759&from=en.

Gellman, B. and Makron, J. (2013) Edward Snowden Says Motive Behind Leaks Was to "Expose Surveillance State". *Washington Post*, June 10, www.washingtonpost.com/ politics/edward-snowden-says-motive-behind-leaks-was-to-expose-surveillance-state/2013/06/09/aa3f0804-d13b-11e2-a73e-826d299ff459_story.html?utm_term=.1 cabd9f22bdf.

Giddens, A. (1991) *Modernity and Self Identity: Self and society in the late modern age*. Cambridge: Polity Press.

González-Fuster, G. (2014) *The Emergence of Personal Data Protection as a Fundamental Right of the EU*. Law, Governance and Technology Series Vol. 16. Cham/ Heidelberg/New York etc.: Springer.

Greenleaf, G. (2017) Renewing Convention 108: The CoE's "GDPR Lite" initiatives. *Privacy Laws and Business International Report*, 142: 14–17; UNSW Law Research Paper No. 17–3. https://ssrn.com/abstract=2892947 https://papers.ssrn.com/sol3/papers.cfm?abstract_id=2892947.

Greenwald, G. (2014) *No Place to Hide: Edward Snowden, the NSA and the surveillance state*. London: Hamish Hamilton/Penguin Books.

Guild, E., Carrera, S. and Balzacq, T. (2008) *The Changing Dynamic of Security in an Enlarged European Union*. Research paper No. 12, CEPS Programme Series. www.ceps.eu http://aei.pitt.edu/11457/1/1746.pdf.

Habermas, J. (1989) *The Structural Transformation of the Public Sphere: An inquiry into a category of bourgeois society* (original work: Strukturwandel der Öffentlichkeit 1962, Hermann Luchterhand Verlag). Cambridge MA: The MIT Press.

Haggerty, K. D. and Samatas, M. (eds.) (2010) *Surveillance and Democracy*. Oxon: Routledge-Cavendish.

Hazari, S. and Brown, C. (2013) An Empirical Investigation of Privacy Awareness and Concerns on Social Networking Sites. *Journal of Information Privacy and Security*, 9(4): 31–51.

Heller, C. (2011) *Prima leben ohne Privatsphäre*. Munchen: C. H. Beco Verlag.

Hildebrandt, M. (2006) Privacy and Identity. In Claes, E., Duff, A. and Gutwirth, S. (eds.), *Privacy and the Criminal Law*. Antwerpen/Oxford: Intersentia, 43–57.

Hildebrandt, M. and Gutwirth, S. (eds.) (2008) *Profiling the European Citizen: Cross-disciplinary perspectives*. Amsterdam: Springer Netherlands.

Hildebrandt, M. and Rouvroy, A. (2011) *Law, Human Agency and Autonomic Computing*. London/New York: Routledge.

Holpuch, A. (2013) Eric Schmidt Says Government Spying is "the Nature of Our Society". *Guardian*, September 13, www.theguardian.com/world/2013/sep/13/eric-schmidt-google-nsa-surveillance.

Hornung, G. and Schnabel, C. (2009) Data Protection in Germany I: The population census decision and the right to informational self-determination. *Computer Law and Security Report*, 25(1): 84–88.

ITU—International Telecommunication Union (2010) *Baseline Identity Management Terms and Definitions. Series X: Data networks, open system communications and security. Cyberspace security—identity management. Recommendation ITU-T X.1252*. www.itu.int/SG-CP/example_docs/ITU-T-REC/ITU-T-REC_E.pdf.

ISO—International Organization for Standardization (2011) *Information Technology—Security Techniques—Privacy Framework*. ISO/IEC 29100:2011(E). First edition 2011: 12–15.

Johnson, B. (2010) Privacy No Longer a Social Norm, Says Facebook Founder. *Guardian*, January 11, www.theguardian.com/technology/2010/jan/11/facebook-privacy.

Jolly, R. and Ray, D. B. (2006) *The Human Security Framework and National Human Development Reports: A review of experiences and current debates*. NHDR occasional paper no. 5, United Nations Development Programme, National Human Development Report Unit. New York: UNDP. www.pogar.org/publications/other/undp/governance/Human-Security-Guidance-Note.pdf.

Kahn, J. D. (2003) Privacy as a Legal Principle of Identity Maintenance. *Seton Hall Law Review*, 33(2): 371–410.

Kant, I. (1785/1997) *Grundlegung zur Metaphysik der Sitten*. Werkausgabe Band VIII (herausgegeben von Weischedel, W.) Erstmals erschienen 1785. Berlin: Suhrkamp Taschenbuch Wissenschaft.

Khurana, T. (2013) Paradoxes of Autonomy: On the dialectics of freedom and normativity. Symposium. *Canadian Journal of Continental Philosophy*, 17: 50–74.

Klitou, D. (2014) Privacy, Liberty and Security. In *Privacy-Invading Technologies and Privacy by Design: Safeguarding privacy, liberty and security in the 21st century.* Information Technology and Law Series. The Hague: Springer/TMC Asser Press, 13–25.

Klopfer, P. H. and Rubenstein, D. I. (1977) Privacy and its Biological Basis. *Journal of Social Issues*, 33(3): 53–65.

Korfmacher, C. (2006) Personal Identity. In *Internet Encyclopaedia of Philosophy.* www.iep.utm.edu/person-i/.

Kubicek, H. and Noack, T. (2010) Different Countries—Different Extended Comparison of the Introduction of eIDs in Eight European Countries. *Identity in the Information Society (IDIS)*, 3(1): 235–245.

Leimbach, T., Hallinan, D., Bachlechner, D., Weber, A., Jaglo, M., Hennen, L., Nielsen, R., Nentwich, M., Strauß, S., Lynn, T. and Hunt, G. (2014) *Potential and Impacts of Cloud Computing Services and Social Network Websites—Study.* Report no. IP/A/STOA/FWC/2008-096/Lot4/C1/SC8; Science and Technology Options Assessment—European Parliamentary Research Service: Brussels.

Lemos, R. (2006) Private Identities Become a Corporate Focus. *SecurityFocus*, February 20, www.securityfocus.com/news/11377.

Lever, A. (2006) Privacy Rights and Democracy: A contradiction in terms? *Contemporary Political Theory*, 5(2): 142–162.

Luepnitz, D. A. (2003) *Schopenhauer's Porcupines. Intimacy and its dilemmas: Five stories of psychotherapy.* New York: Basic Books.

Lyon, D. (2003) *Surveillance as Social Sorting. Privacy, risk and automated discrimination.* London: Routledge.

Lyon, D. (2009) *Identifying Citizens: ID cards as surveillance.* Cambridge: Polity Press.

Lyon, D. (2014) Surveillance, Snowden, and Big Data: Capacities, consequences, critique. *Big Data and Society*, July–December: 1–13. http://journals.sagepub.com/doi/abs/10.1177/2053951714541861.

Marx, G. T. (2001) Identity and Anonymity: Some conceptual distinctions and issues for research. In Caplan, J. and Torpey, J. (eds.). *Documenting Individual Identity.* Princeton: Princeton University Press. http://web.mit.edu/gtmarx/www/identity.html.

McCarthy, K. (2017) Trump Signs "No Privacy for Non-Americans" Order: What Does this mean for the rest of us? *The Register*, January 26, www.theregister.co.uk/2017/01/26/trump_blows_up_transatlantic_privacy_shield.

Moore Jr., B. (1984) *Privacy: Studies in social and cultural history.* New York: Pantheon Books.

Nanz, P. (2007) Multiple Voices: An interdiscursive concept of the European public sphere. In Fossum, J. E., Schlesinger, P. and Kvaerk, G. (eds.), *Public Sphere and Civil Society? Transformations of the European Union.* ARENA Report Series No. 2/07. Oslo, Norway: Centre for European Studies, 11–28.

Nauman, L. and Hobgen, G. (2009) *Privacy Features of European eID Card Specifications.* Position paper, European Network and Information Security Agency ENISA. www.enisa.europa.eu/publications/eid-cards-en/at_download/fullReport.

Nissenbaum, H. (2010) *Privacy in Context: Technology, policy, and the integrity of social life.* Stanford: Stanford University Press.

OECD—Organization for Economic Co-Operation and Development (2013) *The OECD Privacy Framework.* OECD Publishing. www.oecd.org/sti/ieconomy/privacy-guidelines.htm.

Owen, T. (2004) Challenges and Opportunities for Defining and Measuring Human Security, Human Rights, Human Security and Disarmament. *Disarmanet Forum 2004*, 3: 15–24.

Pavone, V. and Degli Esposti, S. (2012) Public Assessment of New Surveillance-Orientated Security Technologies: Beyond the trade-off between privacy and security. *Public Understanding of Science*, 21(5): 556–572.

Pfitzmann, A. and Borcea-Pfitzmann, K. (2010) Lifelong Privacy: Privacy and identity management for life. In Bezzi, M., Duquenoy, P., Fischer-Hübner, S., Hansen, M. and Zhang, G. (eds.), *Privacy and Identity Management for Life, 5th IFIP/PrimeLife International Summer School, Nice, France, September 7–11, 2009, Revised Selected Papers*. Berlin/Heidelberg: Springer, 1–17.

Pfitzmann, A. and Hansen, M. (2010) *A Terminology for Talking about Privacy by Data Minimization: Anonymity, unlinkability, undetectability, unobservability, pseudonymity, and identity*. Version 0.34. http://dud.inf.tu-dresden.de/literatur/Anon_Terminology_v0.34.pdf.

Raab, C. D. (2006) Social and Political Dimensions of Identity. In Fischer-Hübner, S., Duquenoy, P., Zuccato, A. and Martucci, L. (eds.), *Proceedings of the 3rd IFIP/FIDIS International Summer School on The Future of Identity in the Information Society, Karlstad University, Sweden, August 4–10*. Heidelberg: Springer, 3–19.

Raab, C. D. (2009) Identity: Difference and categorisation. In Kerr, I., Steeves, V. and Lucock, C. (eds.), *Lessons from the Identity Trail: Anonymity, privacy and identity in a networked society*. Oxford: Oxford University Press, 227–244.

Reiman, J. H. (1976) Privacy, Intimacy, and Personhood. *Philosophy and Public Affairs*, 6(1): 26–44. www.jstor.org/stable/2265060?seq=1#page_scan_tab_contents.

Ricoeur, P. (1992) *Oneself as Another*. (Translated by Kathleen Blamey). Chicago: University of Chicago Press.

Rouvroy, A. and Poullet, Y. (2009) The Right to Informational Self-Determination and the Value of Self-Development: Reassessing the importance of privacy for democracy. In Gutwirth, S., Poullet, Y., de Hert, P., de Terwangne, C. and Nouwt, S. (eds.), *Reinventing Data Protection?* Dordrecht: Springer, 45–76.

Rundle, M., Blakley, B., Broberg, J., Nadalin, A., Olds, D., Ruddy, M., Guimarares, M. T. M. and Trevithick, P. (2008) At a Crossroads: "Personhood" and digital identity in the information society. *STI Working paper* 2007/7, no. JT03241547 29-Feb-2008, Directorate for Science, Technology and Industry, OECD Publishing. www.oecd.org/dataoecd/31/6/40204773.doc.

Schneier, B. (2003) *Beyond Fear: Thinking sensibly about security in an uncertain world*. New York: Copernicus Books.

Schneier, B. (2006) The Eternal Value of Privacy. Published in *Wired*. May 18. Available at Schneier on Security, www.schneier.com/essays/archives/2006/05/the_eternal_value_of.html.

Solove, D. J. (2004) *The Digital Person: Technology and privacy in the information age*. New York and London: New York University Press.

Solove, D. J. (2006) A Taxonomy of Privacy. *University of Pennsylvania Law Review*, 154(3): 477–560.

Solove, D. J. (2011) *Nothing to Hide: The false tradeoff between privacy and security*. New Haven/London: Yale University Press.

Spivack, N. (2013) The Post-privacy World. *Wired*, July, www.wired.com/insights/2013/07/the-post-privacy-world/.

Strauß, S. (2011) The Limits of Control: (Governmental) identity management from a privacy perspective. In Fischer-Hübner, S., Duquenoy, P., Hansen, M., Leenes, R. and Zhang, G. (eds.), *Privacy and Identity Management for Life, 6th IFIP/PrimeLife International Summer School, Helsingborg, Sweden, August 2–6 2010, Revised Selected Papers*. Dordrecht: Springer, 206–218.

Strauß, S. (2017) A Game of Hide and Seek? Unscrambling the trade-off between privacy and security. In Friedewald, M., Burgess, P. J., Čas, J., Bellanova, R. and Peissl, W. (eds.), *Surveillance, Privacy, and Security: Citizens' perspectives*. London/New York: Routledge, 255–272.

Strauß, S. and Nentwich, M. (2013) Social Network Sites, Privacy and the Blurring Boundary Between Public and Private Spaces. *Science and Public Policy* 40(6): 724–732.

Treiger-Bar-Am, K. (2008) In Defense of Autonomy: An ethic of care. *New York University Journal of Law and Liberty*, 3(2): 548–590.

Trenz, H. J. (2008) In Search of the European Public Sphere: Between normative overstretch and empirical disenchantment. *ARENA Working Paper* 12/08. www.sv.uio.no/arena/english/research/publications/arena-working-papers/2001-2010/2008/wp08_12.pdf.

UDHR (1948) *The Universal Declaration of Human Rights*. www.un.org/en/universal-declaration-human-rights/index.html.

UN—United Nations (1994) *New Dimensions of Human Security. Human development report 1994, United Nations development programme*. New York: Oxford University Press.

Valkenburg, G. (2015) Privacy Versus Security: Problems and possibilities for the trade-off model. In Gutwirth, S., Leenes, R. and De Hert, P. (eds.), *Reforming European Data Protection Law*, 20 of the series Law, Governance and Technology. Dordrecht: Springer, 253–269.

Varela, F. J. (1997) Patterns of Life: Intertwining identity and cognition. *Brain and Cognition*, 34(1): 72–87.

Warren, S. D. and Brandeis, L. D. (1890) The Right to Privacy. *Harvard Law Review* 193 (1890), IV, December 15, 1890, No. 5. http://faculty.uml.edu/sgallagher/Brandeisprivacy.htm.

Watson, S. (2011) The 'Human' as Referent Object? Humanitarianism as securitization. *Security Dialogue*, 42(1): 3–20.

Wehage, J. C. (2013) *Das Grundrecht auf Gewährleistung der Vertraulichkeit und Integrität informationstechnischer Systeme und seine Auswirkungen auf das Bürgerliche Recht*. Dissertation, Universitätsverlag Göttingen. www.univerlag.uni-goettingen.de/bitstream/handle/3/isbn-978-3-86395-123-8/Wehage_Diss.pdf.

Weiser, M. (1991) The Computer of the 21st Century. *Scientific American*, 265(3): 94–104. www.lri.fr/~mbl/Stanford/CS477/papers/Weiser-SciAm.pdf.

Westin, A. (1967) *Privacy and Freedom*. New York: Atheneum.

White, H. C. (2008) *Identity and Control: How social formations emerge* (second edition). Princeton/Oxford: Princeton University Press.

Whitley, E. A., Gal, U. and Kjaergaard, A. (2014) Who Do You Think You Are? A review of the complex interplay between information systems, identification and identity. *European Journal of Information Systems*, 23(1): 17–35.

Wiener, N. (1954) *The Human Use of Human Beings: Cybernetics and society* (first published 1950, reprint of revised edition of 1954). Boston: Da Capo Press.

WP29—Article 29 Data Protection Working Party (2016) Opinion 01/2016 on the EU–U.S. Privacy Shield draft adequacy decision. 16/EN WP 238. http://ec.europa.eu/justice/data-protection/article-29/documentation/opinion-recommendation/files/2016/wp238_en.pdf.

Zhang, Y. and Zhou, Y. (2006) Transparent Computing: A new paradigm for pervasive computing. In Ma, J., Jin, H., Yang, L. T. and Tsai, J. J. P. (eds.), *Ubiquitous Intelligence and Computing. UIC 2006*. LNCS Vol. 4159. Berlin/Heidelberg: Springer, 1–10.

Zimmer, M. (2014) Mark Zuckerberg's Theory of Privacy. *Washington Post*, February 3, www.washingtonpost.com/lifestyle/style/mark-zuckerbergs-theory-of-privacy/2014/02/03/2c1d780a-8cea-11e3-95dd-36ff657a4dae_story.html.

4 Identification practices and the digital transformation of society

The previous chapter dealt with the basic functions of identification as well as the complex interplay of privacy, identity and autonomy. It was shown that privacy provides vital space for free and autonomous identity-building, with informational self-determination (ISD) as a crucial requirement. There is thus a naturally close relationship between identity and privacy. As discussed previously, controversies with security and transparency affect the quality of this relationship. These controversies are mirrored in and are reinforced by socio-technical transformations in the realm of ICTs, which continually pervade and transform society in numerous ways. Socio-technical practices are accompanied by increasing networking structures, connectivity and interactivity of digital information. Among other things, these developments have enabled novel forms of identity representation and of digital identification which are explored in this chapter.

The emergence of ICTs can be generally understood as a socio-technical transition, where technological change entails the occurrence of new functionalities; as well as incremental transformations of existing socio-technical functions and practices. Involved in these transformations is a certain pressure to adapt existing practices to technology. In our case, identification is such a practice which alters with ICTs. Digital identification practices can be found in a variety of contexts and online applications. These different developments are subject to the field of identity management (IDM), which deals with the digital processing and handling of identity information. Certain concepts for authentication and identification are required in various domains and particularly in electronic services to conduct transactions, or in online platforms to manage user profiles. The emergence of IDM is thus closely connected to e-government and e-commerce as well as the rise of personalized online services and social media platforms. IDM approaches generally aim to enhance control over digital information flows that represent personal identities. In this respect, IDM alters (digital) identification writ large. Not less far-reaching are the transformations related to social media platforms: they affect the way individuals interact with each other, and present and perform their identities online. These phenomena are a showcase for the networking structure of ICTs, which enable and foster networked identity representations.

Hence, the emergence of digital identification results from various technical and societal developments, which are presented and discussed here. This starts with a brief overview on the relevant technological developments of ICTs, which influenced the increasing societal role of digital identification. Particularly relevant in this regard is the field of IDM and its major drivers. This is followed by an examination of the emergence of social media platforms and their core functions as regards networked representations of individual identities. As will be shown, there are several overlaps between IDM and social media also as regards their societal functions and usage purposes. Finally, major transition paths of digital identification are explored, which indicate a further extension of identification practices.

The evolution of ICTs in a nutshell

Altogether, ICTs have become integrative parts of society in many respects with significant increases in socio-technical connectivity and interactivity. The following paragraphs provide an overview on the main developments in this regard, which have been driving the digital transformation of society. The different development stages are explored here through the lens of a (metasystem) transition (MST) (as outlined in Chapter 2). This allows the functional transformations related to different technologies and the corresponding trends to be grasped from a wider, systemic perspective. It has to be noted that this is an approximation but not a strict, unambiguous categorization of socio-technical developments into specific stages. The main purpose of this approach is to structure and highlight the dynamics of socio-technical change in the digital transformation of society.

Since the occurrence of the internet, the information society has evolved quickly; driven by technological progress, which induced several changes in the processing of information, as Figure 4.1 shows based on a rough distinction between four development stages. These stages are derived from the three stages of an MST (individuation, interaction, integration). The individuation phase is divided into information and communication for two reasons: first, both are inherent to ICTs; and second, to point out how ICTs—framed as a socio-technical metasystem—turned from a relatively isolated unidirectional tool toward a multidirectional, interactive and integrated networked medium.

These different stages highlight the transformative capacity of ICTs and how they became an integrated part of society in a relatively short period of time. The focus is on the changing modes of interaction exemplified by some key developments which intensified usage patterns of ICTs. While in the early years of Internet usage, the focus was on one-to-one interaction, usage and exchange of information between two entities, this has significantly changed toward sophisticated modes of interaction and increasing integration of systems and applications, as is observable today in many respects.

The first stage sketches the beginnings of ICTs, where new technological means to send, receive, access and distribute information occurred. The internet

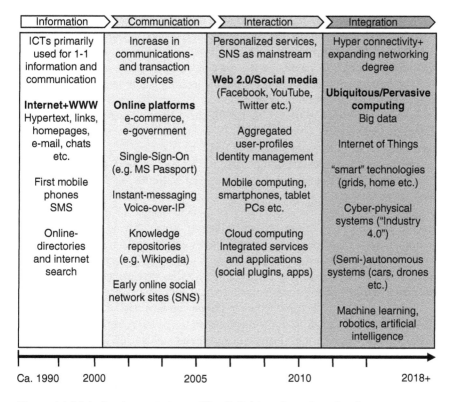

Information	Communication	Interaction	Integration
ICTs primarily used for 1-1 information and communication	Increase in communications- and transaction services	Personalized services, SNS as mainstream	Hyper connectivity+ expanding networking degree
Internet+WWW Hypertext, links, homepages, e-mail, chats etc.	**Online platforms** e-commerce, e-government	**Web 2.0/Social media** (Facebook, YouTube, Twitter etc.)	**Ubiquitous/Pervasive computing** Big data
First mobile phones SMS	Single-Sign-On (e.g. MS Passport) Instant-messaging Voice-over-IP	Aggregated user-profiles Identity management Mobile computing, smartphones, tablet PCs etc.	Internet of Things "smart" technologies (grids, home etc.) Cyber-physical systems ("Industry 4.0")
Online- directories and internet search	Knowledge repositories (e.g. Wikipedia) Early online social network sites (SNS)	Cloud computing Integrated services and applications (social plugins, apps)	(Semi-)autonomous systems (cars, drones etc.) Machine learning, robotics, artificial intelligence

Ca. 1990   2000   2005   2010   2018+

Figure 4.1 Main development stages of the digital transformation of society.

is obviously one of the central technological innovations of this evolutionary development that significantly altered information processing in many respects. Emerging from its forerunner, the ARPANET,[1] during the 1980s, the internet quickly turned into a large-scale system of interconnected computer networks on a global level. The development of the WWW in the early 1990s (Castells 1996/2003; Leiner *et al.* 2003; Lessig 2006) paved the way for a myriad of innovations based on the digital processing of information. With the WWW and hypertext, the internet became widely popular and transformed toward a new mass medium and a crossover technology carrying a broad range of applications, services, platforms, etc. During the 1990s, the web grew quickly with homepages, websites, online directories and so forth. The central online communication medium in that time was e-mail. In parallel to the expansion of the web, mobile phones gained in popularity and increasingly entered the market. During that time, they were not coupled to the internet. In 1992, the first SMS (short message service) (O'Mahony 2012) was sent; the first mobile phone with Internet capabilities, the Nokia Communicator, appeared in 1996 (Pew 2014). Also, one of the first online instant messaging services, ICQ, appeared in that time, which used to be widely popular (Patrizio 2016). In the same period, the search engine market took up. Today's global key player Google was found in 1998 and quickly challenged the former incumbent search engine providers Altavista and Yahoo. Also, the first e-commerce sites appeared: e.g., Amazon has been online since 1995, initially as an online book store; in the same year, the online auction service eBay appeared (ibid.). In this early information stage, ICTs were primarily used for one-to-one interaction and (compared with today) simple information communication services.

In the second stage, starting about 2000, there came an increase in communication and transaction services. The first online platforms were created, which made online services more accessible with the one-stop-shop principle, i.e., a single point of access enabling the usage of different services (e.g., in the fields of e-commerce and e-government). Commercial platforms significantly extended their scope during this stage; for example, Amazon shifted from a book store to a global supplier of various products. Dominant vendors of operating systems such as Microsoft and Apple intensified their efforts to provide software tailored to online applications (e.g., Microsoft Windows 2000, or Apple's Mac OSX). In 1999, Microsoft released an early IDM approach, called "Passport". In 2001, the largest interactive online encyclopedia, Wikipedia, was launched. With Skype occurring in 2003, phone communication via the internet (voice-over-IP) as well as instant messaging became popular online applications. In the same year, myspace.com and linkedin.com were launched as well as other early online SNS that occurred in that period—Facebook appeared in 2004 (Pew 2014).

From about 2005, the third development stage is characterized by the emergence of so-called Web 2.0 (O'Reilly 2005), which led to novel forms of interactions, content-specific platforms and a further growth in the amount of digital information. For instance, the photo-sharing site Flickr or the video portal YouTube appeared in that period. Social media became mainstream platforms with today's major social networking platform Facebook accompanied by various specialized SNS (e.g., LinkedIn, Yammer, Xing, ResearchGate, etc.), various services from Google, micro-blogging site Twitter, news aggregation sites (e.g., Reddit), and many more. Web 2.0 and social media also boosted personalized services, aggregated user profiles and the commercialization of personal information. In about the same period, IDM became increasingly important (see next the section). During this time, mobile and cloud computing also became widely popular; mainly boosted by smartphones and other portable devices. For instance, Amazon launched its first Cloud service in 2006.[2] The first iPhone, appearing in 2007, boosted the smartphone market and mobile computing gained in importance (Pew 2014). These developments also paved the way for integrated services such as apps, i.e., micro-programs, to extend the functionality of applications on smartphones or other devices. They, inter alia, contribute to a closer linkage between online applications and mobile telecommunications.

Today, the fourth and current stage, initiated in about 2010, is present, where the integration of technology (and the generated digital information) into society has reached a new quality. This stage is accompanied by a high and rapidly growing degree of networking and hyper-connectivity in a wide range of domains. Hence, ICTs today do not just play a dominant role in most daily practices from work, private communications, social relationships, etc. They are also increasingly embedded into socio-technological domains that used to function basically without ICTs and the internet. Examples are "smart" technologies entering private households with networked home appliances—smart TV sets, smart grids and smart metering—where ICTs are embedded into energy supply systems or other "traditional" domains that used to be offline. In parallel, there are developments toward autonomic computing, an umbrella term for information systems operating at multiple levels to provide, e.g., "hidden complexity, pervasive computing, context awareness, real time monitoring, proactive computing, and smart human–machine-interfacing" (Hildebrandt 2011: 5). Examples can be found in recent trends in the field of cyber-physical systems and "Industry 4.0" addressing novel forms of further automation. But technologies such as remote-controlled aerial vehicles (drones) or self-driving cars can also be seen as sort of (semi-)autonomous systems. These developments involve a convergence of different technologies; and the extensive arrays of data produced by these technologies feed into the big data paradigm aiming to exploit large data sets. Closely related is an increasing relevance and progress in the field of machine learning (LeCun *et al.* 2015; Strauß 2018). Correspondingly, progress in robotics and recently revitalized trends of so-called artificial intelligence further boost digital automation. Overall, classical visions of pervasive (or ubiquitous) computing (Weiser 1991; ITU 2005), ambient intelligence, the Internet of Things, "smart" networks, etc. with hyper-connected systems become more and more tangible.

Hence, ICTs became deeply integrated into society based on a variety of different but interwoven developments fostering networking structures and connectivity. In general, there is an observable increasing convergence between analog/physical and digital environments stimulated by ICTs and digitization (Floridi 2010/2013; Gillings *et al.* 2016). A major reason for the increasing integration of ICTs in society lies in their core capacity, i.e., to process digital information widely, decoupled from space and time. This capacity significantly changed society and economy on a global scale in many respects. On the one hand, the expansion of a globally acting economy supported the emergence of novel networking domains and increasing need for mobility and connectivity of organizations and individuals. On the other hand, the peculiar characteristics of ICTs fit well to these increasing needs for networking, mobility and connectivity and amplify them. In this regard, ICTs entail a self-dynamic that reinforces further connectivity and integration. In his work on the information age, Castells (1996/2003) dealt with these issues and observed an increasing convergence of specific technologies that may lead to a highly integrative (information) system. Connectivity can be defined as:

> the mechanisms, processes, systems and relationships that link individuals and collectives (e.g., groups, organizations, cultures, societies) by facilitating material, informational and/or social exchange. It includes geophysical

(e.g., space, time and location), technological (e.g., information technologies and their applications) as well as social interactions and artefacts.

(Kolb 2008: 128)

Indeed, as outlined, there are many different but interrelated technologies today that point toward a further integration of ICTs into society. As mentioned in Chapter 1, Floridi (2010: 6) uses the term "infosphere" to subsume the developments in the context of informatization and digitization. He describes ICTs as "re-ontologizing technologies" which represent the emergence and expansion of the infosphere, i.e., the "transition from analog to digital data and the ever-increasing growth of our informational space" (ibid.: 6). With re-ontologization he means "a very radical form of re-engineering, one that not only designs, constructs or structures a system ... anew, but one that also fundamentally transforms its intrinsic nature, that is, its ontology or essence" (ibid.: 6). Consequently, with the further digitization of analog objects or entities, "the digital deals effortlessly and seamlessly with the digital" (ibid.: 7). Information is the essence of this infosphere that enables and fosters connectivity. Floridi (2010: 9) argues: "what we still experience as the world offline is bound to become a fully interactive and responsive environment of wireless, pervasive, distributed, a2a (anything to anything) information processes, that works a4a (anywhere anytime), in real time."

Although Floridi's notion of an infosphere is useful to highlight the rapid progress of ICTs, it is debatable whether it appropriately grasps the manifold challenges of the information society; not least as it suggests the emergence of a hyper-connected society without alternatives (for a critical discussion, see, e.g., Hofkirchner 2010). Nevertheless, there is little doubt that ICTs deeply affect and transform society in an extraordinary fashion. But it is not certain that an interconnectedness or hyper-connectivity of all things in a sense of "anything to anything" emerges, as Floridi assumes. A seamless flow of information between completely digitized entities does not exist yet. In fact, there are various natural frictions in information processing observable in many domains, and daily routines involve completely non-digitized interactions. However, it is true that as soon as ICTs are involved in an interaction, information can be digitized, which may reduce informational frictions (as, e.g., prominently exemplified by smart phones as quasi-pervasive devices), so that it can be easily processed further. Ontological frictions diminish in the sense of a reduced "amount of work and effort required to generate, obtain, process and transmit information" as Floridi (2010: 7) argues. As informatization and digitalization continuingly proceed (including trends such as the Internet of Things, pervasive computing, etc.), societal transformations with diminishing boundaries between different systems are likely. In this regard, ICTs significantly affect society with the increasing potential to seamlessly process information in digital environments from one system to another. This may reduce frictions in information processing but at the same time, it reinforces frictions and tensions between technology and societal core functions.

Already today, ICT-induced connectivity is deeply embedded in various everyday contexts (ranging from standard settings of personal computers to automatically establish an online connection, smart phones being constantly connected via telecommunications networks and increasingly also via the internet, heavy use of social media platforms, networked cars, cyber-physical systems, smart home technologies, etc.). Permanent connectivity of individuals is not least envisioned and constantly promoted by technology vendors and other actors of the digital economy. The already extensive number of networking devices indicates that these visions are incrementally taking shape. The Organization for Economic Cooperation and Development (2013) estimates that by 2022, about 14 billion "smart" devices will be used in households on a global scale. Network provider Cisco (2017) even expects over 27 billion networked devices worldwide by 2021, which is more than three times the world's population. A study on big data (sponsored by data storage enterprise EMC) predicted the amount of digital data produced globally will exceed 40 zettabytes then, which equals 40 trillion gigabytes. This corresponds to more than 5,200 gigabytes per person (Mearian 2012). Although these predictions are naturally linked to the business models of their sponsors, a further extensive growth in the amount of digital data can be expected in all ways. The expansion of networked devices implies a growth in the relations between different informational entities, which produces further digital data. This expansion makes extreme growth in the processing of personal information likely as well, especially when individuals are surrounded by networked devices gathering and processing their information; as suggested by promoted visions in the realm of pervasive computing (e.g., Weiser 1991; ITU 2005) and the corresponding socio-technical developments.

The emergence of (digital) identity management

The presented technological transformations also affect the societal role of digital identities and identification. ICTs basically enhanced connectivity, interactivity and availability of information. This also brought novel means to digitally represent, gather and process identity-related information, and thus altered identification practices for various social, political and economic purposes. Corresponding transformations are mirrored in the increasing importance of these issues in science and society in parallel with the technological developments. Several scholars dealt with digital identities in different respects: for instance, Clarke (1994a/1994b) observed the changing role of identity at the dawn of digital technology, when organizations began to use technological means for identification in e-transactions. He described it as the emergence of a "digital persona", which he defined as "a model of an individual's public personality based on data and maintained by transactions, and intended for use as a proxy for the individual" (Clarke 1994b). Clarke here foresaw early the emergence of what today is addressed by the field of IDM, which several years later became an important domain in research and technology development (see below).

Abelson and Lessig (1998) dealt with the unbundling role of identity in cyberspace and argued for technical design to assist users in controlling "the strength of the link between their real world and cyber-identities". Solove (2004) pointed out that information technology enabled the creation of digital dossiers that refer to digital representations of a person. These digital dossiers "resulted in an elaborate lattice of information networking, where information is being stored, analysed, and used in ways that have profound implications for society" (ibid.: 3). Issues of identity in the information society were the main focus of the EU-funded research project FIDIS,[3] which created a network of excellence to support identification and the management of identities with technology (Halperin and Backhouse 2008; Rannenberg *et al.* 2009). Several scholars explored the effects of ICTs on identity-building and the right to privacy (e.g., Hildebrandt 2006; Hildebrandt and Gutwirth 2008; Rouvroy and Poullet 2009; Nissenbaum 2010). Hildebrandt (2008: 56) argued that society has entered "the age of identification" as governments and enterprises create systems for identification and authentication. Similar also is Lyon (2009), who observed a global growth in the creation of identity cards pushed by governments and the security industry. A number of studies found that Web 2.0 and social media changed self-representation and identity performances online (e.g., Boyd and Ellison 2007; Leenes 2010; Nentwich and König 2012; Ellison 2013). The broad availability of social media profiles is also found to be helpful for surveillance and thus challenges privacy protection (e.g., Acquisti and Gross 2006; Strauß and Nentwich 2013; Fuchs 2015). The implementation of electronic identification systems created new means to foster e-commerce and e-government services, which affects the identification of consumers and citizens (e.g., Aichholzer and Strauß 2010a/2010b; Kubicek and Noack 2010b; Strauß 2011; De Andrade *et al.* 2013). These systems are also instruments of governance, and serve political and economic objectives as well as security and surveillance practices (e.g., Bennett and Lyon 2008; Lyon 2009; Glässer and Vajihollahi 2010; Whitley and Hosein 2010).

Hence, ICTs entail various issues related to digital identities and identification. The field of IDM encompasses different approaches to deal with these issues and serves as an umbrella term. IDM is thus an emerging field of research in the information society, which gains increasing relevance due to the further pervasion of ICTs (e.g., Halperin and Backhouse 2008; Rundle *et al.* 2008; Rannenberg *et al.* 2009; ITU 2010; Kubicek and Noack 2010a; Pfitzmann and Hansen 2010; OECD 2011; Strauß 2011; De Andrade *et al.* 2013; Whitley *et al.* 2014; EU-C 2016a; Grassi *et al.* 2017). The International Telecommunication Union (ITU) defines IDM as:

> [a] set of functions and capabilities (e.g., administration, management and maintenance, discovery, communication exchanges, correlation and binding, policy enforcement, authentication and assertions) used for assurance of identity information (e.g., identifiers, credentials, attributes); assurance of the identity of an entity and supporting business and security applications.
>
> (ITU 2010: 4)

The emergence of IDM is part of the outlined societal transformations related to the deep pervasion of society with ICTs. IDM gained in importance at about the same time ICTs became increasingly interactive, and personalized services began to spread. This indicates a certain societal demand for concepts to manage digital information flows related to personal identities. Digital identification gained in importance with online services, e-transactions and social media becoming mainstream activities. This reinforced trends of service personalization and led to a significant growth in the processing of personal information. Against this background, IDM can be seen as an attempt to improve the controllability of digital information flows related to personal identities (Strauß 2011). Besides their many benefits, these developments entail several tensions and challenges as regards privacy, security and control over personal information (see Chapter 5).

IDM approaches occur in many different shades and applications in the public as well as in the private domains. This may also include areas where practically no strict (hard) identification (disclosure of one's real identity) is required, such as in online services or social media applications. Particular forms of IDM exist in the government and business sectors, as these domains have higher requirements for secure means to ascertain one's identity (such as citizens requesting public services, or customers conducting an online transaction). IDM in these contexts aims to improve identification and authentication procedures between citizens and public administration and/or customers or other parties involved in commercial transactions. A digital identity device here usually fulfills two basic functions: the identification of its holder based on a unique identifier and authentication by providing a digital signature, e.g., to enable legally binding online transactions (Aichholzer and Strauß 2010a; Kubicek and Noack 2010a). But besides these special forms, in a broader sense, IDM is involved in every kind of personalized online service or application which processes identity information. Basically, IDM concepts are employed to provide electronic (or digital) identity (eID) devices such as user profiles and the corresponding login procedures including the relevant architectural components. The extent to which a user is explicitly identified naturally depends on the concrete application.

Basic building blocks of digital identity management

In brief, an identity management system (IDMS) comprises all applications, infrastructures and procedures where identity information is involved. There is a broad scope of technical IDM concepts ranging from different forms of single-sign-on (SSO) solutions enabling access to multiple applications, token-based approaches based on smart cards, mobile phones or other technical devices, equipped with identity information up to biometrics (Halperin and Backhouse 2008; Lips *et al.* 2009; Nauman and Hobgen 2009; Aichholzer and Strauß 2010a; Glässer and Vajihollahi 2010; ITU 2010; Kubicek and Noack 2010b). There are four general IDM architecture models: siloed (or isolated), centralized, federated and user-centric (Bhargav-Spantzel *et al.* 2007; Jøsang *et al.* 2007;

Rundle *et al.* 2008; Strauß and Aichholzer 2010). In a siloed system, identification is isolated from other applications, and therefore it does not provide SSO. Users can choose different credentials (username, password) for each application. Hence, the very same ID is not used for multiple purposes. A centralized approach provides SSO, where the identity information is processed centrally by a single authority. Hence, the same ID is used multiple times and is accessible to different service providers. Federated models, which include siloed and centralized components, are widespread. This federation involves a central identity provider (IdP), who serves as intermediary between the individual user and the different service providers who accept the IdP as a trusted entity. This allows SSO with the same ID in multiple applications and, ideally, identity information is not controlled by a single authority as the IdP provides identity credentials (e.g., a unique identifier) but does not process all personal information. The user-centric model follows a federated approach but aims to provide more user control. This can be, e.g., by providing a particular technical ID device (e.g., a smart card or other hardware token) to the user and/or options to choose between different IdPs independent from applications and services.

In practice, all types can be found in various contexts. One of the first centralized digital IDM approaches was Microsoft's ".NET Passport", created in 1999. It provided an SSO solution to access different Microsoft applications with one central user account. Further attempts to establish Passport as a central IDM system for non-Microsoft applications as well failed as the service was neglected due to its proprietary design and a number of serious privacy and security concerns. In 2001, several privacy and consumer protection groups together with the US Federal Trade Commission brought in legal complaints against Microsoft's Passport system. Similar actions were undertaken by the European Commission (EPIC 2003; Dmytrenko and Nardali 2005). Microsoft abandoned the system in 2006 and re-launched the concept under the label Microsoft Live ID (Dmytrenko and Nardali 2005; Jøsang *et al.* 2007). The current IDM system is called "Microsoft Account", which can be used as SSO to all Microsoft-related applications and platforms.[4] Similar IDM approaches exist from internet and social media enterprises such as Facebook Connect or Google Sign In, which are labeled as "social logins" (as discussed in the following sections). A related approach is the OpenID project[5] formed in 2007, a decentralized, more user-centric IDM concept for web-based authentication, in which several Internet companies are involved (Facebook and Google among others). While OpenID basically provides a low threshold to act as IdP, there are certain risks regarding privacy and trust as well as its vulnerability to phishing attacks (Bonneau *et al.* 2012). Many of the current governmental eID systems follow a federated approach with some user-centric features including smart card technology, which corresponds to token-based (the smart card) and knowledge-based (a PIN code) identification. A reason for this is that smart card technology is widespread in many contexts such as ATM or credit cards, but it can also be used in combination with smartphones, which have enjoyed significant growth in usage rates and have thus become increasingly attractive as eID devices (Kubicek and Noack 2010b; Strauß and

Aichholzer 2010). Each approach has advantages and disadvantages as regards privacy and security, which are discussed in Chapter 5.

Besides the different system design options, there are some basic components relevant in each IDM system. In general, there are at least two basic processes involved (Jøsang *et al.* 2007). In the initial (registration) process, a user is requested to provide personal information and is then issued with a particular identity device (e.g., a user profile or account, an ID document or a similar arti- fact containing a unique identifier and possibly additional identity information). This ID device is then used to authenticate users and to control their access to one or more services in every usage process or user session. Figure 4.2 below sketches a simplified model of a typical user session with the main building blocks of an IDM system.

This model highlights the different components relevant for digital identifica- tion. There are at least two entities involved: the individual entity (Alice), i.e., the identity holder using a service (e.g., an online platform), who is being identi- fied by an (institutional) entity. The latter can be a single person but is usually an organization or institution providing, e.g., the service. The interaction begins with Alice visiting the platform of the provider by using a technical system (e.g., a computer) and being identified based on her (pre-registered) identity device. This device can be merely virtual (such as typical credentials of username and password to access her account or profile) or an additional physical token (e.g., a smart card, mobile phone, etc.). In each case, the ID device carries an identifier or additional ID information. Depending on the service, different types of information related to the user are processed and partially stored in some kind of repository or database which makes it available for further processing (e.g., for

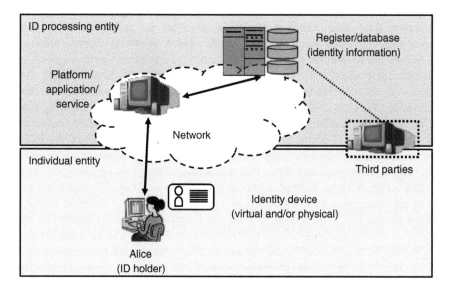

Figure 4.2 Basic building blocks of digital IDM.

eventual third-party entities). In the case of an online or mobile service, the whole interaction involves some kind of network medium (e.g., internet, cellular network, etc.) where the information is processed.

From a systemic perspective, this simple example includes at least six different elements: the (social or human) system A (individual Alice), socio-technical system B (the institution), the information processing system C (the service or application, or front office), the information processing system D (the database, or back office), the network system E, and the ID device F. Hence, compared to face-to-face identification, there are more systems involved (the network at least but usually also the user's machine). This seems trivial but it is important to understand how many entities are basically involved in the digital processing of identity information. The more entities involved, the more relations exist to the individual identity. This has consequences for ISD as identity information may be processed in multiple domains beyond the knowledge and control of the individual. The crucial peculiarity of digital identification, though, is that the whole interaction of an individual with a socio-technical system is reproducible and traceable. The technology and each sub-system involved may create additional information referring to the individual's identity, which can be theoretically gathered and processed further over the involved network. This issue has several privacy implications which are elaborated upon in more depth in Chapters 5, 6 and 7.

Major drivers of digital identification

(Digital) identification serves as a socio-technical "connector" in many respects and has multiple social, political and economic functions. It became increasingly relevant with the possibility of electronic transactions. Organizations began to integrate IDM into business processes in order to provide and conduct e-commerce services where identity verification is involved. Central aims of IDM here are to improve efficiency and security of electronic services as well as to harmonize identification and authentication procedures (Strauß 2011). An expanded distance between individuals and organizations contributed to the relevance of digital identification. This distance increased with the growing size of organizations and administrative bureaucracy in modernity, further reinforced by globalization (Giddens 1984; Clarke 1994a; Castells 1996/2003). As ICTs enable mobility, distant communications and information processing, partially decoupled from space and time, they allow this distance to be overcome in a virtual sense. With its inherent connecting function (see Chapter 3) identification is an essential process in this regard as it creates ties between different entities. In the analog world, anonymity is a standard setting and many transactions are possible without identification as there is no necessity for it to be given. In the digital world, this is much more complicated. If a transaction is completed in a single step (e.g., in the case of instant payment and exchange of goods[6]), usually no identification is needed. With a greater distance between individuals and organizations (e.g., customer and company, citizen and government, user and service, etc.), as found in online services, reliable authentication and identification becomes more important (e.g., for secure transactions). Consequently, this distance contributed to organizations increasingly gathering personal information based on the assumption of its necessity (Clarke 1994a). Hence, digital identification in this regard serves as a means to compensate for this distance by providing an informational link between different entities.

Against this background, it is reasonable that digital identification and IDM are particularly important for a variety of public and private services online (e-business/e-commerce, e-government, e-health, e-procurement, etc.). But this increasing relevance is not merely the result of technological progress. There are also certain political and economic considerations that reinforce the extension of digital identification mechanisms. The digital economy plays an important role, which is observable in national and international policies and strategy documents concerning the information society. For instance, for the OECD as well as the European Union, digital IDM is seen as fundamental for the further development of the digital economy (OECD 2011; EU-C 2016a). A central aim is to stimulate digital markets and improve the efficiency and effectiveness of administrative procedures. In its recent e-government action plan, the European Commission announced they would be strengthening efforts "to accelerate the take up of electronic identification and trust services for electronic transactions in the internal market"; as well as taking further "actions to accelerate the cross-border and cross-sector use of electronic identification (eID), including mobile ID, and trust services (in particular eSignature, website authentication and online registered delivery service)" (EU-C 2016a: 4). Accordingly, the introduction of digital (electronic) identity management systems (eIDMS) is seen as a key driver for online services in public and private sectors. IDM has played an important role for the digital agenda of the EU for many years. Specific directives at EU level were created to regulate the use of electronic signatures[7] and identification.[8] Consequently, most countries adapted their legal frameworks to EU regulation and built the techno-organizational infrastructures needed to implement their eIDMS. During the last decade, many approaches have been taken and a number of governments worldwide (including African, Arab, Asian, European and North American countries) and particularly in Europe have already implemented eIDMS or started relevant initiatives in this regard (CEN 2004; Arora 2008; Nauman and Hobgen 2009; Aichholzer and Strauß 2010a; Kubicek and Noack 2010a; Whitley and Hosein 2010; WH 2011; Gemalto 2014; Whitley *et al.* 2014). In the long run, the EU aims to establish a pan-European eID system. Corresponding large-scale pilot projects STORK and STORK 2.0[9] were already set up to foster interoperability of different eIDMS at national and EU levels (EU-C 2010; De Andrade *et al.* 2013; Brugger *et al.* 2014). In the same vein, the US strategy on IDM aims to establish an operational identity ecosystem including advocacy groups, associations, businesses, governments, individuals and non-profits at all levels (WH 2011). Since 2012, a special identity ecosystem steering group (IDESG[10]) is entrusted with the funding of pilot projects in the field; as part of an initiative of the US National Institute of Standards and

Technology (NIST),[11] which is elaborating guidelines for digital identities (Grassi *et al.* 2017). Hence, there are various activities concerning digital identities on a global level. The largest national electronic identification program so far was implemented in India with over one billion identification numbers issued by the end of 2016.[12]

Digital identities torn between political and economic interests

These developments highlight that the employment of digital identification is related to political and economic interests. Besides these governmental initiatives, which mainly focus on formal identification, social media contributed significantly to a general expansion of digital identification mechanisms. SNS such as Facebook and other social media platforms represent the most common technological phenomenon related to digital identities. They are showcases for personalization in online services. In general, social media stimulate the societal needs to communicate, interact and exchange (personal) information with others as well as to present the self. A mapping of all these activities can provide many details of individual identities. Social media platforms use IDM to handle user registration and create a user profile, which is required to access the platform. This profile equals the digital identity of an individual user. The handling of identity information is obviously important in social media as it naturally enables and fosters personalization, social interactions, user-generated content, etc., where massive amounts of personal information are created and processed. Hence, social media represents a further example of an IDMS, though without the need for a legally binding identification and disclosure of one's real name. In this regard, SNS employ "softer" forms of IDM compared to governmental eIDMS. However, at the same time, identification in social media is more extensive: it is a precondition to access social media platforms and enjoy the broad range of interaction possibilities. Moreover, most SNS providers try to engage users in providing their real names and it is challenging to effectively use SNS anonymously. Before the occurrence of Web 2.0 and social media, explicit identification and provision of identity-related information in online services was rather limited to transactions where identification is legally relevant. Social media changed this significantly as it fostered the use of digital identities for purposes other than transactions. The previously rather occasional processing of personal information bound to particular applications and domains (e.g., for personal communication or transactions online) became widely boosted and "normalized" in social media environments, which are easily accessible. The extensive amounts of information that directly and indirectly refer to an individual provide deep insights into one's interests, relationships, activities, behavior, etc. and thus one's identity (for more details see Chapter 5). While individuals basically use social media for social reasons, there is a strong economic rationale behind the provision of these services. The identity profile thus feeds into numerous business models. The basic business model of global Internet companies like Facebook and Google is service-for-profile (Elmer 2004; Rogers 2009), i.e., the usage is free but users indirectly pay the services with their personal information.

Hence, identification in the government as well as in the private sector is closely connected to the digital economy. A major reason for its relevance in economic contexts is that identification enables the personalization of services for customer relationship management (CRM), targeted advertising, profiling the activities of Internet and social media users, etc. Thus, digital identification is seen as promising a means to exploit new digital markets aiming to monetize personal information.[13] The high economic value of this information and the profitability of the corresponding business models can be derived from the massive annual revenues of global internet companies such as Facebook or Google/Alphabet.[14] According to Forbes, Facebook's market cap in May 2017 was about US$ 407 billion; the corresponding market value of Google's mother company Alphabet is approximately US$ 580 billion.[15]

IDM at the thin line between security and surveillance

Besides these economic aspects, another strong driver of digital identification is security. This includes several objectives ranging from information security to provide secure user accounts and digital identity devices, secure digital signatures to allow for legally valid online transactions, up to cyber security, fighting identity fraud and terrorism and thus protecting national security (CEN 2004; EU-C 2006/2010; Glässer and Vajihollahi 2010; OECD 2011; Strauß 2011; Whitley *et al.* 2014). As regards information security, multiple user accounts are often seen as problematic as users tend to re-use the same passwords for different accounts. This makes security breaches more likely (Metz 2012). The assumed number of accounts per person ranges from 8.5 (Riley 2006) to 25 or more (Egelman 2013). Against this background and the expected further growth in services requiring user accounts, IDM concepts that aim to harmonize login procedures to reduce eventual security risks of multiple user accounts seem plausible. The basic consideration is that a unified IDM approach with a corresponding ID device usable for multiple applications improves efficiency as well as security of online services. A rationale is to develop approaches that ease the problem of the currently dominating "bricolage of isolated, incompatible, partial solutions" of online identification (Leenes *et al.* 2008: 1). However, at the same time, a "pervasive IDM layer" creates additional security and privacy risks (Rundle *et al.* 2008: 19). Although privacy and data protection are particularly essential issues for governmental eID systems, their role in the IDM discourse is rather an implicit one, compared to the emphasis put on service efficiency and security (Strauß 2011).

Besides the central aim to improve security of online services, digital identification is also framed as a means of national security in political contexts. For instance, in some EU policies, the employment of national eIDMS (and in the long term also of interoperable systems across Europe) is also mentioned as a tool to combat crime and terrorism (CEN 2004; EU-C 2006; Bennett and Lyon 2008; Glässer and Vajihollahi 2010; Whitley *et al.* 2014). Bennett and Lyon (2008) provide a critical overview on eID card schemes in different countries in this regard. Several scholars (e.g., De Hert 2008; Lyon 2009; Ajana 2013) observed a global growth in personal data collections and centralized databases for law enforcement and national security including trends to gather biometric information. According to De Hert, the general increase in identification is part of a "global tendency towards ambient intelligence security enforcement scenarios, relying on the massive collection and processing of (personal and non-personal) data in combination with data mining and profiling techniques" (De Hert 2008: 73). Correspondingly, in the past, ideas and claims about establishing digital IDs at a global level to improve information security and/or national security were occasionally expressed: for example, by Eugene Kaspersky, the CEO of a prominent anti-virus company, who raised the idea of a governmental ID for every computer user (Long 2010); or by Interpol about introducing a global digital ID for migration control (HNS 2011). As social media provides extensive arrays of identity information, its value for law enforcement is relatively obvious. Social media activity and thus also its users are increasingly monitored by security agencies (Belbey 2016) and, since the Snowden revelations in 2013, there is hard evidence for global mass surveillance programs of internet activity (Greenwald 2014).

There is a general trend of increasing identification and processing of identity information, which is not limited to IDMS for e-government and e-business, where a need to provide more-sophisticated online identification and authentication to improve service quality is plausible. In general, IDM involves (explicit) attempts to unify the handling of identity information. IDM mostly focuses on easing identification processes and controlling identity information from the perspective of institutions or organizations. However, this does not necessarily comply with the needs of individuals to be identified or to remain anonymous and in any case to have their information protected, especially as an individual may not always be aware of the extent to which her identity information is being processed. An e-commerce provider, for instance, is naturally interested in providing secure transactions to minimize his risks of economic loss. Therefore, gathering personal information from his customers is an obvious approach from his point of view, which may be accepted by the customer as a standard procedure. However, depending on the particular business model, this information may also be used for further purposes (such as targeted advertising). These practices may lead to tensions and conflicts with the needs and rights of consumers. The use of governmental IDM systems for public services is mostly regulated and citizens are usually explicitly requested to identify for a particular, limited purpose. However, this is not exactly the case in social media or similar applications where identity-related information is commercialized. Moreover, as the Snowden case highlighted, digital identity information serves a variety of security and surveillance purposes. Regardless of the variety and multiple functions of IDM approaches, two predominating rationales become apparent which stimulate the increase in digital identification: economic and security aspects. As outlined, economic growth and security objectives play important roles in the implementation and extension of digital identification. Furthermore, due to the extensive availability of identity information in digital environments (such as social media), profiling or what could be called "identity mining" is a lucrative activity for several public and private actors as will be discussed in more depth in Chapter 5. The next section presents and discusses the role of social media for the representation and processing of identity information, which is a showcase for networking dynamics of digital identities.

Social media and how our online identities are networked

Social media and particularly SNS are specific phenomena that have contributed significantly to the trend of online identity representation and expanded identification. First, because the foundation for SNS's basic functionality is the processing of massive amounts of personal information related to individual identities. Second, given the enormous networking degree of SNS and similar platforms, they demonstrate how extensively interconnected online identities are already today. A further expansion of digitally networked environments, and thus of our identities, is very likely, as several developments indicate (e.g., Internet of Things, ambient intelligence, pervasive computing, etc. as outlined previously). In this regard, social media can be seen as a blueprint for our identities becoming highly interactive and dynamic but also transparent and controllable. These issues are not limited to social media and corresponding tensions with privacy can be expected to intensify in other socio-technical contexts as well. The following sections provide an overview on the emergence and core functions of social media platforms. Thereafter it is shown that the scope of social media expands, including tendencies to integrate online user profiles into formal identification procedures.

Social media and SNS occurred in a relatively short period of time and quickly evolved from their beginnings as niche applications toward being global mainstream phenomena. Ellison and Boyd (2013: 158) define SNS as:

> a networked communication platform in which participants (1) have uniquely identifiable profiles that consist of user-supplied content, content provided by other users, and/or system-provided data; (2) can publicly articulate connections that can be viewed and traversed by others; and (3) can consume, produce, and/or interact with streams of user-generated content provided by their connections on the site.

The origins of SNS can be traced back to the 1990s where early community pages (e.g., Geocities), online contact groups and the first instant messaging services (e.g., ICQ) emerged. Initially, these applications were separated from each other and merely part of small niches in the WWW; for example, smaller interest groups or grassroots organizations used community pages to share thoughts and ideas. Instant messaging services provided new options to connect and communicate online. As these different services became accessible via a single webpage and linked to a user profile, the first SNS appeared in 1997 with six-degrees.com. Though this site shut down in 2000 as its business model failed, its general setting including a single user profile as the standard access feature became state-of-the-art and stimulated further development. Since 2000 the number of SNS that covered a variety of different, larger communities or particular interests have grown (ranging from ethnic community building such as business contacts, music, sports and traveling to online dating). In the early 2000s the music-centered network MySpace was the most popular SNS (Boyd and Ellison 2007; Strauß and Nentwich 2013; Leimbach *et al.* 2014). This rapidly changed in 2004 when Facebook appeared; Facebook today is the most popular social media service followed by Google+.[16] Besides these dominant players a number of specialized SNS exist, i.e., for friend finding, dating, job seeking, education, professional business contacts or research (Nentwich and König 2012; Leimbach *et al.* 2014). Moreover, with their rapid evolution and the expansion of Web 2.0, other social media services such as video portals (e.g., YouTube), micro-blogging services (e.g., Twitter), news aggregation sites (e.g., Reddit), photo sharing (e.g., Instagram) and mobile messengers (e.g., WhatsApp) have become increasingly embedded into SNS environments. In this regard, social media technology transforms toward a (quasi-centralized) platform (Gillespie 2010) with a number of integrated services and applications.

Today, SNS, and particularly Facebook as the dominant platform play an important role in the social mainstream with many effects on the interplay between society and ICTs. Several studies observed positive impacts of social media on collaboration, social learning and collective action, community and social capital building, or on participation and activism, stimulating public discourse (e.g., Steinfield *et al.* 2008; Baringhorst 2009; Wimmer 2009; Gillespie 2010; Redecker *et al.* 2010; Benkirane 2012; Dahlgren 2013; Boulianne 2015). Critical studies highlight issues of, inter alia, privacy and trust, manipulation, power and surveillance, the political economy and digital labor, or the blurry boundaries between public and private spheres (e.g., Acquisti and Gross 2006; Debatin and Lovejoy 2009; Leenes 2010; Pariser 2011; Strauß and Nentwich 2013; Fuchs 2015; Fuchs and Sandoval 2015; Milan 2015). Recent studies also deal with the relationship between social media and the "fake news" debate amplified by the US elections in 2016 (Allkott and Gentzkow 2017). Finally, the scandal around Cambridge Analytica, where more than 80 million personal user profiles were misused for targeted profiling and manipulation, got Facebook into serious trouble (Hern and Pegg 2018; Ienca 2018). Currently, it is difficult to assess how much damage this scandal has caused Facebook's reputation and social media in the longer run. Even though trust in the social network decreased, and many users changed their online behavior, there is no large-scale user dropout rate observable so far (Beck 2018).

Possible reasons may be found in the motivational factors of social media users. A number of studies showed that the main motivations of SNS users are to connect to others, maintain contact and relations with friends, relatives and acquaintances, socialize and participate in community building (Brandtdaeg and Heim 2009; Wimmer 2009; Smith 2011; Singh *et al.* 2012; Leimbach *et al.* 2014). Social media thus fits perfectly with the societal need to communicate and exchange with others. This is an explanation for the widespread use of social media globally. A further aspect concerns the entertainment value of social media as a motivational factor (Kim *et al.* 2011; Matikainen 2015). In this regard, SNS usage is partially comparable to traditional mass media consumption such as watching television: users browse through social media content in a similar way to zapping TV channels as a pastime and for entertainment. This is, though, only one usage factor among many others. In social media services primarily covering professional or special interests (such as for business networking, science and research) other usage rationales are likely. Furthermore, the different motivations are interrelated and thus usage patterns cannot be reduced to merely one issue. According to mass communication theory (McQuail 2010), there are four main motivational factors of media usage, i.e., gathering information, entertainment, social interaction, and personal identity representation. These factors and their interplay are visible in social media as well. Furthermore, due to its extensive outreach, social media gains enormous attention in public discourses and thus affects the role of traditional mass communication channels (such as television, radio or newspapers) (Stefanone *et al.* 2010). In this regard, social media may be seen as a quasi-individualized form of mass media although there are many differences: in particular, traditional mass media provide unidirectional communication to a mass audience of individuals. Social media offers a variety of options for many-to-many communication and interaction that can be targeted at specific people as well as groups to foster involvement in discourses, campaigns, issues, etc. Moreover, being a sort of semi-public space (Strauß and Nentwich 2013), social media allow users to present themselves and perform their identities in a variety of ways. In this respect, "social media function as performative 'front stage' for the self" (Milan 2015: 7). While individuals basically use social media for social reasons, there is a strong economic rationale behind the provision of these services. The relatively low threshold to the use of social media and its high degree of interactivity facilitate easy (re-)distribution and co-creation of content as well as its re-contextualization, i.e., embedding existing content into new contexts. These additional values contribute to the popularity of SNS and other social media. Individual users (directly and indirectly) provide vast amounts of information about their personal details, preferences, contacts, networks and modes of interactions within these networks. Global players such as Facebook or Google employ a number of tools such as the social graph (see next sections) to analyze and integrate this information into other applications which are also provided to external entities. This information is highly valuable for business and makes social media a very attractive platform for many economic actors to promote their products and services.[17] Hence, a number of businesses, software providers, marketing companies, etc. have a strong focus on social media channels to exploit this information for targeted, personalized marketing, service-oriented business models, nudging, etc. (as highlighted not least by the Cambridge Analytica case). This includes viral marketing, which is well supported by social media "as the community element embedded in them makes it convenient to transmit the marketing message to a large group of people" (Kaplan and Haenlein 2011: 255). In particular the many young people being active social media users are a very lucrative target group for viral marketing campaigns (e.g., for the music industry, to name just one of many examples). Consequently, celebrities are well represented in a broad scope of social media channels to create and maintain their brand images (Kaplan and Haenlein 2012). The commercialization or economization of social media impacts on its users as the information presented to them is filtered and preselected for direct and indirect advertisement and marketing in order to stimulate consumption. As a result, individuals mostly receive information based on their (assumed) interests, while other information which is assumed to be irrelevant is filtered out. Consequently, SNS users are in a "filter bubble" (Pariser 2011). Hence, from a business perspective, social media is a highly valuable personalized marketing tool. Platform providers argue that tailoring information to individuals improves user experience. However, from an individual's perspective, this may be perceived as a form of surveillance, censorship and manipulation. That the latter are not just theoretical risks is highlighted inter alia by the Cambridge Analytica scandal, which is a symptom of a severe disease of our digital identities (for a further, more thorough discussion on these issues see Chapter 5).

The basics of social media: user profiling and content gathering

McLuhan's (1964) claim that "the media is the message" is certainly valid for social media: already the simple presence of a user profile represents information that is disclosed to others within the social network. Interactivity is similar, as every interaction of a user produces further information that can be linked to her profile. Users can, e.g., create and share information that refers to their interests, opinions, feelings, activities, etc. Network effects facilitate the easy spreading of messages and informational content within the network with a high potential to reach a vast number of users. There is a broad scope of possible activities in SNS ranging from posting comments, opinions or appraisals, sharing hyperlinks, files, pictures, videos or similar, finding friends and managing contacts, synchronous or asynchronous communication (e.g., chatting, instant messaging, group discussions), promoting events, etc. The basic features of SNS thus include several forms of self-representation, contact management, community building, bottom-up activities and the visualization and externalization of data (e.g., by automatically displaying connections, contacts, content, etc. while interacting) (Cachia 2008; Ellison and Boyd 2013; Nentwich and König 2012). Thus, social media bear various pieces of information that refer to individual identities, represented by the SNS user profile. This profile also has a unique identification number (e.g., the Facebook user ID), e.g., used in internal and external applications of the SNS. Consequently, individual users are identifiable by this ID.

Hence, in the sense of McLuhan (1964), the user profile is "the message" to a variety of entities accessing social media platforms to process personal information.

Although SNS differ in design and functionality, there are certain similarities as regards their main structure. The very design of SNS enables and stimulates various new modes of interaction (one-to-one, one-to-many, few-to-few) among users as well as software agents (e.g., websites, software applications, algorithms). Figure 4.3 highlights some of the main building blocks of a typical SNS structure (author's representation, based on Leimbach *et al.* (2014: 100)).

SNS are specific, quasi-exclusive online spaces requiring user registration. Hence, they represent centralized environments which are (at least partially) separated from other domains on the web. What contributed significantly to the success of SNS is the central user profile. It serves as a single access point to a variety of formerly separated services, made available in one single digital environment (the SNS). The provision and maintenance of user profiles represents a form of IDM. As SNS naturally process vast arrays of identity information, they can also be seen as centralized identity platforms (Gillespie 2010; De Andrade *et al.* 2013). From an individual user's perspective, her profile builds the core of an SNS. The user profile represents the digital identity of a user and is perceivable as a sort of multidimensional identity card that provides access to the whole set of SNS features and applications. As social media usage is usually based on the gathering and processing of vast arrays of personal information, the user profile reveals a multitude of identity information ranging from personal details (e.g., age, gender, date and place of birth), contact information (e.g., address, e-mail, phone), record of personal contacts, relationships, group affiliations, pictures and photographs of the user, status messages (e.g., information on personal and professional relationship status, education, etc.), interests,

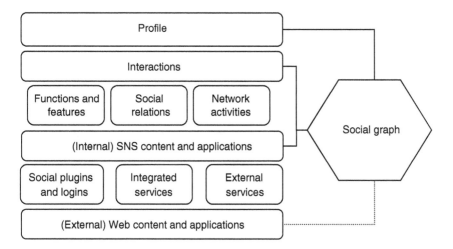

Figure 4.3 Main building blocks of a typical SNS structure.

preferences (likes and dislikes), opinions, attitudes and beliefs, behavior, activities and interactions, favorite places, actual location and movements, participation in events, time of being online, etc. Put simply, social media can provide extensive information about the broad spectrum of an individual's identity, in the present as well as in the past. Many pieces of this information are by default disclosed and thus generally available within the SNS environment. Although users have some options to regulate their degree of visibility by adjusting their profile settings, these are mostly insufficient to effectively protect privacy. Obviously, insufficient privacy controls are a general problem beyond social media, as discussed more thoroughly in Chapters 5 and 6.

Above all, interactivity is a core feature of SNS with the basic idea to enable and foster new modes of (dynamic) interactions between different entities. These entities are not merely individual users but can also be groups or organizations as well as applications or content; or in other words: informational agents. The representation and mapping of social relations and their dynamics build a central component of the manifold functions and activities available via the network. Automatic tools inform users about activities in related domains or promote new ones to stimulate further interactions. This interactivity thus entails the production and distribution of user-generated content. Information consumption became "prosumption" as users can both consume and produce content via social media (Beyreuther *et al.* 2013; Buzzetto-More 2013; Fuchs 2014). The production of content is not necessarily bound to proactive user involvement. Every interaction generates new content that becomes associated with one's user profile. Content emerges, e.g., by posting comments, sharing hyperlinks, photos, videos, etc. with other users; but also without others being involved, such as by using applications, games, watching videos, rating content with the "like" button and so on. Hence, there are multiple options to share and generate content over various integrated services, features, apps, etc. These integrated services can be seen as further (socio-technical) entities (or sub-systems) that are related to the user.

Two forms of content production can be distinguished: internal content resulting from resources within the SNS (interactions, applications, etc.) and external content produced by other sources (e.g., websites, online services, games, apps and so forth) from the web outside the SNS environment. While initially, SNS were relatively closed spaces, separated from the "outer" web, new features enabled the integration of non-SNS domains. External content is increasingly integrated and pulled into the SNS by linking to external services. For developers, most SNS provide application programming interfaces (API) to integrate external applications ("apps"). On Facebook, these apps are often entertainment-focused (e.g., games such as Farmville, Angry Birds, Pokémon, or quizzes, puzzles, music applications, shopping or traveling apps, etc.) and (directly or indirectly) driven by commercial interests.[18] In the Cambridge Analytica scandal, a quiz app called "This Is Your Digital Life" was used to exploit millions of users' data (Hern 2018).

Furthermore, there is a special form of technology for the integration of external context: the so-called social plugins.[19] A social plugin is a standardized micro-program that enables a connection between a social media site and other web content to be established. Prominent examples are the well-known "like", "share", "follow" or "send" buttons of Facebook (as well as Google), which have become integrated in many websites. These features allow users, for example, to express their opinion or share content via a simple click. In the background, they gather and process additional user information also from external sources. Every user interaction with a social plugin such as clicking a like button is traced. If the user has an SNS profile, this information becomes integrated into the user profile. Otherwise, the information is collected by other means (such as by tracking cookies). The social media platform thus gathers information from members and non-members alike. For instance, in 2016, Facebook announced it would intensify tracking of non-members for targeted advertising, for example (Toor 2016). Hence, social plugins enable user activity beyond the systemic boundaries of a social media platform to be tracked.

Particular forms of social plugins enable individual users to access other web services with their social media profiles (prominent examples are Facebook Connect, Google, LinkedIn or Twitter Sign In).[20] These forms are also known as "social login" (Gafni and Nissim 2014; Robinson and Bonneau 2014). Social logins represent a form of IDM where social media platforms act as central IdPs to external sites. External sources applying a social login can access user profile information on the SNS platform, which basically contains name, profile photo, gender, user ID, associated networks and list of friends. Depending on the privacy settings of a user, further information such as status updates, content posted, comments, likes, etc. can be accessed by external sources (Egelman 2013). Altogether, the SNS environment stimulates interactions between personal and non-personal entities within the system but also with external systems.

Social graphs and the mapping of social relations

The interplay of the outlined main building blocks yields enormous amounts of information about users' identities being processed by social media. These extensive arrays of information feed into social graphs, which are applied to analyze and visualize this information. Social graphs make use of network and mathematical graph theory. A social graph aims to identify and map the number of entities (users, content, applications, etc.) and their connections among each other in the network. The social graph is thus a dynamic form of modeling and visualizing the emergence of network relations and interactions. For instance, the number of connections an entity has to others affects its relevance. This can be visualized by nodes or hubs with different size or structure. Figures 4.4 and 4.5 show simple examples of social graph visualization. Among others, Jin *et al.* (2013) differ between four general types of social graphs: (1) friendship graph to show to whom and how a user is related; (2) interaction graph, i.e., to model user interactions with people, content, applications, etc.; (3) latent graph to reveal latent forms of interactions, e.g., site or profile visiting; and (4) following graph to visualize the share of followers and followees such as in micro-blogging

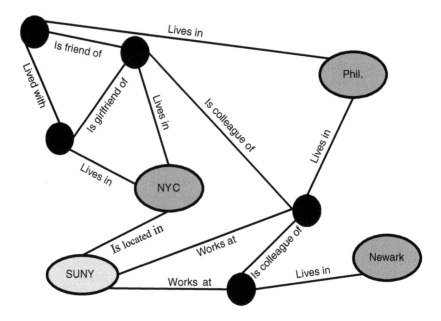

Figure 4.4 Simple graph example visualizing friends, colleagues and locations.

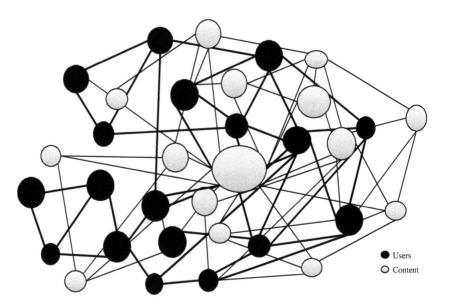

● Users
○ Content

Figure 4.5 Graph visualizing relations between users and web content (such as "liked" or "followed" websites and relations).

services. The exploitation of social graphs is a core instrument in the toolbox of data mining (Leskovec *et al.* 2014).

Given the extensive information available in social media, there are many further types of social graphs that traverse this information and allow deep insights to be gained into user relations, interactions, activities, behavior, etc. While social graphs are primarily employed by providers to analyze their networks, some features are also publicly available or provided to third parties with commercial interests. Facebook, for instance, provides a particular search function[21] that includes many options to conduct particular searches: e.g., for people with particular interests, events visited, content liked, etc. There are also a number of additional tools to explore and visualize social graph data.[22] Via APIs, software developers have many options to use these features (e.g., the open graph protocol[23]) to link other web content outside an SNS with a social graph. The manifold search functions of the graph can be integrated into other applications, e.g., for profiling or customized marketing. Besides other things, the graph protocol also allows predefined actions based on usage behavior to be set: for example, when a user uploads a photo, a particular action can be set such as the presentation of a tailored advertisement suitable to the photo. There is a variety of similar options to exploit user information for marketing, customized profiling, behavioral targeting, or other purposes, which makes the social graph a very powerful tool. Hence, social graphs bear an abundance of information about the relationships of an individual. Having such information even enables exploring relationship patterns of non-members of a social media platform (as e.g., Horvát *et al.* 2013 demonstrate). Hence, individuals' social relations, interactions, interests, activities, behavior, movements, etc. can be mapped on a global level. Given the networking structure and the various ties referring from and to a user profile (e.g., contacts or other related entities), information about a particular person can be gathered via these ties. This can undermine the privacy settings of the person concerned (Bonneau *et al.* 2009). Currently, due to Facebook's enormous popularity and accordingly high user rates, its social graph contains extensive data sets about social interactions and networking structures of individuals worldwide. But Facebook is only one prominent example among others. Several other technology companies have similar approaches, such as Google's knowledge graph,[24] Amazon's Neptune graph engine,[25] or the identity graph of database provider Oracle (for a discussion on these practices see Chapter 5).

From a theoretical stance, social media sheds new light on classical theories about networks and social interactions. Besides graph theory, the social graph also grounds on other theoretical concepts. Milgram's "small world problem" (Milgram 1967) plays a particular role—also known as the "six degrees of separation", which claims that worldwide, each person is related to each other over six contacts.[26] It is thus not coincidence but rather reminiscence that one of the first SNS was labeled sixdegrees.com. Milgram's small world theory was criticized, inter alia, for its bias and lack of sound empirical evidence. While there may be many small world phenomena as part of a large complex world, these small worlds are not necessarily connected (Kleinfeld 2002). Internet communication and social media alleviate the exploration of the small world hypothesis. Some evidence was found, e.g., by Leskovec and Horvitz (2008), who studied the relations of 240 Mio. instant messenger accounts. According to their results, users are related to each other over approximately 6.6 knots. However, even though other studies may have found proof for fewer degrees, social reality differs from these mathematical approaches. Hence, "we may live in a world where everyone is connected by a short chain of acquaintances, but it is hard for most people to find these connections" (Kleinfeld 2002: 66). Nevertheless, considering the power of social graphs and the associated options for analyzing and mapping social relations, today, it may be less relevant whether the chain of connections is more or less than six degrees. Another classical theory dealing with the quality of connections in social networks is the theory of "the strength of weak ties" by Granovetter (1973). According to this theory, the strength of a tie is determined by several factors, i.e., time, emotional intensity, intimacy, and reciprocity. Close relationships (e.g., between friends and relatives) represent rather strong ties that are usually trustworthy, long lasting and stable. Strong ties thus contribute to the stability and consistency of a network. In contrast to that, weak ties are rather loose connections with higher dynamics. Thus, the growth of a social network depends heavily on weak ties as they function as bridges across different network domains or nodes. Compared to strong ties, weak ties allow information to be distributed more widely across greater social distances. Information shared by strong ties "is much more likely to be limited to a few cliques than that going via weak ones; bridges will not be crossed" (ibid.: 1366). However, this information may also be more stable and reliable. In this regard, strong ties contribute to a fluid flow of information in a network. Evidence for the strength of weak ties can be found, for instance, in the micro-blogging service Twitter. This service provides easy forms of information distribution via online media. The relevance of the information (the tweet) depends on the number of followers of a Twitter account: the more followers, the more likely it is that other network domains or communities are reached. The number of followers is highly dynamic and may change quickly. A similar picture is found with contacts in SNS. A high number of weak ties (e.g., the number of Facebook contacts, Twitter followers, etc.) contributes to the size of a social network. However, it may have a negative impact on the quality of the network (e.g., its reliability and trustworthiness) if ties are too weak. Consequently, connections may turn into "absent ties", i.e., "ties without substantial significance" or become irrelevant (ibid.: 1361). Thus, the stability of a network is heavily dependent on the existence of strong ties and their interplay with weaker ones. The strength of a tie can provide, e.g., information about how an individual is embedded in a social network.

Absorbing content and ever-expanding networked identities

All in all, social media and similar applications are very powerful tools, providing an enormous depth of potential insights into individual identities, including relationships and interactions, even beyond the systemic boundaries of the original platform. Social graphs and the like demonstrate how this information is exploited to gain deeply intrusive identity profiles. They basically make use of the connecting function of identity (as explained in Chapter 3) and its ability to create different ties. It is thus no surprise that social media has significantly affected social interactions and entails many societal impacts. They showcase Floridi's notion of the infosphere as everything in their realm is interactively networked. Moreover, even content outside the social media environment becomes increasingly absorbed by social plugins, logins and the like. This results in extensive information collections about individual identities. As shown, by their very design, SNS and other social platforms not only stimulate social interactions online but also significantly foster digital representation of individual users, groups and usage of identity information. Some scholars argue that social media enhances individuals in their self-representation with options to choose which personal details to reveal and which to conceal. Hence, users could construct their online identities or present themselves in ways they would like to be perceived by others (Salimkhan *et al.* 2010; Ellison 2013). However, in fact, there are very limited to options for individuals to keep their (real) identities private. Users who provide little or no personal details can hardly benefit from social media features. Furthermore, every movement or activity in a social media environment creates information that relates to the user. Consequently, the more a user interacts, the more information about her is collected. Moreover, social media encourages and seduces users to present themselves, their interests, etc. and disclose parts of their identity; e.g., this is observable on Facebook where users are prompted to enter their relationship status, employers, interests, feelings, favorite music, films, books, visited events, etc. This already starts during registration as most social media platforms have real-name policies to prompt users to enter their real names (De Andrade *et al.* 2013; Edwards and McAuley 2013; Ellison and Boyd 2013; Whitley *et al.* 2014). For example, Facebook's name policy states:

> Facebook is a community where everyone uses the name they go by in everyday life. This makes it so that you always know who you're connecting with and helps keep our community safe…. The name on your profile should be the name that your friends call you in everyday life. This name should also appear on an ID or document from our ID list.[27]

Google had a similar policy for its social network:

> Google+ profiles are meant for individual people. That's why we recommend using your first and last name on your profile. It will help friends and family find you online, and help you connect with people you know.[28]

Although the providers failed in enforcing a strict real-name policy (Edwards and McAuley 2013), it is widely implemented anyway as the majority of accounts reveal the real names of their holders. Several studies show that online profiles mostly provide a relatively detailed presentation of their users (Weisbuch *et al.* 2009; Ellison 2013; Madden *et al.* 2013). As shown in the previous sections, user profiles build the foundation of social media, usually containing various forms of identity information, often including personal images and photographs, date and place of birth, area of living, education, profession, relationships, friends and acquaintances, etc. Being a semi-public space, social media entails many methods of direct and indirect disclosure of this information (Strauß and Nentwich 2013). As every interaction of a user with her profile is persistent, replicable, scalable and searchable in the social media environment (Boyd 2010), one's identity representation constantly extends. This is, e.g., observable in Facebook's "Timeline" feature (Panzarino 2011; Kupka 2012), which enables a user to browse through her activities ranging from her "birth" in Facebook, i.e., registration and first login, up to the very last action taken in the network environment. Hence, every piece of information provided to the platform is stored and categorized for further processing. For instance, every time a user uploads an image to Facebook, an automated algorithm integrates tags into these images in order to enrich them with additional, searchable information (e.g., people visible, description of the scene such as "eating", "sitting", meta-description of the landscape such as "beach", etc.).[29] These keywords are used to explore content, relationships, activities, etc. of users. Furthermore, the social graph provides many options to exploit social media content and re-use it in other application contexts. Consequently, there are quasi-unlimited contexts in which users' identity information can be processed.

A number of developments contribute to further expansion of the social media landscape. As outlined above, personalization of services and profiling play an important role for its outreach. Providers are not merely acting altruistically; their services are key parts of their business models and, thus, social media basically represents commercial infrastructures. Their design mirrors the peculiarities and dynamics of software development practices that became widespread with Web 2.0: the quick release of new technologies, applications, features, modalities, etc. accompanied by continuous adjustments and reconfigurations depending on user behavior and feedback resulting in a sort of "perpetual beta" status (O'Reilly 2005). In this regard, social media can be seen as a test bed or playground for developers and commercial stakeholders. The internet economy profits in many respects from social media, e.g., for CRM, customized advertising, etc. This is a main reason for the significant increase in personalization of online services in the last decades. A few years ago, the outreach of SNS was limited to entities within the social media environment. However, it grew with the increasing societal relevance and further integration of other applications. As shown, there are plenty of possibilities and tools to use social media and exploit vast arrays of information. APIs, social graphs and social plugins enable various ways to integrate and link services with social media environments and vice versa. This amplified the further expansion of social media toward "outer" spaces on the web. Hence, social media platforms gather identity information even from external sources and thus gain an ever more detailed picture of individual identities. This is boosted by the growth in mobile computing (smart phones, tablets, etc.) that enabled social media usage everywhere. Mobile computing thus serves as an unfolding platform technology for a variety of applications (e.g., due to the integration of apps). Consequently, with mobile usage, the social media universe further expands. Unsurprisingly, it is a rapidly increasing market (Buhl 2015; Perrin 2015). Marketers assume that about 80 percent of social media usage is mobile (see, e.g., Sterling 2016). As part of this, novel services appear which are often absorbed in no time by the major players, such as Facebook's takeover of the photo-sharing application Instagram in 2012 or of the popular mobile messenger WhatsApp in 2014 (O'Connell 2014). A result of these takeovers is that Facebook gains additional user data from these services (such as users' phone numbers), and user profiles grow even further. Among other things, user data from WhatsApp such as mobile phone numbers is forwarded to Facebook (Gibbs 2016a). Other activities of Facebook concern the integration of payment services into its platform (Constine 2016; Russell 2016). A further trend is observable in the field of IDM, where providers attempt to enter this market. Social media platforms used to apply softer forms of IDM limited to their own domains (e.g., to provide and manage user accounts). However, recent developments such as the use of "social logins" (as outlined previously) led to a significant extension: larger providers (such as Facebook, Google, LinkedIn or Twitter) provide tools to integrate their login procedures and thus users' profiles into other (external) web applications. Figure 4.6 shows typical examples thereof, as embedded in many websites.

Other websites, services, platforms, etc. can use these features and outsource the management of their users' identities to social media platforms, who position themselves as central IdPs. As a result, user identities can be integrated in other contexts where, in return, the platforms gain additional identity information from these external sources. With these approaches, social media platforms have the potential to become pervasive online identity systems. Besides these approaches to integrate social media identities in other Web domains, there are also trends to apply them in real-world IDM contexts. The growing relevance and widespread diffusion of social media partially lead to "growing pressures to use this (social network) data about connections and endorsements as part of the identity proofing processes for more formal identification processes" (Whitley *et al.* 2014: 26). Although the creation of online profiles currently does not require formal identity checking, there are approaches to change this. One attempt came from Facebook, which attempted to enforce its real-name policy by de-activating user accounts and prompting users to prove their real identities by providing official

Figure 4.6 Google+ and Facebook social login buttons.

ID (e.g., passport or driving license) to the social network. After heavy user protest, Facebook conceded that they had made a mistake and apologized (Raeburn 2013). However, the real-name policy is still valid but not strictly enforced anymore (Edwards and McAuley 2013). Attempts like this do not come merely from social media providers. In some countries, similar ideas come from political decision-makers. Considerations include, for example, to link social media accounts (such as Facebook) with national identity documents or governmental eIDMS approaches (De Andrade *et al.* 2013; Martin and De Andrade 2013; Whitley *et al.* 2014). Ideas like this raise a number of critical issues, such as: economic dependency and risks of monopolization of identification, threatening its role as a genuine societal and governmental function, lack of control over IDM, problems of data ownership, international legal and regulatory issues, lack of network and technology neutrality, lack of trust and liability, and extensive security and privacy issues to name just a few (De Andrade *et al.* 2013; Whitley *et al.* 2014). Regardless of these risks and problems, there are ongoing trends to merge social media and real-world identities. This is observable in countries like China, inter alia, with problematic situations concerning human rights: Chinese authorities aim to legally force citizens to use their real names in social media (Chin 2015). But similar trends exist in other countries as well: such as the registration of voters via Facebook in the US state of Washington (Farivar 2012); the use of Facebook accounts for official identification to access public online services in the UK (Lee 2012); discussions about integrating the governmental eID system into Facebook in the Netherlands (Martin and De Andrade 2013); recent plans of the US Department of Homeland Security[30] to use social media accounts for border control, i.e., travelers to the US should expose their social media IDs (e.g., on Facebook or Twitter) to law enforcement (Gibbs 2016b; McCarthy 2016); or considerations of the European Commission to link social media and governmental IDs to stimulate the EU digital market (Best 2016; EU-C 2016b). These developments indicate further trends of extending digital identification practices and their application contexts.

Transition paths of digital identification

Basically, a transition (see also Chapter 2) is an enduring evolutionary process which involves various transformations resulting from dynamic interactions between socio-technical niches and regimes (Kemp *et al.* 2001; Geels 2004; Geels and Schot 2007). Hence, a transition is not to be misinterpreted as a shift from an old to a new system. It is a continuous, dynamic transformation pattern where different technological developments influence each other and together affect societal functions and practices. Similar is observable in the case of (digital) identification: as shown, the representation and processing of identity information, i.e., identification practices, are part of a wider socio-technical transformation pattern or transition in the realm of ICTs.

Basically, technological change starts in niches, i.e., "limited domains in which the technology can be applied" (Kemp *et al.* 2001: 274). In these niches, new socio-technical functionalities are explored and employed in specific contexts, which can lead to specialization and further expansion of the technology. With wider usage and diffusion (e.g., by entering new economic markets), a technology can become established in one or more regimes, which then entails wider societal impacts such as changing user practices. Technological regimes "are configurations of science, technics, organizational routines, practices, norms and values, labelled for their core technology or mode of organization" (Kemp *et al.* 2001: 273). A (socio-technical) regime thus comprises the rules and dynamics that result from the complex of processes, organizational and institutional settings, infrastructures, etc. and their dynamics, which shape the socio-technical configuration of a technology or system (Kemp *et al.* 2001; Geels and Schot 2007). Each of the domains involved in a transition has its own dynamics of self-organization processes which enable as well as constrain different development paths (Geels and Schot 2007; Hofkirchner 2013). This means that a technological development may enable a new practice but at the same time complicate others. The dynamic linkages between different system elements create a semi-coherent structure as several tensions may occur such as competing designs, practices, social and economic interests, policies, neglected consumer rights, legal and ethical issues, etc. This may lead to further (intended or unintended) changes regarding structure and organization, reconfigurations or adjustments which affect the design and usage patterns, and thus the societal impacts of a technology.

Similar dynamics of change can be found in the socio-technical transformations related to ICTs. As shown in this chapter, the progress/development of ICTs can be seen as an evolutionary process where socio-technical systems become increasingly integrative parts of society. Furthermore, these different systems are interconnected by digital information. From a wider perspective, ICTs (and primarily the internet) are perceivable as a set of intertwined socio-technical systems or a metasystem, which allows its multiple sub-systems to interact, combine and integrate information from different domains. Formerly rather isolated, siloed systems (e.g., specific websites, single online services, applications, etc.) partially transformed toward highly networked, interactive platforms and infrastructures (as prominently highlighted by social media or e-commerce platforms, etc.). These infrastructures deeply and constantly influence many domains of society as being an integral part thereof. These transformations also affect identification practices and the way identities are represented and managed. Hence, there are certain transformation patterns of digital identification observable: in the early days of the web, before Web 2.0, online applications had no or only few, limited relations and were mostly separated from other application contexts. User profiles and personal information were widely isolated, not extensively networked, and used on occasion but not as part of a strategic IDM concept. With increasing ICT diffusion, and particularly Web 2.0 and social media entering the mainstream, interactions between different application systems increased. In parallel, personalized services gained momentum, requiring or encouraging individual users to provide personal details. At the same time, stimulated by different economic and security interests, IDM emerged with attempts to unify and standardize identification and authentication procedures, enable interchangeable user profiles, etc. Hence, personalization, digital identity representation and identification expanded with digital networks. Consequently, our identities also became networked, socio-technical artifacts.

Today, there is a broad range of different services, platforms and technologies covering various domains of everyday life involving identification. In many respects, ICTs thus represent extensions of personal identities as individuals present themselves in online profiles, and use personalized services as well as technical devices. This entails the processing of extensive amounts of identity-related information, as exemplified by social media platforms and other global internet companies. A boost in smartphone usage underlines the convergence of physical and digital environments with integrated digital identity representation. This is accompanied by accelerated trends of further networking and integration of different online applications and services (social media, IDM systems, apps, social plugins and logins, etc.). There are many tendencies to extend the scope of social media: with social plugins and logins becoming integrated into other systems, the platforms themselves also gather information from applications outside their environments. As a consequence, user profiles are enriched with information from external usage contexts. In this regard, there are meta-profiles emerging, which is also observable in the realm of Web search provider Google, which kept user profiles from all its different services (ranging from search, e-mail, geo-location services, social media, chats, image processing, bulletin boards, etc.) separate from each other. Since 2012, Google has aggregated all user data (Suhl 2012; Reitman 2012) from its broad scope of services and applications (e.g., web search, Gmail, G+, Maps, Google Docs, etc.) into one centralized meta-profile. This meta-profile thus contains extensive collections of individual online activities. But besides Google and Facebook, several other big Internet companies (e.g., Amazon, Microsoft, Apple, Twitter) have extensive amounts of information from their users. Technologies such as the social graph enable analysis and visualization of aggregated user information from multiple sources. Moreover, they allow searching for particular individuals, based on their relationships, activities, interests, behavior, etc. and embedding this func-tionality into other applications as well.

These developments do not imply the emergence of a sort of global meta-ID system, or universal identification mechanisms. Nevertheless, identity informa-tion is broadly and increasingly available, can be aggregated from multiple sources and thus allows for sophisticated meta-profiling. Hence, even though there is no meta-ID, there are extensive identity profiles being created by various actors. Moreover, IDM systems and identification mechanisms generally increase with trends toward (quasi-)centralization. There are also tendencies to integrate identification mechanisms into applications which actually do not need formal user identification; for instance, real-name policies in social media and other online platforms (Whitley *et al.* 2014) or the use of governmental eIDs for libraries, public transport, online games, chat rooms, etc., as exists in some countries (Bennett and Lyon 2008; Lyon 2009), as well as the previously outlined trends to expand the scope of social media identities. With social logins, global internet companies (e.g., Facebook, Google, LinkedIn) began to position themselves as central IdPs for online services: they offer particular login services to integrate their user profiles into websites and applications (e.g., "Login with your Facebook account"). In return, additional web content and users' identity information can flow into the social media platforms. Furthermore, the broad availability of identity information and user profiles triggered desires to combine social media accounts with formal identification. The increasing trends to use social media profiles for identity verification and, e.g., link it with national identity procedures including governmental IDs highlight that digital identities are more and more entering "real world" contexts and vice versa. Also, smartphone technology is increasingly linked to IDM as these phones become popular, multifunctional carrier devices for identification and authentication. This is another example of technological convergence and integration. For instance, e-banking systems employing smartphones as authentication tokens, e-commerce platforms (e.g., Amazon and others) suggesting mobile phone numbers as provided as user credential. Further examples can be found in the field of biometrics (see the next chapter).

Hence, there are many empirical examples for the increasing convergence between analog and digital environments where identification is involved. This is not just a consequence of technological progress but results from several socio-technical transformation processes. The outlined developments involve a number of societal transformations and patterns of change. Digital identification emerged in several technological niches and incrementally gained momentum, which contributed to increasing interactions between different regimes. This is accompanied by various transformations and reconfigurations in social, economic and political domains. The introduction of IDM systems entails socio-technical change processes in public and private sectors, alters the relationship between citizens and their governments as well as between customers and businesses; the dynamics of social interactions in Web 2.0 and social media significantly changed socio-technical interactions and identity representations of individuals in online environments. As shown, the increase in digital identification is driven by a number of interrelated socio-economic and political factors with two dominating domains (or regimes): the digital economy and the security sector. Economic considerations include, e.g., fostering service efficiency, stimulating market development, CRM, behavioral advertising, service-for-profile business models, etc. Security objectives range from providing secure online transactions, reliable identification and authentication up to combating fraud, crime and terrorism, i.e., national security. Considering the self-dynamics of both regimes (economy and security), which may stimulate further identification mechanisms, we can speak of economization and securitization. In our case, economic and security rationales have an influence on the implementation and use of digital identification mechanisms (as discussed in more depth in the next chapter). In general, transitions include enabling as well as constraining mechanisms (Giddens 1984; Hofkirchner 2013). Socio-technical practices change, new ones emerge; and these changes also entail increasing pressure on existing societal functions, which may reinforce existing societal conflicts. Among other things, ICTs enabled new modes of information processing, communication, interaction and networking. They can be seen as socio-technical artifacts which extend the representation of their users' identities and thus enable novel forms of identification. But to some extent, they also constrain individual privacy. The emergence of digital identification puts high pressure on the effective protection of privacy, or more precisely the boundary control function inherent to privacy. The increasingly seamless, frictionless processing of identity information aggravates privacy risks. Digital identification is thus confronted with a certain control dilemma, which is explored in the next chapter.

Notes

1 Advanced Research Projects Agency Network of the US defense department.
2 Announcing Amazon Elastic Compute Cloud (Amazon EC2)—beta, August 4 2006: https://aws.amazon.com/de/about-aws/whats-new/2006/08/24/announcing-amazon-elastic-compute-cloud-amazon-ec2-beta/.
3 Future of Identity in the Information Society: www.fidis.net.
4 For example, https://account.microsoft.com/about.
5 http://openid.net/developers/specs/https://de.wikipedia.org/wiki/OpenID.
6 If a product is bought by direct cash payment, usually no identity information is digitally processed. This is different if a technological device (e.g., a debit card, credit card, etc.) is involved, serving as an identity token. In such cases, there is a distance between buyer and seller as a technical system handles the payment transaction. The same principle is true in online services where technology intermediates an interaction.
7 The e-signature Directive 1999/93/EC created a community framework for the use of electronic signatures in the EU that invited member states to create corresponding national laws: http://eur-lex.europa.eu/legal-content/EN/TXT/HTML/?uri=CELEX:31999L0093&from=DE.
8 The so-called eIDAS act: Regulation (EU) No. 910/2014 of the European Parliament and of the Council of 23 July 2014 on electronic identification and trust services for electronic transactions in the internal market and repealing Directive 1999/93/EC: http://eur-lex.europa.eu/legal-content/EN/TXT/HTML/?uri=CELEX:32014R0910.
9 STORK is the acronym for secure identity across linked borders: www.eid-stork2.eu/.
10 www.idesg.org/.
11 Five Pilot Projects Receive Grants to Promote Online Security and Privacy. *NIST News Post*, September 20, 2012: www.nist.gov/news-events/news/2012/09/five-pilot-projects-receive-grants-promote-online-security-and-privacy.
12 Unique identification authority of India, https://uidai.gov.in; for an overview on the program see also https://en.wikipedia.org/wiki/Aadhaar.
13 For example, consulting companies like the Gartner group give advice to companies on how to monetize their customer data: Gartner (2015) How to Monetize Your Customer Data, December 10: www.gartner.com/smarterwithgartner/how-to-monetize-your-customer-data/.
14 Google's revenue in the first quarter 2016 was over US$20 billion (see, e.g., CNBC 2016a). Facebook's revenue in the first quarter 2016 was over US$5 billion (e.g., CNBC 2016b). The estimated global advertisement revenue of Facebook in 2015 is over US$17 billion (e.g., Statista 2017a). Google's total revenue was over US$74 billion in 2015 (e.g., Statista 2017b).

15 Forbes Ranking of the world's biggest public companies #119 Facebook as of May 2017, www.forbes.com/companies/facebook/. Forbes Ranking of the world's biggest public companies #24 as of May 2017: www.forbes.com/companies/alphabet/.

16 According to rough estimations as of the first quarter of 2017, Facebook had over 1.9 billion users worldwide; in 2010, it was about 600 million (Statista 2017c). As of September 2016, Google+ was assumed to have about 375 million users (StatB 2016). In October 2018, Google announced it would shut down the service for consumers due to a serious security bug: www.blog.google/technology/safety-security/project-strobe/.

17 Facebook, for instance, encourages advertisers to develop and integrate apps into social media for monetization of user data: https://developers.facebook.com/products/app-monetization/.

18 A variety of apps is, e.g., available via Facebook's App center (www.facebook.com/games/), Google's play store (https://play.google.com/), or Twitter's site for app management (https://apps.twitter.com/).

19 For example, from Facebook: https://developers.facebook.com/docs/plugins/, or Google: https://developers.google.com/+/web/.

20 Facebook Connect/Login: https://developers.facebook.com/docs/facebook-login, Google Sign In: https://developers.google.com/+/web/signin/, Sign In LinkedIn: https://developer.linkedin.com/docs/signin-with-linkedin, Twitter Sign In: https://dev.twitter.com/web/sign-in.

21 http://search.fb.com/.

22 For example, 6 Facebook Search Engine and Data Visualization Tools, www.toprankblog.com/2010/08/6-facebook-search-engine-data-visualization-tools/.

23 https://developers.facebook.com/docs/sharing/opengraph https://developers.facebook.com/docs/graph-api/.

24 www.google.com/intl/es419/insidesearch/features/search/knowledge.html.

25 https://aws.amazon.com/neptune.

26 An entertaining approach addressing the small world phenomenon is the so-called Bacon number, referring to US actor Kevin Bacon. The number indicates the distance to the actor: the higher the number the greater the distance. For instance, an actor who did not occur in a movie with Bacon but played with an actor who did has the number 2. In the sense of "I know somebody that knows somebody … that knows Kevin Bacon." For an online tool exploring the Bacon number see, e.g., https://bacon.mybluemix.net/.

27 Facebook's real-name policy: www.facebook.com/help/292517374180078.

28 Google+ profile name information: https://support.google.com/plus/answer/1228271?hl=en.

29 An open source browser add-on called "Show Facebook Computer Vision Tags" visualizes the tags of an image: https://github.com/ageitgey/show-facebook-computer-vision-tags and http://nymag.com/selectall/2017/01/see-what-facebook-thinks-is-in-your-photos.html.

30 The US Department of Homeland Security already conducts surveillance of social media such as Facebook, Twitter and online blogs as well as news organizations. The monitoring activities are outsourced to a private contractor. The US-located Electronic Privacy Information Center (EPIC) pursues a lawsuit against the department: http://epic.org/foia/epic-v-dhs-media-monitoring/.

References

All URLs were checked last on October 23, 2018.

Abelson, H. and Lessig, L. (1998) Digital Identity in Cyberspace. White paper Submitted for *6.805/Law of Cyberspace: Social Protocols*. http://groups.csail.mit.edu/mac/classes/6.805/student-papers/fall98-papers/identity/linked-white-paper.html.

Acquisti, A. and Gross, R. (2006) Imagined Communities: Awareness, information sharing, and privacy on the Facebook. In Danezis, G. and Golle, P. (eds.), *Privacy Enhancing Technologies*. PET 2006. LNCS Vol. 4258. Berlin/Heidelberg: Springer, 36–58.

Aichholzer, G. and Strauß, S. (2010a) Electronic Identity Management in e-Government 2.0: Exploring a system innovation exemplified by Austria. *Information Polity: An International Journal of Government and Democracy in the Information Age*, 15(1–2): 139–152.

Aichholzer, G. and Strauß, S. (2010b) The Austrian Case: Multi-card concept and the relationship between citizen ID and social security cards. *Identity in the Information Society (IDIS)*, (3)1: 65–85.

Ajana, B. (2013) *Governing through Biometrics: The biopolitics of identity*. Basingstoke/ New York: Palgrave Macmillan.

Allkott, H. and Gentzkow, M. (2017) Social Media and Fake News in the 2016 Election. *Journal of Economic Perspectives*, 31(2): 211–236. https://web.stanford.edu/~gentzkow/research/fakenews.pdf.

Arora, S. (2008) National e-ID Card Schemes: A European overview. *Information Security Technical Report*, 13(2): 46–53.

Baringhorst, S. (2009) Introduction: Political campaigning in changing media cultures: Typological and historical approaches. In Baringhorst, S., Kneip, V. and Niesyto, J. (eds.), *Political Campaigning on the Web*. Bielefeld: transcript, 9–30.

Beck, J. (2018) People Are Changing the Way they Use Social Media. *The Atlantic*, June 7, www.theatlantic.com/technology/archive/2018/06/did-cambridge-analytica-actually-change-facebook-users-behavior/562154/.

Belbey, J. (2016) Crime and Social Media: Law enforcement is watching. *Forbes Magazine*, August 31, www.forbes.com/sites/joannabelbey/2016/08/31/crime-and-social-media-law-enforcement-is-watching/#6cf1d7cd541d.

Benkirane, R. (2012) The Alchemy of Revolution: The role of social networks and new media in the Arab Spring. *GCSP Policy Paper*, No. 2012/7, edited by Geneva Center for Security Policy.

Bennett, C. J. and Lyon, D. (2008) *Playing the Identity Card: Surveillance, security and identification in global perspective*. London/New York: Routledge.

Best, S. (2016) Will You Soon Need a Government ID to Log into Facebook? Europe Commission proposes controversial scheme to access social media sites. *Daily Mail Online*, June 3, www.dailymail.co.uk/sciencetech/article-3623396/Will-soon-need-government-ID-log-Facebook-Europe-Commission-proposes-controversial-scheme-access-social-media-sites.html#ixzz4JedgLpcu.

Beyreuther, T., Eismann, C., Hornung, S. and Kleemann. F. (2013) Prosumption of Social Context in Web 2.0. In Dunkel, W. and Kleemann, F. (eds.), *Customers at Work: New perspectives on interactive service work*. London: Palgrave MacMillan/AbeBooks, 223–252.

Bhargav-Spantzel, A., Camenisch, J., Gross, T. and Sommer, D. (2007) User Centricity: A taxonomy and open issues. *Journal of Computer Security*, 15(5): 493–527.

Bonneau, J., Anderson, J., Anderson, R. and Stajano, F. (2009) Eight Friends Are Enough: Social graphs approximation via public listings. In *Proceedings of the Second ACM EuroSys Workshop on Social Network Systems (SNS)*, 13–18. www.cl.cam.ac.uk/~rja14/Papers/8_friends_paper.pdf.

Bonneau, J., Herley, C., van Oorschot, P. C. and Stajano, F. (2012) The Quest to Replace Passwords: A framework for comparative evaluation of web authentication schemes.

In *IEEE Symposium on Security and Privacy.* www.cl.cam.ac.uk/~fms27/papers/2012-BonneauHerOorSta-password-oakland.pdf.

Boulianne, S. (2015) Social Media Use and Participation: A meta-analysis of current research. *Information, Communication and Society*, 18(5): 524–538.

Boyd, D. M. and Ellison, N. B. (2007) Social Network Sites: Definition, history, and scholarship. *Journal of Computer-Mediated Communication*, 13(1): 210–230.

Boyd, D. (2010) Social Network Sites as Networked Publics: Affordances, dynamics, and implications. In Papacharissi, Z. (ed.), *Networked Self: Identity, community, and culture on social network sites.* New York: Routledge, 39–58.

Brandtdaeg, P. B. and Heim, J. (2009) Why People Use Social Networking Sites. In Ozok, A. A. and Zaphiris, P. (eds.), *Online Communities*, LNCS 5621. Berlin/Heidelberg: Springer, 143–152.

Brugger, J., Fraefel, M. and Riedl, R. (2014) Raising Acceptance of Cross-Border eID Federation by Value Alignment. *Electronic Journal of e-Government*, 12(2): 179–189.

Buhl, M. (2015) Millennials Boast Huge Social Networking Growth and Engagement on Smartphones, But Older Users Surprisingly Outpace Them on Tablets. *Comscore*, August 12, www.comscore.com/Insights/Blog/Millennials-Boast-Huge-Social-Networking-Growth-and-Engagement-on-Smartphones.

Buzzetto-More, N. A. (2013) Social Media and Prosumerism. *Issues in Informing Science and Information Technology*, 10: 67–80. http://iisit.org/Vol.10/IISITv10p067-080 Buzzetto0040.pdf.

Cachia, R. (2008) *Social Computing: Study on the Use and Impact of Online Social Networking. IPTS Exploratory Research on the Socio-economic Impact of Social Computing.* JRC Scientific and Technical Reports—Institute for Prospective Technological Studies (IPTS)—European Commission. Luxembourg: office for official publications of the European Communities. http://ftp.jrc.es/EURdoc/JRC48650.pdf.

Castells, M. (1996) *The Rise of the Network Society: The information age: Economy, society, and culture volume I.* Oxford: Blackwell.

Castells, M. (2003) *Das Informationszeitalter. Der Aufstieg der Netzwerkgesellschaft.* Opladen: Leske+Budrich.

CEN—Comité Européen Normalisation (2004) Towards an Electronic ID for the European Citizen, a Strategic Vision. *CEN/ISSS Workshop eAuthentication, Brussels.* www.umic.pt/images/stories/publicacoes/Towards%20eID.pdf.

Chin, J. (2015) China Is Requiring People to Register Real Names for Some Internet Services. *Wall Street Journal*, February 4, www.wsj.com/articles/china-to-enforce-real-name-registration-for-internet-users-1423033973.

Cisco (2017) The Zettabyte Era: Trends and analysis, white paper, www.cisco.com/c/en/us/solutions/collateral/service-provider/visual-networking-index-vni/vni-hyperconnectivity-wp.html.

Clarke, R. (1994a) Human Identification in Information Systems: Management challenges and public policy issues. *Information Technology and People*, 7(4): 6–37. www.rogerclarke.com/DV/HumanID.html.

Clarke, R. (1994b) The Digital Persona and its Application to Data Surveillance. *The Information Society*, 10(2): 77–92. www.rogerclarke.com/DV/DigPersona.html#DP.

CNBC (2016a) Alphabet Earnings: $7.50 per share, vs expected EPS of $7.97. *CNBC*, April 21, www.cnbc.com/2016/04/21/alphabet-reports-first-quarter-results.html.

CNBC (2016b) Facebook Shatters Wall Street Estimates, Proposes New Share Structure. *CNBC*, April 27, www.cnbc.com/2016/04/27/facebook-reports-first-quarter-earnings.html.

Constine, J. (2016) Facebook Messenger Now Allows Payments in its 30,000 Chat Bots. *Techcrunch*, September 12, https://techcrunch.com/2016/09/12/messenger-bot-payments/.

Dahlgren, P. (2013) Do Social Media Enhance Democratic Participation? The importance and difficulty of being realistic. Policy Paper No. 4/2013, edited by Rosa Luxemburg Stiftung Berlin. www.rosalux.de/fileadmin/rls_uploads/pdfs/Standpunkte/policy_paper/PolicyPaper_04-2013.pdf.

De Andrade, N. N. G., Monteleone, S. and Martin, A. (2013) *Electronic Identity in Europe: Legal challenges and future perspectives (e-ID 2020).* JRC Scientific and Policy Reports. Joint Research Centre, European Commission.

De Hert, P. (2008) Identity management of e-ID, Privacy and Security in Europe: A human rights view. *Information Security Technical Report*, 13: 71–75.

Debatin, B. and Lovejoy, J. P. (2009) Facebook and Online Privacy: Attitudes, behaviors, and unintended consequences. *Journal of Computer-Mediated Communication*, 15(1): 83–108.

Dmytrenko, O. and Nardali, A. (2005) Net Passport under the Scrutiny of U.S. and EU Privacy Law: Implications for the future of online authentication. *Journal of Law and Policy for the Information Society*, 1(2–3): 619–645. https://kb.osu.edu/dspace/bitstream/handle/1811/72710/ISJLP_V1N2-3_619.pdf?sequence=1.

Edwards, L. and McAuley, D. (2013) What's in a Name? Real name policies and social networks. In *Proceedings of the 1st Workshop on Internet Science and Web Science Synergies, Paris, May 2013.* www.cs.nott.ac.uk/~pszdrm/papers/2013_NamesHavePower%20paris%20vn.pdf.

Egelman, S. (2013) My Profile is My Password, Verify Me! The privacy/convenience tradeoff of Facebook connect. In *Proceedings of the SIGCHI Conference on Human Factors in Computing Systems, April 27–May 02*, 2369–2378. www.guanotronic.com/~serge/papers/chi13a.pdf.

Ellison, N. (2013) *Future Identities: Changing identities in the UK—the next 10 years. DR3: Social media and identity.* Government Office for Science Foresight United Kingdom. Research report. www.gov.uk/government/uploads/system/uploads/attachment_data/file/275752/13-505-social-media-and-identity.pdf.

Ellison, N. B. and Boyd, D. M. (2013) Sociality through Social Network Sites. In Dutton, W. H. (ed.), *The Oxford Handbook of Internet Studies*. Oxford: Oxford University Press, 151–172.

Elmer, G. (2004) *Profiling Machines*. Cambridge/MA: MIT Press.

EPIC—Electronic Privacy Information Center (2003) Sign Out of Passport! https://epic.org/privacy/consumer/microsoft/.

EU-C—European Commission (2006) i2010 eGovernment Action Plan: Accelerating eGovernment in Europe for the benefit of all. COM (2006) 173 final. Brussels, April 25, http://ec.europa.eu/smart-regulation/impact/ia_carried_out/docs/ia_2006/sec_2006_0511_en.pdf.

EU-C—European Commission (2010) *Digitizing Public Services in Europe: Putting ambition into action, 9th benchmark measurement.* December 2010, Directorate General for Information Society and Media, Unit C.4 Economic and Statistical Analysis. http://ec.europa.eu/newsroom/document.cfm?action=display&doc_id=747.

EU-C—European Commission (2016a) *EU eGovernment Action Plan 2016–2020 Accelerating the digital transformation of government.* COM (2016) 179 final. Brussels, April 19, http://ec.europa.eu/newsroom/dae/document.cfm?doc_id=15268.

EU-C—European Commission (2016b) *Online Platforms and the Digital Single Market Opportunities and Challenges for Europe.* Communication from the Commission to the

European Parliament, the Council, the European Economic and Social Committee and the Committee of the Regions, COM (2016) 288 final. Brussels, May 25, http://eur-lex. europa.eu/legal-content/EN/TXT/PDF/?uri=CELEX:52016DC0288&from=EN.

Farivar, C. (2012) Washington State Will Enable Voter Registration via Facebook. *Ars Technica*, July 18, http://arstechnica.com/business/2012/07/washington-residents-to-be-able-to-register-to-vote-via-facebook.

Floridi, L. (2010) Ethics after the Information Revolution. In Floridi, L. (ed.), *The Cambridge Handbook of Information and Computer Ethics*. Cambridge/UK: Cambridge University Press, 3–19.

Floridi, L. (2013) *The Ethics of Information*. Oxford: Oxford University Press.

Fuchs, C. (2014) Digital Prosumption Labour on Social Media in the Context of the Capitalist Regime of Time. *Time and Society*, 23(1): 97–123. http://fuchs.uti.at/wp-content/time.pdf.

Fuchs, C. (2015) Social Media Surveillance. In Coleman, S. and Freelon, D. (eds.), *Handbook of Digital Politics*. Cheltenham: Edward Elgar, 395–414.

Fuchs, C. and Sandoval, M. (2015) The Political Economy of Capitalist and Alternative Social Media. In Atton, C. (ed.), *The Routledge Companion to Alternative and Community Media*. London: Routledge, 165–175.

Gafni, R. and Nissim, D. (2014) To Social Login or Not Login? Exploring factors affecting the decision. *Issues in Informing Science and Information Technology*, 11: 57–72. http://iisit.org/Vol. 11/IISITv11p057-072Gafni0462.pdf.

Geels, F. W. (2004) Understanding System Innovations: A critical literature review and a conceptual synthesis. In Elzen, B., Geels, F. W. and Green, K. (eds.), *System Innovation and the Transition to Sustainability: Theory, evidence and policy*. Cheltenham, UK/Northampton: Edward Elgar, 19–47.

Geels, F. W. and Schot, J. (2007) Typology of Sociotechnical Transition Pathways. *Research Policy*, 36: 399–417.

Gemalto (2014) National Mobile ID Schemes: Learning from today's best practices. White paper, www.securitydocumentworld.com/creo_files/upload/article-files/wp_mobileid_overview_en.pdf.

Gibbs, S. (2016a) WhatsApp to Give Users' Phone Numbers to Facebook for Targeted Ads. *Guardian*, August 25, www.theguardian.com/technology/2016/aug/25/whatsapp-to-give-users-phone-number-facebook-for-targeted-ads.

Gibbs, S. (2016b) US Border Control Could Start Asking for your Social Media Accounts. *Guardian*, June 28, www.theguardian.com/technology/2016/jun/28/us-customs-border-protection-social-media-accounts-facebook-twitter.

Giddens, A. (1984) *The Constitution of Society: Outline of the theory of structuration*. Cambridge: Polity Press.

Gillespie, T. (2010) The Politics of "Platforms". *New Media and Society*, 12(3): 347–364.

Gillings, M. R., Hilbert, M. and Kemp, D. J. (2016) Information in the Biosphere: Biological and digital worlds. *Trends in Ecology and Evolution*, 31(3): 180–189.

Glässer, U. and Vajihollahi, M. (2010) Identity Management Architecture. In Yang, C. C., Chau, M. C., Wang, J.-H. and Chen, H. (eds.), *Security Informatics, Annals of Information Systems Vol. 9*. Boston: Springer: pages 97–116.

Granovetter, M. S. (1973) The Strength of Weak Ties. *American Journal of Sociology* 78(6): 1360–1380.

Grassi, P. A., Garcia, M. E. and Fenton, J. L. (2017) *Digital Identity Guidelines. NIST special publication 800-63-3*. NIST—US National Institute of Standards and Technology. www.nist.gov/itl/tig/special-publication-800-63-3.

Greenwald, G. (2014) *No Place to Hide: Edward Snowden, the NSA and the surveillance state*. London: Hamish Hamilton/Penguin Books.

Halperin, R. and Backhouse, J. (2008) A Roadmap for Research on Identity in the Information Society. *Identity in the Information Society*, 1(1): 71–87.

Hern, A. (2018) How to Check whether Facebook Shared your Data with Cambridge Analytica. *Guardian*, April 10, www.theguardian.com/technology/2018/apr/10/facebook-notify-users-data-harvested-cambridge-analytica.

Hern, A. and Pegg, D. (2018) Facebook Fined for Data Breaches in Cambridge Analytica Scandal. *Guardian*, July 11, www.theguardian.com/technology/2018/jul/11/facebook-fined-for-data-breaches-in-cambridge-analytica-scandal.

Hildebrandt, M. (2006) Privacy and Identity. In Claes, E., Duff, A. and Gutwirth, S. (eds.), *Privacy and the Criminal Law*. Antwerpen/Oxford: Intersentia, 43–57.

Hildebrandt, M. (2008) Profiling and the Rule of Law. *Identity in the Information Society (IDIS)*, 1(1): 55–70. http://link.springer.com/article/10.1007/s12394-008-0003-1#Fn1.

Hildebrandt, M. (2011) Introduction: A multifocal view of human agency in the era of autonomic computing. In Hildebrandt, M. and Rouvroy, A. (2011), *Law, Human Agency and Autonomic Computing*. London/New York: Routledge, 1–11.

Hildebrandt, M. and Gutwirth, S. (eds.) (2008) *Profiling the European citizen: Cross-disciplinary perspectives*. Amsterdam: Springer Netherlands.

HNS—HelpNetSecurity (2011) Interpol Chief Calls for Global Electronic Identity Card System. *Help Net Security*, April 6, www.helpnetsecurity.com/2011/04/06/interpol-chief-calls-for-global-electronic-identity-card-system/.

Hofkirchner, W. (2010) How to Design the Infosphere: The fourth revolution, the management of the life cycle of information, and information ethics as a macroethics. *Knowledge, Technology and Policy*, 23(1–2): 177–192.

Hofkirchner, W. (2013) *Emergent Information: A unified theory of information framework*. World Scientific Series in Information Studies: Vol. 3. New Jersey/London: World Scientific.

Horvát, E. Á., Hanselmann, M., Hamprecht, F. A. and Zweig, K. A. (2013) You Are Who Knows You: Predicting links between non-members of Facebook. In Gilbert, T., Kirkilionis, M. and Nicolis, G. (eds.), *Proceedings of the European Conference on Complex Systems 2012*. Dordrecht/Heidelberg/New York/London: Springer, 309–315.

Ienca, M. (2018) Cambridge Analytica and Online Manipulation. *Scientific American*, March 30, https://blogs.scientificamerican.com/observations/cambridge-analytica-and-online-manipulation/.

ITU—International Telecommunication Union (2005) *Privacy and Ubiquitous Network Societies*. Background paper, ITU workshop on ubiquitous network societies, ITU new initiatives programme April 6–8. UNS/05. www.itu.int/osg/spu/ni/ubiquitous/Papers/Privacy%20background%20paper.pdf.

ITU—International Telecommunication Union (2010) *Baseline Identity Management Terms and Definitions. Series X: Data networks, open system communications and security. Cyberspace security: Identity management. Recommendation ITU-T X.1252*. www.itu.int/SG-CP/example_docs/ITU-T-REC/ITU-T-REC_E.pdf.

Jin, L., Chen, Y., Wang, T., Hui, P. and Vasilakos, A. V. (2013) Understanding User Behavior in Online Social Networks: A survey. *IEEE Communications Magazine*, 50(9): 144–150.

Jøsang, A., AlZomai, M., and Suriadi, S. (2007) Usability and Privacy in Identity Management Architectures. In *Proceedings of the 5th Australasian Symposium on ACSW Frontiers, Vol. 68*, Australian Computer Society, 143–152.

Kaplan, A. M. and Haenlein, M. (2011) Two Hearts in Three-Quarter Time: How to waltz the social media/viral marketing dance. *Business Horizons*, 54: 253–263.

Kaplan, A. M. and Haenlein, M. (2012) The Britney Spears Universe: Social media and viral marketing at its best. *Business Horizons*, 55: 27–31.

Kemp, R., Rip, A. and Schot, J. (2001) Constructing Transition Paths Through the Management of Niches. In Garud, R. and Karnoe, P. (eds.), *Path Dependence and Creation*. Mahwa/London: Lawrence Erlbaum, 269–299.

Kim, Y., Sohn, D. and Choi, S. M. (2011) Cultural Difference in Motivations for Using Social Network Sites: A comparative study of American and Korean college students. *Computers in Human Behavior*, 27: 365–372.

Kleinfeld, J. S. (2002) The Small World Problem. *Society*, 39(2): 61–66. www.stat.cmu.edu/~fienberg/Stat36-835/Kleinfeld_SWP.pdf.

Kolb, D. G. (2008) Exploring the Metaphor of Connectivity: Attributes, dimensions and duality. *Organization Studies*, 29(1): 127–144.

Kubicek, H. and Noack, T. (2010a) The Path Dependency of National Electronic Identities: A comparison of innovation processes in four European countries. *Identity in the Information Society (IDIS)*, 3(1): 111–153.

Kubicek, H. and Noack, T. (2010b) Different Countries—Different Extended Comparison of the Introduction of eIDs in Eight European Countries. *Identity in the Information Society (IDIS)*, 3(1): 235–245.

Kupka, A. (2012) Facebook Timeline Now Mandatory for Everyone. *Forbes Magazine*, January 24, www.forbes.com/sites/annakupka/2012/01/24/facebook-timeline-now-mandatory-for-everyone/.

LeCun, Y., Benigo, Y. and Hinton, G. (2015) Deep Learning. *Nature*, 521: 436–444.

Lee, D. (2012) Facebook Surpasses One Billion Users as it Tempts New Markets. *BBC News*, October 5, www.bbc.co.uk/news/technology-19816709.

Leenes, R. (2010) Context Is Everything: Sociality and privacy in online social network sites. In Bezzi, M., Duquenoy, P., Fischer-Hübner, S., Hansen, M. and Zhang, G. (eds.), *Privacy and Identity Management for Life*. IFIP AICT Vol. 320. Heidelberg/Berlin/New York: Springer, 48–65.

Leenes, R., Schallaböck, J. and Hansen, M. (2008) Prime (Privacy and Identity Management for Europe) white paper. Third and final version. EU: The PRIME consortium.

Leimbach, T., Hallinan, D., Bachlechner, D., Weber, A., Jaglo, M., Hennen, L., Nielsen, R., Nentwich, M., Strauß, S., Lynn, T. and Hunt, G. (2014) *Potential and Impacts of Cloud Computing Services and Social Network Websites—Study*. Report no. IP/A/STOA/FWC/2008-096/Lot4/C1/SC8; Science and Technology Options Assessment. Brussels: European Parliamentary Research Service.

Leiner, B. M., Cerf, V. G., David, D., Clark, D. D., Kahn, R. E., Kleinrock, L., Lynch, D. C., Postel, J., Roberts, L. G. and Wolff, S. (2003) *Brief History of the Internet*. Internet Society. www.internetsociety.org/internet/what-internet/history-internet/brief-history-internet.

Leskovec, J. and Horvitz, E. (2008) Worldwide Buzz: Planetary-scale views on a large instant-messaging network. In *Proceedings of the 17th International Conference on World Wide Web, April 21–25, Beijing*, 915–924.

Leskovec, J., Rajaraman, A. and Ullman, J. D. (2014) *Mining of Massive Datasets*. Second edition. Cambridge: Cambridge University Press.

Lessig, L. (2006) *Code Version 2.0*. New York: Basic Books.

Lips, A. Miriam, B., Taylor, John A. and Organ, J. (2009) Managing Citizen Identity Information in E-Government Service Relationships in the UK: The emergence of a surveillance state or a service state? *Public Management Review*, 11(6): 833–856.

Long, D. (2010) Eugene Kaspersky: Introduce ID system for all Internet users. *PC Authority*, May 17, www.pcauthority.com.au/News/174767,eugene-kaspersky-introduce-id-system-for-all-internet-users.aspx.

Lyon, D. (2009) *Identifying Citizens: ID Cards as Surveillance*. Cambridge: Polity Press.

Madden, M., Lenhart, A., Cortesi, S., Gasser, U., Duggan, M., Smith, A. and Beaton, M. (2013) *Teens, Social Media and Privacy*. Research Report, Pew Research Center Internet and Technology. www.pewinternet.org/2013/05/21/teens-social-media-and-privacy/.

Martin, A. K. and De Adrane, N. N. G. (2013) Friending the Taxman: On the use of social networking services for government eID in Europe. *Telecommunications Policy*, 37(9): 715–724.

Matikainen, J. (2015) Motivations for Content Generation in Social Media. *Participations: Journal of Audience and Reception Studies*, 12(1): 41–58.

McCarthy, K. (2016) Privacy Advocates Rail against US Homeland Security's Twitter, Facebook Snooping. *The Register*, August 23, www.theregister.co.uk/2016/08/23/homeland_security_social_media_snooping/.

McLuhan, M. (1964) *Understanding Media. The Extensions of Man*. London: Routledge & Kegan Paul.

McQuail, D. (2010) *Mass Communication Theory: An introduction*. Sixth edition 2005 (first edition published 1983). London: Sage Publications.

Mearian, L. (2012) By 2020, There Will Be 5,200 GB of Data for Every Person on Earth. *Computerworld*, December 11, www.computerworld.com/article/2493701/data-center/by-2020-there-will-be-5-200-gb-of-data-for-every-person-on-earth.html.

Metz, R. (2012) More Passwords, More Problems. *Technology Review*, September 21, www.dailymail.co.uk/sciencetech/article-2174274/No-wonder-hackers-easy-Most-26-different-online-accounts-passwords.html.

Milan, S. (2015) When Algorithms Shape Collective Action: Social media and the dynamics of cloud protesting. *Social Media + Society (SM + S)*, 1(2) (Online first December 30): 1–10. http://journals.sagepub.com/doi/pdf/10.1177/2056305115622481.

Milgram (1967) The Small World Problem. *Psychology Today*, 2(1): 60–67.

Nauman, L. and Hobgen, G. (2009) *Privacy Features of European eID Card Specifications*. Position paper, European Network and Information Security Agency ENISA. www.enisa.europa.eu/publications/eid-cards-en/at_download/fullReport.

Nentwich, M. and König, R. (2012) *Cyberscience 2.0: Research in the age of digital social networks*. Series Interactiva, Vol. 11. Frankfurt/New York: Campus.

Nissenbaum, H. (2010) *Privacy in Context: Technology, policy, and the integrity of social life*. Stanford: Stanford University Press.

O'Connell, A. (2014) Facebook Buys WhatsApp: What does it mean for WhatsApp privacy? *The Online Privacy Blog*, March 5, www.abine.com/blog/2014/whatsapp-privacy-and-facebook-acquisition/.

O'Mahony, J. (2012) Text Messaging at 20: How SMS changed the world. *Telegraph*, December 3, www.telegraph.co.uk/technology/mobile-phones/9718336/Text-messaging-at-20-how-SMS-changed-the-world.html.

O'Reilly, T. (2005) What is Web 2.0? Design patterns and business models for the next generation of software. *O'Reilly Media*, September 30, www.oreilly.com/pub/a/web2/archive/what-is-web-20.html.

OECD—Organization for Economic Co-Operation and Development (2011) *National Strategies and Policies for Digital Identity Management in OECD Countries*. OECD Digital Economy Papers, No. 177. Paris: OECD Publishing. http://dx.doi.org/10.1787/5kgdzvn5rfs2-en.

OECD—Organization for Economic Co-Operation and Development (2013) *Building Blocks for Smart Networks*. OECD Digital Economy Papers, No. 215, DSTI/ICCP/CISP(2012)3/FINAL. Paris: OECD Publishing. http://dx.doi.org/10.1787/5k4dkhvnzv35-en.

Panzarino, M. (2011) Facebook Introduces Radical New Profile Design Called Timeline: The story of your life. *The Next Web*, September 22, http://thenextweb.com/facebook/2011/09/22/facebook-introduces-timeline-the-story-of-your-life/.

Pariser, E. (2011) *The Filter Bubble: What the internet is hiding from you*. New York: Penguin Press.

Patrizio, A. (2016) ICQ, the Original Instant Messenger, Turns 20. *NetworkWorld*, November 18, www.networkworld.com/article/3142451/software/icq-the-original-instant-messenger-turns-20.html.

Perrin, A. (2015) Social Media Usage 2005–2015. Report, Pew Research Center Internet and Technology, October 8, www.pewinternet.org/2015/10/08/social-networking-usage-2005-2015/.

Pew (2014) World Wide Web Timeline. Pew Research Center Internet and Technology, March 11, www.pewinternet.org/2014/03/11/world-wide-web-timeline/.

Pfitzmann, A. and Hansen, M. (2010) *A Terminology for Talking About Privacy by Data Minimization: Anonymity, unlinkability, undetectability, unobservability, pseudonymity, and identity*. Version 0.34. http://dud.inf.tu-dresden.de/literatur/Anon_Terminology_v0.34.pdf.

Raeburn, S. (2013) Fury at Facebook as Login Requests "Government ID" from Users. *The Drum News*, October 29, www.thedrum.com/news/2013/10/29/fury-facebook-login-requests-government-id-users#0SAYzdXek51viRHm.99.

Rannenberg, K., Royer, D. and Deuker, A. (eds.) (2009) *The Future of Identity in the Information Society: Challenges and opportunities*. Berlin: Springer.

Redecker, C., Ala-Mutka, K. and Punie, Y. (2010) *Learning 2.0: The Impact of Social Media on Learning in Europe*. Policy Brief, Joint Research Centre of the European Commission, JRC56958. Luxembourg: European Communities Publications. www.ict-21.ch/com-ict/IMG/pdf/learning-2.0-EU-17pages-JRC56958.pdf.

Reitman, R. (2012) What Actually Changed in Google's Privacy Policy. *EPIC*, February 1, www.eff.org/deeplinks/2012/02/what-actually-changed-google%27s-privacy-policy.

Riley, S. (2006) Password Security: What users know and what they actually do. *Usability News*, February 14, Software Usability Research Laboratory, Wichita State University, http://usabilitynews.org/password-security-what-users-know-and-what-they-actually-do/.

Robinson, N. and Bonneau, J. (2014) Cognitive Disconnect: Understanding Facebook Connect login permissions. In Sala, A., Goel, A. and Gummadi, K. P. (eds.), *Proceedings of the 2nd ACM Conference on Online Social Networks (COSN), Dublin, Ireland, October 1–2*, pages 247–258. doi: 10.1145/2660460.2660471.

Rogers, R. (2009) The Googlization Question, and the Inculpable Engine. In Stalder, F. and Becker, K. (eds.), *Deep Search: The politics of search engines*. Edison, NJ; Innsbruck: StudienVerlag/Transaction Publishers, 173–184.

Rouvroy, A. and Poullet, Y. (2009) The Right to Informational Self-Determination and the Value of Self-Development: Reassessing the importance of privacy for democracy. In Gutwirth, S., Poullet, Y., de Hert, P., de Terwangne, C. and Nouwt, S. (eds.), *Reinventing Data Protection?* Dordrecht: Springer, 45–76.

Rundle, M., Blakley, B., Broberg, J., Nadalin, A., Olds, D., Ruddy, M., Guimarares, M. T. M. and Trevithick, P. (2008) *At a Crossroads: "Personhood" and Digital Identity in the Information Society.* STI Working paper 2007/7, no. JT03241547 29-Feb-2008, Directorate for Science, Technology and Industry, OECD Publishing. www.oecd.org/dataoecd/31/6/40204773.doc.

Russell, J. (2016) Facebook is Testing Social Commerce Payments in Southeast Asia. *Techcrunch,* June 9, https://techcrunch.com/2016/06/09/facebook-is-testing-social-commerce-payments-in-southeast-asia/.

Salimkhan, G., Manago, A. and Greenfield, P. (2010) The Construction of the Virtual Self on MySpace. *Cyberpsychology: Journal of Psychosocial Research on Cyberspace,* 4(1), Article 1. www.cyberpsychology.eu/view.php?cisloclanku=2010050203.

Singh, N., Lehnert, K. and Bostick, N. (2012) Global Social Media Usage: Insights into reaching consumers worldwide. Wiley Online Library, doi: 10.1002/tie.21493. http://beople.es/wp-content/uploads/2013/04/GLOBAL-SOCIAL-MEDIA-USAGE-INSIGHTS-INTO-REACHING-CONSUMERS-WORLDWIDE.pdf.

Smith, A. (2011) Why American Use Social Media. Report. *Pew Research Center Internet and Technology,* November 15, www.pewinternet.org/2011/11/15/why-americans-use-social-media/.

Solove, D. J. (2004) *The Digital Person: Technology and privacy in the information age.* New York: NYU Press.

StatB—Statistic Brain (2016) Google Plus Demographics and Statistics. *Statistic Brain,* September 4, www.statisticbrain.com/google-plus-demographics-statistics/.

Statista (2017a) Facebook's Advertising Revenue Worldwide from 2009 to 2016 (in million U.S. dollars). *Statista,* www.statista.com/statistics/271258/facebooks-advertising-revenue-worldwide/.

Statista (2017b) Advertising Revenue of Google Websites from 2001 to 2016 (in billion U.S. dollars). *Statista,* www.statista.com/statistics/266242/advertising-revenue-of-google-sites.

Statista (2017c) Number of Monthly Active Facebook Users Worldwide As of 1st Quarter 2017 (in millions). *Statista,* www.statista.com/statistics/264810/number-of-monthly-active-facebook-users-worldwide/.

Stefanone, M. A., Lackaff, D. and Rosen, D. (2010) The Relationship between Traditional Mass Media and "Social Media": Reality television as a model for social network site behavior. *Journal of Broadcasting and Electronic Media,* 54(3): 508–525. doi: 10.1080/08838151.2010.498851.

Steinfield, C., Ellison, N. B. and Lampe, C. (2008) Social Capital, Self-Esteem, and Use of Online Social Network Sites: A longitudinal analysis. *Journal of Applied Developmental Psychology,* 29(6): 434–445.

Sterling, G. (2016) Nearly 80 Percent of Social Media Time Now Spent on Mobile Devices. *Marketing Land,* April 4, http://marketingland.com/facebook-usage-accounts-1-5-minutes-spent-mobile-171561.

Strauß, S. (2011) The Limits of Control: (Governmental) Identity management from a privacy perspective. In Fischer-Hübner, S. Duquenoy, P., Hansen, M., Leenes, R. and Zhang, G. (eds.), *Privacy and Identity Management for Life, 6th IFIP/PrimeLife International Summer School, Helsingborg, Sweden, August 2–6 2010, Revised Selected Papers.* Dordrecht: Springer, 206–218.

Strauß, S. (2018) From Big Data to Deep Learning: a leap towards strong AI or "intelligentia obscura"? *Big Data and Cognitive Computing,* 2(3), 16. www.mdpi.com/2504-2289/2/3/16.

Strauß, S. and Aichholzer, G. (2010) National Electronic Identity Management: The challenge of a citizen-centric approach beyond technical design. *International Journal on Advances in Intelligent Systems*, 3(1/2): 12–23.

Strauß, S. and Nentwich, M. (2013) Social Network Sites, Privacy and the Blurring Boundary between Public and Private Spaces. *Science and Public Policy* 40(6): 724–732.

Suhl, S. O. (2012) Google führt Dienste trotz Datenschutzbedenken zusammen. *Heise Online*, 1. März, www.heise.de/newsticker/meldung/Google-fuehrt-Dienste-trotz-Datenschutzbedenken-zusammen-1446292.html.

Toor, A. (2016) Facebook Begins Tracking Non-Users around the Internet. *The Verge*, May 27, www.theverge.com/2016/5/27/11795248/facebook-ad-network-non-users-cookies-plug-ins.

Weiser, M. (1991) The Computer of the 21st Century. *Scientific American*, 265(3): 94–104. www.lri.fr/~mbl/Stanford/CS477/papers/Weiser-SciAm.pdf.

Weisbuch, M., Ivcevic, Z. and Ambady, N. (2009) On Being Liked on the Web and in the "Real World": Consistency in first impressions across personal webpages and spontaneous behavior. *Journal of Experimental Social Psychology*, 45(3): 573–576.

WH—The White House (2011) *National Strategy for Trusted Identities in Cyberspace: Enhancing online choice, efficiency, security, and privacy*, April 2011, The White House, Washington DC. www.hsdl.org/?view&did=7010.

Whitley, E. and Hosein, G. (2010) *Global Challenges for Identity Policies*. London: Palgrave Macmillan.

Whitley, E. A., Gal, U. and Kjaergaard, A. (2014) Who Do You Think You Are? A review of the complex interplay between information systems, identification and identity. *European Journal of Information Systems*, 23(1): 17–35.

Wimmer, J. (2009) The Publics behind Political Web Campaigning: The digital transformation of "classic" counter-public spheres. In Baringhorst, S., Kneip, V. and Niesyto, J. (eds.), *Political Campaigning on the Web*. Bielefeld: transcript, 31–51.

5 The privacy control dilemma of digital identification

The previous chapter analyzed the emergence of digital identification. This chapter now sheds light on the privacy implications and challenges resulting from this development. As elaborated in Chapter 3, there is a naturally close relationship between identity and privacy. Privacy is vital for identity-building and autonomy. With its inherent boundary control function, privacy enables individuals in regulating and self-determining the extent to which they provide informational details of their identities to other individuals or institutions. Identification comprises control functions as well, though, for other purposes: identification has an inherent control mechanism that serves the function of establishing a connection between two or more entities. It contributes to gaining certainty about particular characteristics of a person making her distinct from others. A central aim of identification is the controlled processing of identity information, which is particularly relevant for digital identification and IDM approaches, less in the sense of fostering privacy controls for the individual concerned, but rather in the sense of ascertaining her identity.

Identification processes are an essential part of socio-technical systems in many respects, and are vital for the functioning of society, the state and the economy. They can contribute to building ties relevant for various societal functions (see Chapter 3). Means of identification are thus crucial to build trust among different entities interacting with each other in social, political and economic contexts, support administrative procedures, connect different technical systems, etc. Hence, identification is an important instrument of governance, but it also contains forms of control (White 2008). In general, striving for control involves a quest for security and stability for a particular matter. This is valid for political and administrative power and national security as well as for economic growth. Identification is a means toward this quest basically aiming to reduce uncertainty and improve security in particular settings. As shown previously, the field of IDM emerged as a consequence of informatization. It entails attempts to regain control over the processing of digital identity information and to tackle the increasing complexity thereof. A general aim is to enable more-secure identification for a variety of purposes in digital environments. However, security here has various roles and meanings. As the state also governs by identity (Amoore 2008; Whitley *et al.* 2014), governments set up IDM systems to integrate standardized citizen identification in public administration, and stimulate e-commerce and the development of digital markets. Security authorities apply identification mechanisms to control individuals and protect the interests of their states. Economic actors, online platforms, social media, etc. use digital identification to protect and control login procedures, to provide personalized services as well as to create new business models.[1] A crucial aim in each case is to govern information flows related to digital identities. These information flows serve many commercial interests, such as CRM, monitoring of potential customers for market research, targeted advertising and behavioral profiling. Hence, there is a variety of actors benefiting from identification practices for various purposes ranging from fostering administrative procedures and stimulating economic development, as well as for political objectives. In all these approaches, the processing of identity information is primarily controlled by institutional/organizational actors (e.g., businesses, public sector institutions, security authorities, social media providers, etc.).

Although there are several plausible reasons for identification, an imbalanced control over identity information at the cost of the individual and consequently lacking ISD (see Chapter 3) hampers privacy protection. Furthermore, even when IDM is designed to enhance user control (e.g., where people can proactively decide when and how to be identified), this may not prevent the misuse of information for other purposes (De Hert 2008; Strauß 2011). The information stored in centralized databases and registers applied in public and private sectors may provide a detailed picture about the trails and contexts of individuals' identities. A similar situation is found in the case of the broad array of identity information collected and processed in digital environments such as social media and the like. This serves a wide range of purposes that often remain unknown to the individual concerned. The de- and re-contextualization of this information for purposes other than those originally intended is often barely controllable; identification can occur in manifold ways with or without the consent of the individual. Personal information can generally flow in a limitless way between information systems in the public as well as private sectors. Big data, datafication and the ongoing trend in large-scale data collections aggravate this situation (Strauß 2018). Individuals are thus significantly hampered in ISD as regards the processing of their information. Attempts to improve control over digital information, such as IDM aiming to standardize the handling of identity information, bear some potential in this regard. However, when they serve mainly institutional entities, they contribute little to improving ISD, especially as IDM implementations tend to neglect privacy: compared to security and economic interests, the protection of privacy is often not a primary issue of IDM (De Hert 2008; Nauman and Hobgen 2009; Strauß 2011). Although some efforts in the field of governmental eIDMS exist in this regard, they have serious limits and mostly lack in effective privacy protection. While institutional entities benefit from IDM, the advantages for the individuals concerned are rather marginal (Kubicek and Noack 2010; Strauß and Aichholzer 2010); at least as regards privacy and ISD. Hence, there is an imbalance of power between individual and institutional entities as regards control over identity information. This problem can be described as a privacy control dilemma of digital identification: although IDM creates digital identification mechanisms in order to regain control over personal information flows in digital environments, it may ironically lead to a further loss of control over this information, at least from an individual's perspective (Strauß 2011). Effective privacy protection requires some friction in the processing of personal information with unlinkability as an important requirement. In this regard, there is a smoldering tension between the connecting function of identification and the boundary control function of privacy requiring informational frictions.

Many socio-political, economic and technical issues shape this dilemma: basically, digital identification is an important tool of governance in public and private sectors. However, there are also several tensions as regards the imbalanced control over information between individuals (people, citizens, customers, etc.) and institutional entities (organizations, governments, businesses, etc.) who apply identification processes. This control gap between individual and institutional entities is a general problem of imbalanced power structures inherent to the surveillance discourse, as discussed in the following. As will be shown, there are certain overlaps between identification practices and the functions and mechanisms of surveillance, i.e., panopticism. Core issues in this regard are information asymmetries, reinforced by ICTs and digital identification. The implementation of IDM and digital identification mechanisms is conveyed by securitization and economization of personal information, which contribute to a further extension of identification practices. Conflicting interests as regards individual privacy, economic objectives and national security complicate the challenge to conciliate the interests of the individual with those of the institutions processing her identity information. Embedded in the privacy control dilemma is an inherently conflictual relationship between privacy protection, security and surveillance, which is mirrored in the discourse about digital identification. Accordingly, empirical results from the EU research project SurPRISE provide insights into the perceptions of European citizens on the interplay between surveillance, privacy and security in relation to surveillance-oriented security technology. The growing concerns and fears about privacy intrusion among European citizens underline that there are several tensions between individual and institutional transparency as regards the processing of personal information. Furthermore, the design and use of ICTs reinforce these tensions as they boost (personal) information processing and stimulate a further expansion of explicit and implicit forms of identification. A central problem of contemporary privacy protection is thus socio-technically enforced identifiability. Tackling this problem requires enhanced privacy controls, ISD and effective protection instruments. These issues and their interrelations are discussed in the following parts of this chapter.

Surveillance, identification and control

Basic functions, practices and consequences of surveillance

Surveillance is a common cluster term to describe practices of observation, monitoring and controlling individuals which involve the gathering and processing of information. As a hierarchical modality of power and disciplinary practice, surveillance entails societal impacts in various (public and private) domains (e.g., Foucault 1977; Clarke 1988; Lyon 1994/2001/2003/2009; Haggerty and Ericson 2000; Bennett and Haggerty 2011; Ball *et al.* 2012; Marx 2015; Wright and Kreissl 2015). Identification practices are closely related to power structures and modes of surveillance. Hence, the gathering of "some form of data connectable to individuals (whether as uniquely identified or as a member of a category)" is a central feature of human surveillance (Marx 2015: 734). For Lyon (2009: 4) all forms of surveillance begin with identification. But this does not imply that all forms of identification are equivalent to surveillance. Nevertheless, identification can be used for and can result in surveillance practices; both can be implicitly and explicitly linked. Haggerty and Ericson (2000: 610) argue that "surveillance is driven by the desire to bring systems together, to combine practices and technologies and integrate them into a larger whole". With its connecting function, identification can contribute to implementing this combination of practices, technologies and systems in many respects. This often occurs implicitly. Identification is thus not to be misunderstood as a form of surveillance per se; or as mechanism to serve surveillance purposes. However, the boundary between appropriate identification and excessive surveillance is not always clear but often ambiguous. The more intrusive security and surveillance practices become, the more individual identities can become affected. The question is thus of utmost importance: to what extent can identification processes overlap with functions of surveillance? My basic premise here is that identification, i.e., the processing of information referring to an individual, is a core process of privacy-affecting surveillance. Hence, if a surveillance practice includes the identification of individuals, then the privacy of these individuals is affected. Conversely, central mechanisms of surveillance (such as panopticism and asymmetry of power) can also be mirrored in identification practices. Before these issues are discussed in more depth, the basic functions and modalities of surveillance are outlined.

Giddens (1984) argued that surveillance is a common practice of modern national states to exercise administrative power. It includes a machinery of processing large amounts of information which enables and supports control mechanisms across space and time. Correspondingly, for Giddens, surveillance is "the coding of information relevant to the administration of subject populations, plus their direct supervision by officials and administrators of all sorts" (1984: 183f. cited from Fuchs 2010). Today, this machinery is observable in many respects. Numerous institutions (e.g., businesses, governments, intelligence agencies, public or private organizations, security authorities, etc.) collect and use information about individuals for purposes of administration as well as of control. Surveillance is an intrinsic part of modern bureaucracy, though often more than simply a practice of organizing information to serve administrative procedures in the realm of governance. It is employed inter alia to protect national security and can entail various mechanisms of population control. As a form of disciplinary power (Foucault 1977), surveillance provides several options to influence and manipulate individual as well as collective behavior. Surveillance thus entails serious risks of social sorting and discrimination as, e.g., Lyon (2003) pointed out. Inherent to surveillance is the existence, creation or reinforcement of asymmetrical power between the observers and those that are being observed. This power is not necessarily exercised instantly or visibly. However, it can include a sort of preparatory action in terms of pre-emptive and preventive security measures (such as surveillance measures increasingly aimed at preventing crime and terrorism). This may include preventive information gathering and monitoring of individual behavior.

Surveillance can both enable and constrain power (Lyon 1994; Fuchs 2010). It enables as it gives power to those that conduct surveillance and allows the exercising of this power over those that are monitored. This power can include physical power (direct violence at worst, punishment, etc.), control over information, violations of privacy, or discrimination and power of repression that leads to overwhelming self-control or self-discipline of the individuals being subject to surveillance and their behavior (Foucault 1977; Lyon 2003; Fuchs 2010; Ball *et al.* 2012). In many cases, surveillance is "implemented as a security mechanism so that surveillance and self-control are used as two mechanisms (one of direct violence and one of ideological violence) for reproducing and securing domination" (Fuchs 2010: 11). In totalitarian regimes, surveillance is employed to identify, classify, control, discriminate and repress civil society. There are thus risks inherent to surveillance that discrimination reinforces with population control and social sorting. As highlighted by many scholars, history provides various examples of violent social discrimination and population control, drastically demonstrating how surveillance can serve destructive forces (such as in the Nazi regime, the Stasi dictatorship in East Germany, or in South Africa during the apartheid era, to name just a few). In the worst cases, this can even lead to deportation, murder and genocide with millions of people killed based on their ethnic identity. The abuse of population registration and census data played a significant role in Nazi Germany (Lyon 2003/2009; Bennett and Lyon 2008; Ball *et al.* 2012). It is therefore essential to have effective forms of checks and balances to continuously question surveillance practices (Wright *et al.* 2015) in order to control and stem its destructive capacity.

How contemporary surveillance affects privacy

Irrespective of its manifold forms, purposes and risks, surveillance generally represents a security practice aiming to reduce uncertainty and foster control. To achieve these aims, the gathering of information is a core feature of surveillance. Although often understood in that sense, surveillance is not the nemesis of privacy per se; and vice versa, privacy was never meant to be "the 'antidote to surveillance'" (Bennett 2011: 493). In a broad sense, the term "surveillance" (deriving from the French word *surveiller*, which means to watch over) addresses the "close watch kept over someone or something".[2] Not every form of surveillance directly targets individuals; e.g., surveillance in the field of public health, environmental protection or aviation control, where personal information is usually not gathered directly. Aviation control, for example, conducts surveillance to monitor planes and other objects in airspace. Privacy is not an issue here as long as there is no processing of identity information involved. When aviation control includes the collection of information about flight passengers, it represents a surveillance practice with a privacy impact. This simple example points out that the privacy impact of surveillance depends on the processing of personal information and, thus, the capacity for identification. Some forms of identification processes are often inherent to surveillance. Traffic control, e.g., includes monitoring of streets in order to ensure that speed limits are observed. There is no identification process involved in this monitoring as long as number plates of vehicles are not automatically gathered. But identification is triggered when a vehicle breaks the legal speed limit. Then, the police or a speed camera automatically takes a picture of the vehicle's number plate. This picture is then used to identify the holder of the vehicle in order to deliver the speeding ticket. Hence, this practice involves conditional identification. The use of surveillance technology can complicate conditional identification when it permanently gathers information about individuals. Traffic control with automated number plate recognition without any limitation (i.e., permanent recording) is more privacy-intrusive than a practice with conditional identification. A typical example of a surveillance technology is closed circuit television (CCTV), which usually captures images of people by default. As a consequence, information referring to the identity of that person is gathered, which is a form of unconditional identification. These examples point out that the modalities of identification as well as the design and use of a technology determine the extent to which privacy is affected by surveillance.

Contemporary surveillance benefits in many respects from the employment of technology, as many surveillance scholars have highlighted. For instance, Clarke (1988) used the term "dataveillance", which he defined as "the systematic monitoring of people's actions or communications" to describe electronic surveillance practices. For Gary Marx (2002: 12) the "new surveillance" is more extensive than traditional surveillance, characterized by the "use of multiple senses and sources of data" and includes "the use of technical means to extract or create personal data". Some years later, he defined new surveillance as "scrutiny of individuals, groups, and contexts through the use of technical means to extract or create information" (Marx 2015: 735). Examples of "new" technological surveillance practices are, e.g., "computer matching and profiling, big data sets, video cameras, DNA analysis, GPS, electronic work monitoring, drug testing, and the monitoring made possible by social media and cell phones" (ibid.: 735). Marx assumes that contemporary (or "new") surveillance is more extensive because of technology but he does not explain for what exact reasons. In my view, an important reason concerns the modality of information processing. The gathering of identity information basically creates the possibility of intruding into privacy. Depending on the storage capacity of a technology, the factual intrusion can happen instantly or at a later moment. ICTs provide various ways to process information widely decoupled from space and time. This enables and amplifies surveillance practices in many respects. In its most general sense, surveillance involves the gathering of information to reduce uncertainty about an issue and thus gain in power and control. This rationale remains the same with or without the employment of technology. However, ICTs inter alia enable the gathering and reproduction of information remotely, decoupled from the physical location of a surveillance subject. A further aspect concerns the networking structure of ICTs: it allows aggregating different kinds of information from different domains and collecting them unbound from the physical presence of the observed object or subject. Hence, through ICTs, surveillance gains an additional, non-physical dimension, which contributes to extend its outreach.

Besides these technological aspects, networking structures are also observable among the actors of surveillance. In a traditional sense, surveillance was mainly conducted by the state and public sector institutions for all kinds of administration and governance modalities including internal and external security. Contemporary surveillance is somewhat different, representing a complex nexus of many different actors in the public as well as in the private domains. With the so-called "surveillant assemblage" and its rhizomatic surveillance, Haggerty and Ericson (2000) use an interesting model to highlight this nexus. In this regard, surveillance spreads over various branches where there are two essential characteristics of the surveillant assemblage: "its phenomenal growth through expanding uses, and its leveling effect on hierarchies" (ibid.: 614). Hence, in many cases, surveillance does not merely include a single, operating entity (e.g., the state) but a variety of different, partially interrelated actors. Surveillance practices can thus result from a functional conglomerate of multiple actors. The surveillant assemblage

> operates by abstracting human bodies from their territorial settings and separating them into a series of discrete flows. These flows are then reassembled into distinct "data doubles" which can be scrutinized and targeted for intervention. In the process, we are witnessing a rhizomatic leveling of the hierarchy of surveillance, such that groups which were previously exempt from routine surveillance are now increasingly being monitored.
>
> (Ibid.: 606)

In the view of Haggerty and Ericson (ibid.), the different actors "work" together as "a functional entity" meaning that the gathered information feeds into this system of surveillance. Cohen (2012: 9) describes the surveillant assemblage as "a heterogeneous, loosely coupled set of institutions that seek to harness the raw power of information by fixing flows of information cognitively and spatially".

Regardless of the multitude of constituting actors, the actions of the surveillant assemblage basically include control mechanisms, driven mainly by political and economic interests in the public as well as in the private sectors. Or in other words: the surveillant assemblage is often accompanied by public–private–partnerships. Surveillance and monitoring practices play an important role in national security as well as in the digital economy. Put simply, governmental actors aim to improve (national) security and economic actors to serve their business models and secure their commercial interests. Indeed, these interests are often intertwined and therefore barely distinguishable.

There is a prominent showcase of a globally acting surveillant assemblage with complex interrelations between security authorities and private companies: namely the as-yet biggest case of electronic surveillance revealed in 2013 by whistleblower Edward Snowden. Since the Snowden revelations, there is hard evidence for global mass surveillance programs that exploit ICTs in many respects. These programs are conducted by the US intelligence service the NSA, the British intelligence organization GCHQ (Government Communications Headquarters) as well as other security agencies worldwide, being their strategic partners (Greenwald 2014). This case made the NSA a major synonym for surveillance. However, in fact, irrespective of its powerful role, the agency is by no means the only entity conducting surveillance. Intelligence agencies in Europe (such as the GCHQ) and in other regions are also deeply involved in global surveillance activities. Furthermore, the variety of surveillance programs serves as a hub for other security agencies in the US as well as for countries with special spying agreements. This primarily includes the so-called "Five Eyes" partners: Australia, Canada, New Zealand, the UK and the US. Besides these so-called Tier A allies, there are also Tier B allies, which involves focused cooperation with a variety of countries in Europe as well as in Asia.[3] The spying partnerships also include a number of international organizations and enterprises that are involved in the surveillance programs (Greenwald 2014). Among the multitude of surveillance programs is the PRISM[4] program, which gathers data from the servers of the most prominent online services (such as Apple, Facebook, Google, Microsoft, Skype, YouTube, etc.). The massive data collection enables intelligence agencies to spy in real time on their targets. Put shortly, PRISM monitors all kinds of online communications including e-mail, voice and video chat, photos, videos, stored data, social networking and so on (ZDNet 2013; Greenwald 2014). In the same vein, the GCHQ operates programs striving for all-encompassing surveillance such as MTI—"mastering the internet" (MacAskill *et al.* 2013) and Tempora,[5] which gathers raw data directly from fiber-optic cables. The Snowden files in general drastically highlight how sophisticated and deeply privacy-intrusive global mass surveillance has become. These surveillance practices demonstrate how ICTs are exploited to monitor the personal communications of everyday life. However, irrespective of its enormous impact on society, the Snowden case should not blur the view on the very mechanisms and drivers of contemporary surveillance, which have existed for much longer than the revealed programs, and which function in many other contexts as well.

The securitization and economization of digital identification

Contemporary surveillance practices and the implementation and use of the corresponding technology are driven by several socio-political and economic developments. Security and economic interests are core determinants of surveillance as well as of identification practices. Both interests overlap in many respects. Therefore, the terms securitization and economization are used here to point out the predominant role of security and economic rationales. Both rationales had strong influence on the emergence of digital identification and IDM (as outlined in Chapter 4). Hence, there is an observable securitization and economization of digital identification as the processing of information (directly or indirectly) referring to individual identities serves a complex mixture of security and economic interests. In many respects, this flows into surveillance contexts, which benefit from identification processes. Hence, metaphorically speaking, securitization and economization of identity information meet in the shadows of surveillance.

As outlined in Chapter 3, a wider paradigm shift in security policy took place in the 1990s, which is carried forward by securitization. Securitization describes the phenomenon of an expanding security discourse spanning multiple domains. It frames security as a perpetual process which then, apparently, justifies extensive security and surveillance activities. At the political level, this paradigm shift is accompanied by intensified use of surveillance technology to cope with novel security threats and challenges. In the aftermath of the 9/11 terrorist attacks, there was a significant extension of surveillance on a global scale. However, similar developments with a stronger focus on holistic security approaches including pre-emptive and preventive surveillance activities had already emerged beforehand, as many scholars observed (e.g., Ball and Webster 2003; Lyon 2003; Bigo 2008; Haggerty and Samatas 2010; Bennett and Haggerty 2011). The arbitrary self-dynamic of securitization, i.e., the continuous pursuit of security, reinforces surveillance. Consequently, surveillance practices increasingly strive for the preventive detection of risks before they become factual threats. The use of surveillance technology with its capability to easily gather large amounts of information fits perfectly into this framing and is thus presented as the preferable "weapon of choice" to tackle all kinds of security threats (Strauß 2017a). Furthermore, there are overlaps between economic drivers, the industries implementing security technology and security policy asking for this technology. In this regard, the logic of securitization with its perpetual striving for security widely corresponds to the quest for economic growth. Thus, securitization and economization are intertwined. Several scholars (e.g., Haggerty and Ericson 2000; Ball and Webster 2003; Lyon 2009; Bennett and Haggerty 2011; Ball *et al.* 2012) pointed out the global growth in security and surveillance modalities and the strong influence of economic mechanisms to stimulate new markets. The framing of security as a holistic concept and "moving target" stimulates demand for security and surveillance technology which benefits the corresponding markets and vendors. The Organization for Economic Co-Operation and

Development uses the term "security economy" (OECD 2004) for the intertwining between the economic and the security sectors. Examples of the influential security economy can be found in the enormous efforts made for security and surveillance at large-scale events such as the Olympic Games or World Cups. As Bennett and Haggerty (2011) highlighted, such mega-events obviously provide a good occasion for vendors to demonstrate their latest technology and experiment with its usage in monitoring people and places, which then may be adopted by security authorities. Hence, the economic rationale behind the implementation of security technology is often to stimulate new security markets and innovation.

A further issue is the widespread belief in technology as the best means to foster security in the political discourse (Guild *et al.* 2008). Hence, the technological push reinforces securitization and vice versa. The broad scope of technologies and the nature of ICTs seem to tempt policy makers to believe that complex security measures could simply be improved or even automated by technology. The basic rationale here often is an economic one in the sense of lowering costs, and improving efficiency and effectiveness of security measures (Wright and Kreissl 2015). The employment of security technologies often happens without assessing their effectiveness or risks to privacy, other human rights and liberty. This can even generate more insecurity (Guild *et al.* 2008). Consequently, there are certain tensions between surveillance practices and human rights (ibid.; Ball *et al.* 2012; De Hert 2012; Wright and Kreissl 2015). An example of these controversies of securitization related to ICTs is the European Data Retention Directive[6] which obliged EU member states to pre-store communication data of all citizens for at least six months. On the one hand, law enforcement repeatedly proclaimed necessity of this technological measure to combat crime and terrorism; on the other, the high and growing number of critics from experts and civil society alike argued that this practice of mass surveillance violates human rights. Among the risks is the inversion of the presumption of innocence as every citizen becomes a potential surveillance target without concrete suspicion (FRA 2016). In 2014, the EU Court of Justice declared the directive as illegal for its violation of fundamental human rights and particularly the right to privacy (CJEU 2014). Irrespective of this landmark verdict, some countries (e.g., Germany) did not fully abandon data retention but made some legal readjustments to continue this form of surveillance (FRA 2016). In 2016, though, the EU Court again declared that data retention is incompatible with fundamental rights (CJEU 2016). The data retention case is one of many examples of increasing pre-emptive surveillance practices which naturally affect all citizens regardless of their factual relation to illegal behavior. These practices are particularly critical as they intrude deeply into fundamental human rights and bear certain risks of discrimination. The highly intrusive capacity of data retention in particular results from the possibilities gained to create extensive identity profiles of all citizens based on their communications and online activities.

Basically, privacy-intrusive surveillance implies the processing of information referring to an individual's identity. Consequently, identity and identification play a certain linking function in the complex relationship between privacy, security and surveillance. The nexus between securitization, extended surveillance and identity is observable in many respects. Identity represents a referent object of securitization related to the collective identity of a community or a national state (Buzan *et al.* 1998; Bigo 2000; CASE 2006; Ajana 2013). National identity schemes such as passports are instruments of security governance, showing that a person has a particular nationality, and thus is a citizen of the corresponding country. This identity representation allows the categorization of individuals into citizens and non-citizens, which is a typical security practice of border control. Similar deployment of (digital) identification as a security practice is observable in many other contexts as well, where identity information is gathered to, e.g., control access to borders, buildings, or services; or to categorize individuals based on their characteristics. This includes a broad range of applications and objectives: e.g., measures for national security such as border control with ID documents or plans toward "smart", automated border control systems ("entry–exit") with biometric scanning,[7] data retention approaches to preventively collect individual communications data or flight passenger records, secret surveillance programs, as well as identification procedures and IDM systems to improve the security of e-commerce, e-government or other online services (as outlined in Chapter 4).

The push of digital identification and IDMS is related to the security economy and the overlap between political and economic domains (Bennett and Lyon 2008; Lyon 2009). Lyon (2009) uses the term "card cartel" to highlight the overlaps between these sectors and the "oligopolization of the means of identification", i.e., several players pushing and implementing eID cards (Lyon 2009: 16). Electronic identity cards thus "have become the tool of choice for new forms of risk calculation" (Amoore 2008: 24) which facilitate a "mode of pre-emptive identification" (ibid.). In many countries, the planning of governmental eIDMS was linked to debates about national security and cybersecurity, reinforcing counter-terrorism, fighting organized crime, identity fraud as well as illegal immigration (Bennett and Lyon 2008; Lyon 2009; Whitley and Hosein 2010). For instance, the US in their role as a member of the International Civil Aviation Organization, a sub-organization of the United Nations, induced the creation of a standard for a travel ID (passport) with a radio frequency identification (RFID) chip and biometrical data (Stanton 2008). Some EU member states considered this standard while planning and implementing their national eID systems. For instance, in Germany, Portugal and Spain the national eID is equipped with biometrical data and can be used both as travel document as well as for online transactions (ibid.; Bennett and Lyon 2008; Kubicek and Noack 2010). Hence, national security considerations also had some impact on the creation of governmental eIDMS, although these systems were mainly created to stimulate e-government and the digital economy. The political strategies inducing the emergence of these systems include an often-indistinct mix of economic and security objectives. On the one hand, digital identification is seen as a key enabler for different kinds of online services in public and private sectors. On the other hand, it is framed as a tool to achieve national security objectives. IDM approaches are also seen as a means to improve the ability of governments and intelligence agencies to identify potential security threats such as fake identities in the realm of crime and terrorism (Glässer and Vajihollahi 2010). From a wider perspective, the increase in (digital) identification corresponds with fears and uncertainties in society as regards global risks and security threats. The employment of digital identification is thus also linked to security issues, and preventive and pre-emptive surveillance mechanisms.

Besides the complex interrelations between national security and economic rationales in the government sector, there are many other forms of surveillance related to the securitization and economization of digital identity information. Economization here means that identity information is primarily treated as an economic factor, including its processing for commercial purposes but also, beyond that, its framing as a quantitative figure. Basically, big data and boundless information flows are framed as an economic core value. Big data serves as a cluster term for a new technological potential to exploit digital information for a broad scope of applications. It boosts the digital economy in the spirit of a "digital gold rush" to gather and exploit maximum data for socio-political and economic purposes of various kinds; including analysis of consumer preferences, predicting behavior, to automated risk calculation and predictive policing (Mayer-Schönberger and Cukier 2013; Strauß 2018). A working group of the World Economic Forum promoted cross-border data flows to foster the global trade and investment system in the digital economy (WEF 2015). Personal data in general represents a crucial asset for a growing number of digital markets of any kind (Spiekermann *et al.* 2015; Acquisti *et al.* 2016; Christl and Spiekermann 2016). Consequently, identity information is exploited for an extensive range of economic purposes. In contrast to its originally decentralized nature with some possibilities of anonymous interactions, the internet has become a central hub for a variety of options to capture vast arrays of information about personal identities, behavior and actions, interests, etc. (Acquisti *et al.* 2016). "As a result, chronicles of peoples' actions, desires, interests, and mere intentions are collected by third parties, often without individuals' knowledge or explicit consent, with a scope, breadth, and detail that are arguably without precedent in human history" (ibid.: 3). The Web 2.0, social media and the like are prominent showcases for extensive clusters of information that enable deep insights into their users' identities, which serve various commercial purposes (see Chapter 4). The very design of social media platforms entails permanent availability of personal information. This availability makes social media but also other ICTs a very attractive source for all kinds of economic purposes.

The gathering and trading of personal information is literally big business: according to figures from 2015, the company BlueKai (a sub-firm of Oracle) had about 750 million profiles of Internet users with approximately 30,000 attributes about these individuals (Spiekermann *et al.* 2015). This example is only one among many others. There are several enterprises specialized as data brokers conducting large-scale profiling as their business model. Enterprises like, e.g., Acxiom, Datalogix, Experian or LexisNexis offer services that focus on exploiting massive amounts of information about individual consumers (Christl and Spiekermann 2016). The data comes from various sources and particularly from ICTs and online platforms. Many online services have several third parties involved (e.g., online marketers and advertising networks like DoubleClick or ScorecardResearch, content delivery network providers such as Akamai, etc.) which gather information, e.g., for targeted advertising to serve their customers. Specialized data brokers aggregate information from many sources to create in-depth profiles. Similar to SNS like Facebook building social graphs (as discussed in Chapter 4), data brokers employ identity graphs to map, structure and aggregate information about individuals. Oracle, for instance, promotes its graph[8] as a targeting tool to "get to the heart of the matter, the heart of your customer" (Oracle 2015a: 1). To achieve this, the tool allows one to "unify addressable identities across all devices, screens and channels" as well as to "create a comprehensive consumer profile including what people say, what they do and what they buy" (Oracle 2015b). Moreover, it "connects offline and online ID spaces with the goal of maintaining an industry-leading, comprehensive, and accurate ID graph in which all links are 'probabilistically validated'" (Oracle 2016: 20). This is at least what the company claims.

Oracle is one among several companies with access to large sources of personal information and that is a strategic partner of the NSA (Greenwald 2014). Features like the identity graph thus serve economic as well as security and surveillance purposes. Besides data brokers that mainly conduct consumer profiling, there are other companies like Palantir[9] technologies with a special focus on data analysis and profiling for security authorities. Among its clients are several US security authorities such as the Air Force, CIA, Department of Homeland Security, Federal Bureau of Investigation (FBI), NSA, etc. (Burns 2015). Palantir thus has close connections to the intelligence community, has a strategic partnership with the NSA and was involved in developing its surveillance software XKeyscore (Biddle 2017). XKeyscore is a sophisticated search tool allowing intelligence agencies to explore all kinds of information about particular people (including social media activity or online communications) based on their Internet usage (Greenwald 2014).

Hence, social media and ICT usage in general provide vast sources of all kinds of information about personal identities, which feed into the surveillant assemblage. As shown, the Snowden case exemplifies this in many respects. As highlighted in some of the Snowden slides, online social networks are attractive to intelligence agencies because they provide "insights into the personal lives of targets" including "communications, day to day activities, contacts and social networks, photographs, videos, personnel information (e.g., addresses, phone, e-mail addresses), location and travel information" (Greenwald 2014: 158). They represent "a very rich source of information on targets" such as "personal details, 'pattern of life', connections to associates, media" (ibid.: 161). But social media is only one of many other sources to follow the ambitions of the NSA and its partners to "collect it all" (ibid.: 90). As outlined, PRISM exploits information from very widespread online services. Other surveillance practices even include the capturing of raw data streams (so-called upstream collections, as in the Tempora or the Stormbrew project, which includes tapping of network devices) (ibid.). With tools like XKeyscore, analysts can use search queries similar to a web search to seek information about their targets (Greenwald 2013/2014). This tool enables "nearly everything a typical user does on the internet" to be found (ibid.: 153). In order to find a particular person, keywords (so-called "selectors") that refer to individual identities can be used (e.g., IP address, phone number, e-mail address, usernames, etc.), which then allow learning more about, e.g., the personal communications of a target.

Hence, there are numerous options for a variety of actors of the surveillant assemblage to monitor and track the behavior of billions of individuals by exploiting digital information about them. The increasing availability of digital identity information stimulates surveillance desires in many respects. Our digital identities are thus the subject of manifold forms of surveillance. These surveillance practices are particularly driven by a complex nexus of economic rationales and objectives in the realm of national security. The Snowden disclosures underline that big data generally has a "supportive relationship with surveillance" (Lyon 2014: 1). Platforms, services and technologies with inherent identification mechanisms of various kinds can be very supportive to the practices of the surveillant assemblage. Entailed is an increasingly difficult distinction between personal and non-personal information, which facilitates de-anonymization and re-identification techniques (Chapter 5 takes a closer look at these issues). Regardless of whether identity information is exploited for economic or security purposes, these practices are mostly hidden to the individuals concerned. In this regard, there are certain similarities between forms of identification and panopticism as presented and discussed in the following section.

Panopticism and the asymmetric use of identity information

It has been shown that there is a strong interplay between surveillance and digital identification. This interplay also concerns the functioning of surveillance and its panoptic features. Besides the all-seeing character "Big Brother" from George Orwell's novel *Nineteen Eighty-four*, Jeremy Bentham's panopticon (dating back to 1791) is the most prominent metaphor for surveillance. This prominence is mainly due to the work of Michel Foucault, particularly his book *Discipline and Punish* (1977) in which he analyses the emergence of the prison and mechanisms of control. Foucault interpreted the panopticon as "a generalizable model of functioning; a way of defining power relations in terms of the every day life of men" (Foucault 1977: 205).

The aim of the panopticon is to create a state of conscious and permanent visibility for the automatic functioning of power. At the same time, as the insides of the watchtower remain opaque, "this model of undetected surveillance keeps those watched subordinate by means of uncertainty" (Lyon 1994: 60). Panoptic power is automated and de-individualized as the principle of power is not in the hands of a single entity but instead results from organizational settings, i.e., a

Figure 5.1 Presidio Modelo, prison built in the design of the panopticon, located on the Island de la Juventud, Cuba.

Source: Wikipedia: user Friman 2005, licensed as CC-BY-SA 3.0.

hierarchical order with a permanently visible watchtower as a centralized control unit, which entails a lack of private sphere for the observed. With its strict hegemonic structure, the panopticon divides community and instead constitutes a sorted collection of separated individuals which are subjected to disciplinary power. Its aim is to control and normalize social behavior through permanent (at least perceived as such) surveillance. Panoptic features of surveillance thus undermine the boundary control function of privacy. Individuals are significantly hampered in their efficacy in self-determining their interactions with others without being controlled.

With the emergence of ICTs and their quasi-ubiquitous features, surveillance scholars began to rethink the panopticon metaphor in this altered technological context and introduced neologisms such as "electronic panopticon" (Gordon 1987), "superpanopticon" (Poster 1990), "panoptic sort" (Gandy 1993) or similar. There are several studies about the manifold aspects of electronic surveillance technologies (e.g., CCTV, Internet and telecommunications, location tracking, RFID, wiretapping, etc. to name just a few) creating "panoptic" situations in everyday-life contexts, often entailing evident threats of surveillance such as social sorting, discrimination, exclusion, etc. (Lyon 1994; Haggerty and Ericson 2000; Marx 2002/2015; Bennett and Haggerty 2011). However, irrespective of their relevance in particular, there is a "general tendency in the literature to offer more and more examples of total or creeping surveillance, while providing little that is theoretically novel" (Haggerty and Ericson 2000: 607). Lyon (1994) argued that there is no common understanding about the extent to which electronic surveillance has panoptic features. "Different analysts focus on different aspects of panopticism" (Lyon 1994: 67) and, thus, the relationship between electronic surveillance and panoptic power remains relatively diverse. In the same vein, Haggerty (2006: 26) notes that "the panopticon now stands for surveillance itself", which makes it difficult to understand "the complexity and totality of contemporary surveillance dynamics" (ibid.: 38). As a consequence, it often remains unclear to what extent a technology actually enables or amplifies surveillance and which modalities are relevant in this regard.

Some scholars argue that the panopticon metaphor is invalid as ICTs would relativize panoptic power and enable everyone to conduct surveillance. Consequently, there are novel options for bottom-up surveillance, called inter alia "sousveillance" (Dupont 2008) or "participatory surveillance" (Albrechtslund 2008). Dupont (2008: 265f.) even claims that there would be a "democratization of surveillance" as civil society (individuals as well as NGOs, etc.) can, e.g., use the internet to monitor the activities of governments or large corporations. In his view, the internet is rather an anti-panopticon due to its decentralized architecture and democratic capacity. But how realistic is this view? Indeed, phenomena such as the Occupy movement, Wikileaks, or Anonymous (despite the critical issues these phenomena partially entail) exemplify the potential of ICTs to empower civil society and enforce more transparency by scrutinizing political and economic activities. These and similar approaches have some impact on public opinion questioning surveillance. However, at the same time, global mass surveillance steadily proceeds and power structures remain widely stable. Hence, the assumption that ICTs, online services, etc. would be widely independent and decoupled from surveillance control attempts of public and private authorities (e.g., Dupont 2008) is a fallacy. The actions of the surveillant assemblage instead demonstrate the opposite. Global mass surveillance programs drastically highlight that there is no need to control an entire online service as long as digital information flows are gathered. This is among the essential lessons of the Snowden revelations. Hence, even though there is no doubt about the enormous democratic and innovative potential of ICTs, this does not imply that panoptic power ceases to exist. The framing of ICTs as sort of anti-panopticon is as misleading as the view of ICTs as primary instruments of surveillance. Social media, for instance, highlights that ICTs bear the potential to serve democracy and hegemony alike. An example is the Arab Spring, which used to be falsely presented as a result of social media empowerment. While social media served as a tool to convey pre-existing democratic movements, the technology as such did not induce a democratic shift. Moreover, other regimes (e.g., in Syria, Egypt or Tunisia) used social media to monitor and control the activities of counter-movements (Benkirane 2012; Dewey *et al.* 2012; Skinner 2012). Similar to this are the surveillance programs revealed by Snowden, which make heavy use of social media and ICTs. These examples highlight the rather simple fact that power structures are complex and not simply changeable by technological means only. Changes of power require a deeper change of socio-technical practices. Thus, hegemonic power structures may be reproduced, reinforced as well as relativized by the use of technology but, essentially, they do exist and function without technology. In this regard, Foucault's interpretation of the panopticon is still very useful to explore modalities of power without a need to focus on technology. There seems to be a certain misleading tendency in surveillance studies to reduce the panopticon metaphor to an issue of the architecture and design of a technology in order to explain its panoptic potential. Such attempts seeking architectural analogies between the panopticon and surveillance technology are rather doomed to fail, especially in the case of ICTs. Of course, the internet and other ICTs are mostly multimodal, widely decentralized networks while the panopticon is centralized by its very design. In this regard, the panopticon metaphor is of limited use to explain the modalities of contemporary surveillance. However, there seems to be a misunderstanding about the universal character and functioning of the panopticon. As, e.g., Fuchs (2010) pointed out, Foucault's theory does not exclude decentralized forms of surveillance. In his book *Discipline and Punish*, Foucault (1977) analyzed the prison system, which is not and never was completely centralized. There is no permanent connection between different prisons, but a prison as such is still a panoptic unit that exercises panoptic power. The same is true for surveillance technology and ICTs, neither of which are fully centralized control units. The internet, for instance, is decentralized with myriad websites, services, platforms, etc. But this decentralized architecture does not change the fact that some providers may centralize their services or that information is gathered and stored in a centralized form. Much more important than the architectural design of the panopticon is the way it enables and reinforces disciplinary power. In this regard, Foucault's interpretation provides a valuable analytical lens to reveal the general functioning of surveillance and of control mechanisms. While a broad range of surveillance practices exist, their basic functionality is widely similar: namely to create asymmetry of power in order to exercise control.

Information processing obviously plays a crucial role in panoptic power and the way it exercises control over individuals. As argued, there is a close relationship between surveillance and identification, i.e., the processing of information affecting the individual. Thus, when linked to surveillance practices, identification practices can have similar effects to panoptic power. Lyon (2001: 2) defined surveillance as "any collection and processing of personal data, whether identifiable or not, for the purposes of influencing or managing those whose data have been garnered". Although surveillance can include information that does not directly identify a person, some form of (perceived or factual) identification occurs as soon as a particular individual is exposed to privacy-intrusive surveillance. At some stage in the surveillance process, information about the very individual being monitored is required to exercise power over her. This power can have different shades and can function when surveillance has the effective capability of identification or gives the impression of having this capability. This is true for traditional as well as for electronic surveillance. This does not necessarily imply that the identified person is aware of being identified, particularly not when surveillance aims to secretly control or manipulate people. At the same time, surveillance does not have to effectively identify the individual to exercise control. It can be sufficient to create the notion of identifiability among individuals. This can trigger the so-called "chilling effect" meaning that individuals tend toward self-censorship and avoid exercising their rights such as free speech when perceived to be under surveillance (Lyon 2003; Raab and Wright 2012). Traditional surveillance usually includes observation, which, if targeted at a particular person, also implies some (cognitive) processing of information about this person. For instance, the guard in the panoptic watchtower exercises control over an individual via an informational advantage: he has more information about the individual than vice versa. This gives him the power to factually decide to observe a particular individual as well as to let the individual believe they are observable, which creates uncertainty for this individual. The same principle is true for modern surveillance. But in contrast to traditional surveillance, observation is only one of many other surveillance practices. Modern surveillance does not necessarily involve observation but all forms of surveillance (if targeted at individuals) imply the processing of information about individuals. Identification mechanisms thus can have similar effects to observation in the panopticon. Table 5.1 below shows some similarities between panopticism and (digital) identification. It compares basic characteristics of the panopticon (as identified by Foucault 1977) on the left column alongside common characteristics of digital identification in the right.

The panopticon represents a political technology as its functioning can be used in manifold ways to support and reinforce control. Identification in general is an organizational mechanism aimed at reducing uncertainties in different interactions between individual and institutional entities. As shown, digital identification is also used as a governance tool and its mechanisms serve both political as well as economic objectives to implement various forms of control. In this regard, it is an effecting tool (Hood and Margetts 2007; Bennett and Lyon 2008). Centralization is a crucial aspect of the panopticon, which consists of a centralized control unit (i.e., the watchtower). Identity information is often stored and processed in centralized databases and registers. Moreover, as shown

Table 5.1 Similarities between digital identification and panopticism

Panopticism	(Digital) identification
Political technology	Tool of political and economic governance
Centralized control unit (watchtower)	Centralized data processing and meta-profiling
Trap of permanent visibility	(Quasi-)obligation to provide identity information; identifiability
Automation and de-individualization of power	Pre-defined identity criteria, automated categorization and risk calculation
Asymmetry of power as core principle	Opacity of information processing and imbalanced control over information

in Chapter 4, ICTs in general and the extension of digital identification specifically reinforce meta-profiling and the aggregation of information from various sources. The panopticon features a twofold state of permanent visibility and transparency: given the constant presence of the watchtower and the invisibility of the guard, individuals literally have no place to hide and thus perceive that they are under permanent observation but can never be certain whether they are being observed or not. Foucault (1977: 203) called this the "trap of visibility". Similar situations may occur when individuals are requested to reveal their identities or provide identity information without knowledge about the actual purpose and use of the information they provide. Identification puts the spot light on the individual as it (directly or indirectly) aims to reveal her identity. At the same time, it is often highly opaque and features transparency in the sense of hiding information (as discussed in Chapter 3). Contexts in which the provision of identity information is factually or quasi-obliged are increasing incrementally, e.g., to use a service, access a platform, etc. Furthermore, as shown, identity information is exploited for various contexts often beyond the knowledge and control of the individual concerned. The information processing inherent to digital identification is often standardized and automated based on predefined criteria to, e.g., categorize users, customers, etc., serving various purposes such as CRM, profit calculation, scoring or risk management (Bennett and Lyon 2008; Lyon 2009). Hence, to some extent, individuals become de-individualized by organizational and structural settings as in a panopticon. Against the background of big data and similar trends, individuals may increasingly become subjected to automated control and risk calculation based on their digital identity information.

Finally, the foundation of the panopticon lies in its asymmetry of power between the watchers and the watched. More precisely, this asymmetry is an informational one as the watchers have more information about the observed than vice versa. As the chilling effect demonstrates (Lyon 2003; Raab and Wright 2012), just the perception or fear among individuals of being under surveillance, i.e., observable or identifiable, may have a controlling effect. This asymmetry of information is the basic motor of panoptic power. Identification can create similar effects. This is particularly the case, when an asymmetry of power over identity information occurs, which implies some form of information asymmetry. This includes insufficient ISD as well, i.e., when an individual is identified (or perceives that they are identifiable) but lacks in knowledge or control over this process of identification and its purposes. Therefore, identifiability, i.e., the possibility to become identified, can lead to a form of information asymmetry from an individual's perspective. Hence, identification as well as identifiability of individuals can be related to forms of panoptic power. As there is an increasing tendency toward digital identification in various contexts, this development may entail an even further strengthening of information and power asymmetries in many respects.

Information asymmetries, agency problems and discrimination

As argued, the essence of panoptic power is the creation and maintenance of information asymmetry. Information asymmetries occur in various contexts which are not panoptic per se. In general, this imbalance is a classic problem likely to occur between individual and institutional entities; but also between interaction partners in economic markets. Information economics deals with information asymmetries in relation to macro- and micro-economic issues such as market development and contracting. Asymmetric information is present if entities with different amounts of knowledge about an issue interact with each other (Akerlof 1970; Stiglitz 2002). A simple example is an economic transaction such as a consumer buying a good from a vendor. The consumer usually has less information about the product (e.g., ingredients, origin, production process, supply chain, etc.) than the vendor. Agency theory (also known as principal–agency theory) differs between two roles: the principal and the agent. The agent usually has more information than the principal and thus more power to take advantage of the principal. This setting is also known as the principal–agent or agency problem (Shapiro 2005). The fact that the agent has more information does not necessarily imply that he exploits the principal. However, there is a certain risk in this regard, i.e., moral hazard. To reduce this risk, transparency and accountability of the agent, his motives and actions are essential.

Similar problems are mirrored in ICT usage in general and more specifically in digital identification practices and the privacy discourse. Digital environments are often accompanied by various information asymmetries; for instance, between users and providers of commercial social media platforms, which also bear tensions between collective and individual agency (Milan 2015). In contrast to optimistic views on social media (seen as a means of prosumption, user empowerment, etc.), several scholars (e.g., Comor 2010; Fuchs 2014; Milan 2015) argue that the commercialization of social media and ICTs reinforces alienation and increases disparities. Hence, the empowering potential of social media and other ICTs became quickly assimilated by existing power structures and market mechanisms. In general, the way technology is developed and applied often reproduces and reinforces existing power and information asymmetries.

Institutional entities usually have an informational advantage while the individual concerned lacks in knowledge about whether and how her information is used. Entailed in this is a state of insecurity and uncertainty for the individual. Consequently, there is an imbalanced control over identity information between the individual and the various institutional entities gathering and processing her information. Digitally networked environments, technologies and applications complicate this problem. Today, identity information is used in various contexts by a conglomerate of numerous institutional actors. While there is an observable general growth in identification systems and institutional control over digital identities, its purposes and functions are increasingly blurred for individuals who have to reveal their identity often without knowing whether and how it is used.

This form of information asymmetry thus entails a lack in ISD and individual control over digital identities. The increase in centralized databases, national registers, online platforms, etc. and identification practices enhances the informational power of those entities holding information about individuals. This is particularly the case when different databases and systems all use the very same identification method; as, e.g., intended by some governmental IDM approaches (De Andrade *et al.* 2013) as well as IDM concepts of social media platforms (as discussed in Chapter 4). With an increase in standardized IDM implementations, there is thus a risk of an incremental quasi-centralization of identification systems or development toward a "pervasive IDM layer" (Rundle *et al.* 2008: 19). Tendencies to centralize data storage or use a single identification system for multiple purposes facilitate cross-linking and aggregating identity information from different sources, and thus profiling. But besides explicit IDM implementations, information can also be aggregated from multiple contexts without the knowledge of the individuals concerned. The manifold forms to explicitly and implicitly identify individuals thus reinforce information asymmetries, and hamper and undermine effective privacy protection.

Information asymmetries can entail multiple forms of social control up to discrimination and manipulation. Individuals mostly lack options to reduce these asymmetries. Regardless of their relevance for various governance modalities, identification mechanisms, IDM, etc. bear certain risks of social sorting, i.e., a means of verifying and classifying individuals to determine special treatment, e.g., for purposes of administration, CRM or risk management (Lyon 2003/2009; Bennett and Lyon 2008; Ball *et al.* 2012). This "special treatment" can involve several forms of discrimination such as social, racial or ethnic exclusion and thus reinforce social disparities, mistrust and racism (Lyon 2003). False positives from surveillance activities are evident, where innocent people were secretly monitored and suspected to be involved in criminal activity. Various examples exist where people became falsely classified as suspicious and were subject to surveillance without concrete evidence, such as false positives on the "no fly list" of the US (Schneier 2006b; Krieg 2015) or cases in the UK where innocent people become suspects due to profiling activities employing DNA databases (Travis 2009). Another example is the case of a public servant and pro-democracy activist in New Zealand being accused of planning a terrorist attack in 2012. Based on surveillance of his online activities (as monitored in the context of the PRISM program) the NSA treated him as a suspicious person and passed the data to the New Zealand security agencies. As a consequence, he became a suspect on a top-secret surveillance list. The authorities revoked his passport and raided his home. According to reports in the media, all this happened without legal grounds (Gallagher and Hager 2016). These examples demonstrate threats inherent to mass surveillance. Hence, not without irony, extensive modes of security and surveillance can undermine and disable the essence of human security, i.e., the protection of the integrity of the individual and her rights to protection from different kinds of threats (as discussed in Chapter 3). Thus, to some extent, the human security concept becomes inverted.

Instead of being protected, individuals may be exposed to the risk of being classified as security threats and discriminated against by security and surveillance practices. Hence, there is often a thin line between applying identification mechanisms for efficient and secure provision of services and overwhelming social control. The securitization and economization of identity information facilitate the maintenance and reinforcement of information asymmetries: security authorities and companies alike benefit from informational advantages. For instance, what businesses understand as CRM, to personalize services and advertisements, may include profiling and tracking of individuals' behavior, activities, etc. and lead to scoring as well as price discrimination from the individual consumer's perspective. The measures and programs that security agencies conduct to protect national security may involve surveillance, reducing privacy and ISD and entailing censorship.

Practical examples of discrimination are profiling and scoring activities, i.e., the statistical classification and sorting of individuals based on information about them. For instance, in the banking and insurance sector, credit scoring is used to classify customers based on their financial situation and consumer patterns (Dixon and Gellman 2014). Personal information in social media, inter alia, is used for so-called "personality mining" to predict user behavior and recommend products. Such an approach is, e.g., proposed by Buettner (2016) who (akin to other marketers) shares the belief that personality would be computable and thus also predictable. The approach uses a five-factor model from behavioral psychology (with the factors agreeableness, conscientiousness, extraversion, neuroticism and openness to experience) to determine one's personality. The factors are explored by conducting a detailed statistical analysis of user information (e.g., profile information, time spent online, number of logins, contacts, interests, posts, pictures, etc.) that is, inter alia, provided by the social graph (as presented in Chapter 4). As a result, the factors are represented by probabilities which then can be fed into applications to, e.g., recommend different products or customize tariffs. For example, a British insurance company planned to calculate its tariffs based on Facebook posts of its customers: the idea is to analyze the personality profile of first-time drivers. People that are assumed by the algorithm to be conscientious and well-organized can expect a higher score than, e.g., those assumed to be overconfident (Ruddick 2016). It is also evident that social media classifies its users based on their profile information, which, in some cases, even leads to ethnic and racial profiling: for example, Facebook's system provides a feature for its marketing customers "to exclude black, Hispanic, and other 'ethnic affinities' from seeing ads" (Angwin and Parris 2016).

As already mentioned, security and intelligence agencies exploit ICTs and online communications data for all kinds of surveillance activities. Social media is a particularly easy target and is thus increasingly monitored by law enforcement and security agencies (Greenwald 2014; Belbey 2016; Bromwich *et al.* 2016). Besides the various mass surveillance practices, users of privacy tools can become special targets of surveillance programs. An example is the previously mentioned NSA software tool "XKeyscore": the tool allows searching for particular people based on predefined criteria. Security researchers and journalists who analyzed the tool's source code revealed that it categorizes users of privacy-friendly software (e.g., the Tor browser or other anonymization tools) as "extremists". These users are thus treated as potential targets of surveillance (Doctrow 2014). Privacy tools like Tor are used inter alia by journalists, lawyers, human right activists and other sensitive professions in order to protect their communications from surveillance (for a discussion on issues of privacy tools see Chapter 6).

Another example of social sorting on a large scale can be found in the republic of China, which is currently testing an as-yet voluntary social credit scoring system planned to be mandatory for the whole population by 2020. The system aims to collect as much information about citizens' interests, actions, behavior, etc. as possible from all kinds of electronic sources. The system is backed by, inter alia, the national ID card system as well as several e-commerce and credit companies like Alibaba and Tencent, who also run all Chinese social networks and thus have extensive personal data collections. The concept is partially similar to credit scoring systems which are used to verify one's credit rating, but are much more intrusive. Based on information it has about the population, the system creates a score for every citizen (ranging between 350 and 950), which alters with good and bad behavior. The system determines various forms of bad behavior such as running a red light (costing, e.g., 50 points), posting a political comment online without prior permission, buying a video game, etc. Even bad behavior in one's relationships may lead to a reduction of one's score. People with higher scores gain benefits (such as lower costs for car rental at a score of 650 or permission to travel to Singapore when reaching the score 700), while people with lower values receive restrictions and have fewer chances to get jobs (Storm 2015; Denyer 2016). This scoring system can be seen as a digital panopticon par excellence. Besides its deep intrusiveness, this example can be seen as part of a general trend to quantify personal information and use it for different scoring systems in line with the global big data paradigm. Ideas to apply scoring not just for financial issues but also for law enforcement and crime prevention can, e.g., be found in Germany where the Minister of the Interior made similar proposals (Krempl 2016). Related concepts already exist in the field of predictive policing, which aims to identify "likely targets for police intervention and prevent crime or solve past crimes by making statistical predictions" (Perry *et al.* 2013). Predictive policing systems such as IBM's "blue CRUSH" (Criminal Reduction Using Statistical History) or the software "TrapWire" are already in use, e.g., in the US and the UK. Threat scenarios in the sense of the movie *Minority Report* may be overestimated. In the movie plot, people are arrested based on statistical predictions that they will commit a crime in the future. However, the use of automated predictive analytics entails several risks and complicates finding the right balance between appropriate computation and excessive social control (Strauß 2018).

Algorithmic authorities or the incremental scoring of our identities

As shown, there are many cases where personal information is used for purposes that are unknown and uncontrollable for the individuals concerned. Such approaches raise serious ethical concerns and can include various forms of discrimination, stereotyping, manipulation and abuse of power. Moreover, the activities of profiling, scoring, monitoring, etc. are widely automated by data mining and pattern-recognition algorithms that analyze vast arrays of digital information. In this regard, "code is law" (Lessig 2006), as software and algorithms increasingly affect and determine society and thus entail a certain controlling capacity. This controlling capacity is often vague, hidden and opaque and is far from being open to public scrutiny and oversight. Shirky (2009) used the term "algorithmic authority" to describe this phenomenon. Today, algorithmic authorities already occur in various forms. Considering a further increase in this regard, a digital identity may become increasingly co-referential with its (algorithmic) environment (as observable, e.g., in social media). Hence, in some contexts it may even be seen as a sort of self-referential machine, because it is permanently determined by the dynamics of its constituting digital information flows. Algorithms of many online platforms, for instance, process user information to calculate what users may be interested in and then present customized information to them. This is a form of strict-determinism as information about (assumed) interests of the past is used to determine the amount of information presented to a particular user. To some extent, this can limit individuals' views on reality at least within the scope of the information system. Practical examples can be found in many digital systems of everyday use (e.g., online consumer or social media platforms, Internet search engines, etc.), where personal information is used to customize and filter the amount of information an individual receives from the system. This can be, e.g., useful for marketing purposes where the detection of specific patterns in consumer habits may include soft manipulation to seamlessly create demands such as in Amazon's recommendation algorithm (Van Dijk 2014). In the view of platform providers, these practices are reasonable in order to improve service quality and user experience. However, these practices also lead to the creation of a "filter bubble" (Pariser 2011) or "echo chamber" (Hosanagar 2016), which automatically determines what kind of information is presented to the user. Individuals then repeatedly receive information about their assumed interests based on automatically gathered user profiles while other information is automatically filtered out. Consequently, users mostly receive information based on their assumed interests as well as information aimed at creating particular demands. Hence, individuals are significantly hampered in gaining access to unfiltered information and can thus be trapped even in their own filter bubbles. Providers may argue that users are not trapped as they have various options of free and self-determined content production. However, this can be very restrictive as social media platforms highlight: content which platform providers such as Facebook perceive as inappropriate is regularly filtered, censored or erased. There are various examples where providers censored content even when no violation of its content policy was observable (Heins 2014; York 2016). Furthermore, the Cambridge Analytica scandal highlights that algorithmic power and identity information can be misused for purposes of manipulation: according to media reports, big data analysis conducted by the company Cambridge Analytica (now renamed to Emerdata)[10] was used to predict and influence the behavior of voters in the US presidential election in 2016 in support of president-elect Donald Trump (Confessore and Hakim 2017; Hern and Pegg 2018).

The increasing trend to employ automated profiling, scoring, risk calculation, etc. includes approaches to quantify information about individuals which feeds into various forms of social control. Entailed in these developments are manifold societal risks and above all, there is a certain risk that individual identities are reduced to the sum of their (digitally represented) informational parts and thus to quantitative, computable factors. If a person's identity is merely recognized based on her computable digital representation, the non-computable parts of identity (*ipse*) may be statistically normalized. This partially refers to the de-individualization mechanism of panoptic power, as the uniqueness of an identity may diminish with its expanding digital representation. The aforementioned plans of the citizen score system carries this to its extremes as an individual's score may determine significant parts or socio-technical contexts of her life. But less drastic examples also bear many societal risks. While automated information processing aims to foster efficiency and effectiveness, automated decisions affecting individuals are highly critical from a privacy perspective, as they facilitate social sorting, stereotyping and manipulation. The outlined examples highlight these problems. Additional problems occur as these automated socio-technical practices of big data may entail a drastic growth in complexity induced by massive data collections which can amplify the probability of errors, false positives and spurious correlations (Strauß 2015a; Calude and Longo 2016). For instance, Hamacher and Katzenbeisser (2011) demonstrated that the preventive gathering of data to, e.g., predict criminal activities does not lead to better results as expected from big data and predictive analytics. The increase in complexity of information processing and the costs to reveal and correct errors may even entail opposing effects. There are efforts to detect and correct failure which do not merely involve economic but above all many social costs (Wright and Kreissl 2015; Strauß 2017b). But in economic terms the financial burden of surveillance is also enormous: for instance, the economic impact of NSA surveillance is expected to exceed US$35 billion, as estimated by the US Information Technology and Innovation Foundation (Castro and McQuinn 2015).

As identity is not static but dynamic, approaches to gather identity information naturally entail some uncertainty as regards the validity of this information. This is particularly true for dynamic parts of identity information (i.e., *ipse*), which are naturally hard to quantify. Besides other things, reductionist attempts aiming to quantify *ipse*-information bear risks of misleading interpretations, which may even harm the individual represented by this information. For instance, incorrect behavioral patterns or false correlations may lead to discrimination or false accusations of innocent individuals (as shown in the previous sections). Furthermore, the dynamic character of identity in general is vital for individual experiences, and personal and societal development alike. Any limitation or restriction thus entails manifold social and ethical problems for personal and societal well-being. Attempts to increase data quality contribute little to reducing these problems when identification is employed for unethical purposes.

As shown, there are several similarities between panoptic power and forms of digital identification. While there is no universal identification system and neither is identity information per se exploited for surveillance and panopticism, there are many examples that highlight how identification serves panoptic forms of power. Lyon (1994: 67) argued that with the panopticon metaphor applied to ICTs "we see here nothing less than the near-perfection of the principle of discipline by invisible inspection via information-gathering." The myriad of global mass surveillance activities seems to underline Lyon's view. Lyon (1994) also discussed the question of whether panoptic power is present as a generalizable model over different social spheres, which cannot be easily answered as society as such is too complex. I argue that the employment of identification mechanisms contributes in various ways to the emergence of panoptic power in different social spheres. ICTs foster the inherent function of identification to connect and link different entities and systems. From this view, digital identification may be seen as a conductor of panoptic power. Identification here is not meant in a strict sense of uniquely identifying a person, but rather of processing information about an individual which can be used to reveal her identity. In the original concept of the panopticon, individuals are literally observed as they cannot move their bodies without being watched. This is not the case with modern surveillance where physical presence is not a necessary condition anymore. But the core feature, i.e., the construction of information asymmetry, is widely alike. Instead of potentially permanent observation, modern surveillance practices exploit the various identity traces individuals create when using technologies, applications, etc. These identity traces are widely available decoupled from space and time, though often invisible and uncontrollable for the individuals themselves. Considering the growth in big data and predictive analytics, the individual does not just become increasingly controllable in the present, but to some extent even in the future as her behavior can be predicted and thus manipulated based on semi-automated systems and their embedded algorithms.

Overall, there are many privacy risks resulting from information asymmetries entailed in means of identification in surveillance contexts. The problem does not result from identification per se, which is an important governance instrument serving many socio-political and economic purposes. But the contexts and purposes it is applied to are often opaque, and lack in transparency and accountability. Consequently, this favors moral hazard, i.e., immoral practices, and individuals have limited options to control their information. Therefore, privacy does not suffer merely from extensive information gathering and surveillance, but also from the entailed lack of transparency and accountability of information processing. This is also mirrored in the perceptions of European citizens, as will be shown in the following.

Citizens' perceptions on privacy, security and surveillance

Although security and surveillance measures directly affect individuals, little is known about their perceptions and opinions on contemporary surveillance. The EU-funded SurPRISE project[11] contributed to narrowing this gap and explored the perceptions of European citizens on the interplay between surveillance, privacy and security with a focus on surveillance technology. A core part of the empirical work included a large-scale participatory approach with citizen summits held (in 2014) in nine European countries with about 200 participants each.[12] In total, the summits had 1,780 people participating with $N=1,772$ valid responses. The participants were recruited differently across the countries involved. In Austria, Hungary, Italy, Spain and the UK, external contractors conducted the recruitment. In Denmark, Germany, Norway and Switzerland, a mix of channels (such as postal invitations, announcements in online and print media) was applied to get people involved. In each case, the recruitment was based on particular criteria (age, educational level, gender, geographical area and occupation) to avoid bias and achieve a heterogeneous panel structure. People with particular expertise in the project issues of privacy, security, surveillance or similar were excluded in order to avoid expert-driven opinions. A relatively even panel distribution could be achieved based on these criteria. As regards gender, there was a slightly higher share of male (52 percent) than of female (48 percent) participants. The age distribution ranged from 18 to 70+ with a slight majority (44 percent) of people belonging to the categories ranging from 40 to 59. The participation processes followed the same basic design with a combination of quantitative and qualitative methodology: a predefined interactive survey was the basic instrument to gather quantitative data and, in addition, three thematically structured group discussions were held during each summit to gain more insights into the rationales behind the perceptions of the participants. To explore eventual differences in the perceptions as regards technology, a particular focus was set on surveillance-oriented security technologies (SOSTs). This term was introduced in the project to describe security technologies with inherent surveillance capabilities. The participants were confronted with the three different SOSTs: smart CCTV (sCCTV), deep packet inspection (DPI: a specific form of Internet surveillance) and smartphone location tracking (SLT). These technologies served as examples representing different issues such as visual privacy, privacy of information and communication as well as locational privacy (Strauß 2015b). Some of the main quantitative results of the citizen summits (ibid.; Strauß 2017b) are presented and discussed.[13]

Major attitudes and concerns about surveillance technologies

Figure 5.2 illustrates various attitudes and concerns of participants concerning privacy and security issues of SOSTs. The results show that for the majority, 64 percent, there is some necessity of using surveillance technology in order to improve security. Only a minority of the respondents (26 percent) thinks that

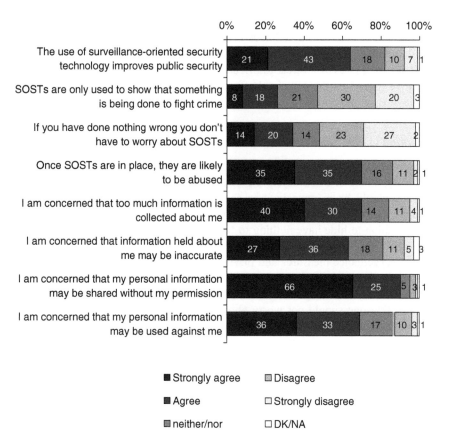

Figure 5.2 Major attitudes and concerns about SOST usage.

SOST usage rather has the function to demonstrate action against crime. However, the general position that using surveillance technology can contribute to security does not imply a general acceptance of privacy intrusions and surveillance (Strauß 2015b/2017a). The highly expressed fears and concerns indicate that the problem of information asymmetries is also perceived among the survey participants. Fifty percent of the respondents do not share the opinion that worries about surveillance technology are unfounded if one has done nothing wrong (this refers to the classical "nothing to hide" argument, which is discussed in the next section). For 70 percent, it is likely that SOSTs contribute to an abuse of power. The concerns about the misuse of personal information point to perceived uncertainty and insecurity as regards information processing: 70 percent are concerned that too much information is gathered about them; 63 percent worry about inaccurate and thus misleading information held about them; about 80 percent are concerned about their personal information being used against them and 91 percent expressed concerns about their information being shared without their permission[14] (Strauß 2015b/2017a). Thus, there are several fears of privacy violations among the respondents due to the misuse of personal information as processed by surveillance-oriented security technology. Overall, the results indicate that the majority perceives the intrusiveness of security and surveillance measures as a threat to privacy. As a consequence this can also have a negative impact on the perceived effectiveness of a security measure, as visible in the next set of results.

"Nothing to hide" unscrambled

Privacy is often falsely framed as a form of secrecy, which reduces it to a means of hiding things or information. This framing supports the misleading view that privacy would be in opposition to security and transparency (as discussed in Chapter 3). A very common argument in this regard is the statement "those who have nothing to hide have nothing to fear" (Solove 2004/2011; Schneier 2006a; Strauß 2017a). This statement is frequently used in the security discourse to justify surveillance measures and privacy intrusions. The rhetorical trick of this argument is to present privacy as equivalent to secrecy, which conveys the impression of something shady and suspicious. As a consequence, the argument implies that one should not worry about surveillance and privacy infringement as long as one behaves correctly and does not have the desire to keep information secret. In this regard the argument corresponds with disciplinary power in a Foucauldian sense. It restricts options to express concerns against surveillance (such as limitations to privacy, freedom of thought and expression, etc.) as they are automatically framed as something suspicious, as those who worry may have done something wrong. Consequently, the nothing-to-hide (NTH) argument also implies that those who have concerns have something to fear.

In order to learn what citizens think about this line of argument a similar statement (see statement two in Figure 5.2) was made: "If you have done nothing wrong, you don't have to worry about SOSTs." The results show that 50 percent reject this statement while only 34 percent share this opinion. As shown previously, the majority expressed strong concerns about malpractice regarding personal information, i.e., that too much information is collected, information is used against them and information is shared without the permission of the individuals concerned.[15] These results were cross-linked with those about the perceptions on the NTH statement (see Figure 5.3 and Table 5.2) (Strauß 2015b/2017a).

It is to be expected that most NTH opponents (85 percent) have concerns about the collection of their personal information. But it is rather surprising that the majority of NTH supporters (52 percent) share the same concerns about too much information being collected about them. Moreover, the same contradiction is observable as regards the other concerns: 54 percent of the NTH supporters expressed concerns about their information being used against them and 83 percent are concerned that their information is shared without their permission. Hence, even those people who perceive they have nothing to hide, and thus

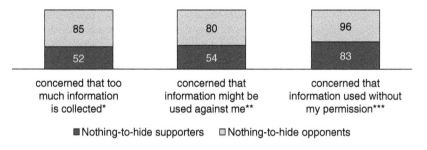

concerned that too
much information
is collected*

concerned that
information might be
used against me**

concerned that
information used without
my permission***

■ Nothing-to-hide supporters   □ Nothing-to-hide opponents

* N=549 supporters, N=804 opponents. ** N=541 supporters, N=807 opponents.
*** N=549 supporters, N=803 opponents.

Figure 5.3 Concerns among NTH supporters and opponents (percentages).

Table 5.2 Concerns of NTH supporters and opponents (percentages)

		Concerned	*Not concerned*	*Neither/nor*	*NA*
Too much information is	Supporters	52	29	18.5	0.5
collected	Opponents	85	6	8.5	0.5
Information might be	Supporters	54	23	23	0
used against me	Opponents	80	7	12	1
Information is shared	Supporters	83	9	8	0
without my permission	Opponents	96	1	2	1

claim not to worry about SOSTs, in fact worry about extensive information collection and abuse. These results further confirm that the NTH argument is,
similar to the assumed privacy/security trade-off (see Chapter 3), misleading.
Thus, the perceptions of citizens on privacy and security are more differentiated
than suggested by a narrow framing of privacy which neglects its public value.
These results instead indicate that citizens do not accept the gathering of their
information for surveillance purposes without plausible reasons (Strauß 2017a).
Keeping information private seems to be an important issue among respondents,
especially *because* of concerns about unjustified and uncontrolled information
gathering for surveillance. Consequently, ISD and self-controlled handling of
their information is an important issue as well as to what extent and for what
purposes this information is being processed.

Perceived intrusiveness and effectiveness of surveillance technology

The degree of intrusiveness, i.e., the extent to which surveillance technology
intrudes into an individual's privacy can be expected to have an impact on how
the individual perceives the use of the technology. Different technologies usually
have different intrusive qualities and surveillance modalities, which may also

affect their perceived effectiveness concerning security. To explore people's perceptions on these different intrusive qualities as well as on the perceived effectiveness, the participants were asked to assess statements for each of the three
SOSTs (as shown in Table 5.3). Each technology represents a different mode of
intrusion and thus affects privacy differently: sCCTV mainly involves visual
surveillance, SLT monitors one's movement and thus intrudes into locational
privacy, and DPI represents surveillance of Internet activity and thus includes
intrusions into the privacy of information and communications (Strauß
2015b/2017a). Hence, these technologies process different types of personal
information which effect perceptions on privacy intrusions. The results indicate
that the more intrusive a technology is perceived to be the more concern it raises,
which can also influence the perceived effectiveness.

As shown, respondents were relatively ambivalent in their perception on
security provisions by the technologies. While at least sCCTV and SLT were
assessed as effective security tools by a majority, more than two-thirds also said
they felt uncomfortable with these technologies. In the case of DPI, the position
was clearly opposed as only 43 percent perceived it as an effective tool while

Table 5.3 Major views on intrusiveness and effectiveness of SOSTs (percentages)

		Agree	Neither/nor	Disagree	NA
… is an effective national security tool	sCCTV	64	18	17	1
	DPI	43	24	32	1
	SLT	55	25	20	0
The idea of … makes me feel uncomfortable	sCCTV	39	20	40	1
	DPI	66	16	17	1
	SLT	45	24	31	0
I feel more secure when … is in operation	sCCTV	43	25	32	0
	DPI	12	25	61	2
	SLT	27	29	43	1
… is forced upon me without my permission	sCCTV	60	16	23	1
	DPI	87	7	5	1
	SLT	68	14	16	2
… can reveal sensitive information about me	sCCTV	52	15	32	1
	DPI	80	10	10	0
	SLT	60	20	19	1
… can lead to misinterpretations of my behavior	sCCTV	67	13	19	1
	DPI	77	12	10	1
	SLT	66	16	17	1
… can reveal to strangers where I am or was	sCCTV	57	16	26	1
	DPI	73	14	12	1
	SLT	68	16	16	0
I worry about how the use of … could develop in the future	sCCTV	67	13	19	1
	DPI	84	9	7	0
	SLT	65	18	17	0

66 percent felt uncomfortable with the use of this technology. None of the SOSTs was perceived as increasing security when in operation. DPI as the most intrusive technology was also assessed by the participants as such. Furthermore, it is also received the lowest values as regards its perceived effectiveness in improving security. Only for 12 percent did this technology contribute to a feeling of a security gain while the clear majority of 61 percent perceived the opposite. A similar pattern, though less distinct, is observable for the other SOSTs as well. Security gains are perceived by 43 percent in the case of sCCTV and by 27 percent for SLT. This reluctant view on security gains with the use of the SOSTs indicates that privacy intrusions to serve security purposes are not (as is often assumed) simply accepted but can even lead to an increase in subjective insecurity. This insecurity is mirrored in more-concerning aspects: for each SOST, the vast majority perceives that the technology is forced upon them. The same is true for concerns about the technologies revealing sensitive information, or information about one's location, as well concerns about misinterpretations of behavior. Considering the different values for each SOST, it is conspicuous that DPI raises the highest concerns and has the lowest acceptance followed by SLT and then sCCTV. This indicates an interrelation between intrusiveness and effectiveness (Strauß 2015b/2017a): the more intrusive the technology is perceived to be the less effective it is perceived to be. While all three SOSTs are assessed as privacy critical, sCCTV raised slightly lower concerns in most cases compared to the other two technologies. One explanation is that CCTV is well known, it is perceivable what the technology does (i.e., a camera that gathers images) and it is limited to particular areas in public while the others are more abstract, hidden and intrusive, and they can gain much deeper insights into one's private sphere. At the same time, the technologies behind SLT and DPI are more present in everyday life as most people carry smartphones at all times and use the internet every day. The related surveillance practices can gain very deep insights into one's identity by, e.g., gathering information on one's movements, social relationships, communications, interests, etc. These results thus indicate that the more details gathered about individual identities from their very private sphere, such as permanent monitoring of individual behavior, communications and interests, the higher the individual concerns about the collection and misuse of information. Information asymmetries also play a role here. The information asymmetry associated with a deeply intrusive technology (such as DPI) with multiple surveillance options may be perceived as higher compared to technologies with a clearer focus on gathering particular information (for example, CCTV primarily gathers images). Overall, the clearly expressed concerns provide a strong statement against privacy-intrusive security and surveillance practices. Moreover, the vast majority is worried about how the technologies could develop in the future, which indicates a certain fear about a further expansion of surveillance, and function or mission creep (i.e., uncontrolled, extensive surveillance).

These results allow the conclusion to be drawn that the intrusive quality of a technology, i.e., the way it interferes with privacy, also has an effect on its perceived acceptability (Strauß 2017a). To some extent, privacy intrusion seems to be tolerable for the respondents if it is necessary for a security gain. However, as Figure 5.4 shows, improving security is a necessary but not sufficient condition for the acceptance of privacy-intrusive practices.

The types of information a technology gathers makes a difference as does how deeply it can intrude into an individual's life. This is not just a matter of the technology and its design but also of the socio-technical practices in which it is applied and the usage contexts. The crux is that the usage of surveillance technology is mostly opaque and obscure, which was intensively debated in the group discussions at the citizen summits. Discussants often mentioned the importance of legal control and oversight to ensure that surveillance is appropriate, lawful and not abused (Strauß 2015b/2017a). However, there is little trust that laws and regulations are sufficient to protect against malpractice and misuse of the technologies as shown: in each case, less than 30 percent think that this is the case while for the vast majority protection is insufficient. Hence, these results point out that transparency, accountability and effective oversight are among the essential issues for privacy protection.

Trust in security authorities

In accordance with the lack of trust in regulation, the respondents also expressed great uncertainty as regards trust in security authorities to use the surveillance technologies with respect for human rights. As illustrated in Figure 5.5, there is only a relative tendency to perceive security authorities as trustworthy with some differences as regards the SOSTs (36 percent smart CCTV, 36 percent DPI, 46 percent SLT). However, only a minority of respondents expressed no doubts about the authorities abusing their power while there is a clear tendency toward the opposite: 46 percent in the case of smart CCTV, 34 percent for SLT and 52 percent regarding DPI. Hence, the respondents have a certain fear that security authorities take advantage of surveillance technology and abuse their power (Strauß 2017a).

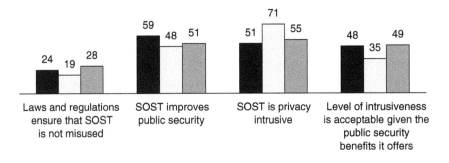

Figure 5.4 Intrusiveness and acceptability (percentages).

Security authorities which use ...

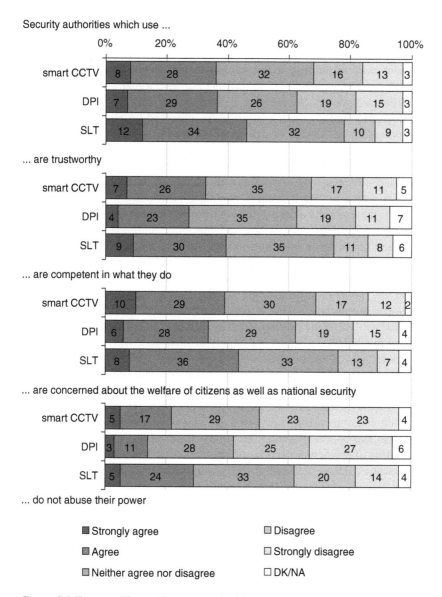

Figure 5.5 Trustworthiness of security authorities.

Furthermore, these results have the highest values in the category "neither/nor" in the whole survey, mostly exceeding 30 percent. This indicates a high level of uncertainty and insecurity among the respondents as regards trusting the authorities. As the previous results reveal, for most of the participants, the use of SOSTs represents a very intrusive measure which raises enormous concerns about the misuse of personal information via extensive surveillance activities.

Although security measures as such are not rejected but are to some extent perceived as being relevant and useful, concerns about misuse dominate. Particular fears are observable about function creep and the authorities abusing their power by employing the technologies (Strauß 2015b/2017a). These fears result from privacy-intrusive technology usage, extensive surveillance as well as a lack of accountability and oversight of security authorities, which altogether hamper trust. What complicates the building of trust is that security and surveillance practices mostly imply certain mistrust in the observed people. This is particularly problematic in the case of untargeted measures such as mass surveillance where everyone represents a potential suspect. Consequently, such measures raise insecurity and uncertainty, not least because mistrust can reinforce itself: security and surveillance practices that mistrust citizens likely lead to mistrust of these citizens by the authorities conducting these practices.

Overall, these results disprove the assumption that the majority of citizens lacks awareness of privacy issues and has only marginal concerns about security and surveillance activities. Indeed, some of the perceptions presented may partially differ from the participants' opinions in "real world" settings. Nevertheless, exploring the perceptions of citizens is very important to improve the general understanding of the interrelations between privacy, security and surveillance. This is particularly relevant as regards traditional conceptualizations of the privacy–security interplay in terms of a trade-off (as discussed in Chapter 3), which are largely refuted here. Several other studies dealing with related issues came to similar findings[16] (see, e.g., Friedewald *et al.* 2017). There are thus several strong indications that security and surveillance measures which neglect privacy protection do not contribute to raising perceived security but can even create opposite effects. This is particularly the case when these measures are based on extensive collections of personal information and operate beyond the scrutiny of the public. Hence, in short, the effectiveness of privacy protection suffers from extensive security and surveillance measures. These measures directly and indirectly affect individual identities, as privacy is intruded into in manifold ways while there is a lack of effective protection. Therefore, critical issues concern insufficient control for individuals over their information (referring to ISD) as well as a lack of transparency and control of surveillance practices and their operating entities. These issues are of increasing public concern, as other studies about online information processing confirm. For instance, the special Eurobarometer 431 of June 2015 on data protection shows that citizens have major concerns regarding the control and protection of their personal data (EB 2015): 67 percent of EU citizens perceive a lack of control over the information they provide online and for 37 percent there is no control at all over their information. The majority of respondents (57 percent) disagree with the statement that "providing personal information is not a big issue" and 53 percent feel uncomfortable about the use of information about their online activity by Internet companies. For 90 percent of Europeans it is important that their personal information is thoroughly protected irrespective of the country where a public authority or private company processing the information is located. Only a minority of 24 percent trusts providers of SNS to set appropriate privacy settings. Seventy percent of respondents say that personal information should not be collected and processed without their explicit permission. In general, there are widespread concerns among Europeans about their information being misused (ibid.). The flash Eurobarometer 443 of July 2016 on e-privacy provides similar findings (EB 2016): for over 70 percent, guaranteed confidentiality of their Internet communications is very important. Ninety percent) are in favor of having their communications (messages and calls) encrypted so that only the recipients can read them. Seventy-eight percent of the respondents find it very important that the use of their personal information on their devices (e.g., computers, smartphones and tablets) requires their permission. Near to two-thirds (64 percent) find it unacceptable that they only get unrestricted access to a website or service by having their online activities monitored. Eighty-nine percent of the respondents think that the default settings of Internet browsers should be sufficient to protect from tracking (ibid.). These aspects underline the need for more effective protection mechanisms in-built in digital technology. This refers to issues of privacy by design (PbD), which will be discussed in more depth over the course of this chapter.

Altogether, the presented results correspond with the premise that information and power asymmetries are among the core problems of contemporary privacy protection. Individuals generally lack control over their information as well as effective agency to reinforce their right to privacy. As shown, this has less to do with low privacy awareness and more to do with deficient options for ISD; as well as lacking transparency and accountability of the institutions that gather information about individuals beyond their scrutiny. Easing this problem requires more effective privacy controls as well as oversight and scrutiny of privacy-intrusive socio-technical systems and practices. However, the crux is that it is often unclear to what extent a socio-technical system or practice effectively intrudes into privacy and how privacy impacts emerge. It is thus important to come to a deeper understanding of the emergence of impacts on individual privacy to improve impact assessments and consequently also privacy protection. The next sections are dedicated to these issues with the main argument that (socio-technically induced and reinforced) identifiability is a core criterion in this regard.

Reducing identifiability by default as core challenge

It was shown that identification is an intrinsic part of privacy-intrusive surveillance and there are many examples where identity information is exploited for a variety of purposes beyond the control of the individuals concerned. Problems of insufficient individual control are also mirrored in the perceptions of citizens on the interplay between privacy, security and surveillance. There are certain overlaps between panopticism and identification, in particular as regards the emergence and expansion of information asymmetries. The occurrence of information asymmetries is not limited to surveillance but is a classic agency problem between individual and institutional entities. Individuals frequently experience informational disadvantages, lack in control over their information and have few options to protect and enforce their right to privacy. Information asymmetries and agency problems are likely to occur in digital identification processes, where identity information can be used in multiple, uncontrolled contexts.

While the exploitation of identity information for different forms of surveillance is evident, the diversity of privacy-intrusive practices and technologies involved complicates the relevant factors enabling privacy intrusion. Irrespective of this diversity, a crucial determinant of the emergence of a privacy impact is identifiability, i.e., the availability of information suitable to identify an individual. Identifiability entails one or more possibilities to process information that refers or relates to the identity of a person. It is thus the precondition of identification. This aspect is important for several reasons. First, because it implies the existence of one or more pieces of identifiable information, suitable to directly or indirectly identify an individual. Consequently, identifiability determines the occurrence of a privacy-affecting information asymmetry. This asymmetry occurs when an individual is identifiable and cannot control whether she is identified, i.e., lacks in ISD. Only in a state of anonymity, there is no such information. Second, identifiability is particularly relevant in socio-technical contexts as ICTs significantly reinforce options for identification. Many of the outlined surveillance practices benefit from the wide availability of digital information in social media and other online platforms, and basically from the identifiability inherent to ICTs.

At first glance, the nexus between identifiability and privacy is obvious as the focus of privacy and data protection was always on personal information. However, ICTs altered this nexus: as shown in the previous chapters, different forms of identification mechanisms are embedded in a number of socio-technical contexts, entailing an expansion of identifiability and thus a reduction in anonymity. Today, our identities are largely and increasingly exposed to the dynamics of ICTs. Basically, every interaction of an individual produces information that can refer or relate to her. However, in analog settings, without the involvement of ICTs, this information diminishes and is not persistently available. For example, conversations, movements, activities, etc. are usually neither recorded nor in any other way easily reproducible without technological means. Digital technology significantly changed this setting and reduced natural areas of anonymity, as physical and digital interactions are observable and reproducible. ICTs generally have contributed to a further growth in the amount of personal information not just because they reinforce its processing across multiple domains; but also because their usage can create additional information which may refer to individual identities. Hence, every interaction in a digital environment usually creates explicit and implicit informational traces, often suitable for identification. In the following, this issue is described as identity shadow.

Trapped between explicit and implict identification

The extent to which a person is identifiable depends heavily on whether the information is sufficient for unique identification. If this information is not already an identifier, further information may be needed about the person. In that case, a combination of different sets of information can enable identification. ICTs provide many options in this regard to combine and aggregate information, and thus facilitate different forms of identification. Identification may occur as an explicit as well as an implicit part of an information process. Explicit identification means that identity information of a person is being processed with her knowledge. In contrast to that is implicit identification, which can also occur as a "side-effect" of an interaction in a socio-technical context; e.g., while a person is using a technology or service, or visiting a website or searching the web, etc. Implicit identification such as targeted advertising, user tracking or profiling happens *en passant*, e.g., during an online session. Hence, identity information is often not gathered directly from an individual, but rather from the applications, technical devices, etc. referring to her, which are then aggregated. The collection of different metadata, for instance, is a common practice of online providers, who frequently argue in their privacy policies that this kind of information is collected merely to improve service quality and user experience.[17] In fact, this kind of information is often used for profiling activities of third parties as well. System-immanent or implicit forms of digital identification mostly proceed undetected by the individual and are therefore difficult to grasp. An important issue is that technological design can provide identifiable information as a by-product, which significantly fosters implicit identification. A simple example is caller-ID with a phone call. This technology was introduced in 1988 (Marx 2002) and before that phone calls were usually anonymous by default. The caller-ID changed this practice of phone communication to the opposite as the phone number (which is an identifier) became visible by default. This made it easier to identify a caller, and complicates anonymous phone calls as a caller then has to proactively hide her number. Moreover, the call-receiver may perceive this as suspicious. This is a simple example of a technology having an embedded identification mechanism. Certainly, in this case, a privacy problem does not exist as individuals want to communicate with each other and mostly know each other anyway. Nevertheless, this case demonstrates how technology changed the default setting to being identifiable. Similar examples can be found in ICTs and always-on devices, though more complex and with greater implications for privacy.

This setting inherent to ICTs can be called an identifiability-by-default mechanism. From a privacy perspective, this mechanism is critical as it enables a myriad of ways to exploit information about individuals beyond their knowledge and control. In this regard, identifiability by default may be seen as antagonistic to PbD. To conceptually highlight the problem of hidden or implicit identification, I introduced the term "identity shadow" (Strauß 2011: 210) in recognition the data shadow of Alan Westin (1967), who broadly framed data availability as a general privacy problem. However, data per se does not affect individual privacy but the processing of data referring to an individual's identity does. Thus, the identity shadow "comprises all the data appearing in a digital environment which can be used to (re-)identify an individual beyond her control and/or infringe her privacy" (Strauß 2011: 210). The term "identity shadow" takes up the panopticon metaphor and the problem of information asymmetries. Basically, the interplay of light and darkness determines the cast of a shadow, which is mostly beyond one's control. For an individual, her shadow is mostly invisible and impossible to catch. The only option is to gain control over the amount of light by which one's identity is illuminated. In practical terms this means control over one's flows of identity information, which is significantly hampered in many respects.

Re-identification or de-anonymization can be achieved by, e.g., aggregating different data attributes from multiple contexts which enable the gathering of semi-identifying data or quasi-identifiers (Sweeney 2002; Henriksen-Bulmer and Jeary 2016). Although these data are not necessarily unique, they can at least reduce uncertainty about an identity as they refer to an individual. Thus, even seemingly harmless (non-personal) information can affect one's privacy as it enables cross-linkage of identity information over different (normally separated) contexts. A typical example is a combination of date of birth, gender and zip code, which can be used to create identifiers that are likely unique enough to, e.g., even determine major parts of the population in the US, as Sweeney (2002) demonstrated. Consequently, the absence of typical identity information such as a person's name is not a barrier to identification. Similar approaches are feasible by combining other data sets. The use of ICTs in general entails manifold options for re-identification as many (semi-identifying) data attributes are required or created as a by-product during a user session. These data sets are here called common data (CD) and a distinction can be made between person-specific (typically name, date of birth, address, ZIP, etc.) and technology-specific data (e.g., IP address, network address, device identifiers, metadata, etc.) (Strauß 2011).

Figure 5.6 illustrates the identity shadow on the example of Alice using a digital identity device for a wide array of different services such as e-government services, health services or accessing a social media platform. Each of these services may have either a specific IDM approach or the ID device applies an unlinkability concept (e.g., with sector- or domain-specific identifiers (dsID)) for each service as in some governmental eIDMS. A separation of usage contexts can be achieved with both approaches, if the use of a unique ID is avoided. However, the main problem addressed here is that regardless of the use of domain-specific identifiers to avoid linkability of digital information over separated contexts, there is a risk of gathering quasi-identifiers to break the unlinkability concept and cross-link information, e.g., by exploiting common data. Even if information directly referring to one's identity is removed from a data set, there are other options for re-identification. A simple example concerns log files

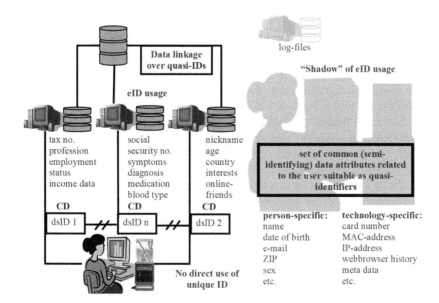

Figure 5.6 The identity shadow.
Source: adapted from Strauß (2011: 211).

and protocols. Although their aim is mostly to detect unauthorized access and protect from abuse, they can be exploited for privacy-intrusive profiling as they usually provide detailed information about user activities. The depth of the identity shadow in a particular usage context depends on the amount of common data available in that context and the technologies involved (Strauß 2011). For instance, online activities usually leave a number of data traces that can be exploited for de-anonymization: besides the very common form of user tracking based on web-cookies or click-tracking, etc., web browser data (e.g., bookmarks, history of visited sites, browser configuration, etc.) allows the generation of a digital "fingerprint" for unique identification of a person (Eckersley 2010; Schritt-wieser *et al.* 2011). A recent study demonstrated a fingerprinting-based identification rate of over 90 percent without using IP addresses or cookie data (Cao *et al.* 2017). Besides fingerprinting techniques based on web browser data there are similar approaches such as using time stamps of applications for de-anonymization (Bager 2016), or even the battery status of a technical device (Kleinz 2016). Social media in general processes massive amounts of identity information, gives deep insights into personal details and provides many options to gather quasi-identifiers. Integrative technologies such as social plugins (see Chapter 4) enable websites to gather and process identity information of a user from her social media profile. Hence, user details are also available to external services, e.g., name, profile photo, gender, networks, user ID, list of friends as well as status updates, comments, shared content, etc. Moreover, different ways to re-identify individuals out of anonymized data ranging from analyzing group associations, user preferences, online activities, social graphs, face recognition based on user photos, to location data, etc. were demonstrated by several security scholars (e.g., Narayanan and Shmatikov 2009; Wondracek *et al.* 2010; Nilizadeh *et al.* 2014; Gulyás *et al.* 2016). As social media extends its scope with social plugins and graphs, user details are also available for external sources outside the platforms. Further issues result from mobile computing. Compared to a smart card, mobile devices such as smart phones entail a lot of additional information (e.g., device identifier, geo-location, phone number, SIM-card number, IDs of wi-fi networks, etc.). As smart phones can access the internet, they also have corresponding network identifiers, e.g., IP and MAC[18] address. Also, IDs of a favorite wi-fi network can be used for user tracking (Vaas 2013).

A crucial part of the identity shadow problem results from identification mechanisms as integral parts of ICTs, i.e., identifiability by default, which can involve several sub-systems such as hardware devices, databases, software applications, etc. The connecting function inherent to identification (as described in Chapter 3) is basically important to enable interactions between different entities or systems. When different entities (e.g., humans, technologies or applications) interact with each other (e.g., exchange information, communicate, cooperate), some forms of identification are typically involved. The processing of a piece of identifiable information (such as an identifier) is a precondition for networked systems to establish a connection. Therefore, technical devices are usually equipped with identifiers (e.g., a card number, network address, IP address, etc.). This allows one particular entity (a technical system or device) to be distinguished from another and enables interaction. Hence, identification creates an informational link between two or more entities. This is true for Internet connections[19] but, in principle, some form of identification process occurs in every kind of network. Technical devices are thus usually equipped with an identifier enabling their identification in particular contexts. For instance, a personal computer connects to a network such as the internet via an IP address; a website is accessible under a particular (unique) domain (e.g., www.internetsociety.org); e-mail communication requires a valid e-mail address identifying a client; a mobile phone has a particular serial number (IMEI[20]) and SIM[21] cards have a unique identifier (IMSI[22]) to interact with the phone network and a unique phone number to enable communication; even a simple Bluetooth device such as a headset is identified by the computer device it is linked to; RFID tags can be used to equip all kinds of objects such as clothes with an identifier. Further examples can be found easily.

Thus, as these common examples highlight, identification is an intrinsic process of ICTs or socio-technical systems shaping their connectivity and interactivity. Identification allows creating a sort of strong tie that links different systems in analog or physical as well as digital environments. As identifiability is a necessary condition for identification in general, it represents a universal issue of all socio-technical systems. Indeed, technical forms of identification are different from human identification of individual people. Hence, they do not necessarily lead to the identification of an individual person. However, as the identity shadow highlights, both forms can overlap, as technical identifiers provide potential links to the people using a technology. Identifiability-by-default mechanisms inherent to technological design thus also affect the identifiability of the person. As identity is a relational concept, digital identities of individual people can be expected to become increasingly networked with the use of technical devices or interacting with informational entities or agents (e.g., a device, a service, an application or any other kind of information system). These entities can then directly or indirectly refer to the individual. This may be a technical device such as a smartphone, but also a software application such as a social media or cloud computing account. Hence, put simply, the "identity" of a technological system can refer to the personal identity of its users. Through interactions with digital information systems, the properties of an individual's identity may be extended as the information representing her becomes available virtually. Moreover, technology also enables the use of this digital identity representation decoupled from its source. Therefore, the number of socio-technical (sub-)systems involved in a user interaction or processing of user-related information has an impact on the identity shadow of this particular user. With a growing number of socio-technical (sub-)systems, the identity shadow is likely to grow as well, as every usage context can potentially generate additional identity information. Hence, ICTs entail an incremental extension of the representation of our identities and affect identification. This identity representation is not always visible but, metaphorically speaking, mostly hiding in the shadows and thus exposed to identification practices.

Contextual identity layers

An identity shadow can have many different shades. It may be seen as a reflection of an individual's identity, which continuously morphs by enabling new space for de- and re-contextualization beyond her control. This undermines the privacy principle of purpose binding and hampers Nissenbaum's (2010) concept of contextual integrity (as discussed in Chapter 3). Increasing digital environments and thus digital information brings further possibilities to (re-)identify and de-anonymize individuals; even when they do not provide personal information directly. Hence, the boundaries between personal and non-personal information, public and private spheres, blur as, e.g., observable in social media. Consequently, socio-technical contexts conflate previously separate spheres, which results in expanding identifiability and various forms of implicit identification.

From a wider perspective, the problem highlighted with the identity shadow can be illustrated as a model, consisting of expanding contextual identity layers. As outlined in Chapter 3, identity in general does not shrink. Consequently, identifiable information is likely to continuously grow with every usage over the course of time. At a particular moment in (space and) time, an individual may be represented by a particular number of identity attributes, i.e., a set of identifiable information. For instance, when a child is born, the initial information gathered about her includes a set of bodily characteristics (such as height, weight, gender, biometric features) as well as temporal, spatial and relational information (e.g., date of birth, place of birth, birth name and names of parents) that depicts birth. This is identifiable information referring to an individual and the amount of this kind of information usually expands over time as its socio-technical usage contexts grow as well. Given the dynamics of identifiable information and the multiplicity of contexts, the exact amount of information that identifies an individual in a particular context is mostly not strictly determinable. This aspect is crucial to grasp how identifiable information in general emerges and develops (see Chapter 7 for a detailed discussion).

Metaphorically, an identity life cycle can be seen as a sort of spiral where the individual is the very entity that is represented by a flow of identifiable information expanding across multiple, circular layers (contextual identity layers) with multiple entities and application contexts involved (as illustrated in Figure 5.7). These entities can be individuals (such as family and friends, acquaintances, colleagues, clerks, etc.) as well as institutional (e.g., government agencies, employers, private companies, law enforcement, intelligence agencies, etc.). Most of the institutional entities use applications with repositories (e.g., dossiers, registers, databases, etc.) to store and process identifiable information. The involvement of ICTs expands the identity spiral because, due to the nature of digital information, contexts can easily overlap irrespective of their boundaries. Additional, multiple layers emerge that involve also virtual, non-physical entities (e.g., applications, databases, services, repositories, technical hard- and software devices, etc.). In this regard, the representation of a personal identity incrementally turns into a digitally networked identity. This digital identity can provide deep insights into individual privacy, i.e., who a person is, what she does, where she is and was, her personal and professional relationships, preferences, interests, behavior, etc.

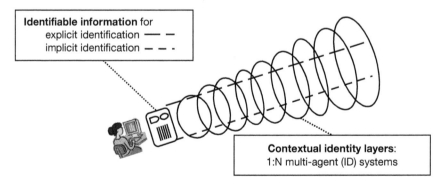

Figure 5.7 Spiral of digital identification. The circles of the spiral represent contextual (identity) layers and point out that identifiable information can be repeatedly processed in different contexts.

On a meta-level, the totality of identifiable information referring to or representing a particular individual and the increasing conflation of usage contexts may be perceived as the virtual embodiment of a meta-ID. Norbert Wiener (1954: 96) stated: "We are not stuff that abides, but patterns that perpetuate themselves." This aspect of (self-)perpetuation is particularly relevant against the background of digital identification and identifiability. As shown, there are many forms of implicit and explicit identification mechanisms in a variety of contexts. Context can be understood as the condition of an application (Nissenbaum 2010: 140ff.) or informational process. From an individual's view, in many cases there may be only a one-dimensional context perceivable as she is only aware of the current application she is interacting with while in fact there may be a 1:n relation with multiple contexts in which her information is being processed. These additional, hidden contexts refer to the identity shadow problem as outlined previously. From a systemic perspective, a contextual layer can be seen as a relational entity (or sub-system) that may be linked to other subsystems which may further process identifiable information. For the individuals concerned, these multiple contextual identity layers mostly imply information asymmetries and lack of ISD: first, because the individual can hardly avoid being subject to implicit identification (occurring in hidden, uncontrollable contexts); and second, because the thresholds between different contexts and related (sub-) systems may be unknown or beyond control as well.

For privacy protection, it makes a significant difference whether identifiable information is bound to a particular context only or whether it is used in other contexts as well. The possibility for re-contextualization is thus a privacy risk, which is in contradiction to a basic privacy principle, namely purpose limitation (or binding). The crux here is to clearly determine what counts as a context or a system that processes identifiable information. In general, a privacy-relevant context involves the processing of identifiable information. In this regard, the processing of identifiable information is a necessary condition for a privacy-affecting application context. In many cases, a context may be a single application (e.g., an e-government or e-commerce transaction, the submission of a registration form, etc.) in which identifiable information (e.g., name, date of birth, e-mail address) is processed with direct involvement or interaction of the individual. However, in addition to the primary context of the initial application, there may be other systems involved as well. Hence, other contextual layers or sub-systems (e.g., technical devices, hard- and software systems) may affect privacy but remain undetected. Furthermore, each system (or contextual layer) processes identifiers which can refer to an individual identity and thus can also be used for privacy intrusion. Thus, even without direct involvement, a user can be identifiable as her information is associated with a technical device. As shown previously with the identity shadow, the same process can be found in other technologies and applications, where multiple types of technical identifiers may refer to a particular user. This information emerges from the information systems (sub-systems) that are associated with an application context. For instance, a standard Web session involves at least three different information systems:

a personal computing device, the operating system and the Web browser. Via interfaces, information may also be transferred from one information system to another (as, e.g., observable in social media platforms providing APIs to external entities for the use of social plugins, logins, etc. as outlined in Chapter 4).

Hence, through the potentially unlimited flow of identifiable information, a digital identity can be involved in multiple processing contexts of multiple (individual and institutional as well as technical) entities, without the knowledge of the person concerned. In the case of explicit identification, the individual is involved in the emergence of the input information (e.g., by entering personal information into an information system or triggering a corresponding event). On the contrary, implicit identification happens without direct involvement of the individual whose information is processed. Implicit identification can occur during a user session regardless of whether the person is also explicitly identified by personal information. Instead of the person, an application, system, etc. may gather or generate identifiable information about that person and pass it on to another system, for example when an application automatically gathers a user profile and transmits it to another system. These system-immanent interrelations can trigger a cascade of processes in which input and output of identifiable information can oscillate between multiple systems. Depending on the temporal availability of identifiable information, there may be longer time spans between input and output without any direct involvement or awareness of the person whose identity information is being processed. In a worst-case scenario, the uncontrolled processing of identifiable information entails a cascade of identification processes where the individual is uncontrollably identified in many contexts without even noticing it.

Between continuity and change: how identifiability expands

Technology usage and technological progress entail a further expansion of the identity shadow and contextual identity layers in many respects. An increasing number of networked always-on devices reinforce permanent availability of digital information flows and thus identifiability. An important example concerns the constant growth in mobile computing with portable devices such as smart phones, or wearable technologies (e.g., smart watches etc.). These devices can serve as technological hubs to steer other technologies and provide additional applications such as location-based services as well as information about geolocation and movements of individuals. Hence, mobile devices significantly extend user tracking, which is not limited to digital spaces but now also includes a person's movement in the real world. Consequently, it becomes increasingly difficult to avoid being tracked (Clarke 2012). Tracking information allows the creation of identity profiles including location and movements, which is another indicator for increasing overlaps between physical and digital environments. There already are a number of business models in the realm of big data aimed at monetizing telecom data (IBM 2013; Leber 2013; Kannenberg 2016). Big data and datafication in general boost the trend to digitally gather and process maximum data from everyday-life contexts (Mayer-Schönberger and Cukier 2013; Lyon 2014; Strauß 2015a). The myriad of "smart" technologies, networked devices toward trends such as the Internet of Things, ambient intelligence, pervasive computing, etc. yield further ICTs that feed the big data paradigm.

With these developments, the realm of possibilities expands to gather unique patterns in digital (or digitized) information sets. Once a unique pattern is found, it can be used to create a quasi-identifier and apply de-anonymization techniques. Thus, the identity shadow is obviously of high value for the surveillant assemblage including the NSA and other security and surveillance actors. The cases of ICT-related surveillance presented in the previous sections range from targeted advertising and various forms of profiling, up to global mass surveillance programs as well as a growth in data brokerage. Basically, all these activities exploit the identity shadow of their targets by, e.g., creating and employing identity graphs for extensive profiling activities. Identity graphs (as well as social graphs, see Chapter 4) are based on graph theory and computational models. They comprise all kinds of information about individuals from multiple sources aimed at drawing a comprehensive identity profile based on numerous categories and scores. That ICTs and networked technologies of various kinds are valuable for surveillance was highlighted not least by James Clapper, the chief of US intelligence, who mentioned that the NSA and other intelligence agencies will probably exploit the Internet of Things to spy on individuals: "In the future, intelligence services might use the internet of things for identification, surveillance, monitoring, location tracking, and targeting for recruitment, or to gain access to networks or user credentials" (Ackerman and Thielman 2016).

Besides developments fostering the extension of technology-specific identifiable information, the amount of person-specific information is also increasing in many respects, not least as regards biometrics. The employment of biometric systems is a high-ranked issue in many security strategies (Lyon 2009; Ajana 2013). For several years, there has been an observable growth in the use of biometrics and face recognition. Biometrics in a technical sense is defined as "the automated recognition of individuals based on their behavioural and biological characteristics" (ISO 2010: 2). The scope of usage of biometric technologies ranges from access control in security areas to border and migration control, law enforcement, or different kinds of profiling activities. Biometrics has also gained in importance as an integrative feature of laptops or smart phones equipped with fingerprint scanners (e.g., Apple's "TouchID"). The proponents of biometrics see it as a sophisticated and highly secure means of identity verification or authentication. However, in fact, biometric identification is a form of pattern recognition that calculates a probability: a biometric system is basically an automated pattern-recognition system that uses information about one's body, e.g., for identification, access control, etc. It either makes an identification or verifies an identity by establishing the probability that a specific physiological or behavioral characteristic is valid (Wilson 2010). Hence, biometrics approximates the validity of identity information based on a probability pattern. This also implies that a certain degree of false positives or errors is possible. Several studies pointed out that biometrics entails security and privacy risks (e.g., Clarke 2001; Prabhakar *et al.* 2003; Lyon 2009; Acquisti *et al.* 2014; Sharif *et al.* 2016). Besides that, biometric information can be copied and abused. For instance, security researchers demonstrated the insecurity of fingerprint sensors embedded in smartphones with relatively simple means: based on the photo of a fingerprint from a glass, the hackers created a synthetic digit (Arthur 2013). In other demonstrations, hackers show how to gather biometric information using a standard digital camera. With relatively simple methods, even iris information could be reproduced (Krempl 2015). It is thus questionable whether approaches using biometric features for authentication are as secure as they are promoted to be.

While the employment of biometrics used to be rather limited to special security domains (e.g., for access control in high-security areas), there are trends to include these technologies in other domains. For example, authentication via fingerprint in mobile apps,[23] or novel forms of payment via facial image ("pay-by-selfie") (Leyden 2016) are promoted in the banking sector.[24] In particular facial recognition is gaining in importance in the public as well as private sectors (Acquisti *et al.* 2014). Security and law enforcement agencies increasingly employ facial recognition for preventive surveillance activities. In 2011 the US FBI initiated the so-called "next generation identification" program (NGIP) to set up the largest biometric database worldwide (Reardon 2012; EPIC 2016). Among the stored information will be, e.g., DNA profiles, fingerprints, iris scans, palm prints, photographs and voice identification profiles. Facial recognition is among the core features of this surveillance system. The information is gathered from external sources such as police databases, CCTV systems, and similar systems from public as well as private entities (EPIC 2016). According to a study by the Georgetown University in Washington in 2016, about 117 million facial images are stored in governmental databases in the US. The collection consists of images gathered from, inter alia, driving licenses, passports as well as police databases. The majority of these images refer to normal citizens that have never been involved in criminal activity (Garvie *et al.* 2016). The US Government Accountability Organization (GAO) evaluated the facial recognition system of the NGIP and found several flaws as regards the accuracy of the technology. The GAO came to the conclusion that NGIP raises concerns about the protection of privacy and individual civil liberties (GAO 2016).

Facebook introduced a facial recognition system in 2010 (Isaac 2010). According to media reports, the software is more accurate than the FBI's NGIP (LaChance 2016). This system exploits the broad availability of images online (as, e.g., boosted by digital cameras and smartphones). It enables recognition of a person based on her presence in photos uploaded to Facebook as well as automatic tagging which allows, e.g., searching for particular people. The app "Facedeals" (related to Facebook) uses facial recognition "to provide a 'seamless method' for customers to announce their presence at restaurants, cafés, bars and other venues on Facebook" (De Andrade *et al.* 2013: 61). Google and Apple also have similar software in their photo apps (Brandom 2016; Monckton 2017). Another application called SceneTap uses facial recognition for age and gender determination in bars, etc. to provide people with information about suitable places to meet others (De Andrade *et al.* 2013: 61). Facebook was confronted with heavy protest from privacy and data protection authorities in Europe but also in the US due to its facial recognition system. Facebook's reaction to the strong opposition and complaints of regulators in Europe was to turn off the facial recognition feature in the EU for new users in 2012 (De Andrade *et al.* 2013). With this strategic measure, Facebook avoided lawsuits with the EU. However, it does not really solve the manifold privacy problems as Facebook is a global service located in the US. In 2016, Facebook started to promote a new photo app which includes its facial recognition technology "DeepFace"[25] in Europe, though with limited functionality due to repeated heavy protest and legal issues with European regulation (Hern 2016). This feature is automatically activated by default. Hence, users in other countries who do not want their face being exposed to this system have to change their privacy settings (O'Donnell 2017).

Further trends in the field of virtual and augmented reality can be expected to amplify the identity shadow and its privacy impacts. Smart devices such as wearable computers (e.g., "Google Glass" or other smart glasses) may indicate the next generation of mobile social media. Such devices may have the capability of bidirectional tracking via an integrated camera and thus could gather one's movements as well as what one looks at, including facial recognition, etc. (Strauß and Nentwich 2013). But virtual and augmented reality could also be used to trick facial recognition: just recently, a technique to spoof facial recognition by employing a virtual reality model was demonstrated (Cuthbertson 2016). Furthermore, with speech recognition, a further technology based on biometric information is on the rise as, e.g., the increasing number of digital assistants, ranging from Apple's "Siri", Microsoft "Cortana", Google "Now", to smart speakers (e.g., Amazon echo and its assistant "Alexa") and similar gadgets demonstrate. As all these technologies are increasingly equipped with machine learning algorithms and so-called "artificial intelligence", their intrusive capacity on privacy is potentially enormous. Consequently, the identity shadow is likely to grow steadily if privacy protection is neglected.

Overall, these developments indicate a further convergence of physical and digital environments involving identification technologies. The more physical and digital worlds converge, the more networked our identities become, which further strains privacy protection. This is mainly because it becomes increasingly difficult to control the information flow from one system or environment to another and, thus, ISD suffers from this increasing convergence. Biometrics is a particular form of identification that underlines this issue. Biometrics demonstrates that "the line between technology and the body is blurring; identities are defined in terms of bodily features as—a fingerprint or a facial image—captured in an algorithm" (Lyon 2009: 17). As a consequence, the body itself becomes a sort of code. Clarke (2001) warned early about the manifold risks of biometrics to privacy, as their extensive use can significantly reduce anonymity and could lead to threats of dehumanization as individuals may be reduced to a set of bio-metric information. Although the latter risks may seem overstated, a scenario where biometric information is extensively processed indeed raises serious privacy issues. Considering different forms of biometrics as a core technology of everyday life, then our bodily characteristics become the main representations of our identities. At the same time, identity representations are exposed to the risk of being permanently available for uncontrolled identification. This would reduce the options of individuals to autonomously express their identities and freely decide whom to reveal what informational parts of it to and in which con-texts. The permanent possibility of being identified by biometric recognition drastically worsens one's chance of avoiding being observable and traceable online as well as offline because one can hardly opt-out from one's bodily char-acteristics. Consequently, the increasingly blurred contexts and boundaries of the public and the private spheres also affect the human body. These blurry bound-aries are also an issue in contemporary art and activism, which seek ways to deal with privacy threats. For example, an "identity prosthesis", i.e., a facial mask to undermine facial recognition systems, was developed for an art project.[26] Similar approaches exist to trick fingerprint sensors with, e.g., synthetic fingers[27] or to hide from surveillance systems by using specific clothing, i.e., stealth wear.[28] Facial recognition systems can also be undermined by using colorful glasses as security researchers recently demonstrated (Doctrow 2016; Sharif *et al.* 2016). These approaches indicate an ongoing societal discourse about privacy and the increase in digital identification where civil society seeks ways to deal with these issues, among other things.

As shown, there are manifold socio-technical developments that contribute to a further growth in our identity shadows and identifiability. Hence, ultimately, ICTs and digital technology in general significantly affect identity representa-tions, particularly when processing contexts are basically unrestricted. Given the possibilities of digital information processing, technology can transform initially non-persistent information produced during an interaction and enrich it with a certain property of continuity. The information is then digitally represented and can be made available outside the context of the original interaction as well. As outlined in Chapter 3, continuity (as well as change) characterizes an intrinsic part of identity as regards self-development and identity-building (Ricoeur 1992; Hildebrandt 2006). But there is a significant difference between analog and digital environments here: as identity information is usually not explicitly mapped or documented in the analog world, it is not permanently available by default. This continuity is thus context-specific but not misinterpreted as a form of totality. Moreover, in an ontological sense, continuity is incompatible with identity, as Sartre (2014: 263f.) stated. In this regard, permanent availability of identity information without any frictions or discontinuity may complicate self-determination. In line with privacy, identity development needs some (onto-logical) frictions (Floridi 2013). Hence, identity also implies a certain solitude and seclusion so that it is unique and distinguishable from other entities. To some extent, the digital world strains this natural discontinuity, e.g., exemplified by social media platforms, where one's interests, actions, behavior, etc. in the past and in the present can be observable. An example to highlight this issue is Facebook's "Timeline" feature introduced in 2011, which visualizes how any particular user profile emerged and developed over the course of time (Panzarino 2011; Kupka 2012). The Timeline can contain all details and stages of an individual user's life on Facebook, i.e., a sort of automatic autobiography including all events, photos, shared content, posts, etc. This kind of information is not available merely for the particular user but can be accessed by external sources as well. Considering Ricoeur's (1992) distinction between the two basic types of identity—*idem* and *ipse* (see Chapter 3)—the dynamic character of digital information enables further growth in both types while, at the same time, the distinction increasingly blurs, as the Timeline example illustrates. The availability of information referring to ipse, i.e., social relations, associations, interactions, expressed thoughts and feelings, postings, likes, behavior, shared thoughts and feelings, etc., can be particularly problematic from a privacy perspective. This kind of information provides deep insights into one's identity and also bears risks of misinterpretation and prejudice. For instance, the idea to use Facebook profiles for national security (as mentioned in Chapter 4) entails a high risk that irrelevant information about a person is used to classify this person, which may convey a low threshold to discrimination.

ICTs significantly extended the scope of identity information and of its naturally limited availability. Identity information can be processed regardless of whether the original context of an identification process ceases to exist. As a consequence, identity information from multiple contexts can be explicitly visible, accessible, observable, collectible, and to some extent also manipulable beyond the control of the individual concerned (as shown in the previous sections). This also has conceptual implications for the quality and scope of privacy, not least as regards its temporal and spatial dimensions. Privacy provides a space free from (factual and perceived) interference, which implies a certain distance between the individual and society. In a traditional sense, privacy may be seen as a concept determined by certain zones or territories (Kahn 2003), which have always been linked to social convention and norms and included spatial as well as virtual domains. Although this setting still exists, it is altered and challenged by increasingly pervasive ICTs. Hence, these "classical" privacy territories have become digitized and thus informationally enriched. Spatial and temporal dimensions (e.g., the physical space in which an individual is located at a certain point in time) of identity representations are more easily reproducible and accessible. Digital identities are exposed to the transparency reinforced by ICTs (see also Chapter 3). Hence, a technological device does not have to be *at the same physical location* as an individual *at the same time* to gather and process her information. Paradoxically, this can entail a form of permanent virtual proximity or closeness between technology and individual; a sort of quasi-persistent informational link (as, e.g., already observable in smart phones). Besides other things, this virtual proximity enabled distant identification of an individual, irrespective of the spatial and temporal distance to the person, as her digital identity representation can be processed at multiple locations at the same time. This multidimensional, networked character of digital identity has many benefits. But the inherent co-referentiality between technology and identity (Floridi 2013) also complicates privacy protection as the informational boundaries of those contexts, in which an individual's identity is processed (by personal as well as socio-technical entities) partially diminish. These diminishing boundaries further challenge the achievement of contextual integrity as a digital identity can be subject to multiple processing contexts. An elementary characteristic and precondition of privacy and contextual integrity is their contextual separation or informational friction. This means that the flow of personal information is (ideally) not uncontrollably streaming from one context to another. The concept of unlinkability is a crucial requirement to technically implement these frictions (see Chapter 3). While this is mostly the case in the physical or analog world, digital environments challenge unlinkability, and the individual's capabilities of ISD are hampered if not impeded. Against the background of a continuing convergence between physical and digital environments with expanding identifiability, a further reduction in ISD is very likely. Permanent identifiability thus repeals the boundary control function of privacy and hampers self-determined inclusion and seclusion in particular socio-technical contexts. An individual then cannot control whether to be identified or not. Therefore, enhancing the boundary control function of privacy by regaining control over identifiability and digital identity representations is among the core challenges of privacy. The next chapter presents and discusses the extent to which approaches in the realm of PbD and PIA provide suitable options in this regard.

Notes

1 Identity information is also seen as a lucrative business factor, as these promotion articles exemplify: "Monetizing Identity: Pay by Face", TMForum, March 25, 2014, https://inform.tmforum.org/nfv-it-transformation/2014/03/monetizing-identity-pay-by-face/; "How to Monetize your Customer Data", Gartner, December 10, 2015, www.gartner.com/smarterwithgartner/how-to-monetize-your-customer-data/.

2 As, e.g., the Merriam Webster Dictionary defines: www.merriam-webster.com/dictionary/surveillance.

3 For example Austria, Belgium, Croatia, Czech Republic, Denmark, Germany, Greece, Hungary, Iceland, Israel, Italy, Japan, Norway, Saudi Arabia, South Korea, Spain, Sweden, Switzerland, Turkey.

4 Trivia: a prism is an optical item to decompound a ray of light into its constituent spectral colors: https://en.wikipedia.org/wiki/Prism.

5 For instance, the GCHQ ran the Tempora project to gather raw data directly from fiber-optic cables; see, e.g., "GCHQ Taps Fibre-Optic Cables for Secret Access to World's Communications", *Guardian*, 21 June, 2013: www.guardian.co.uk/uk/2013/jun/21/gchq-cables-secret-world-communications-nsa.

6 Directive 2006/24/EC of the European Parliament and of the Council on the Retention of Data Generated or Processed in Connection with the Provision of Publicly Available Electronic Communications Services or of Public Communications Networks: http://eur-lex.europa.eu/LexUriServ/LexUriServ.do?uri=OJ:L:2006:105:0054:0063:EN:PDF.

7 Plans are to use four fingerprints as well as facial images, e.g.: EU Commission (2016): Stronger and Smarter Borders in the EU: Commission proposes to establish an Entry-Exit System, press release, April 6, 2016: http://europa.eu/rapid/press-release_IP-16-1247_en.htm.

8 For example, data management platform ID graph: www.oracle.com/marketingcloud/products/data-management-platform/id-graph.html.

9 Palantir is co-founded by Peter Thiel, who is one of the technological advisers to US president Donald Trump. According to media reports, the company is involved in plans of the US Trump administration to deport millions of immigrants (Woodman 2017).

10 https://en.wikipedia.org/wiki/Cambridge_Analytica.

11 The project received funding from the EU's Seventh Framework Programme for research, technological development and demonstration under grant agreement number 285492.

12 In Austria, Denmark, Germany, Hungary, Italy, Norway, Spain, Switzerland, and United Kingdom. Further information about these national participation processes is available at http://surprise-project.eu/events/citizen-summits/.

13 For further details about the methodology and synthesis of the summits, see, Strauß (2015b). Further information about all national participation processes, individual country reports, etc. is available at http://surprise-project.eu/dissemination/research-results/.

14 Fear of unauthorized information usage also refers to issues of informed consent and limited user control as discussed in Chapter 6.

15 This broad disagreement to the NTH argument is also mirrored in the results of the different countries with the strongest opposition in Germany. Exceptions were Hungary and the UK, where respondents tended to agree with the statement. However, also there, the participants expressed concerns about extensive information collection and fears of misuse.

16 Such as of the EU projects PRISMS (Privacy and Security Mirrors: http://prisms project.eu/) and PACT (public perception of security and privacy: www.projectpact. eu/). Akin to SurPRISE, these projects also analyzed the traditional trade-off between privacy and security, though with different foci on technologies and practices. For a broader discussion, the three projects organized a joint conference in 2014. For selected papers from this event, see, Friedewald *et al.* (2017).

17 This common argument refers to issues of limits of user control, as discussed in Chapter 6.

18 The Media Access Control (MAC) address identifies a technical component in a network such as a network interface.

19 Such as TCP, e.g., Kozierok (2005).

20 International Mobile Equipment Identity: https://de.wikipedia.org/wiki/International_Mobile_Equipment_Identity.

21 Subscriber Identity Module: https://en.wikipedia.org/wiki/Subscriber_identity_module.

22 International Mobile Subscriber Identity: https://en.wikipedia.org/wiki/International_mobile_subscriber_identity.

23 For instance, the fingerprint authentication of the federal credit union: www.gfafcu.com/fingerprint-authentication, or the Unicredit group, see, e.g., Sayer (2013).

24 A very drastic case exists in China, where female students were requested to provide nude photographs of themselves as a condition to obtain a loan (Connor 2016).

25 The technology was presented in 2014 by Facebook developers at a conference on computer vision and pattern recognition; see, Taigman *et al.* (2014).

26 URME Personal Surveillance Identity Prosthetic: www.urmesurveillance.com/urme-prosthetic/.

27 Identity counter-surveillance kit: http://mian-wei.com/#/identity/.
28 Privacy Gift Shop: Stealth Wear collection: http://privacygiftshop.com/shop/stealth-wear/.

References

All URLs were checked last on October 23, 2018.

Ackerman, S. and Thielman, S. (2016) US Intelligence Chief: we might use the internet of things to spy on you. *Guardian*, February 9, www.theguardian.com/technology/2016/feb/09/internet-of-things-smart-home-devices-government-surveillance-james-clapper.

Acquisti, A., Gross, R. and Stutzman, F. (2014) Face Recognition and Privacy in the Age of Augmented Reality. *Journal of Privacy and Confidentiality*, 6(2): 1–20. http://repository.cmu.edu/jpc/vol. 6/iss2/1.

Acquisti, A., Taylor, C. and Wagman, L. (2016) The Economics of Privacy. *Journal of Economic Literature*, 54(2): 442–492. www.aeaweb.org/articles?id=10.1257/jel.54.2.442.

Ajana, B. (2013) *Governing through Biometrics. The biopolitics of identity*. Basingstoke/New York: Palgrave Macmillan.

Akerlof, G. (1970) The Market for "Lemons": Quality uncertainty and the market mechanism. *Quarterly Journal of Economics*, 84(3): 488–500.

Albrechtslund, A. (2008) Online Social Networking as Participatory Surveillance. *First Monday*, 13(3) March. http://firstmonday.org/article/view/2142/1949.

Amoore, L. (2008) Governing by Identity. In Bennett, C. J. and Lyon, D. (eds.), *Playing the Identity Card: Surveillance, security and identification in global perspective*. London/New York: Routledge, 21–36.

Angwin, J. and Parris Jr., T. (2016) Facebook Lets Advertisers Exclude Users by Race. *ProPublica*, October 28, www.propublica.org/article/facebook-lets-advertisers-exclude-users-by-race.

Arthur, C. (2013) iPhone 5S Fingerprint Sensor Hacked by Germany's Chaos Computer Club. *Guardian*, September 23, www.theguardian.com/technology/2013/sep/22/apple-iphone-fingerprint-scanner-hacked.

Bager, J. (2016) Timing-Attacke deanonymisiert Website-Besucher teilweise. *Heise Online*, September 13, www.heise.de/newsticker/meldung/Timing-Attacke-deanonymisiert-Website-Besucher-teilweise-3319599.html.

Ball, K. and Webster, F. (2003) *The Intensification of Surveillance: Crime, terrorism and warfare in the information age*. London: Pluto.

Ball, K., Haggerty, K. and Lyon, D. (eds.) (2012) *Handbook on Surveillance Studies*. Abingdon/New York: Routledge.

Belbey, J. (2016) Crime and Social Media: Law enforcement is watching. *Forbes Magazine*, August 31, www.forbes.com/sites/joannabelbey/2016/08/31/crime-and-social-media-law-enforcement-is-watching/#6cf1d7cd541d.

Benkirane, R. (2012) The Alchemy of Revolution: The role of social networks and new media in the Arab Spring. *GCSP Policy Paper*, No. 2012/7, edited by Geneva Center for Security Policy.

Bennett, C. J. (2011) In Defence of Privacy: The concept and the regime. *Surveillance and Society*, 8(4): 485–496.

Bennett, C. J. and Haggerty, K. D. (eds.) (2011) *Security Games: Surveillance and control at mega-events*. New York: Glasshouse.

Bennett, C. J. and Lyon, D. (2008) *Playing the Identity Card: Surveillance, security and identification in global perspective*. London/New York: Routledge.

Biddle, S. (2017) How Peter Thiels Palantir Helps the NSA to Spy on the Whole World. *The Intercept*, February 22, https://theintercept.com/2017/02/22/how-peter-thiels-palantir-helped-the-nsa-spy-on-the-whole-world/.

Bigo, D. (2000) When Two Become One: Internal and external securitisations in Europe. In Kelstrup, M. and Williams, M. (eds.), *International Relations Theory and the Politics of European Integration: Power, security and community*. London: Routledge, 171–204.

Bigo, D. (2008) Globalized (In)Security: The field and the Ban-Opticon. In Bigo, D. and Tsoukala, A. (eds.), *Terror, Insecurity and Liberty: Illiberal practices of liberal regimes after 9/11*. Oxon/New York: Routledge, 10–48.

Brandom, R. (2016) Apple's New Facial Recognition Feature Could Spur Legal Issues. *The Verge*, June 16, www.theverge.com/2016/6/16/11934456/apple-google-facial-recognition-photos-privacy-faceprint.

Bromwich, J. E., Victor, D. and Isaac, M. (2016) Police Use Surveillance Tool to Scan Social Media, A.C.L.U. Says. *New York Times*, October 11, www.nytimes.com/2016/10/12/technology/aclu-facebook-twitter-instagram-geofeedia.html.

Buettner, R. (2016) Predicting User Behavior in Electronic Markets Based on Personality-Mining in Large Online Social Networks: A personality-based product recommender framework. *Electronic Markets: The International Journal on Networked Business*: 27(3), 247–265. doi:10.1007/s12525-016-0228-z.

Burns, M. (2015) Leaked Palantir Doc Reveals Uses, Specific Functions and Key Clients. *Techcrunch*, November 1, https://techcrunch.com/2015/01/11/leaked-palantir-doc-reveals-uses-specific-functions-and-key-clients/.

Buzan, B., Weaver, O. and de Wilde, J. (1998) *Security: A new framework for analysis*. Boulder: Lynne Rienner.

Calude, C. S. and Longo, G. (2016) The Deluge of Spurious Correlations in Big Data. *Foundations of Science*, 22(3): 595–612. doi:10.1007/s10699-016-9489-4. http://link.springer.com/article/10.1007/s10699-016-9489-4.

Cao, Y., Song, L. and Wijmans, E. (2017) (Cross-)Browser Fingerprinting via OS and Hardware Level Features. In *Proceedings of the 24th NDSS Symposium, 26 February–1 March 2017, San Diego, CA*. Internet Society. http://dx.doi.org/10.14722/ndss.2017.23152.

CASE Collective (2006) Critical Approaches to Security in Europe: A networked manifesto. *Security Dialogue* 37(4): 443–487.

Castro, D. and McQuinn, A. (2015) Beyond the USA Freedom Act: How U.S. surveillance still subverts U.S. competitiveness. *Information Technology and Innovation Foundation*, June, www2.itif.org/2015-beyond-usa-freedom-act.pdf?_ga=1.114044933.369159037.1433787396.

Christl, W. and Spiekermann, S. (2016) *Networks of Control: A report on corporate surveillance, digital tracking, big data and privacy*. Vienna: Facultas. www.privacylab.at/wp-content/uploads/2016/09/Christl-Networks__K_o.pdf.

CJEU—Court of Justice of the European Union (2014) The Court of Justice Declares the Data Retention Directive to be Invalid. Press release no. 54/14. Luxembourg, 8 April 2014. Judgment in Joined Cases C-293/12 and C-594/12 Digital Rights Ireland and Seitlinger and Others. http://curia.europa.eu/jcms/upload/docs/application/pdf/2014-04/cp140054en.pdf.

CJEU—Court of Justice of the European Union (2016) The Members States May Not Impose a General Obligation to Retain Data on Providers of Electronic Communications Services. Press release no. 145/16, Luxembourg, 21 December 2016. Judgment in Joined Cases C-203/15 Tele2 Sverige AB v Post-och telestyrelsen and C-698/15 Secretary of State for the Home Department v Tom Watson and Others. http://curia.europa.eu/jcms/upload/docs/application/pdf/2016-12/cp160145en.pdf.

Clarke, R. (1988) Information Technology and Dataveillance. *Communications of the ACM*, 31(5): 498–512. www.rogerclarke.com/DV/CACM88.html.

Clarke, R. (2001) *Biometrics and Privacy*. www.rogerclarke.com/DV/Biometrics.html.

Clarke, R. (2012) Location Tracking of Mobile Devices: Uberveillance stalks the streets. *Computer Law and Security Review*, 29(3): 216–228. www.rogerclarke.com/DV/LTMD.html.

Cohen, J. E. (2012) *Configuring the Networked Self: Law, code, and the play of everyday practice*. Yale: Yale University Press.

Comor, E. (2010) Digital Prosumption and Alienation. *Emphemera: Theory and Politics in Organization*, 10(3/4): 439–454. Available at: www.ephemerajournal.org/contribution/digital-prosumption-and-alienation.

Confessore, N. and Hakim, D. (2017) Data Firm Says "Secret Sauce" Aided Trump; Many Scoff. *New York Times*, March 6, www.nytimes.com/2017/03/06/us/politics/cambridge-analytica.html.

Connor, N. (2016) Female Chinese Students "Asked to Hand Over Nude Photos to Secure Loans". *Telegraph*, June 15, www.telegraph.co.uk/news/2016/06/15/female-chinese-students-asked-to-hand-over-nude-photos-to-secure/.

Cuthbertson, A. (2016) Facial Recognition Can Be Tricked with Facebook Photos. *Newsweek Europe*, August 22, http://europe.newsweek.com/facial-recognition-can-be-tricked-facebook-photos-492329?rm=eu.

De Andrade, N. N. G., Monteleone, S. and Martin, A. (2013) *Electronic Identity in Europe: Legal challenges and future perspectives (e-ID 2020)*. JRC Scientific and Policy Reports. Joint Research Centre, European Commission.

De Hert, P. (2008) Identity Management of e-ID, Privacy and Security in Europe: A human rights view. *Information Security Technical Report*, 13: 71–75.

De Hert, P. (2012) A Human Rights Perspective on Privacy and Data Protection Impact Assessments. In Wright, D. and De Hert, P. (eds.), *Privacy Impact Assessment*. Springer: Dordrecht, 33–76.

Denyer, S. (2016) China Wants to Give All Its Citizens a Score—and Their Rating Could Affect Every Area of Their Lives. *The Independent*, October 22, www.independent.co.uk/news/world/asia/china-surveillance-big-data-score-censorship-a7375221.html.

Dewey, T., Kaden, J., Marks, M., Matsushima, S. and Zhu, B. (2012) *The Impact of Social Media on Social Unrest in the Arab Spring*. Final report prepared for: Defense Intelligence Agency. Stanford University. https://stanford.box.com/shared/static/c5v3umqoc7oa2b9p6qjb.pdf.

Dixon, P. and Gellman, R. (2014) *The Scoring of America: How secret consumer scores threaten your privacy and your future*. Research Report, World Privacy Forum. www.ftc.gov/system/files/documents/public_comments/2014/04/00007-89171.pdf.

Doctrow, C. (2014) If you Read BoingBoing, the NSA Considers you as Target for Deep Surveillance. *BoingBoing*, July 3, http://boingboing.net/2014/07/03/if-you-read-boingboing-the-n.html.

Doctrow, C. (2016) Researchers Trick Facial Recognition Systems with Facial Features Printed on Big Glasses. *BoingBoing*, November 2, http://boingboing.net/2016/11/02/researchers-trick-facial-recog.html.

Dupont, B. (2008) Hacking the Panopticon: Distributed online surveillance and resistance. *Sociology of Crime Law and Deviance*, 10: 259–280.

EB—Eurobarometer (2015) *Special Eurobarometer 431: Data protection*. EU. http://ec.europa.eu/commfrontoffice/publicopinion/archives/ebs/ebs_431_en.pdf.

EB—Eurobarometer (2016) *Flash Eurobarometer 443: Report e-privacy*. TNS political and social, EU. Available at: https://ec.europa.eu/digital-single-market/en/news/eurobarometer-eprivacy.

Eckersley, P. (2010) How Unique Is Your Web Browser? In Atallah, M. and Hopper, N. (eds.), *Proceedings of the 10th International Conference on Privacy Enhancing Technologies (PETS'10)*. Heidelberg: Springer, 1–18. https://panopticlick.eff.org/static/browser-uniqueness.pdf.

EPIC—Electronic Privacy Information Center (2016) *EPIC v. FBI—Next generation identification—Seeking documents about the FBI's expansive biometric identification database*. http://epic.org/foia/fbi/ngi/.

Floridi, L. (2013) *The Ethics of Information*. Oxford: Oxford University Press.

Foucault, M. (1977) *Discipline and Punish: The birth of the prison*. (Translated from the French by A. Sheridan, 2nd edition 1995). New York: Vintage Books/Randomhouse.

FRA—European Union Agency for Fundamental Rights (2016) *Fundamental Rights Report 2016*. Luxembourg: Publications Office of the EU. http://fra.europa.eu/sites/default/files/fra_uploads/fra-2016-fundamental-rights-report-2016-2_en.pdf.

Friedewald, M., Burgess, P. J., Čas, J., Bellanova, R. and Peissl, W. (eds.) (2017) *Surveillance, Privacy, and Security: Citizens' perspectives*. London/New York: Routledge.

Fuchs, C. (2010) How Can Surveillance Be Defined? Remarks on theoretical foundations of surveillance studies. *The Internet and Surveillance: Research Paper Series* (no. 1). Unified Theory of Information Research Group. www.sns3.uti.at/wp-content/uploads/2010/10/The-Internet-and-Surveillance-Research-Paper-Series-1-Christian-Fuchs-How-Surveillance-Can-Be-Defined.pdf.

Fuchs, C. (2014) Digital Prosumption Labour on Social Media in the Context of the Capitalist Regime of Time. *Time and Society*, 23(1): 97–123. http://fuchs.uti.at/wp-content/time.pdf.

Gallagher, R. and Hager, N. (2016) The Raid: In bungled spying operation, NSA targeted pro-democracy campaigner. *The Intercept*, August 15, https://theintercept.com/2016/08/14/nsa-gcsb-prism-surveillance-fullman-fiji/.

Gandy, O. (1993) *The Panoptic Sort: A political economy of personal information*. Boulder: Westview.

GAO—US Government Accountability Organization (2016) *Face Recognition Technology: FBI should better ensure privacy and accuracy*. Report to the Ranking Member, Subcommittee on Privacy, Technology and the Law, committee on the Judiciary, U.S. Senate. www.gao.gov/assets/680/677098.pdf.

Garvie, C., Bedoya, A. M. and Frankle, J. (2016) *The Perpetual Line-Up: Unregulated police face recognition in America*. Washington DC: Georgetown Law Center for Privacy and Technology. www.perpetuallineup.org.

Giddens, A. (1984) *The Constitution of Society: Outline of the theory of structuration*. Cambridge: Polity Press.

Glässer, U. and Vajihollahi, M. (2010) Identity Management Architecture. In Yang, C. C., Chau, M. C., Wang, J.-H. and Chen, H. (eds.), *Security Informatics, Annals of Information Systems Vol. 9*. Boston: Springer, 97–116.

Gordon, D. (1987) The Electronic Panopticon: A case study of the development of the National Crime Records System. *Politics and Society*, 15(4): 483–511.

Greenwald, G. (2013) XKeyscore: NSA tool collects "nearly everything a user does on the internet". *Guardian*, July 31, www.theguardian.com/world/2013/jul/31/nsa-top-secret-program-online-data.

Greenwald, G. (2014) *No Place to Hide: Edward Snowden, the NSA and the surveillance state.* London: Hamish Hamilton/Penguin Books.

Guild, E., Carrera, S. and Balzacq, T. (2008) *The Changing Dynamic of Security in an Enlarged European Union*. Research paper No. 12, CEPS Programme Series. www.ceps.eu http://aei.pitt.edu/11457/1/1746.pdf.

Gulyás, G. G., Simon, B. and Imre, S. (2016) An Efficient and Robust Social Network De-anonymization Attack. In *Proceedings of the ACM Workshop on Privacy in the Electronic Society, October 2016, Vienna, Austria*, 1–11. doi: 10.1145/2994620.2994632.

Haggerty, K. D. (2006) Tear Down the Walls: On demolishing the panopticon. In Lyon, D. (ed.), *Theorizing Surveillance: The panopticon and beyond*. Cullompton: Willan Publishing, 23–45.

Haggerty, K. D. and Ericson, R. V. (2000) The Surveillant Assemblage. *British Journal of Sociology*, 51(4): 605–622.

Haggerty, K. D. and Samatas, M. (eds.) (2010) *Surveillance and Democracy*. Oxon: Routledge-Cavendish.

Hamacher, K. and Katzenbeisser, S. (2011) Public Security: Simulations need to replace conventional wisdom. In *Proceedings of the New Security Paradigms ACM Workshop (NSPW11), September 2–15, Marin County, US*, 115–124.

Heins, M. (2014) The Brave New World of Social Media Censorship. *Harvard Law Review*, 127(8): 325–330.

Henriksen-Bulmer, J. and Jeary, S. (2016) Re-identification Attacks: A systematic literature review. *International Journal of Information Management*, 36(6): 1184–1192.

Hern, A. (2016) Facebook Launches Facial Recognition App in Europe (without Facial Recognition). *Guardian*, May 11, www.theguardian.com/technology/2016/may/11/facebook-moments-facial-recognition-app-europe.

Hern, A. and Pegg, D. (2018) Facebook Fined for Data Breaches in Cambridge Analytica Scandal. *Guardian*, July 11, www.theguardian.com/technology/2018/jul/11/facebook-fined-for-data-breaches-in-cambridge-analytica-scandal.

Hildebrandt, M. (2006) Privacy and Identity. In Claes, E., Duff, A. and Gutwirth, S. (eds.), *Privacy and the Criminal Law*. Antwerpen/Oxford: Intersentia, 43–57.

Hood, C. C. and Margetts, H. Z. (2007) *The Tools of Government in the Digital Age* (second edition). Public Policy and Politics. Hampshire: Palgrave Macmillan.

Hosanagar, K. (2016) Blame the Echo Chamber on Facebook. But Blame Yourself, Too. *Wired*, November 25, www.wired.com/2016/11/facebook-echo-chamber/.

IBM (2013) Data Monetization: Telco's bit-pipe dystopia, cloud and the redistribution of value. *IBM Telecom, Media and Entertainment Blog*, May 2, www.ibm.com/blogs/insights-on-business/telecom-media-entertainment/data-monetization-telcos-bit-pipe-dystopia-cloud-and-the-redistribution-of-value/.

Isaac, M. (2010) Facebook to Add Facial Recognition Software to Photo Tagging. *Forbes Magazine*, December 15, www.forbes.com/sites/mikeisaac/2010/12/15/facebook-to-add-facial-recognition-software-to-photo-tagging.

ISO—International Organization for Standardization (2010) *Information Technology—Identification Cards—On-Card Biometric Comparison.* ISO/IEC 24787:2010(E). First edition 2010–12–15. http://bcc.portal.gov.bd/sites/default/files/files/bcc.portal.gov.bd/page/adeaf3e5_cc55_4222_8767_f26bcaec3f70/ISO_IEC_24787.pdf.

Kahn, J. D. (2003) Privacy as a Legal Principle of Identity Maintenance. *Seton Hall Law Review*, 33(2): 371–410.

Kannenberg, A. (2016) Telefónica Deutschland will Bewegungsdaten von Mobilfunkkunden vermarkten. *Heise Online*, September 22, www.heise.de/newsticker/meldung/Telefonica-Deutschland-will-Bewegungsdaten-von-Mobilfunkkunden-vermarkten-3329545.html.

Kleinz, T. (2016) Datenschutzbedenken: Mozilla entfernt Akku-Fingerprinting aus Firefox. *Heise Online*, Oktober 31, www.heise.de/newsticker/meldung/Datenschutzbedenken-Mozilla-entfernt-Akku-Fingerprinting-aus-Firefox-3405099.html.

Kozierok, C. M. (2005) The TCP/IP Guide, Version 3, www.tcpipguide.com/free/t_TCP-PortsConnectionsandConnectionIdentification.htm.

Krempl, S. (2015) 31C3: CCC-Tüftler hackt Merkels Iris und von der Leyens Fingerabdruck. *Heise Online*, December 28, www.heise.de/security/meldung/31C3-CCC-Tueftler-hackt-Merkels-Iris-und-von-der-Leyens-Fingerabdruck-2506929.html.

Krempl, S. (2016) "Terror Score": Ex-Bundesdatenschützer greift Innenminister an. *Heise Online*, October 7, www.heise.de/newsticker/meldung/Terror-Score-Ex-Bundesdatenschuetzer-greift-Innenminister-an-3343177.html.

Krieg, G. (2015) No-fly Nightmares: The program's most embarrassing mistakes DNA database. *CNN*, July 12, http://edition.cnn.com/2015/12/07/politics/no-fly-mistakes-cat-stevens-ted-kennedy-john-lewis/index.html.

Kubicek, H. and Noack, T. (2010) Different Countries—Different Extended Comparison of the Introduction of eIDs in Eight European Countries. *Identity in the Information Society (IDIS)*, 3(1): 235–245.

Kupka, A. (2012) Facebook Timeline Now Mandatory for Everyone. *Forbes Magazine*, January 24, www.forbes.com/sites/annakupka/2012/01/24/facebook-timeline-now-mandatory-for-everyone/.

LaChance, N. (2016) Facebook's Facial Recognition Software Is Different from the FBI's. Here's why. National Public Radio (NPR), May 18, www.npr.org/sections/alltechconsidered/2016/05/18/477819617/facebooks-facial-recognition-software-is-different-from-the-fbis-heres-why.

Leber, J. (2013) How Wireless Carriers Are Monetizing Your Movements. *Technology Review*, April 12, www.technologyreview.com/s/513016/how-wireless-carriers-are-monetizing-your-movements/.

Lessig, L. (2006) *Code Version 2.0.* New York: Basic Books.

Leyden, J. (2016) Mastercard Rolls Out Pay-by-Selfie across Europe. *The Register*, October 5, www.theregister.co.uk/2016/10/05/mastercard_selfie_pay/.

Lyon, D. (1994) *The Electronic Eye: The rise of surveillance society.* Minneapolis: University of Minnesota Press.

Lyon, D. (2001) *Surveillance Society: Monitoring everyday life.* Oxford: University Press.

Lyon, D. (2003) *Surveillance as Social Sorting: Privacy, risk and automated discrimination.* London: Routledge.

Lyon, D. (2009) *Identifying Citizens: ID cards as surveillance.* Cambridge: Polity Press.

Lyon, D. (2014) Surveillance, Snowden, and Big Data: Capacities, consequences, critique. *Big Data and Society*, July–December: 1–13. http://journals.sagepub.com/doi/abs/10.1177/2053951714541861.

MacAskill, E., Borger, J., Hopkins, N., Davies, N. and Ball, J. (2013) Mastering the Internet: How GCHQ set out to spy on the World Wide Web. *Guardian*, June 21, www.theguardian.com/uk/2013/jun/21/gchq-mastering-the-internet.

Marx, G. T. (2015) Surveillance Studies. In Wright, J. D. (ed.), *International Encylopedia of the Social and Behavioral Sciences*, Second Edition Vol. 23, 733–741. doi: 10.1016/B978-0-08-097086-8.64025-4.

Marx, G. T. (2002) What's New About the "New Surveillance?" Classifying for Change and Continuity. *Surveillance and Society*, 1(1): 9–29.

Mayer-Schönberger, V. and Cukier, K. (2013) *Big Data: A Revolution that will transform how we live, work and think*. New York: Houghton Mifflin Harcourt.

Milan, S. (2015) When Algorithms Shape Collective Action: Social media and the dynamics of cloud protesting. *Social Media + Society (SM+S)*, 1(2) (Online first December 30): 1–10. http://journals.sagepub.com/doi/pdf/10.1177/2056305115622481.

Monckton, P. (2017) Is Google About to Start Sharing Your Facial Recognition Data? *Forbes Magazine*, April 28, www.forbes.com/sites/paulmonckton/2017/04/28/google-photos-ramps-up-facial-recognition/.

Narayanan, A. and Shmatikov, V. (2009) De-anonymizing Social Networks. In *Proceedings of the 30th IEEE Symposium on Security and Privacy*, 173–187. doi: 10.1109/SP.2009.22.

Nauman, L. and Hobgen, G. (2009) *Privacy Features of European eID Card Specifications*. Position paper, European Network and Information Security Agency ENISA. www.enisa.europa.eu/publications/eid-cards-en/at_download/fullReport.

Nilizadeh, S., Kapadia, A. and Ahn, Y. (2014) Community-enhanced De-anonymization of Online Social Networks. In Ahn, G., Yung, M. and Li, N. (eds.), *Proceedings of the 2014 ACM SIGSAC Conference on Computer and Communications Security*. ACM: New York.

Nissenbaum, H. (2010) *Privacy in Context: Technology, policy, and the integrity of social Life*. Stanford: Stanford University Press.

O'Donnell, A. (2017) How to Disable Facebook's Facial Recognition Feature. *Lifewire*, June 26, www.lifewire.com/how-to-disable-facebooks-facial-recognition-feature-2487265.

OECD—Organization for Economic Co-Operation and Development (2004) *The Security Economy*. OECD, Paris: OECD Publishing. www.oecd.org/futures/16692437.pdf.

Oracle (2015a) Oracle Data Cloud: The new driving force of data-driven marketing, online brochure. www.oracle.com/us/products/applications/brochure-data-driven-marketing-odc-2894231.pdf.

Oracle (2015b) Oracle Buys Datalogix Creates the World's Most Valuable Data Cloud to Maximize the Power of Digital Marketing. Company presentation, January 23. www.oracle.com/us/corporate/acquisitions/datalogix/general-presentation-2395307.pdf.

Oracle (2016) Oracle Data Cloud. *The Data Source Magazine*, Issue No. 3, Fall 2016, https://cloud.oracle.com/opc/saas/resources/the-data-source-magazine-fall-2016.pdf.

Panzarino, M. (2011) Facebook Introduces Radical New Profile Design Called Timeline: The story of your life. *The Next Web*, September 22, http://thenextweb.com/facebook/2011/09/22/facebook-introduces-timeline-the-story-of-your-life/.

Pariser, E. (2011) *The Filter Bubble: What the internet is hiding from you*. New York: Penguin Press.

Perry, W. L., McInnis, B., Price, C. C., Smith, S. and Hollywood, J. S. (2013) *Predictive Policing: The role of crime forecasting in law enforcement operations*. RAND Cooperation: Santa Monica, CA, USA. www.rand.org/pubs/research_reports/RR233.

Poster, M. (1990) *The Mode of Information*. Chicago: University of Chicago Press.

Prabhakar, S., Pankanti, S. and Jain, A. K. (2003) Biometric Recognition: Security and privacy concerns. *IEEE Security and Privacy*, 99(2): 33–42.

Raab, C. D. and Wright, D. (2012) Surveillance: Extending the limits of privacy impact assessment. In Wright, D. and De Hert, P. (eds.), *Privacy Impact Assessment*. Dordrecht: Springer, 363–383.

Reardon, S. (2012) FBI Launches $1 Billion Face Recognition Project. *New Scientist*, September 7, www.newscientist.com/article/mg21528804-200-fbi-launches-1-billion-face-recognition-project/.

Ricoeur, P. (1992) *Oneself as Another*. (Translated by Kathleen Blamey). Chicago: University of Chicago Press.

Ruddick, G. (2016) Admiral to Price Car Insurance Based on Facebook Posts. *Guardian*, November 2, www.theguardian.com/technology/2016/nov/02/admiral-to-price-car-insurance-based-on-facebook-posts.

Rundle, M., Blakley, B., Broberg, J., Nadalin, A., Olds, D., Ruddy, M., Guimarares, M. T. M. and Trevithick, P. (2008) At a Crossroads: "Personhood" and digital identity in the information society. *STI Working paper* 2007/7, no. JT03241547 29-Feb-2008, Directorate for Science, Technology and Industry, OECD Publishing. www.oecd.org/dataoecd/31/6/40204773.doc.

Sartre, J. P. (2014) *Das Sein und das Nichts. Versuch einer phänomenologischen Ontologie*. 18. Auflage Januar 2014 (Original 1943). Hamburg: Rowohlt.

Sayer, P. (2013) Fujitsu Names Unicredit as First European Customer for Palm-Scan Authentication. *NetworkWorld*, March 4, www.networkworld.com/article/2164100/byod/fujitsu-names-unicredit-as-first-european-customer-for-palm-scan-authentication.html.

Schneier, B. (2006b) No-Fly List. *Schneier on Security*, October 6, www.schneier.com/blog/archives/2006/10/nofly_list.html.

Schneier, B. (2006a) The Eternal Value of Privacy. Published in *Wired*, May 18, *Schneier on Security*. www.schneier.com/essays/archives/2006/05/the_eternal_value_of.html.

Schrittwieser, S., Kieseberg, P., Echizen, I., Wohlgemuth, S., Sonehara, N. and Weippl, E. (2011) An Algorithm for k-Anonymity-Based Fingerprinting. In Y. Q. Shi, H. J. Kim and F. Perez-Gonzalez (eds.), *Proceedings of the 10th International Conference on Digital-Forensics and Watermarking—IWDW, LCNS 7128*. Heidelberg: Springer, 439–452. www.sba-research.org/wp-content/uploads/publications/k_anonymity_algorithm_2011.pdf.

Shapiro, S. (2005) Agency Theory. *Annual Review of Sociology*, 31: 263–284. www.annualreviews.org/doi/abs/10.1146/annurev.soc.31.041304.122159.

Sharif, M., Bhagavatula, S., Bauer, L. and Reiter, M. K. (2016) Accessorize to a Crime: Real and stealthy attacks on state-of-the-art face recognition. In *Proceedings of the 2016 ACM SIGSAC Conference on Computer and Communications Security, October 24–28, Vienna, Austria*, 1528–1540. www.cs.cmu.edu/~sbhagava/papers/face-rec-ccs16.pdf.

Shirky, C. (2009) A Speculative Post on the Idea of Algorithmic Authority. *Blogpost*, November 15, www.shirky.com/weblog/2009/11/a-speculative-post-on-the-idea-of-algorithmic-authority/.

Skinner, J. (2012) Social Media and Revolution: The Arab Spring and the Occupy movement as seen through three information studies paradigms. *Sprouts Working Papers on Information Systems* 483. http://aisel.aisnet.org/cgi/viewcontent.cgi?article=1482&context=sprouts_all.

Solove, D. J. (2004) *The Digital Person: Technology and privacy in the information age.* New York and London: New York University Press.

Solove, D. J. (2011) *Nothing to Hide: The false tradeoff between privacy and security.* New Haven/London: Yale University Press.

Spiekermann, S., Acquisti, A., Böhme, R. and Hui, K. L. (2015) The Challenges of Personal Data Markets and Privacy. *Electronic Markets* 25(2): 161–167.

Stanton, J. M. (2008) ICAO and the Biometric RFID Passport: History and analysis. In Bennett, C. J., Lyon, D. (eds.), *Playing the Identity Card: Surveillance, security and identification in global perspective.* London/New York: Routledge, 253–267.

Stiglitz, J. E. (2002) Information and the Change in the Paradigm in Economics. *The American Economic Review*, 92(3): 460–501.

Storm, D. (2015) ACLU: Orwellian Citizen Score, China's Credit Score System, Is a Warning for Americans. *Computerworld*, October 7, www.computerworld.com/article/ 2990203/security/aclu-orwellian-citizen-score-chinas-credit-score-system-is-a-warning- for-americans.html.

Strauß, S. (2011) The Limits of Control: (Governmental) identity management from a privacy perspective. In Fischer-Hübner, S. Duquenoy, P., Hansen, M., Leenes, R. and Zhang, G. (eds.), *Privacy and Identity Management for Life, 6th IFIP/PrimeLife International Summer School, Helsingborg, Sweden, August 2–6 2010, Revised Selected Papers.* Dordrecht: Springer, 206–218.

Strauß, S. (2015a) Datafication and the Seductive Power of Uncertainty: A critical exploration of big data enthusiasm. *Information*, 6: 836–847. www.mdpi.com/2078- 2489/6/4/836/pdf.

Strauß, S. (2015b) *Citizen Summits on Privacy, Security and Surveillance: Synthesis report. Deliverable 6.10 of the SurPRISE project.* http://surprise-project.eu/wp-content/ uploads/2015/02/SurPRISE-D6.10-Synthesis-report.pdf.

Strauß, S. (2017a) A Game of Hide and Seek? Unscrambling the trade-off between privacy and security. In Friedewald, M., Burgess, P. J., Čas, J., Bellanova, R. and Peissl, W. (eds.), *Surveillance, Privacy, and Security: Citizens' perspectives.* London/ New York: Routledge, 255–272.

Strauß, S. (2017b) Privacy Analysis: Privacy impact assessment. In Hansson, S. O. (ed.), *The Ethics of Technology: Methods and approaches.* London/New York: Rowman & Littlefield International, 143–156.

Strauß, S. (2018) Big data: Within the tides of securitisation? In Saetnan, A. R., Schneider, I and Green, N. (eds.), *The Politics of Big Data: Big data, big brother?.* Oxon: Routledge, 46–67.

Strauß, S. and Aichholzer, G. (2010) National Electronic Identity Management: The challenge of a citizen-centric approach beyond technical design. *International Journal on Advances in Intelligent Systems*, 3(1/2): 12–23.

Strauß, S. and Nentwich, M. (2013) Social Network Sites, Privacy and the Blurring Boundary Between Public and Private Spaces. *Science and Public Policy* 40(6): 724–732.

Sweeney, L. (2002) k-anonymity: A model for protecting privacy. *International Journal on Uncertainty, Fuzziness and Knowledge-based Systems*, 10(5): 557–570. https://epic. org/privacy/reidentification/Sweeney_Article.pdf.

Taigman, Y., Yang, M., Ranzato, M. A. and Wolf, L. (2014) DeepFace: Closing the gap to human-level performance in face verification. *Facebook Research*, June 24, https:// research.facebook.com/publications/480567225376225/deepface-closing-the-gap-to- human-level-performance-in-face-verification/.

Travis, A. (2009) Innocent Suspects' Profiles Still Reaching DNA Database. *Guardian*, October 28, www.guardian.co.uk/politics/2009/oct/28/dna-database-innocent-profiles.

Vaas, L. (2013) Nordstrom Tracking Customer Movement Via Smartphones' Wifi Sniffing. *Naked Security*, May 9, https://nakedsecurity.sophos.com/2013/05/09/nordstrom-tracking-customer-smartphones-wifi-sniffing/.

Van Dijk, J. (2014) Datafication, Dataism and Dataveillance: Big data between scientific paradigm and ideology. *Surveillance and Society*, 12(2): 197–208.

WEF—World Economic Forum (2015) Addressing Barriers to Digital Trade. E15 Expert Group on the Digital Economy—Strengthening the global trade and investment system for sustainable development, Think piece, December 2015. Cologne/Geneva: World Economic Forum. http://e15initiative.org/wp-content/uploads/2015/09/E15-Digital-Ahmed-and-Aldonas-Final.pdf

Westin, A. (1967) *Privacy and Freedom*. New York: Atheneum.

White, H. C. (2008) *Identity and Control: How social formations emerge* (second edition). Princeton/Oxford: Princeton University Press.

Whitley, E. A., Gal, U. and Kjaergaard, A. (2014) Who Do You Think You Are? A review of the complex interplay between information systems, identification and identity. *European Journal of Information Systems*, 23(1): 17–35.

Whitley, E. and Hosein, G. (2010) *Global Challenges for Identity Policies*. London: Palgrave Macmillan.

Wiener, N. (1954) *The Human Use of Human Beings: Cybernetics and society*. (First published 1950, reprint of revised edition of 1954). Boston: Da Capo Press.

Wilson, C. (2010) *Biometric Modalities. Vein Pattern Recognition: A privacy-enhancing biometric.* C. Wilson, New York: CRC Press.

Wondracek, G., Holz, T., Kirda, E. and Kruegel, C. (2010) A Practical Attack to De-anonymize Social Network Users. In *IEEE Symposium on Security and Privacy (SP), Washington D.C.*, 223–238. doi: 10.1109/SP.2010.21 www.syssec.rub.de/media/emma/veroeffentlichungen/2011/06/07/deanonymizeSN-Oakland10.pdf.

Woodman, S. (2017) Palantir Provides the Engine for Donald Trump's Deportation Machine. *The Intercept*, March 2, https://theintercept.com/2017/03/02/palantir-provides-the-engine-for-donald-trumps-deportation-machine/.

Wright, D. and Kreissl, R. (eds.) (2015) *Surveillance in Europe*. London/New York: Routledge.

Wright, D., Rodrigues, R., Raab, C., Jones, R., Székely, I., Ball, K., Bellanova, R. and Bergersen, S. (2015) Questioning Surveillance. *Computer Law and Security Review*, 31(2): 280–292.

York, J. C. (2016) Censorship on Social Media: 2016 in review. *EFF: Electronic Frontier Foundation*, December 24, www.eff.org/de/deeplinks/2016/12/censorship-social-media-2016-review.

ZDNet (2013) PRISM: Here's how the NSA wiretapped the internet. *ZDNET*, June 8, www.zdnet.com/article/prism-heres-how-the-nsa-wiretapped-the-internet/.

6 How to regain control?

Assessing privacy by design and privacy impact assessment

The previous chapters dealt with the emergence of digital identification and its complex mechanisms as well as socio-technically amplified identifiability being a core problem of contemporary privacy protection. As shown, this problem is involved in a privacy control dilemma of digital identification. This dilemma is accompanied by information asymmetries at the cost of individual privacy and ISD. Hence, the boundary control function of privacy is significantly hampered by uncontrolled flows of identifiable information and diminishing informational boundaries between different socio-technical systems. To ease this situation, fostering instruments of privacy control is in all ways crucial. There is thus particular need for privacy-enhancing technologies, privacy by design (PbD) approaches and privacy impact assessment (PIA). But what are the current options to implement these instruments and to what extent are PbD and PIA interrelated? This chapter seeks answers to these questions by assessing current approaches related to PbD and PIA. First, the prospects and perils of PbD in tackling the problem of identifiability and uncontrolled identity information are discussed. This is followed by a discussion on the limits of user control. As shown, besides technical issues, there are trends toward what I call a "privatization of privacy", which seriously hampers privacy protection. Overall, there is demand for better knowledge about the flows of identifiable information and thus approaches to assess privacy impacts. Therefore, the basic functions, scope and limits of PIA are examined in the subsequent sections. This includes a discussion on existing approaches to grasp the different dimensions of privacy and privacy-affecting activities.

Prospects and perils of privacy by design

The rapid growth of ICTs and digitally networked technology in general reinforced the demand for approaches to make technology privacy-friendly. PbD is thus often mentioned as crucial a means to improve the quality of privacy and data protection in relation to the use of digital technology. But what does PbD actually mean, and how promising is it as an antidote to identifiability by default inherent to technology design, ever-expanding identity shadows and increasing identifiability? These issues are discussed in the following.

PbD can be understood as an attempt to entrench privacy-friendly technology development and use in the informational ecosystem (Rubinstein 2011; Cavoukian 2012a/2012b; Cavoukian *et al.* 2014; Danezis *et al.* 2014). Although approaches for so-called privacy-enhancing technologies (PETs) have existed for several years, they are as-yet used in niches but not on a larger scale. PbD aims to stimulate PET development and usage as well as to ensure that technology is by default equipped with privacy-preserving mechanisms (Rubinstein 2011). It concerns the implementation of mechanisms to safeguard privacy as a built-in feature of technology. However, it is less of a technical approach and more a broad concept that embraces PETs and carries forward its approach to organizational handling of personal information.

According to Cavoukian[1] (2012a: 3ff.) there are seven foundational principles of PbD:

1 proactive not reactive, and preventive not remedial, meaning that privacy protection is to be proactively considered and implemented in advance to reduce risks and not just when a risk or breach occurs
2 privacy as the default setting, i.e., the standard mode of technology should be to protect privacy and not to disclose personal information
3 privacy embedded into design, i.e., as an activated, built-in feature of information systems and practices
4 full functionality—positive-sum, not zero-sum, i.e., dichotomized views and constructed trade-offs such as privacy versus security should be avoided as far as possible so that both issues are seen as equally relevant for system functionality, which also implies that PbD is not to be implemented in a way that hampers the functionality of a system
5 end-to-end security life-cycle protection, i.e., a consistent protection of personal information at all processing stages from collection, use and storage to erasure of information
6 visibility and transparency, so that information processing is comprehensible and it is verifiable whether privacy is respected
7 user centricity, i.e., respect for individual user privacy so that privacy protection is designed in a user-friendly way where the user and her personal information are understood as central parts of the system.

A central aim of PbD is to make privacy protection a standard feature of every technology. However, as the outlined general principles also indicate, the PbD concept is rather a broad organizational guideline. Therefore, it does not provide detailed technical requirements to improve privacy protection. Privacy engineers criticized this issue as it hampers the development of effective technical PbD approaches (Gürses *et al.* 2011). Cavoukian (2012b) advocates broadness of PbD because different organizations may have different specific requirements for privacy protection. While this seems plausible, the concept as such could at least refer to common privacy principles and standards which are largely accepted; such as the fair information practices of the OECD (OECD 2013). Gürses *et al.*

(2011) argue that the principle of data minimization in particular is an essential requirement for PbD. This is particularly relevant in times where big data and similar developments boost the permanent availability and processing of information. A counter-paradigm that highlights the positive effects of vanishing information is thus important to re-balance the privacy discourse. Privacy-by-default settings could contribute a lot in this regard, though these are not very widespread at the moment. Although most applications have privacy settings, they are often set to full and permanent information disclosure by default. This is highly counterproductive for privacy protection. A change of this common practice with privacy standards by design contributes a lot to avoiding unintended information disclosure and thus identifiability. But what are the factual possibilities of implementing PbD concepts and reducing the risks of identifiability? In order to make the broad concept of PbD more tangible, this question is discussed in the following, based on some examples of privacy-friendly tools and concepts.

Inspecting the general toolbox of privacy enhancement

Basically, there is a diverse range of PbD-related approaches and privacy-enhancing tools addressing privacy issues in various domains. For instance, many Web browsers have "do not track" features or can be equipped with plugins or add-ons to limit advertising, user tracking, etc. Common examples are, e.g., Adblock Plus, BetterPrivacy, Facebook Blocker, Ghostery, NoScript, TrackMeNot, and many more. There are also some privacy-friendly search engines (e.g., Startpage.com, Duckduckgo.com) and SNS (e.g., Diaspora—diasporafoundation.org). Akin to Web browsers, e-mail clients can also be equipped with specific privacy add-ons, such as for e-mail encryption (e.g., Pretty Good Privacy—PGP or openpgp.org). Anonymous mail clients allow the sending and receiving of e-mails without the need to prove one's identity to a mail provider (e.g., Hushmail.com). Privacy-friendly online messengers with encryption features (e.g., Signal, crypto.cat) protect communication content; encrypted cloud services (e.g., Spideroak) provide privacy-friendly file sharing; and there are several anonymization services (e.g., proxy servers or anonymization tools such as JonDonym,[2] or the Tor network) up to privacy-friendly operating systems (e.g., Tails), to name just a few. Despite this rich privacy toolbox there are certain limits with respect to PbD. These as well as other tools often serve very specific purposes for privacy-aware, skilled users. Consequently, less-experienced users have limited options to benefit from them. Moreover, in most cases, a tool covers only one specific aspect. There is a lack of combined concepts in the sense of a broad implementation of PbD, not least as the use of privacy tools in general is the responsibility of individual users and not, as PbD intends, the responsibility of institutional actors, producing technology and/or processing personal information. Nevertheless, a closer look at the basic features of privacy tools helps to shed light on the technical options and concepts to effectively protect identity information. These options can then be seen as basic requirements for PbD to be implemented at institutional level.

In fact, there are several technical options for PbD to achieve data minimization to reduce identifiability. This particularly concerns the implementation of anonymity and de-identification, pseudonymity and unlinkability (Chaum 1985; Pfitzmann and Hansen 2010; Cavoukian 2012a/2012b; Danezis *et al.* 2014). For anonymization and de-identification techniques, the concept of k-anonymity is essential, which means that a set of information is indistinguishable from at least k−1 other information sets to be anonymous (Sweeney 2002). Enhanced approaches are l-diversity and t-closeness, which aim to increase the degree of anonymity with greater diversity and less accuracy of data properties (Li *et al.* 2007; Machanavajjhala *et al.* 2007). A further, relatively novel concept is differential privacy, which uses noisy data to normalize information and thus reduce identifiability (Dwork and Roth 2014). An important basis of all these different approaches is the aim to decrease the applicability of information for identification; e.g., by erasing, masking or obfuscating identifiers or parts of identifiable information, grouping values, or adding noise to increase information ambiguity. One option is to reduce the temporal availability of information; for instance, by implementing the idea of an expiration date for digital information in technical systems.[3] This can be an in-built mechanism to partially or completely erase information which is not permanently required after a certain period of time (e.g., communication content), an automatic revocation of information access for external users, or a randomly changing identifier. In many contexts, though, a complete erasure of information is neither feasible nor of practical use. Therefore, mechanisms to remove parts of identifiable information are crucial. With such mechanisms, the functionality of a technology or application can be kept while the risk of unintended information disclosure is reduced, at least to some extent.

A very simple example is a dynamic IP address, which randomly changes. This can help to avoid a person being permanently traced on the internet by the same address. Another simple, related example concerns the storage setting of web-cookies which are often persistently stored or with an expiration date lying decades in the future. Modern Web browsers enable users to decide whether cookies are treated as session cookies, which expire with the session they refer to, and are then automatically deleted. This simple feature is a low-level example of an expiration date. But there are also more-sophisticated technical approaches with incorporated expiration dates available: an early approach was the software Vanish, which combined bit-torrent technology with cryptographic techniques to equip data with a mechanism to self-destruction (Geambasu *et al.* 2009). Although Vanish had several flaws and was itself vulnerable to attacks as, e.g., Wolchok *et al.* (2010) demonstrated, the approach as such can be useful in many respects. A more recent example of a similar mechanism can be found in the popular instant messenger app Snapchat, with an in-built feature of automatic deletion of messages within a defined period of time. However, this does not sufficiently prevent from third-party access to user content as, e.g., pointed out in a study on encryption and human rights protection (AI 2016). Other messengers with similar approaches are Telegram and Signal, which offer more security and privacy features than Snapchat (ibid.). A further principle to limit temporal availability of information is applied in the concept of so-called "perfect forward secrecy" (e.g., Greenberg 2016a). Systems with perfect forward secrecy frequently change the keys used to encrypt and decrypt information (Krawczyk 2005). This improves information security and privacy, because even with a compromised key, an attacker can only gather a small piece of information, e.g., of a chat, phone conversation or of an online service.

Fundamental to implementing information security and privacy is the methodological toolkit of cryptography. It offers a variety of protection mechanisms and is thus very promising for PbD in accordance with the previously outlined concepts. Cryptographic functions can be used in manifold ways to encrypt content and safeguard or anonymize information. There are different options to implement encryption with a basic difference between asymmetric techniques using only one encryption key and the more common (and more secure) symmetric encryption methods using public and private key-pairs. A specific form of the latter are methods based on so-called elliptic curves (for details, e.g., Menezes *et al.* 1996). Encryption has always been essential for information security and privacy. But since the Snowden revelations, it has gained in popularity (e.g., Kuchler 2014; Finley 2014). The encryption of content is a typical application of cryptography in order to keep information and communication confidential. This can be, e.g., achieved by cryptographic hash functions, which are a very common security practice. A hash function inter alia enables confidential storage of information without knowing its meaning. This practice is basically used to protect passwords from abuse, since they are not stored directly as plain text but only as a hash value. The same principle can be used to protect personal information, e.g., by avoiding direct use of identifiers and storing only their hash values instead. This can help to reduce the identifying capacity of an information set and improve unlinkability. However, a hash value itself is mostly unique (akin to a pseudonym). Therefore, it can also be misused to breach security and infringe on privacy. For example, the hash value of a password and the username can be sufficient for an attacker to gain access to a user account. Besides that, hash functions can be vulnerable to so-called collision attacks (e.g., Klíma 2005; Preneel 2005), which attempt to find an identical hash value to undermine protection. A prominent, classic example of content encryption is the software PGP,[4] originally developed by Phil Zimmermann in order to empower individuals in their right to privacy.[5] PGP is based on symmetric encryption (using a public and a private key) and became relatively widespread in the crypto-community. Today, there are several variants available (such as the open source software OpenPGP or GNUPG[6]) as well as add-ons for e-mail clients (e.g., Enigmail for Thunderbird[7]). PGP is just one among many examples of content encryption. Further examples are encrypted instant messengers or cloud services, as mentioned above. Basically, different forms of encryption features can be integrated into all kinds of ICTs.

A prominent example of an anonymization tool making use of cryptography is the Tor project,[8] which develops software to protect privacy and anonymity online. Tor is well known among privacy and security experts and recommended by civil rights organizations such as the EFF (Electronic Frontier Foundation). Its core piece is the Tor browser, making use of a dynamic network of servers which avoids direct connections by applying randomly changing, encrypted links. This approach called onion routing allows private network paths to be used, to increase security of data transmission and to improve anonymity when accessing the internet. The Tor network provides alternative servers to avoid direct connections between a user's computer and webservers, e.g., visited websites. This enables the use of an alternative IP address to the original one when browsing through the Web. Consequently, a user cannot be directly tracked via the IP address of her device. However, a user can be still identified and tracked via Web browser data. To reduce this risk and protect from online tracking, the Tor browser provides private browsing as an integrative feature (e.g., by blocking cookies and other tracking technologies). Besides these practical examples, there are further, as-yet experimental approaches to implement homomorphic[9] encryption schemes (such as Enigma[10] or Ethereum[11]) by employing blockchain[12] technology in order to protect personal information by applying decentralized, cryptographic data structures. The basic idea is to set up decentralized technical architectures to avoid a concentration of power and control by a single party. In this regard it aims to establish a technical approach to foster checks and balances of a decentralized mode of governance (Zyskind *et al.* 2015). These and similar concepts are somewhat promising, for example, to ease technical privacy problems in the realm of big data and cloud computing.

As shown, there is basically a broad scope of technical approaches and developments facilitating PbD. As every approach obviously has advantages and disadvantages it is crucial that PbD is implemented consistently and not in an occasional, arbitrary manner. Otherwise, it offers only marginal protection. To achieve a thorough PbD implementation, it is important to understand what protecting privacy basically means. Irrespective of their peculiarities and differences, PbD approaches ideally share a common foundation as regards the mechanism of protection: they feature protection mechanisms so that identifiable information cannot easily and seamlessly flow from one application context or information system to another. As outlined in the previous chapter, the aspect of friction in the information flow is crucial in order to come toward effective technical protection mechanisms providing unlinkability. Hence, from a systemic perspective, PbD can be understood as an attempt to foster the boundary control function of privacy by providing mechanisms and creating frictions in the information flow which can result in a decoupling of different information systems. Conceptually, cryptography provides the same mechanism and creates such informational frictions because encrypted information is not interpretable without decryption. In this regard, encrypted information is equipped with an inherent friction. The tools mentioned exemplify this: Tor, e.g., creates informational frictions by applying the onion-routing technique, where Internet traffic is distributed across a randomized mix of cascading servers. One result is that direct connections between user clients and visited servers are avoided so that users cannot be easily traced by visited websites. A further example is the encrypted online messenger Signal. Besides encryption of communication content, it blocks inter alia the creation of screenshots (Greenberg 2016b). This is because a screenshot could be taken when the sender or the receiver reads a decrypted message. The result is a friction protecting from visual privacy intrusion of a text-based application which, otherwise, could undermine the content encryption feature. Put more generally, this approach reduces the options to gather and represent information processed by the application with alternative forms of representation (here visualization). Or in other words: this feature creates a friction or boundary between the intended contextual layer (secure messaging between specific parties) and a non-intended further contextual layer (visual information gathering by an additional third party) to improve the security of the tool. Another approach to create frictions is sandboxing, as, e.g., employed in the recent version of the Tor browser.[13] Sandboxing is a technique of computer security to decouple different processes from each other so that, e.g., malware cannot easily intrude into a running application (Prevelakis and Spinellis 2001). It is a form of virtualization which allows the creation of virtual hard- and software environments. Approaches of this kind are promising to achieve higher information security and establish informational frictions. This aspect of informational frictions and systemic boundaries between different application contexts is essential to improve the conceptual understanding of privacy protection and thus also for the development of more effective safeguards.

Identity management: friend or foe to privacy by design?

As the uncontrolled handling of identity information is among the core problems of privacy, an important question is to what extent identity management (IDM) can contribute to PbD. Theoretically, IDM has some potential here and is discussed as a privacy-enhancing approach by some scholars (e.g., Hansen *et al.* 2004; Jøsang *et al.* 2007; Leenes *et al.* 2008; Nauman and Hobgen 2009; Danezis *et al.* 2014). This potential relates to the possibilities of incorporating basic PbD mechanisms and requirements (as discussed earlier). A general requirement for privacy-enhancing IDM is user centricity, i.e., the provision of controls to support users in handling their information. However, there are some serious problems that complicate coming toward privacy-enhancing IDM. First of all, maximum anonymity and data minimization are the primary aims of protecting privacy. However, there are many cases where this is neither feasible nor practicable in the case of IDM. A partial solution would be to at least integrate features enabling anonymous and pseudonymous user sessions in services wherever possible. Currently, there is a clear lack of IDM approaches in this regard. For cases that require the processing of some identifiable information, IDM can be used to standardize user identification and authentication. This can contribute to improving information security and thus raising the level of protection of an application or system. However, the level of protection depends heavily on the IDM architecture and implementation. There are four general IDM architecture models: siloed (or isolated), centralized, federated and user-centric (Bhargav-Spantzel *et al.* 2007; Jøsang *et al.* 2007; Rundle *et al.* 2008; Strauß and Aichholzer 2010). In a siloed system, information processing is separated from other systems and therefore information cannot be easily linked over different domains. This separation provides unlinkability and is important for privacy protection (as outlined previously and in Chapter 3). However, a siloed approach complicates information exchange with other systems, which may not satisfy the needs of efficient information processing. In contrast to a siloed approach, a centralized system stores all personal data in one repository (a database) handled by a central entity or provider. Service providers can integrate this central repository into their applications. Here, user authentication can be handled over one centralized account, which offers more convenience than, e.g., a siloed system. However, users are completely dependent on the central provider and a centralized system entails high risks for privacy and security, because all personal information is centrally accessible. The federated model combines the siloed and centralized approaches. Identity information is managed by a central identity provider (IdP) that acts as an intermediary between the user and different applications. This federation enables a single account to be included for user authentication into multiple applications. The benefit is more convenience and fewer privacy risks than with centralization, as an IdP usually provides identifiers but does not process all personal information. However, the IdP has the knowledge about all unique identifiers and usage contexts of a specific person, which enables profiling and thus privacy infringement. Therefore, reliability, accountability and trustworthiness of the IdP are crucial issues in a federated model. The user-centric model tries to reduce the problems of a centralized IdP by offering the user more control. Here, users do not have to fully rely on a central IdP but can select one or more different IdPs, and thus have at least some choice whom to trust in processing her identity information. Depending on the concrete implementation, users can manage their (encrypted) identity information with a technical device (e.g., a smart card) that can be used for applications where identification and authentication are needed. This should foster user control and ISD. The flipside of the coin here is that users need advanced technical skills to handle their identity information and understand its processing in order to make informed decisions about its usage. Moreover, privacy and security problems remain as the involved providers still have deep insights into identity information and thus abuse is possible. Although this approach seems somewhat promising, there are a number of open issues also regarding its technical implementation to provide a solid mix of convenience, usability, security and effective privacy protection (see, e.g., Bhargav-Spantzel *et al.* 2007; Strauß and Aichholzer 2010). No approach, neither federated nor user-centric IDM models, provides sufficient mechanisms to safeguard information after it has been shared (e.g., among federation members or third parties). In each case, users have only marginal control over their information. The user-centric approach with the option to choose between multiple IdPs may overburden individual users and also bears risks of market concentration (De Andrade *et al.* 2013). Hence, overall, core problems of information asymmetries and issues of insufficient protection and user control remain.

In practice, IDM approaches often occur as hybrid forms with several characteristics of these different models. But, in general, there is a lack of approaches that effectively improve user control and privacy protection in the sense of PbD. The implementation of privacy-enhancing IDM implies a combination of privacy protection and authentication (Hansen *et al.* 2004), to foster the protection and controllability of identity information and thus reinforce ISD. Crucial requirements in this regard concern the implementation of PbD features where the incorporation of unlinkability is of particular relevance to provide anonymous and pseudonymous use and appropriate user control (Strauß 2011). However, these essential requirements for a privacy-enhancing IDM are most often not implemented in practice. This is observable in public and private sectors alike. The insufficiency of privacy protection of social-media-based IDM is obvious as users factually have no effective option to protect their privacy. But even in the government sector, where enormous efforts have been made to implement IDM systems for citizen identification there is a broad scope of different implementations with varying protection levels regarding privacy and security (Nauman and Hobgen 2009; Kubicek and Noack 2010; Strauß and Aichholzer 2010; Strauß 2011). A technical study on governmental eID systems in Europe pointed out that none of the examined approaches provided sufficient privacy safeguards (Nauman and Hobgen 2009). The study found that some systems even used unencrypted global identifiers (such as a social security number). Similar privacy issues were found by other studies as well (Sapelova and Jerman-Blažič 2014). But more-sophisticated approaches representing best practices of e-government were also criticized by experts; such as the Austrian and the German eIDMS. Each of these systems applies unlinkability concepts. The Austrian eIDMS is a sophisticated approach with a mix of federated and user-centric elements. It uses so-called sector-specific identifiers to provide unique identification in specific contexts or sectors (e.g., health or tax) but avoids that personal information, referring to the eID holder, being easily linked across different sectors. This solution provides some protection and higher levels of security compared to other approaches. However, the Austrian system was criticized for its complexity, lack of usability and insufficient privacy protection, as serious privacy problems remain. One aspect concerns the sector-specific identification, which in principle contributes to reducing the risk of linkability and profiling. But as one of the different sector-specific identifiers is involved in almost every usage context, this undermines the unlinkability concept as personal information can then be aggregated via this identifier (Strauß and Aichholzer 2010; Strauß 2011). Some may argue that these are design flaws which can be remedied. Indeed, the use of sector-specific identifiers provides a relatively solid level of protection. However, even a flawless approach is exposed to the core problem of the identity shadow, i.e., the existence of other possibilities to link information across different contexts by using "semi-identifying" information. Unlinkability is a very crucial privacy requirement. However, its implementation is ineffective when it only reduces linkability of direct identifiers and does not protect from linking other types of semi-identifying information.

A further critical issue concerns the notion of a core or universal identity incorporated in many IDM approaches aimed at facilitating identification based on quasi-centralization. Accordingly, IDM is then often seen as a means to provide "one identity per individual" (e.g., Waters 2004). This perception is common in technology development, where identity is seen as a generalizable, abstract representation of an entity and/or person (e.g., Glässer and Vajihollahi 2010). The basic idea is that the "core identity" of a person can be simply represented by a specific set of identifiers used in multiple application contexts. This assumed core identity is then represented by a digital artifact, a carrier device, an identity token, etc. aimed at standardizing identification procedures with some gains in security and efficiency of information processing. In general, it is a plausible intention to standardize identification procedures. However, the idea of a universal or core identity is reductionist and is in conflict with an (often neglected) fact: that there is no single universal identity because identity is a relational and dynamic concept. Identity is context-sensitive and, thus, every individual can have multiple (partial) identities in different contexts (see Chapter 3). IDM approaches neglecting this aspect cannot offer options of anonymous or pseudonymous usage and are thus not privacy-enhancing. Pfitzmann and Hansen (2010) highlight this aspect and define privacy-enhancing IDM as "managing various partial identities (usually denoted by pseudonyms) of an individual person, i.e., administration of identity attributes including the development and choice of the partial identity and pseudonym to be (re-)used in a specific context or role". This notion of IDM is essential to allow for unlinkablity. A lack of understanding and consideration of this issue obstructs effective privacy protection. An individual then has no real choice about which information to provide and no option other than revealing her (real) identity, which further reduces anonymity and thus is a problem rather than a solution in privacy protection.

A core-identity approach may be appropriate for some services (e.g., legally binding e-government and e-commerce transactions), where formal or hard identification is required and legally restricted. However, it is problematic for all kinds of services where identification is inappropriate or itself problematic from a privacy perspective (such as for information services). For example, unique identification and the disclosure of information such as full name, address, social security number, etc. may be appropriate for a particular e-government service where a transaction is involved. But it is completely inappropriate for a common online application (e.g., social media, browsing or searching the Web, etc.). Identification is often employed for plausible reasons, but, as shown, there are several tendencies to expand (digital) identification mechanisms, observable in various contexts. Trends to foster digital identification entail risks of function and mission creep, meaning here the incremental extension of identification resulting in a quasi-obligation for individuals to reveal their identities even in contexts where identification is not needed (Lyon 2009). Examples include intentions to combine different identification systems such as governmental

IDMS and social media, as mentioned in Chapter 4. The quasi-obligation for ID is partially conveyed by a "nothing to hide" logic (as discussed in previous parts of this book). Even though identification is necessary and important in many societal contexts, it is neither adequate nor necessary in every context. Moreover, anonymity used to be the standard case in most contexts of everyday life although there may be contrary trends. As this chapter has shown, IDM implementations are driven mainly by a complex mix of economic and security objectives. This securitization and economization of digital identification significantly hampers the implementation and use of privacy-friendly IDM systems. In line with the principle of data minimization, identification and identifiability have to be avoided as far as possible in order to reduce privacy risks. Consequently, in those contexts where identification is needed (e.g., in formal transactions), the processing of identity information requires contextual integrity in line with the principle of purpose binding. Hence, privacy-friendly IDM approaches require integrated features enabling anonymity and pseudonymity as well as protection from uncontrolled use of information. Otherwise, IDM bears certain risks to undermine privacy protection by even reinforcing identifiability.

The limits of user control

As shown, for PbD and effective privacy protection in general, user centricity and particularly user control are essential. However, there are several limits and barriers to achieving more control for users. Moreover, it is debatable whether enhancing user control alone is sufficient to effectively improve privacy protection. One issue among many here is that the proper technical implementation of PbD mechanisms can be very challenging for developers. Hence, even technical safeguards providing some control for users often lack in protecting from unintended, privacy-infringing identification and identity shadow exploitation. Some may think that better technical safeguards and more-sophisticated IDM concepts such as in the governmental domain could ease the situation. However, as shown, IDM entails a number of privacy risks and a (quasi-)centralized IDM layer would reinforce the risk that IDM is abused as a surveillance infrastructure (Rundle *et al.* 2008; Lyon 2009; Strauß 2011). Furthermore, even if an effective privacy-enhancing IDM system was available, its scope would be seriously limited if its proper usage was mostly the responsibility of the individual user alone. Certainly, encouraging individuals in the self-controlled handling of their information is crucial. But it is insufficient to merely equip technology with some user control mechanisms, which reduces PbD to a purely technical concept. One aspect concerns so-called security usability issues: when a system is too complex for the user and lacks in usability, this may undermine its protection concept. Several studies argue that users avoid IDM tools that are perceived as complex and inconvenient (Jøsang *et al.* 2007; Bhargav-Spantzel *et al.* 2007; Strauß and Aichholzer 2010). For instance, a comparative study on governmental IDM systems in Europe found that high system complexity is a great burden for citizens, which results in rather low usage rates (Kubicek and Noack

2010). Furthermore, the systems may improve the security for service providers but not for the individual users (ibid.). Hence, insufficient usability of IDM may undermine the information security and privacy of individual users, especially when the primary focus lies on the interests of the service providers. Consequently, individual users have limited options to protect their privacy.

Besides the technical challenges, crucial problems result from insufficient or ineffective privacy protection among institutional actors processing personal information. This refers to issues regarding information asymmetries and agency problems (as discussed in the previous chapters). These issues are observable in, inter alia, privacy settings and privacy policies, which underlines the limits of user control. Privacy settings basically enable users in customizing the processing of their personal information in technologies and applications. In this respect, they may be seen as simple, practical PbD examples. However, in most cases, these settings are very limited in scope and often lack in effective privacy protection for several reasons. A prominent example is Facebook, where users can customize their profiles and define, e.g., which information is available and which is private. While this is useful in general, it does not change the fact that Facebook itself as well as its many external partners exploit users' information and infringe upon their privacy. Figure 6.1 shows a comparison of Facebook's default privacy settings between 2005 and 2010.

The aim of privacy settings is to enable users in controlling the disclosure of their personal information. However, the standard setting already undermines this as the visualization demonstrates.[14] In its beginnings, Facebook provided at least a basic level of protection. With frequent updates of its privacy policy this has drastically changed. Access to personal information was limited in 2005 and mostly exclusive for direct contacts or members of the network (as the illustration

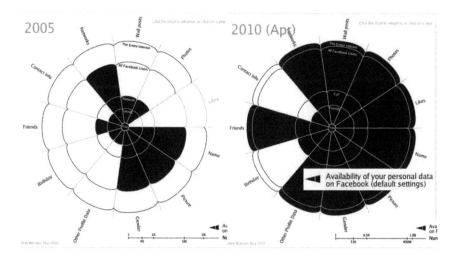

Figure 6.1 Facebook's default privacy setting over time.

Source: adapted from Matt McKeon 2010: http://mattmckeon.com/facebook-privacy.

shows with the inner circles). However, since 2010, no such limits exist anymore: since then, entities outside the social media environment can also access several parts of user information by default. Users who do not proactively change their privacy settings automatically disclose their profile information including contacts, photos, preferences, etc. Besides the high complexity of the settings users are confronted with, the option to reduce profile visibility in general is more "a quick fix than a systematic approach to protecting privacy" (Debatin and Lovejoy 2009: 103). Evidently, the situation for privacy did not improve over the years. Referring to another policy change, in 2013, the *New York Times* commented that "Facebook's new policies make clear that users are required to grant the company wide permission to use their personal information in advertising as a condition of using the service" (Goel and Wyatt 2013). In fact, even privacy-aware users have little chance of preventing their profile information from being exploited by third parties such as marketers, security agencies or other entities of the surveillant assemblage. That this is not just a theoretical risk to privacy is evident since the Cambridge Analytica scandal (Hern and Pegg 2018) and the recent data breach affecting over 50 million users (Solon 2018). Furthermore, there has been a growing number of data breaches observable on several large online platforms in the last few years on a global scale. Prominent examples are, e.g.:

- the compromised information of 77 million customers of the Sony PlayStation Network in 2011
- the as-yet biggest case of a security breach, affecting over 500 million user accounts of the Internet company Yahoo in 2014
- in 2016, Yahoo reported that about 1 billion accounts may already have been compromised in 2013
- the theft of 4 million customer records from a British telecom provider in 2015
- nearly 60 million customers of transport-sharing provider Uber were exposed to a cyber-attack in 2016
- a Facebook data breach affecting over 50 million users in 2018
- social network Google+ closed due to serious risks of data breach
- two million T-Mobile customers affected from data breach.

(Newman 2016; Dunn 2017)

These are just a few examples of a growing list of incidents.

Hence, Facebook is only a prominent example among many of the numerous problems individuals are confronted with when attempting to protect their privacy. A core problem of insufficient privacy controls results from socio-technical identifiability as demonstrated previously with the identity shadow. The identifiability-by-default setting inherent to many ICTs offers various ways to gather identity information. Accordingly, privacy policies make use of the insufficiency of privacy settings and reinforce identifiability. In theory, the primary aim of a privacy policy is to inform users about how their data is treated and how their privacy is respected. This relates to the privacy principle of transparency to enable users in comprehending the processing of their information (see also Chapter 3). However, in practice, this is mostly insufficient as privacy policies are often difficult to understand and instead provide general descriptions of the variety of ways in which a maximum of personal information is collected but not how privacy is protected. Service or application providers usually justify their extensive collections of user information with user experience and high quality of services. This is highlighted by major players on the Web like Google, Facebook and others, who gather large arrays of user information from their services as well as from all kinds of Web content where their services are involved. An excerpt from Google's privacy policy,[15] for instance, indicates the enormous magnitude of information collection:

> We collect information to provide better services to all of our users—from figuring out basic stuff like which language you speak, to more complex things like which ads you'll find most useful, the people who matter most to you online, or which YouTube videos you might like.

Information is collected in various ways, beginning with all the information provided by users such as name, e-mail address, phone number, credit card number; all the information of user profiles including name or nickname, photos, etc.; information from service usage including what is used, how, when and so forth; device-specific information including hardware model, software versions, unique identifiers; information from mobile usage such as phone number, device number, etc., which can be associated with a user account; also, from Google's privacy policy, "usage data and preferences, Gmail messages, G+ profile, photos, videos, browsing history, map searches, docs, or other Google-hosted content" is gathered and analyzed by automated systems. Similar to this is the case of search queries or online activities such as searching a restaurant on Google Maps or watching a YouTube video; information about the activity or content (search term, video, etc.) is processed as well as user location, device details, etc. Furthermore, besides cookies and log information, location information and unique application numbers, among others, are also collected, and tracking technologies (e.g., pixel tags) are used and may be stored on a user's computer or similar device. These technologies also enable partners of Google (such as online marketers) to process user information. Hence, put simply, individual identity shadows are exploited as much as possible. Similar information collection practices can be found in many other privacy policies as well. Users are confronted with complicated statements while at their core, privacy policies frequently declare that in many cases, maximum information is collected.

But how is this possible? The foundation for these extensive information collections lies in the concept of informed consent, which is a basic part of privacy and data protection laws (as outlined in Chapter 3). In most countries, collecting and processing of personal information for commercial self-purposes is legally prohibited and only allowed if the individual concerned agrees. Hence, service providers and other information processing entities have to ask their potential users for permission, which is obtained via the informed-consent mechanism. This idea of informed consent is crucial. However, the crux is that often user acceptance is constructed to legalize personal information processing, e.g., for commercial purposes. But individual users mostly have no other choice than to fully accept the privacy conditions, and thus the processing of their information irrespective of whether third parties are involved or not. In the case of dissent, the individual cannot use the service, application or technology. Options to partially agree are usually not foreseen, such as to allow a service used directly to process information but prohibit third-party access. Therefore, due to the lack of choice, informed consent often equals a "like it or lump it" approach as criticized by several privacy scholars (Nissenbaum 2010; De Andrade *et al.* 2013; Danezis *et al.* 2014; EGE 2014; Zuiderveen-Borgeswius 2016). All in all, informed consent thus often entails an enforced agreement to accept privacy intrusion with an inherent quasi-obligation to permit explicit or implicit identification.

Who is in charge? Privacy divides and the "privatization" of privacy

Against this background, privacy settings as well as more-sophisticated privacy control mechanisms are per se limited in scope. Further issues concern additional privacy tools or PETs. As shown, basically, there are a number of PETs available to support individuals in protecting their privacy. However, a general issue is that in many cases these tools are rather expert-centered and have a low familiarity among non-experts. Moreover, although usability has increased, usage often requires high privacy awareness and technical knowledge and entails a lot of effort. The classic problems of e-mail encryption tools like PGP, for instance, including high complexity for standard users, lack of convenience, awareness, no "real" use cases and thus low usage rates, still exist today (Ruoti *et al.* 2016). Thus, in fact, many privacy tools are still rather limited to a small group of experienced users. Furthermore, skilled users may also encounter several difficulties to achieve protection as the case of the anonymization software Tor highlights. Tor offers a relatively high level of protection but also has certain limits. One aspect concerns usability issues: basically, the Tor browser is easy to use, widely similar to a standard web browser. One of its peculiarities is default features restricting certain tracking features of websites (e.g., cookies, web bugs, embedded JavaScript, iframes, etc.) to enhance privacy protection. However, an unintended side-effect is that this can impair the functionality of websites. Although this is not an issue due to Tor design or usage but of insufficient design of several websites, it can complicate individual usability of privacy tools. Another aspect is that protection ends at a user's "final" destination. Several security researchers demonstrated certain risks of de-anonymization of Tor users. A major issue is the problem that exit nodes of the Tor network can be abused to spy on individual users (Le Blond *et al.* 2011; Sun *et al.* 2015). Nevertheless, Tor is a solid tool offering some protection from profiling and tracking in general, but not in specific contexts as user data can still be gathered from the

Web content a user interacts with. For instance, Tor provides few options to prevent social media platforms from exploiting user profiles or tracking user activities. Because as soon as, e.g., a user accesses her profile on an online platform with her user credentials (e.g., username, password), she becomes identifiable. Thus, even when using sophisticated privacy tools like Tor, situations can occur where users are confronted with the option to either accept privacy intrusion or avoid the use of platforms requiring identification. A further option is to use alternative platforms in addition to Tor such as the decentralized, privacy-friendly SNS Diaspora or Friendica,[16] PGP-based e-mail encryption and an encrypted cloud service (e.g., Spideroak). A combined approach provides additional protection but also increases the efforts of individual users. Moreover, privacy-friendly alternative services in general are rather niche applications with a very low number of users. For instance, compared to Facebook's about two billion users, Diaspora had less than 400,000 users in 2014.[17] This highlights the crux of PETs: low usage rates complicate interaction with people who do not use these services (e.g., sending an encrypted e-mail is ineffective if the receiver cannot decrypt it; the circle of friends active on Facebook is significantly higher than in Diaspora). Consequently, the lack of a critical mass of privacy-aware and skilled users also limits the scope of privacy-friendly approaches and hampers unfolding of their potential to strengthen privacy protection.

Their limited outreach is a general problem of privacy tools. Among others, Papacharissi and Gibson (2011) detected a particular form of digital divide, a privacy divide, between privacy haves and privacy have-nots in the context of SNS. Members of the former group are privacy-aware, have technical skills and are thus cautious in providing their personal information. Members of the latter, though, lack in privacy awareness as well as in computer literacy and thus carelessly disclose personal information. Moreover, with the predominating commercial processing of personal information "privacy gradually attains the characteristics of a luxury commodity" as "it becomes a good inaccessible to most … is disproportionately costly to the average individual's ability to acquire and retain it" (Papacharissi and Gibson 2011: 85). Furthermore, a lack of privacy protection can create a social disadvantage. This privacy divide is not limited to social media but is generally observable between privacy-aware and skilled users; i.e., those with the knowledge and ability to, e.g., use privacy tools and average users with a lack thereof. Moreover, another aspect is that privacy-aware individuals may experience social disadvantages precisely *because* they use PETs. There are tendencies among several providers to prevent users from employing privacy tools and creating user accounts without the provision of their real IDs. For instance, the registration of a free e-mail account without the need to provide valid identity information has become rather difficult. A number of free mail providers request real IDs or the provision of a phone number to double check the validity of a user account.[18]

From the providers' perspective, this measure is partially plausible as long as it aims to protect from abuse, spam, etc. and increase service security. However, from a privacy perspective, it is critical when the identity information processed by these measures is stored and used for additional purposes such as commercial profiling, etc., entailing further privacy intrusion. Basically, this information enriches the identity profiles a provider has about its users. Although some providers (e.g., Gmail) claim that the phone number is not shared for marketing purposes, third-party use is not excluded per se and may be a matter of purpose definition. Irrespective of their plausibility, measures like these also contribute to further constraints of online anonymity. That some providers perceive the use of privacy tools as a burden to their business models is, e.g., observable in the case of Facebook frequently trying to prevent the use of ad-blockers (e.g., Tynan 2016). Similar is observable with the increasing tendency of online newspapers to exclude users with ad-blockers. Also, the real-name policies of Internet companies are not just a security measure but are tied to economic interests as more-detailed user profiles are more valuable for marketers. Privacy-aware people who want to protect their personal information by, e.g., avoid revealing more information than necessary for service usage (e.g., their phone number or other additional identity information), in order to avoid tracking, spam and to protect their privacy, are excluded from usage.

Furthermore, some providers prevent users from accessing their services via anonymous networks such as the previously mentioned Tor network. The expression of political rights and prevention from political repression are strong drivers of Tor usage in repressive regimes and liberal democracies alike (Jardine 2016). It is evident that the use of privacy tools like Tor or the crypto-messenger Signal can be difficult in countries with problematic issues regarding human rights protection, where online activities are censored or constrained. For example, Bahrain, China, Egypt, Iran, Russia, Saudi Arabia and Turkey attempt to restrict or block these privacy tools (BBC 2016; Osborne 2016; McCarthy 2017). These blocking activities are particularly problematic in countries where regime critics, journalists, human rights activists, etc. may encounter repression and thus have high demand for PETs and anonymization tools. However, also in other countries, users may encounter difficulties when using PETs. For instance, some IP addresses from the Tor network are occasionally blocked by some internet service providers as well as online providers.[19] Some security agencies such as the FBI or the NSA claim that Tor and other anonymization networks are used mostly by criminals and terrorists (Ball *et al.* 2013; Froomkin 2015). This may be one reason why Tor users are classified as "extremists" by some NSA surveillance programs (Doctrow 2014). While Tor is used for criminal activities as well (McGoogan 2016), this does not change the fact that anonymization services are essential tools for non-criminal, privacy-aware individuals, human rights activists, journalists, security researchers and other sensitive professions alike. In this regard, there is a certain "Dark Web dilemma", which may be resolved with more cautious policing activities in the Dark Web to stem criminal activity (Jardine 2015). Mass surveillance of Tor and other privacy tools is highly critical from a human rights perspective. Hence, more promising are cooperative approaches, e.g., between Tor developers and law enforcement, to improve mutual understanding of the motives of privacy-aware users and law enforcement alike: developers of the Tor project cooperate with law enforcement to, e.g., offer training to enable better comprehension of the network.[20] This and similar measures can support law enforcement to target criminal activity without criminalizing the whole network and its users. A criminalization of Tor or other privacy tools as well as efforts to restrict them would harm human rights and (civil) society in many respects.

The cases presented and the tendencies to limit online anonymity and block privacy tools underline that there are many serious barriers for individuals in safeguarding their privacy. A particular problem occurs when PbD is reduced to a means of individual privacy control only, while the responsibility of information processing entities (e.g., public and private institutions) to protect privacy is neglected. This relates to an exaggerated focus on technical issues of user centricity and control. Besides technical issues, several conflicting interests complicate effective protection. From a wider perspective, agency problems between individuals and institutional entities become apparent. Hence, the uncontrolled processing of identity information is obviously not an issue merely of the individual but rather is an institutional problem. The general increase in identification practices results from a complex interplay of technological design and socio-political factors where securitization and economization of identification are among the core drivers of this development. The expansion of identification mechanisms is problematic because it entails an incremental increase in (quasi-) mandatory identification and thus a reduction in anonymity. Security agencies and law enforcement tend to see privacy tools providing anonymity as barriers to their work, and thus strengthen efforts to limit their use. Providers of online services aim to protect their services from abuse as well as have additional economic interests to foster identification and identifiability. Every interest as well as their entailed activities is plausible to some extent. However, privacy-affecting activities are often opaque, and lack in transparency and accountability. Therefore, it can be difficult to assess their factual plausibility as well as their legal and ethical justifications. Furthermore, there is a certain risk of what I call "privatization of privacy", i.e., where the responsibility to protect privacy is mainly shifted toward the individual concerned. As shown, there are several limits to avoiding unwanted information processing and reducing identifiability. Basically, it is barely possible for a single individual to manage her identity information in all the manifold contexts it is being processed.

As shown in Chapter 3, privacy is an individual human right but also a common good, i.e., a societal value of public interest, vital for democratic societies. This public or common value is at risk if privacy is reduced to a private value that is of individual concern only. As, e.g., Kahn (2003: 388) pointed out, individual control over privacy cannot be fully detached from social norms because such a separation would result in a fragmented society. While the aspect of individual control over privacy is basically essential, this does not necessarily imply that an individual alone carries the full responsibility that her identity information is not misused. On the contrary, social reality and practices of information processing make clear that this is neither applicable nor desirable.

The previously outlined privacy divides indicate a certain fragmentation in digital environments. However, the main problem is not a gap between privacy haves and have-nots but rather is a gap as regards the responsibility to protect privacy between individuals and institutions. A focus only on user centricity and user control is not sufficient to ease this situation; especially not when privacy is falsely reduced to a purely private issue.

Reasons for the reinforced tendency to "*privatize*" privacy can be derived from the traditional notion of privacy as the right to be let alone (Warren and Brandeis 1890), which emerged from ownership and property rights. This notion still plays an important role today. Warren and Brandeis (1890) inter alia argued that information about a person such as an image belongs to that person and is her property. They argued for privacy to be a stand-alone right disentangled from property rights (Kahn 2003). However, this classical framing of privacy lacks in considering it as a multidimensional concept and particularly its function as a public value (Nissenbaum 2010; Cohen 2012). Hence, privacy is not only a sort of "materialistic" good and matter of personal concern. However, if privacy is reduced in this regard, this may result in a paradox situation: individuals as original holders of their information entrust others to use their "property" by giving informed consent, which then often entails a loss of control over their information as they have no chance to avoid eventual further use. At the same time, they are overburdened with the responsibility to control their information to protect from misuse, which is often inconceivable. This is a little bit like a house holder entrusting a house keeper to take care of his home, who then sells all his belongings and blames the holder for not taking care of his home. This polemic scenario should point out that privacy protection cannot be effective when platform providers and institutions are not accountable for their activities. Currently, there is lack of accountability and responsible information processing with respect to privacy. This is reinforced by the dynamics of the digital economy where the free flow of (personal) information is framed as a core value, which feeds into commercial interests. In line with this logic, the gathering and processing of personal information is a (semi-automated) standard procedure of most ICTs and online services. In this framing, privacy is rather perceived as a burden. Consequently, the responsibility to protect privacy is forwarded to the individual user. At the same time, there is a lack of transparency of information processing and accountability of the involved entities, who neglect privacy responsibility.

Thus, from an individual's perspective, the privatization of privacy complicates effective protection of personal information and (digital) identity in many respects. As shown, there are some promising approaches in the realm of PbD. As economic interests are among the core drivers for privacy infringement, PbD bears potential to counteract this situation by creating and stimulating economic incentives to protect privacy. However, there is also a certain risk of a further privatization of privacy. User-centric PbD approaches and PETs are no panacea even for experienced users. A general burden results from the strong focus on technology and the often high complexity of technical solutions. Moreover, the problem is less a technical and more a societal one. While average users per se have little chance to remain anonymous in online environments, experienced, privacy-aware users have to face eventual discrimination because of their privacy affinity. Indeed, individuals have the main responsibility to protect their privacy. However, against the background of imbalanced control over identity information, increasing identification, information asymmetries between individuals and institutions, etc., there is very limited room for maneuver in this regard. Therefore, to compensate, insufficient privacy protection requires combined approaches to revitalize the public value of privacy. Crucial in this regard is shared responsibility between individuals and institutions, with particular focus on the latter. As regards technical approaches, this implies a need to improve PbD beyond some occasional control features. PbD is not limited to the provision of user control mechanisms but ideally is an approach to implement privacy safeguards with the main aim to minimize privacy intrusion by information processing institutions. Hence, a crucial requirement for effective PbD approaches is data minimization. More specifically, this implies a reduction of identifiability wherever possible. A central technical issue concerns the expanding identity shadow offering various methods of implicit identification which entail even more identifiability. These problems in particular are insufficiently addressed by PbD. The effectiveness of technical solutions is seriously impaired because of the enormous complexity of the problem and the entailed conflicting societal interests and practices. Particular issues are insufficient knowledge about the flows of identifiable information and control thereof, as information can be easily de- and re-contextualized. Hence, technical solutions alone are not sufficient to ease the problem. Instead there is a demand for socio-technical governance including organizational, regulatory and technical measures to compensate for information asymmetries resulting from identifiability. While user control is without doubt essential too, it is not sufficient to merely shift the responsibility to protect privacy to individuals. Therefore, there is a need to foster accountability and responsibility in information processing entities as regards the protection of privacy.

The crux is that the implementation of PbD can be challenging: engineers and developers need particular guidelines and requirements to design privacy-friendly technologies and applications; companies and other institutions taking their privacy responsibility seriously need detailed knowledge about the functioning of the information processes in their organizations including the employed technologies and applications. Although PbD principles and guidelines are generally useful, several scholars have criticized them for being too vague and thus difficult to consider for engineers (Gürses *et al.* 2011). One issue is that PbD requires privacy awareness at an organizational as well as individual level. Existing PbD guidelines are important to raise this awareness and stimulate the creation of a privacy-friendly culture, which is a precondition for the implementation of PbD. However, these guidelines address general management issues rather than more concrete organizational and technical requirements. The factual implementation needs to consider the peculiarities of a technology or application as well as of the organization applying them.

Assessing privacy impact assessment

As argued previously, a key issue to improve privacy protection is how to identify the basic requirements for PbD in general that apply to particular institutions as well. PIA is an instrument to identify these requirements which can support and stimulate the development of PbD. In this regard, it is a prerequisite for the informed implementation of PbD. In the longer run, both concepts—PIA and PbD—can mutually reinforce each other and contribute to creating a higher level of privacy protection standards. Therefore, a combined approach between both is essential. This also corresponds with the novel EU privacy regulation, where the complementarity of PIA and PbD is implicitly included. Article 25 of the GDPR regulates PbD (labeled data protection by design and by default): data controllers (entities who define the purpose of processing) are encouraged to

> implement appropriate technical and organizational measures, such as pseudonymization, which are designed to implement data-protection principles, such as data minimization, in an effective manner and to integrate the necessary safeguards into the processing in order to meet the requirements of this Regulation and protect the rights of data subjects.
>
> (Article 25 GDPR)

Among others, the implementation of these measures should take into account the "nature, scope, context and purposes of processing as well as the risks of varying likelihood and severity for rights and freedoms of natural persons posed by the processing" (Article 25 GDPR). Hence, the implementation of PbD requires proper knowledge of the scope and impacts of data processing, which refers to PIA as regulated in Article 35 GDPR, which encourages data controllers to "carry out an assessment of the impact of the envisaged processing operations on the protection of personal data" in advance of the processing. Therefore, PIA plays an important role in tackling many of the explored contemporary privacy problems, and is explored in more depth in the following.

To improve privacy protection, not just occasionally but to a greater extent, requires a combination of regulatory and socio-technical measures. Besides the technical barriers of complex solutions, a main problem results from the previously discussed trends toward a further "privatization" of privacy entailing a shift in responsibility to the individuals concerned. At the same time, agency problems remain and are aggravated, in particular when there is a lack of transparency and accountability among the entities processing and controlling identifiable information. As a consequence, the effective implementation of essential privacy requirements such as unlinkability is impeded. Therefore, enhancing transparency and accountability is crucial to ease the privacy control dilemma by compensating for, or at least reducing, information asymmetries resulting from uncontrolled identifiability. From a wider, systemic perspective, this implies making informational boundaries of socio-technical systems more transparent and verifiable. In this regard, PIA plays an essential role to improve the understanding of identity information processing conducted by institutions, and thus to raise their transparency and accountability. This is of utmost importance for the development of more effective PbD concepts. PIA and PbD are thus complementary and on the same side of the coin.

The initial aim of PIA is to examine the privacy impacts of socio-technical practices and check whether they are in accordance with privacy and data protection regulation. This does not necessarily imply detection of privacy violations but of potential risks thereof. However, technological progress challenges PIA in many respects as traditional approaches have a limited capability to grasp the privacy impacts of ICTs. Basically, PIA is a core instrument in the toolbox of data protection authorities (DPAs) and other privacy-protecting institutions. However, these institutions often have very limited resources and capacities to effectively enforce privacy and set counteractions in cases of privacy abuse or infringement (FRA 2010; Wright and Kreissl 2015; Strauß 2017). Furthermore, they need a legal mandate to become active and, until recently, there was no legal obligation at all (in Europe and in many other regions) for companies to conduct PIA or prove privacy compliance. The problem of limited effectiveness of DPAs and other oversight bodies to enforce privacy rights is not just an issue at the EU level but on a global scale. To ease the situation in Europe, the European data protection supervisor proposed the creation of a digital clearinghouse. This should stimulate the coherent enforcement of digital rights in the EU by fostering cooperation between national DPAs and other oversight bodies. The primary aim is to improve the protection of privacy in the age of big data. Among the planned activities of this institution is the assessment of impacts on digital rights and particularly on privacy (EDPS 2016). This proposal is one among several indicators about PIA being about to gain more importance. Until recently, it played a rather marginal role particularly in the European context. This is about to change especially with the still-ongoing European privacy reform which, among other things, aims to institutionalize PIA in the privacy and data protection regime. The GDPR (effective since May 2018) inter alia foresees a mandatory conducting of data protection impact assessments for public and private institutions under certain conditions, when specific risks occur as regards individual rights (Article 35: GDPR). As a consequence, businesses in particular have to deal more thoroughly with their information systems and their modalities of personal information processing. Against this background, an increasing relevance of PIA becomes apparent including the need for approaches facilitating the implementation of a PIA process.

As the requirements for PIA may vary in different institutions, it is difficult to develop a standard procedure applicable in multiple domains. However, irrespective of particular institutional settings, as shown, the emergence of a privacy impact is essentially affected by identifiability and the processing of identifiable information. Taking this aspect into consideration is thus important for every PIA process. An enhancement of PIA, with accordingly improved options to detect privacy risks and demand for protection, can support the development of more effective protection measures. More precisely, a perspective on privacy protection understood as protection of an information process, i.e., a flow of identifiable information, could contribute to gaining a more systemic framework of protection. In accordance with the boundary control function of privacy, such a systemic view on privacy enables systemic boundaries to be located. This allows better understanding of the extent to which privacy intrusion might occur. It thus can contribute to develop approaches for a decoupling of different but interwoven systems vital for more effective privacy protection. The basic premise here is that fostering the conceptual understanding of (socio-technical) identifiability contributes to enhancing the assessment of privacy impacts. As a consequence, (more) appropriate strategies and socio-technical mechanisms can be developed to reduce certain privacy risks, and comprehend and avoid unnecessary or unintended privacy intrusions.

The following sections present and discuss the main aspects of PIA, arguing for more emphasis on issues of identifiability understood as the main determinant of information processes with a privacy-intrusive capacity. The next section begins with a brief review on the role of PIA and existing concepts in this regard. As will be shown, existing PIA frameworks have certain limits and there is a need for more systematic approaches in order to deal with contemporary privacy challenges.

Basic functions and scope of privacy impact assessment approaches

According to Clarke (2009: 123), PIA is "a systematic process for evaluating the potential effects on privacy of a project, initiative or proposed system or scheme". Wright and De Hert (2012a: 5) define PIA broadly as

> a methodology for assessing the impacts on privacy of a project, policy, programme, service, product or other initiative which involves the processing of personal information and, in consultation with stakeholders, for taking remedial actions as necessary in order to avoid or minimize negative impacts.

Ideally, this process is not conducted *ex post* but *ex ante*, and is already involved in the development of a technology, application, etc., so that privacy and data protection issues can be detected early. PIA is thus a means to identify and assess potential effects and risks of information processing on privacy, which contributes to reducing corresponding vulnerabilities. This latter aspect refers to the development and implementation of PbD. For organizations, conducting a PIA can serve multiple aims: a primary aim is to verify whether the information processing of the organization is in compliance with privacy and data protection law. This verification can improve the trustworthiness of the organization in the public and the enhanced knowledge of its information processing can contribute to reducing costs and increasing efficiency (Strauß 2017). Overall, PIA can help to foster transparency and accountability of an organization, serving the organization, the individuals concerned in the information processing, as well as the wider public.

For several years, PIA has gained in importance on a global level. Interestingly, in countries like Canada, Australia and New Zealand, PIA has some tradition. In Australia, the first approaches to assess privacy impacts in the public sector date back to the 1990s (Bayley and Bennett 2012; Clarke 2012b; Wright and De Hert 2012b). Canada also started early and was among the first countries to consider PIA as an instrument of privacy policy which has been legally regulated and foreseen as mandatory for government agencies under certain conditions since 2002 (Bayley and Bennett 2012). In the US, the Internal Revenue Service issued a PIA model in 1996 and today also has some legal obligation for government agencies to conduct PIA (Wright and De Hert 2012b). In Europe, PIA as such has a relatively short history so far. This does not imply that the assessment of privacy impacts is less important in Europe. But in contrast to the Anglo-Saxon countries, there were no guidelines or conceptual models available before 2007, when the first PIA handbook was published in the UK. A reason for this is that, until recently, the term PIA[21] was not explicitly used in legal frameworks. However, a related concept is prior checking, which used to be more familiar in Europe. Article 20 of the EU Data Protection Directive 95/46/EC (DPD 1995) addresses prior checking and asks member states to determine processing operations that are likely to entail privacy risks and to examine these processing operations before their implementation. The task of prior checking is the main responsibility of national DPAs who check the legality of applications reported by the data processing entities (e.g., companies, organizations, etc.). In practice, as with PIA, this procedure varies significantly from country to country (Clarke 2009; Le Grand and Barrau 2012).

In 2009, PIA gained more attention in Europe as the EU Commission asked the member states for input into the development of a PIA framework for the deployment of RFID technology. The Article 29 Working Party[22] endorsed the RFID PIA framework in 2011. The EU Commission also announced plans to include PIA approaches in new legal frameworks on data protection (Wright and De Hert 2012b). In specific cases, conducting a PIA should be obligatory, "for instance, when sensitive data are being processed, or when the type of processing otherwise involves specific risks, in particular, when using specific technologies, mechanisms or procedures, including profiling or video surveillance" (EU-C 2010b: 12). The EU Commission enforced these plans and induced, inter alia, the creation of a task force with experts from the industry to develop a template for PIA in the context of smart grid and smart metering. This template intends to give guidance to smart grid operators or other stakeholders on how to perform an impact assessment for corresponding systems (SGTF 2014). Neither the template nor the performing of PIA is mandatory but with an official recommendation[23] published in 2014 the EU Commission invited member states to encourage their stakeholders to perform a PIA on smart metering. The development of this template has to be seen against the background of the EU privacy and data protection reform. The smart metering PIA template is a showcase for a planned, further institutionalization of PIA in the European privacy and data protection regime. The new regulation inter alia foresees a mandatory conducting of data protection impact assessments when specific risks occur as regards individual rights (Article 35 GDPR). A PIA is mandatory in the following cases:

- when "a systematic and extensive evaluation of personal aspects ... based on automated processing, including profiling" occurs
- when "special categories of data referred to in Article 9(1), or of personal data relating to criminal convictions and offences" are processed on a large scale
- and when publicly accessible areas are systematically monitored on a large scale.

(Article 35 (3) GDPR)

The data categories listed in Article 9 are

> personal data revealing racial or ethnic origin, political opinions, religious or philosophical beliefs, or trade-union membership, and the processing of genetic data, biometric data for the purpose of uniquely identifying a natural person, data concerning health or data concerning a natural person's sex life or sexual orientation

(Article 9(1) GDPR)

Against the background of the GDPR being effective since May 2018, it is likely that PIA will become an even more important issue in the EU within the next few years.

The conditions defined in the GDPR help public and private institutions to determine when PIA is mandatory. However, the GDPR merely provides a legal minimum standard as regards PIA and does not include specific rules about its concrete implementation. This is obvious as the purpose of the law is to define legal rights and obligations but not to provide procedural guidelines. Nevertheless, the availability of frameworks and guidelines is important to enable organizations in carrying out PIA. There is a number of useful PIA guidelines and handbooks available, which often vary in scope and approach. But there are some basic requirements which are relevant for every PIA approach, irrespective of its eventual peculiarities. De Hert (2012: 40) argues that from a human rights perspective there are three generic requirements for privacy-affecting information processing: "legality (Is there a legal basis in law for a technology that processes data?), legitimacy (Is the processing pursuing legitimate aims?) and necessity (Is the processing necessary in a democratic society?)". Although PIA is not limited to legal aspects and not to be misunderstood purely as an instrument of the law, these basic requirements for lawful data processing contribute to a vital foundation for PIA in general. But as De Hert (2012) notes, given the high complexity of legal issues, understanding and interpreting these requirements can be quite difficult. Equally important requirements are basic privacy principles (as outlined in Chapter 3) such as purpose und usage limitation of personal information collection, transparency and accountability, quality of information, concepts for storage, access and protection to personal information, etc. (OECD 2013).

Irrespective of the variety of PIA approaches and guidelines, there are some basic elements which can be found in most PIA models (e.g., Oetzel *et al.* 2011; Wright and De Hert 2012a; ICO 2014; CNIL 2015a/2015b; Bieker *et al.* 2016; Strauß 2017). Hence, a PIA basically incorporates the following issues:

- scope and objectives of the assessment (e.g., legal requirement, privacy compliance, fostering of transparency of information processing, etc.)
- description of the context, application or technology to be assessed
- identification and assessment of personal information flows

  - what personal information is processed and how is it used (from creation/collection to processing, storage and deletion)?

- identification and assessment of privacy risks

  - what are the risks and how likely are they?

- identification of existing controls and recommendation of means to mitigate the risks (developing ways to avoid or reduce the detected privacy risks)
- documentation of measures to resolve the risks and record eventual remaining risks.

These basic steps provide useful guidance on a general level. However, several issues complicate the important role PIA could play to improve privacy protection. As mentioned, the function and meaning of PIA can vary significantly from country to country. This is explainable by, inter alia, the complexity of the topic with varying national legal frameworks, many different national and international organizations, stakeholders, their interests and procedures, etc., as well as an as-yet lacking legal obligation in most countries. The strong role of policy and regulation in particular is a double-edged sword. The development and employment of PIA approaches is closely linked to privacy policy, including legal and regulatory issues. PIA is often used as an instrument of policy with the motivation to create public trust (Clarke 2009). On the one hand, this is obvious as the law defines rules for privacy and data protection to differentiate between legal and illegal intrusion. Public and private institutions conducting PIA have an interest in respecting these rules in their workflows and processes to avoid legal problems. For them, PIA is mostly a tool of privacy compliance, which supports the organization itself as well as for the societal role of privacy protection. However, on the other hand, there is also a risk that PIA is misused as a fig leaf to distract from eventual privacy concerns of the public about novel technologies. For instance, Bamberger and Mulligan (2012) analyzed the role of PIA in the US. PIA is a legal obligation for US government agencies when PII is included in developing or procuring information-technology systems. However, there are many problems and flaws of PIA in the US such as insufficient procedures, conflicting political interests, lack of independency of the agencies conducting the process, etc. (ibid.). Clarke (2009: 128) came to a similar conclusion and described the US as "a wasteland from the viewpoint of privacy policy". However, insufficient procedures and the like are not just a national problem of the US but also of other countries where similar problems as regards the effectiveness of PIA exist. Furthermore, as many ICT developments are located in the US, this has negative effects for privacy and data protection in Europe. Examples such as the case "Europe vs. Facebook"[24] or the regulatory issues in the EU concerning the dominance of Google (e.g., Boffey 2017) underline this aspect. These issues are part of a regulatory problem on an international level[25] as the efficacy of privacy protection depends heavily on the agency of the privacy regime, i.e., its ability to act on a global scale. With the GDPR as a major instrument, the novel privacy regulation in Europe paves the way for easing the situation in many respects. A common basic legal framework contributes to harmonizing privacy and data protection regulation in the member states, which can strengthen the European privacy regime in general. This development is promising to foster the role of PIA as a standardized instrument of privacy policy in Europe. In the longer run, this may have positive effects on privacy protection in the US and other countries as well.

However, the general issue remains that policy and regulation may lag behind technology, which complicates privacy protection. It is rather obvious that the law cannot cover all aspects of socio-technical reality, because the main task of the law is to provide applicable rules that allow for a stable society, irrespective of particular technologies. In an ideal setting, the law enables society to react accordingly to new technologies. However, technology alters society and vice versa, and this interplay can create needs for additional regulation and standardization. Nevertheless, it would be a great fallacy to occasionally adapt the law every time a new technology emerges. More important is ensuring that technology is developed and used in accordance with the law. The crux is to identify those issues resulting from technology and related socio-technical practices that impair the effectiveness of existing regulation. In such cases, adapting regulation is reasonable. As agency problems limit the effectiveness of privacy protection, reinforcing institutional transparency and accountability regarding information processing is an important measure. Here, new regulation can contribute to easing the situation as the European privacy reform with the GDPR exemplifies. Regardless of its controversial issues, the GDPR is about to ease some of the problems mentioned and strengthen privacy regulation, particularly with the obligation to conduct PIA under certain conditions (Article 35 GDPR) as well as the mandatory installation of a data protection officer for larger companies (Article 37 GDPR). Before this new regulation, most European countries had no such legal obligations for companies at all.[26] Consequently, many businesses did not even consider employing PIA, either due to a lack of awareness of its purpose or in order to avoid efforts perceived as unnecessary. In this regard, the GDPR can improve the situation to some extent as institutions are encouraged to reflect on their privacy compliance. The GDPR fosters PIA in general. But for good reason, it cannot determine strict rules and detailed guidelines on how to conduct PIA covering every technology, application or practice, and that is useful for every institution. This is not the task of the regulation but of the actors of the privacy regime.

Although regulation is of fundamental importance, for PIA to be an effective tool, it is crucial to come toward approaches that allow privacy issues to be grasped not from merely a legal, but also from a wider, ethical and societal perspective in relation to technology. A narrow focus on legal issues can reduce the effectiveness of PIA as relevant privacy risks may be overlooked (Wright and De Hert 2012c). PIA can be particularly challenging in the case of ICTs which are a hybrid technology, involved in nearly every domain (Strauß 2017). Raab and Wright (2012) analyzed a number of different PIA methodologies and found several flaws. Besides other things, the main issues are that most PIA concepts offer limited options to apply them to surveillance practices and ICTs. A basic reason for this is the relatively narrow focus of PIA on legal issues of data protection (Wright and De Hert 2012c). Although this focus is important and reasonable, it may be insufficient when the different types and dimensions of privacy are neglected, because socio-technical reality can bear privacy impacts that are not accordingly addressed by law.

Many factors and issues determine whether an individual's privacy is affected. As shown in the previous chapters, privacy-intrusive activities can be conducted by many different actors. Some privacy impacts result from surveillance practices exploiting identity information, others as a by-product of common forms of information processing in various socio-technical contexts. Hence, some activity does not have to be a modality of surveillance to be privacy-intrusive. Socio-technical practices in general can affect privacy when they involve the collection, processing or storage of personal information. The European Court of Human Rights thus declared that "[m]ere storing of data relating to the private life of an individual amounts to an interference within the meaning of Article 8 (right to respect for private life) of the European Convention on Human Rights" (EU-CHR 2017). As shown, technology design and usage entail and reinforce privacy challenges and risks. The progress in technology and privacy-intrusive techniques complicates gathering the extent to which a particular technology entails a privacy impact. Moreover, as with digital information, the boundaries between different technologies also blur. Hence, there are many socio-technical issues complicating PIA. Against this background there is demand for more systematic PIA approaches.

Overall, PIA suffers from a lack of standards and theoretical concepts that address privacy impacts from a systemic perspective. Consequently, there is a certain risk that PIA processes vary in quality and from topic to topic, technology to technology, etc. while at the same time leaving crucial privacy risks and issues unregarded. Although there are a number of useful PIA guidelines and handbooks available, they are mostly either very specific to a particular topic (e.g., RFID, smart metering), or too broad, providing general organizational steps with emphasis on legal issues. For instance, the PIA template mentioned concerning smart grids and metering (SGTF 2014) offers useful guidelines for a specific domain. The intention of the EU Commission to use this template as a blueprint in order to stimulate PIA in other domains as well is reasonable. However, its specific character limits its scope and applicability. Other, more basic, PIA guidelines (e.g., ICO 2014; CNIL 2015a) are broader but with varying approaches. Some focus more on risk assessment, others more on organizational issues and procedural steps, etc. In each case, general obstacles result from relatively narrow, legally focused or diverse conceptualizations of privacy impacts. In this respect, the effectiveness of PIA suffers from a certain lack of common theoretical grounds about its key issues, i.e., the emergence of a privacy impact. This is particularly the case as regards ICTs. A critical issue is that the extent to which a socio-technical practice triggers a privacy impact varies with the institutions and technologies involved. When there is no common understanding of the emergence of a privacy impact, there is a certain risk that PIA arbitrarily considers some privacy threats but overlooks others. Therefore, in any case, PIA needs to be specified and tailored to the domain in which it is applied (including relevant organizational practices, technologies, etc.). This necessary tailoring process could be alleviated by a more solid theoretical backing. As shown above, an integral element of every PIA approach concerns the analysis of personal information flows. However, the crux is often how to conduct this analysis. This can be a particular burden for organizations that may intend to conduct PIA (even without legal obligation) but shy away from the effort. Regardless of their usefulness, most PIA guidelines focus on analyzing the explicit processing of personal information by a particular technology or application. Given the complexity of ICTs or digital technology in general, it can be challenging to assess what types of privacy are affected by what kind of activities processing personal information. The following section presents and discusses two approaches dealing with these issues.

Privacy types and privacy-affecting activities

There are different options to grasp privacy impacts and assess the risks privacy is exposed to. A precondition is a basic conceptual understanding of the (socio-technical) modalities that may affect privacy. This then enables a closer look at technology in particular. As outlined, the analysis of (personal) information processing is a core part of PIA. Irrespective of the technology, privacy impacts can result from many different activities and, moreover, privacy as such can have multiple dimensions. One attempt to grasp these dimensions is to differentiate between types of privacy.

The seven types of privacy

Clarke (2006) provides a valuable classification of four major types of privacy: privacy of the person, privacy of personal behavior, privacy of social communications and privacy of personal data. The first type of privacy makes reference to what is also known as bodily privacy, and aims to protect the physical space and the body of a person. The second type of privacy aims to safeguard the personal behavior of individuals, such as religious practices and sexual activities. The third type covers some of the relationships and social ties that any individual builds and operates in. Finally, the privacy of personal data refers to the integrity and protection of all the sensitive data about an individual. Finn *et al.* (2013: 6ff.) complement Clarke's approach with additional dimensions and suggest seven types of privacy:

1 Privacy of the person: addresses issues of keeping body functions and body characteristics (such as biometrics or genetic information) private. This type also refers to the strong cultural meaning of the physical body.

2 Privacy of behavior and action: one's "ability to behave in public, semi-public or one's private space without having actions monitored or controlled by others". This type includes "sensitive issues such as sexual preferences and habits, political activities and religious practices" (ibid.: 6f.).

3 Privacy of communication: the ability to communicate freely via different media without fear of interception, wiretapping or other forms of surveillance of communication.

4 Privacy of data and image: this type includes issues about protecting personal data so that it is not automatically available to other individuals and organizations. Individuals should have the right to substantially control that data and its use. An image represents a particular form of personal data that can be used to identify and observe people based on their visual characteristics.

5 Privacy of thoughts and feelings: this type addresses one's freedom to think and feel whatever one likes without restriction. It is distinguishable from privacy of the person, similar as "the mind can be distinguished from the body" and distinctions "between thought, feelings and behaviour. Thought does not automatically translate into behaviour" (Ibid: 7).

6 Privacy of location and space: addresses an individual's ability to move freely in public or semi-public space without being identified, tracked or monitored. "This conception of privacy also includes a right to solitude and a right to privacy in spaces such as the home, the car or the office" (ibid.: 7). Considering a growth in mobile computing devices such as smartphones and location data, the protection of locational privacy can be expected to increase in importance (Blumberg and Eckersley 2009; Clarke 2012a).

7 Privacy of association (including group privacy): affects one's right to associate with whomever one wishes without being monitored. Included are involvements in or contributions to groups or profiles. This type of privacy is closely linked to other fundamental rights such as freedom of association, movement and expression.

This typology can be useful to reflect on privacy impacts resulting from technologies or applications. Using these types as categories can point out the extent to which a particular technology may have multiple privacy impacts. Table 6.1 exemplifies this with some common technologies. A distinction between different privacy types provides a more detailed picture of how privacy is affected, which may facilitate the creation of appropriate protection measures.

The most common privacy-intrusive technology is CCTV. At first glance, CCTV mainly affects two types of privacy: that of the person and that of location and space. It may also affect privacy of association, namely if a group of people is captured on CCTV. However, considering the combination of CCTV and a database for processing the images, this technology also touches privacy of data and image. When CCTV systems record activities, they also affect privacy of behavior and action. New forms of "smart" CCTV being able to recognize, e.g., faces or patterns of behavior (such as how a person moves) create additional impacts on this type of privacy. CCTV equipped with a microphone can also intrude into privacy of communication. Another example with increasing relevance is biometrics, i.e., technological means of recognizing individuals based on measurement of their physical characteristics (see also Chapter 5). In its broadest sense, biometrics focuses on (physical) information about the human body; most commonly the term refers to technologies such as fingerprint and iris scanners and increasingly face and vein pattern recognition and even DNA profiling. A biometric system is basically an automated pattern-recognition system that uses information about one's body, e.g., for identification and access control. Further processing of biometric information for profiling, pattern recognition and other forms of data mining is becoming more and more common in the security domain. While these technologies have an obvious impact on privacy of the person or body, biometrics in a wider sense also affects other types of privacy such as privacy of data and image, as well as privacy of location and space (Strauß 2017). A further example with multiple types affected is social media as, e.g., demonstrated by Strauß and Nentwich (2013) in the case of SNS. In line with the core aims of SNS and other social media (see Chapter 4) to communicate, share information, create different forms of content and interact

Table 6.1 Privacy types affected by different technologies

Technology/Privacy of ...	(Smart) CCTV	Biometrics	Social media	Smart phones
Person	(X)	X	(X)	(X)
Behaviour and action	(X)		(X)	(X)
Communication			X	X
Data and image	X	(X)	X	X
Thoughts and feelings			(X)	(X)
Location and space	X	(X)	(X)	X
Association	(X)	(X)	X	X

Note
Author's presentation (adapted from Strauß 2017: 150) based on the typology of Finn *et al.* (2013). An "X" indicates that the privacy type is widely affected; "(X)" means that this privacy type is partially or potentially affected.

with others, privacy of communication, data and image, and association are affected by this technology. Depending on what information a user reveals, social media can potentially reveal many details of a person's life and thus also provide insight into that person's behavior, shared thoughts or locations and places. The smartphone is another prominent technology that serves multiple purposes. It can be understood as a conglomerate of different intertwined technologies that entail a number of privacy impacts. The most obvious types are communication and association, as a phone primarily serves as a communication tool which then can also give insight into one's connections with other people. But smartphones also serve many other purposes: they can reveal one's location and can be tracked, they can be equipped with a camera, used for online services to share information, e.g., via social networks or apps, or can even be used to scan biometrics, etc. Hence, smartphone surveillance can give deep insights into the surveyed person's behavior, thoughts and feelings.

However, as the examples indicate, this mapping can only provide a general overview but not a strict assignment. Although the seven types of privacy provide a useful means to grasp the multiple dimensions of privacy, there are several limits which make them rather unsuitable for a more detailed impact assessment. The conceptual distinction between the different types allows a quick, practical overview to be gained on the multiple ways a technology can be privacy-affecting. However, this benefit of a general overview is at the cost of a more detailed picture: as visible on the examples of social media and smart phones, it is rather difficult to grasp the extent to which ICTs affect privacy in depth. Contemporary and emerging technologies are increasingly interrelated and interoperable. As the examples of social media and smartphones in particular highlight, one socio-technical system can include a number of different technologies with accordingly broad privacy impacts. The nature of digital information and the convergence of technologies (e.g., a smartphone also has an integrated camera, SNS features include text-, audio- and video-based modes of interaction) make it likely that in several cases every type of privacy might be affected. Hence, in such cases where a technology affects most or all types, there is little analytical gain without a further, more detailed analysis about how the different types are affected. Therefore, this typology merely represents a baseline to examine in more depth the extent to which a technology entails or reinforces privacy impacts (Strauß 2017).

Furthermore, a detailed view is complicated because the approach does not include issues of identifiability and identifiable information. Each of these privacy types ultimately represents a form of identifiable information. However, the typology is basically a differentiation of personal information but it becomes complex when considering identifiable information resulting from technology usage. Therefore, it provides limited options to analyse privacy impacts that result from implicit identification (as highlighted in Chapter 5). Consequently, less-obvious or implicit forms of privacy intrusion may be unrecognized. This is problematic because, as shown in the previous chapters, implicit forms of identification in particular can entail significant privacy impacts.

Privacy-affecting activities

Another approach is to focus on privacy-affecting activities. Privacy impacts can occur in manifold ways triggered by different activities. In his taxonomy on privacy, legal scholar Daniel Solove (2006) made an attempt to elaborate the various activities that affect privacy. He differs between four basic groups of activities that can be harmful to privacy: (1) information collection, (2) information processing, (3) information dissemination and (4) invasion. Each of these groups has related subgroups as shown in Figure 6.2.

Solove's model begins with the individual (data subject) who is directly affected by the different activities. These activities can be conducted by various entities (e.g., other people, government, and businesses), which are clustered as "data holders". These entities collect information related to the individual, which is then processed for further usage, e.g., storage, combination, searching, manipulation, etc. The next group, information dissemination, includes activities of data holders to transfer information to other entities or release it. The final group, called invasions, addresses activities that impinge directly on the individual concerned and her private affairs. In contrast to the first three groups which "pull" information away from the control of the individual, invasions challenge the individual directly and information is not necessarily involved (Solove 2006: 488ff.).

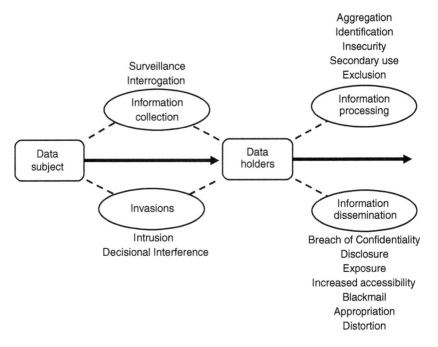

Figure 6.2 Groups of privacy-affecting activities.

Source: author's representation, adapted from Solove (2006: 490ff.).

Each of these activities consists of multiple subgroups. The two subgroups of *information collection* are: surveillance, which is defined as "watching, listening to, or recording of an individual's activities", and interrogation, i.e., "various forms of questioning or probing for information" (ibid.: 490). *Information processing* includes: aggregation, i.e., the combination of different data about a person; identification, which links information to a particular individual; insecurity, by which Solove means insufficient protection of the stored information so that it is vulnerable to leaks and improper access; secondary use, which is the use of information for other purposes without the consent of the individual concerned; and exclusion, which means that the individual is excluded from knowing and controlling how her information is processed, by whom, for what purpose, etc. The subgroup of *information dissemination* describes privacy-affecting issues of transferring or spreading personal information: breach of confidentiality; disclosure, i.e., "the revelation of truthful information about a person that impacts the way others judge her character" (ibid.: 491); exposure, i.e., "the exposing to others of certain physical and emotional attributes about a person" (ibid.: 533); increased accessibility, which is the possibility to access available information without the control of the individual; blackmail, i.e., the threating of an individual to disclose her personal information; appropriation, i.e., the misuse of an individual's identity to serve other interests such as identity theft; and distortion, i.e., "the dissemination of false or misleading information about individuals" (ibid.: 491). The two sub-categories of *invasions* are intrusion, which "concerns invasive acts that disturb one's tranquillity of solitude"; and decisional interference, i.e., "governmental interference with people's decisions regarding certain matters of their lives" (ibid.: 554).

Solove's model is particularly interesting as it sheds light on how the handling of information as part of different types of activities can affect privacy. It is thus another important contribution to grasping the multiple dimensions of privacy impacts. His taxonomy offers a detailed description of the different groups of activities he identified, enriched with many legally relevant examples. However, the model remains relatively vague as regards whether the subgroups are particular activities, or consequences of the main groups they belong to. It is also not always clear why an activity is part of one group and not of another. For instance, surveillance is seen as a part of information collection, which is reasonably separated from aggregation, being a subgroup of information processing. Surely, surveillance inevitably involves collecting information and the scope of surveillance can expand by further information processing. However, the aggregation of once-separated information can also be part of a surveillance activity. Strictly speaking, this relation cannot be derived from Solove's model as surveillance is presented here as an activity of information collection prior to processing. Ambiguous also is the framing of identification as a subgroup of information processing. On the one hand, Solove refers to Clarke (1994) and understands identification as "connecting information to individuals" where identification "enables us to attempt to verify identity" (Solove 2006: 510). On the other hand, in Solove's model, identification is included merely as one activity of information processing among others. Consequently, identification, i.e., the processing of identifiable information, is not seen here as a necessary condition for an impact on privacy or at least is not presented as such. For Solove, identification "entails a link to the person in the flesh" while aggregation can, but does not necessarily, allow for identification (ibid.: 510f.). Although this is basically the case, privacy-affecting aggregation of information concerning an individual inevitably involves some processing of identifiable information; because, otherwise, she (and thus her privacy) cannot be affected directly.

Therefore, as argued throughout this book, the processing of identifiable information is precisely the kind of process that triggers intrusion into the privacy of an individual. Identification certainly implies information processing, but it is more than just one privacy-affecting activity among others: identification is at the core of privacy-affecting activities. This is because it enables a piece of information to be linked to a particular individual so that this individual is distinguishable from others. This is the basis for eventual intrusions into the privacy of this very individual. However, this does not necessarily imply that information directly links to a person "in the flesh". It also does not mean that for privacy intrusion a person has to be uniquely identified, because the real identity of a person (e.g., her full name) is not necessary to have her privacy infringed (e.g., by observation or surveillance). Nevertheless, identifiable information is involved when informational privacy is affected. Ultimately, any information related to a person's identity may be used to intrude into her privacy. Because it can be sufficient that information related to a person's identity is gathered (e.g., against her will or without her awareness) for an activity to be privacy-intrusive. Therefore, identifiability is a core problem of privacy protection.

In fact, Solove's privacy-affecting activities basically involve the processing of some kind of identifiable information. Most obvious are identification and appropriation. But also surveillance and interrogation comprise the collection of information about a person; privacy-affecting information aggregation implies that personal information is involved; secondary use means processing of personal information without the consent of this person; breach of confidentiality implies information that a person perceives as confidential; disclosure involves true information about a person's character; exposure means that physical and emotional attributes about a person are revealed; increased accessibility refers to access to personal information; also blackmailing a person requires information about that person; and distortion, because the dissemination of false or misleading information about a person implies that correct information about that person is held. Hence, even though identification does not play a prominent role in Solove's model, the processing of identifiable information implicitly does. The perspective on privacy-affecting activities is important as it provides a more process-oriented view on privacy. However, the activities are closely interwoven and may be hard to distinguish in particular when ICTs are involved. In many cases, the collection of digital information alone can lead to dissemination of this information more or less at the same time (e.g., in social media). This does not reduce the analytical relevance of these categories. But there is demand for alternative approaches also that incorporate the peculiarities of ICTs and digital information processing.

As shown in the previous chapters, identifiable information can be gathered and processed in various ways, supported and reinforced by technology. In order to understand and conceptually grasp the modalities of information processing that may affect individual privacy, it is thus crucial to perceive identification as a core activity in this regard. Some form of identification is mostly involved when an individual's privacy is affected, at least as regards informational privacy. The crux is that the individual is often not aware of how her identifiable information is being processed or involved in information processing. This does not mean that every form of identification entails a privacy intrusion. For instance, recognizing the face of a person passing by may also include some form of identification, though a volatile, non-persistent one. If technology is involved as, e.g., one takes a photograph or a video of a person for a particular purpose, this has different implications as the identifiable information (the image or footage) becomes somewhat persistent/durable and available for further processing. As shown, with technological development, identifiability expands as the contexts of information processing expand as well. Consequently, there are more and more hazards emerging that challenge and threaten privacy. As identification is context-sensitive, it also depends on the context or purpose and degree of identification whether privacy is affected or not. Nevertheless, the processing of some identifiable information referring to a particular person is a precondition for the emergence of a privacy impact concerning that person. It is thus essential to focus on the multiple dimensions of identifiability and different types of identifiable information. Otherwise, it becomes increasingly difficult to tackle the variety of current and emerging hazards to privacy. Hence, to come toward enhanced forms of PIA, the following chapter proposes an identifiability-based PIA framework including a novel typology of different types of identifiable information.

Notes

1 Ann Cavoukian was the Information and Privacy Commissioner of Ontario, Canada and is among the first advocates of PbD.
2 anonymous-proxy-servers.net.
3 For a detailed discussion about the idea of an expiration date, see, Mayer-Schönberger (2009).
4 https://philzimmermann.com/EN/findpgp/.
5 www.philzimmermann.com/EN/essays/WhyIWrotePGP.html.
6 www.openpgp.org, www.gnupg.org.
7 www.enigmail.net.
8 www.torproject.org/.
9 Homomorphism implies that the structure of an information set is kept. It counts as the holy grail of cryptography, e.g., Micciancio (2010).
10 Such as the Enigma project at the MIT: www.media.mit.edu/projects/enigma/overview/. See also Greenberg (2015).

11 https://ethereum.org/.
12 Blockchain is the technology on which the crypto-currency bitcoin is based, but can also be used for other decentralized systems. See, e.g., Pass *et al.*'s (2016) Analysis of the Blockchain Protocol in Asynchronous Networks: https://eprint.iacr.org/2016/454.pdf.
13 https://blog.torproject.org/blog/tor-browser-70-released.
14 This visualization is only an excerpt and does not show the full scope of disclosed personal information.
15 Google privacy policy: www.google.at/intl/en/policies/privacy/.
16 Diaspora: https://diasporafoundation.org/Friendica: http://friendi.ca/.
17 How many users are in the DIASPORA network? https://diasp.eu/stats.html.
18 As simple practical tests (conducted on September 22, 2018) show. Among the tested providers were Gmail (google.com/gmail), Gmx.net, Web.de and Outlook.com.
19 For a list of services blocking Tor see, e.g., https://trac.torproject.org/projects/tor/wiki/org/doc/ListOfServicesBlockingTor. Reasons for being blocked can be difficult to verify. For instance, during some practical tests of the Tor browser (with different IP addresses involved), conducted on September 24, 2018, access to some websites via Tor such as Google search, Gmx.net, Facebook.com login or Amazon.com was hampered and partially blocked. These problems did not occur in some further tests (September 30, 2018), but did occur again in some others. Reasons can be manifold but this further indicates problems privacy-aware users may encounter when using PETs.
20 Trip Report: Tor Trainings for the Dutch and Belgian Police. Tor Blog, February 05, 2013, https://blog.torproject.org/blog/trip-report-tor-trainings-dutch-and-belgian-police; see also, Dreged (2013).
21 As well as its synonym DPIA—Data Protection Impact Assessment, more common in Europe.
22 An independent advisory body established by Article 29 of the EU Data Protection Directive, consisting of different national and EU data protection representatives.
23 Commission Recommendation of October 10, 2014 on the Data Protection Impact Assessment Template for Smart Grid and Smart Metering Systems: http://eur-lex.europa.eu/legal-content/EN/TXT/HTML/?uri=CELEX:32014H0724&from=EN.
24 www.europe-v-facebook.org.
25 This is related inter alia to the Privacy Shield regulation and Convention 108, as mentioned in Chapter 3.
26 An exception is Germany where the installation of data protection officers is already required for most companies.

References

All URLs were checked last on October 23, 2018.

AI—Amnesty International (2016) For Your Eyes Only? Ranking 11 Technology Companies on Encryption and Human Rights. London: Amnesty International. www.amnesty.org/en/documents/POL40/4985/2016/en/.

Ball, J., Schneier, B. and Greenwald, G. (2013) NSA and GCHQ Target Tor Network that Protects Anonymity of Web Users. *Guardian*, October 4, www.theguardian.com/world/2013/oct/04/nsa-gchq-attack-tor-network-encryption.

Bamberger, K. A. and Mulligan, D. K. (2012) PIA Requirements and Privacy Decision-Making in US Government Agencies. In Wright, D. and De Hert, P. (eds.), *Privacy Impact Assessment*. Dordrecht: Springer, 225–250.

Bayley, R. M. and Bennett, C. J. (2012) Privacy Impact Assessments in Canada. In Wright, D. and De Hert, P. (eds.), *Privacy Impact Assessment*. Dordrecht: Springer, 161–185.

BBC (2016) Turkey Blocks Access to Tor Anonymizing Network. *BBC Online*, December 16, www.bbc.co.uk/news/technology-38365564.

Bhargav-Spantzel, A., Camenisch, J., Gross, T. and Sommer, D. (2007) User Centricity: A taxonomy and open issues. *Journal of Computer Security*, 15(5): 493–527.

Bieker, F., Friedewald, M., Hansen, M., Obersteller, H. and Rost, M. (2016) A Process for Data Protection Impact Assessment under the European General Data Protection Regulation. In Rannenberg, K. and Ikonomou, D. (eds.), *Privacy Technologies and Policy. Fourth Annual Privacy Forum (APF)*, LNCS 9857. Frankfurt/Heidelberg/New York/Dordrecht/London: Springer, 21–37.

Blumberg, A. J. and Eckersley, P. (2009) *On Locational Privacy, and How to Avoid Losing it Forever*. Electronic Frontier Foundation. www.eff.org/wp/locational-privacy.

Boffey, D. (2017) Google Fined Record €2.4bn by EU Over Search Engine Results. *Guardian*, June 27, www.theguardian.com/business/2017/jun/27/google-braces-for-record-breaking-1bn-fine-from-eu.

Cavoukian, A. (2012a) *Privacy by Design and the Emerging Personal Data Ecosystem*. Information and Privacy Commissioner, Ontario, Canada, www.ipc.on.ca/images/Resources/pbd-pde.pdf

Cavoukian, A. (2012b) *Operationalizing Privacy by Design: A guide to implementing strong privacy practices*. www.cil.cnrs.fr/CIL/IMG/pdf/operationalizing-pbd-guide.pdf.

Cavoukian, A., Dix, A. and Emam, K. E. (2014) *The Unintended Consequences of Privacy Paternalism*. Policy paper, Information and Privacy Commissioner, Ontario, Canada. www.comm.utoronto.ca/~dimitris/JIE1001/levin4.pdf.

Chaum, D. (1985) Security Without Identification: Transaction systems to make big brother obsolete. *Communications of the ACM*, 28(10): 1030–1044. https://gnunet.org/sites/default/files/10.1.1.48.4680.pdf.

Clarke, R. (1994) Human Identification in Information Systems: Management challenges and public policy issues. *Information Technology and People*, 7(4): 6–37. www.rogerclarke.com/DV/HumanID.html.

Clarke, R. (2006) *What's "Privacy"?* www.rogerclarke.com/DV/Privacy.html.

Clarke, R. (2009) Privacy Impact Assessment: Its origins and development. *Computer Law and Security Review*, 25(2): 123–135. http://rogerclarke.com/DV/PIAHist-08.html.

Clarke, R. (2012a) Location Tracking of Mobile Devices: Ueberveillance stalks the streets. *Computer Law and Security Review*, 29(3): 216–228. www.rogerclarke.com/DV/LTMD.html.

Clarke, R. (2012b) PIAs in Australia: A work-in-progress report. In Wright, D., De Hert, P. (eds.), *Privacy Impact Assessment*. Springer: Dordrecht, 119–148.

CNIL—Commission Nationale de l'Informatique et des Libertés (2015a) *Privacy Impact Assessment (PIA): Methodology (how to carry out a PIA)*. June 2015 edition. www.cnil.fr/sites/default/files/typo/document/CNIL-PIA-1-Methodology.pdf.

CNIL—Commission Nationale de l'Informatique et des Libertés (2015b) *Privacy Impact Assessment (PIA): Tools (templates and knowledge bases)*. June 2015 Edition. www.cnil.fr/sites/default/files/typo/document/CNIL-PIA-2-Tools.pdf.

Cohen, J. E. (2012) *Configuring the Networked Self: Law, code, and the play of everyday practice*. Yale: Yale University Press.

Danezis, G., Domingo-Ferrer, J., Hansen, M., Hoepman, J., Le Métayer, D., Tirtea, R. and Schiffner, S. (2014) *Privacy and Data Protection by Design: From policy to engineering*. European Union Agency for Network and Information Security (ENISA), December 2014.

De Andrade, N. N. G., Monteleone, S. and Martin, A. (2013) *Electronic Identity in Europe: Legal challenges and future perspectives (e-ID 2020).* JRC Scientific and Policy Reports. Joint Research Centre, European Commission.

De Hert, P. (2012) A Human Rights Perspective on Privacy and Data Protection Impact Assessments. In Wright, D. and De Hert, P. (eds.), *Privacy Impact Assessment.* Springer: Dordrecht, 33–76.

Debatin, B. and Lovejoy, J. P. (2009) Facebook and Online Privacy: Attitudes, behaviors, and unintended consequences. *Journal of Computer-Mediated Communication,* 15(1): 83–108.

Doctrow, C. (2014) If you Read BoingBoing, the NSA Considers you as Target for Deep Surveillance. *BoingBoing,* July 3, http://boingboing.net/2014/07/03/if-you-read-boing-boing-the-n.html.

DPD—Data Protection Directive (1995) EU Directive 95/46/EC of the European Parliament and of the Council of 24 October 1995 on The Protection of Individuals with Regard to the Processing of Personal Data and on the Free Movement of Such Data: http://eur-lex.europa.eu/legal-content/EN/TXT/PDF/?uri=CELEX:31995L0046&from=DE.

Dreged, S. (2013) What is Tor? A beginner's guide to the privacy tool. *Guardian,* November 5, www.theguardian.com/technology/2013/nov/05/tor-beginners-guide-nsa-browser.

Dunn, J. E. (2017) 22 of the Most Infamous Data Breaches Affecting the UK. *Techworld,* July 14, www.techworld.com/security/uks-most-infamous-data-breaches-3604586/.

Dwork, C. and Roth, A. (2014) The Algorithmic Foundations of Differential Privacy. *Foundations and Trends in Theoretical Computer Science,* 9(3–4): 211–407.

EDPS—European Data Protection Supervisor (2016) *Opinion 8/2016: Opinion on coherent enforcement of fundamental rights in the age of big data.* https://secure.edps.europa.eu/EDPSWEB/webdav/site/mySite/shared/Documents/EDPS/Events/16-09-23_BigData_opinion_EN.pdf.

EGE—European Group on Ethics in Science and New Technologies (2014) *Ethics of Security and Surveillance Technologies.* Opinion No. 28 of the European Groups on Ethics in Science and New Technologies. Brussels, May 20.

EU-C—European Commission (2010) *A Comprehensive Approach on Personal Data Protection in the European Union.* Communication from the Commission to the European Parliament, the Council, the Economic and Social Committee and the Committee of the Regions, COM (2010) 609 final, Brussels, November 4. http://ec.europa.eu/justice/news/consulting_public/0006/com_2010_609_en.pdf.

EU-CHR—European Court of Human Rights (2017) *Factsheet: Data protection.* July 2017. www.echr.coe.int/Documents/FS_Data_ENG.pdf.

Finley, K. (2014) Encrypted web traffic more than doubles after NSA revelations. *Wired,* May 16, www.wired.com/2014/05/sandvine-report/.

Finn, R. L., Wright, D. and Friedewald, M. (2013) Seven Types of Privacy. In Gutwirth, S., Leenes, R., De Hert, P. and Poullet, Y. (eds.), *European Data Protection: Coming of age.* Dordrecht: Springer, 3–32.

FRA—European Union Agency for Fundamental Rights (2010) *Data Protection in the European Union: The role of national Data Protection Authorities. Strengthening the fundamental rights architecture in the EU II.* Luxembourg: Publications Office of the European Union.

Froomkin, D. (2015) FBI Director Claims Tor and the "Dark Web" Won't Let Criminals Hide from his Agents. *The Intercept,* October 9, https://theintercept.com/2015/09/10/comey-asserts-tors-dark-web-longer-dark-fbi/.

GDPR—General Data Protection Regulation (2016) Regulation (EU) 2016/679 of the European Parliament and of the Council of 27 April 2016 on the Protection of Natural Persons with Regard to the Processing of Personal Data and On the Free Movement of Such Data, and Repealing Directive 95/46/EC (General Data Protection Regulation). http://eur-lex.europa.eu/legal-content/EN/TXT/HTML/?uri=CELEX:32016R0679&qid =1485427623759&from=en.

Geambasu, R., Kohno, T., Levy, A. and Levy, H. M. (2009) Vanish: Increasing data privacy with self-destructing data. In *Proceedings of the 18th USENIX Security Symposium (SSYM'09), Montreal, Canada*, 299–316. https://vanish.cs.washington.edu/pubs/usenixsec09-geambasu.pdf.

Glässer, U. and Vajihollahi, M. (2010) Identity Management Architecture. In Yang, C. C., Chau, M. C., Wang, J.-H. and Chen, H. (eds.), *Security Informatics, Annals of Information Systems Vol. 9*. Boston: Springer, 97–116.

Goel, V. and Wyatt, E. (2013) Facebook Privacy Change Is Subject of F.T.C. Inquiry. *New York Times*, September 11, www.nytimes.com/2013/09/12/technology/personal tech/ftc-looking-into-facebook-privacy-policy.html.

Greenberg, A. (2015) MIT's Bitcoin-Inspired "Enigma" Lets Computers Mine Encrypted Data. *Wired*, June 30, www.wired.com/2015/06/mits-bitcoin-inspired-enigma-lets-computers-mine-encrypted-data/.

Greenberg, A. (2016a) Hacker Lexicon: What is perfect forward secrecy? *Wired*, November 28, www.wired.com/2016/11/what-is-perfect-forward-secrecy/.

Greenberg, A. (2016b) Signal, the Cypherpunk App of Choice, Adds Disappearing Messages. *Wired*, October 11, www.wired.com/2016/10/signal-cypherpunk-app-choice-adds-disappearing-messages/.

Gürses, S., Troncoso, C. and Diaz, C. (2011) Engineering Privacy by Design. Paper presented at the *Conference on Computers, Privacy and Data Protection (CPDP), 25–28 January 2016, Brussels, Belgium*. www.esat.kuleuven.be/cosic/publications/article-1542.pdf.

Hansen, M., Berlich, P., Camenisch, J., Clauß, S., Pfitzmann, A. and Waidner, A. (2004) Privacy-enhancing Identity Management. *Information Security Technical Report*, 9(1): 35–44.

Hern, A. and Pegg, D. (2018) Facebook Fined for Data Breaches in Cambridge Analytica Scandal. *Guardian*, July 11, www.theguardian.com/technology/2018/jul/11/facebook-fined-for-data-breaches-in-cambridge-analytica-scandal.

ICO—UK Information Commissioner's Office (2014) *Conducting Privacy Impact Assessments: Code of practice*. Version 1.0. https://ico.org.uk/media/for-organisations/documents/1595/pia-code-of-practice.pdf.

Jardine, E. (2015) *The Dark Web Dilemma: Tor, anonymity and online policing. Global Commission on Internet Governance*, paper series: no. 21. Centre for International Governance Innovation and Chatham House: The Royal Institute of International Affairs. www.cigionline.org/sites/default/files/no. 21.pdf.

Jardine, E. (2016) Tor, What Is it Good for? Political repression and the use of online anonymity-granting technologies. *New Media and Society* (March 31, online first) 1–18. http://journals.sagepub.com/doi/10.1177/1461444816639976.

Jøsang, A., Al Zomai, M. and Suriadi, S. (2007) Usability and Privacy in Identity Management Architectures. In *Proceedings of the 5th Australasian symposium on ACSW frontiers, Vol. 68*, Australian Computer Society, 143–152.

Kahn, J. D. (2003) Privacy as a Legal Principle of Identity Maintenance. *Seton Hall Law Review*, 33(2): 371–410.

Klíma, V. (2005) Finding MD5 Collisions: A toy for a notebook. *Cryptology ePrint Archive*, Report 2005/075. https://eprint.iacr.org/2005/075.pdf.

Krawczyk, H. (2005) Perfect Forward Secrecy. In van Tilborg, H. C. A. (ed.), *Encyclopedia of Cryptography and Security*. New York: Springer, 457–458.

Kubicek, H. and Noack, T. (2010) Different Countries—Different Extended Comparison of the Introduction of eIDs in Eight European Countries. *Identity in the Information Society (IDIS)*, 3(1): 235–245.

Kuchler, H. (2014) Tech Companies Step Up Encryption in Wake of Snowden. *Financial Times*, November 4, www.ft.com/content/3c1553a6-6429-11e4-bac8-00144feabdc0.

Le Blond, S., Manils, P., Abdelberi, C., Kaafar, M. A., Claude Castelluccia, C., Legout, A. and Dabbous, W. (2011) One Bad Apple Spoils the Bunch: Exploiting P2P applications to trace and profile Tor users. In *4th USENIX Workshop on Large-Scale Exploits and Emergent Threats (LEET '11), Mar 2011, Boston, US*. https://hal.inria.fr/inria-00574178/en/.

Le Grand, G. and Barrau, E. (2012) Prior Checking, a Forerunner to Privacy Impact Assessments. In Wright, D. and De Hert, P. (eds.), *Privacy Impact Assessment*. Springer: Dordrecht, 97–116.

Leenes, R., Schallaböck, J. and Hansen, M. (2008) Prime (Privacy and Identity Management for Europe), white paper. Third and final version. EU: The PRIME consortium.

Li, N., Li, T. and Venkatasubramanian, S. (2007) t-Closeness: Privacy Beyond k-anonymity and l-diversity. In *Proceedings of the 23rd IEEE International Conference on Data Engineering (ICDE)*, 106–115. doi: 10.1109/ICDE.2007.367856.

Lyon, D. (2009) *Identifying Citizens: ID cards as surveillance*. Cambridge: Polity Press.

Machanavajjhala, A., Gehrke, J. and Kifer, D. (2007) ℓ-Diversity: Privacy beyond k-anonymity. *ACM Transactions on Knowledge Discovery from Data (TKDD)*, 1(1). doi: 10.1145/1217299.1217302. http://arbor.ee.ntu.edu.tw/archive/ppdm/Anonymity/MachanavajjhalaLP06.pdf.

Mayer-Schönberger, V. (2009) *Delete: The Virtue of Forgetting in the Digital Age*. Princeton: Princeton University Press.

McCarthy, K. (2017) Russia, China Vow to Kill Off VPNs, Tor Browser. *The Register*, July 11, www.theregister.co.uk/2017/07/11/russia_china_vpns_tor_browser/.

McGoogan, C. (2016) Dark Web Browser Tor Is Overwhelmingly Used for Crime, Says Study. *Telegraph*, February 2, www.telegraph.co.uk/technology/2016/02/02/dark-web-browser-tor-is-overwhelmingly-used-for-crime-says-study/.

Menezes, A., van Oorschot, P. C. and Vanstone, S. A. (1996) *Handbook of Applied Cryptography*. First edition 1996. London: CRC Press.

Micciancio, D. (2010) Technical Perspective: A first glimpse of cryptography's holy grail. *Communications of the ACM*, 53(3): 96. www.yildiz.edu.tr/~aktas/courses/CE-0112822/06-05-2-2.pdf.

Nauman, L. and Hobgen, G. (2009) *Privacy Features of European eID Card Specifications*. Position paper, European Network and Information Security Agency ENISA. www.enisa.europa.eu/publications/eid-cards-en/at_download/fullReport.

Newman, L. H. (2016) Hack Brief: Hackers Breach a Billion Yahoo Accounts. A Billion. *Wired*, December 14, www.wired.com/2016/12/yahoo-hack-billion-users/.

Nissenbaum, H. (2010) *Privacy in Context: Technology, policy, and the integrity of social Life*. Stanford: Stanford University Press.

OECD—Organization for Economic Co-Operation and Development (2013) *The OECD Privacy Framework*. OECD Publishing. www.oecd.org/sti/ieconomy/privacy-guidelines.htm.

Oetzel, M. C., Spiekermann, S., Grüning, I., Kelter, H. and Mull, S. (2011) *Privacy Impact Assessment Guideline*. Bundesamt für Sicherheit in der Informationstechnik—BSI.

Osborne, C. (2016) How to Access Tor, even when your Country Says you Can't. *ZDNet*, August 4, www.zdnet.com/article/how-to-dance-around-censorship-and-access-tor-even-when-blocked/.

Papacharissi, Z. and Gibson, P. L. (2011) Fifteen Minutes of Privacy: Privacy, sociality, and publicity on social network sites. In Trepte, S. and Reinecke, L. (eds.), *Privacy Online: Perspectives on Self-Disclosure in the Social Web*. Berlin/Heidelberg: Springer, 75–89.

Pfitzmann, A. and Hansen, M. (2010) *A Terminology for Talking About Privacy by Data Minimization: Anonymity, unlinkability, undetectability, unobservability, pseudonymity, and identity*. Version 0.34. http://dud.inf.tu-dresden.de/literatur/Anon_Terminology_v0.34.pdf.

Preneel, B. (2005) Collision Attack. In van Tilborg, H. C. A. (ed.), *Encyclopedia of Cryptography and Security*. New York: Springer, 220–221.

Prevelakis, V. and Spinellis, D. (2001) Sandboxing Applications. In *USENIX 2001 Technical Conference Proceedings: FreeNIX Track*, 119–126.

Raab, C. D. and Wright, D. (2012) Surveillance: Extending the limits of privacy impact assessment. In Wright, D. and De Hert, P. (eds.), *Privacy Impact Assessment*. Dordrecht: Springer, 363–383.

Rubinstein, I. S. (2011) Regulating Privacy by Design. *Berkeley Technology Law Journal*, 26(3):1409–1456. http://scholarship.law.berkeley.edu/cgi/viewcontent.cgi?article=1917&context=btlj.

Rundle, M., Blakley, B., Broberg, J., Nadalin, A., Olds, D., Ruddy, M., Guimarares, M. T. M. and Trevithick, P. (2008) At a Crossroads: "Personhood" and digital identity in the information society. *STI Working paper* 2007/7, no. JT03241547 29-Feb-2008, Directorate for Science, Technology and Industry, OECD Publishing. www.oecd.org/dataoecd/31/6/40204773.doc.

Ruoti, S., Andersen, J., Zappala, D. and Seamons, K. (2016) Why Johnny Still, Still Can't Encrypt: Evaluating the usability of a modern PGP client. Version 2, January 13. *ArXiv e Print*, Cornell University. https://arxiv.org/abs/1510.08555.

Sapelova, S. and Jerman-Blažič, B. (2014) Privacy Issues in Cross-Border Identity Management Systems: Pan-European case. In Hansen, M., Hoepman, J., Leenes, R. and Whitehouse, D. (eds.), *Privacy and Identity Management for Emerging Services and Technologies: 8th IFIP/Primelife International Summer School, Nijmegen, The Netherlands, June 17–21 2013*, Revised Selected Papers, IFIP AICT 421. Berlin/Heidelberg: Springer, 214–223.

SGTF—Smart Grid Task Force (2014) *Data Protection Impact Assessment Template for Smart Grid and Smart Metering Systems*. Expert Group 2: Regulatory recommendations for privacy, data protection and cyber-security in the smart grid environment. Brussels, European Commission. https://ec.europa.eu/energy/sites/ener/files/documents/2014_dpia_smart_grids_forces.pdf.

Solon, O. (2018) Facebook Faces $1.6bn Fine and Formal Investigation over Massive Data Breach. *Guardian*, October 3, www.theguardian.com/technology/2018/oct/03/facebook-data-breach-latest-fine-investigation.

Solove, D. J. (2006) A Taxonomy of Privacy. *University of Pennsylvania Law Review*, 154(3): 477–560.

Strauß, S. (2011) The Limits of Control: (Governmental) identity management from a privacy perspective. In Fischer-Hübner, S., Duquenoy, P., Hansen, M., Leenes, R. and Zhang, G. (eds.), *Privacy and Identity Management for Life, 6th IFIP/PrimeLife International Summer School, Helsingborg, Sweden, August 2–6 2010, Revised Selected Papers*. Dordrecht: Springer, 206–218.

Strauß, S. (2017) Privacy Analysis: Privacy impact assessment. In Hansson, S. O. (ed.), *The Ethics of Technology: Methods and approaches*. London/New York: Rowman & Littlefield International, 143–156.

Strauß, S. and Aichholzer, G. (2010) National Electronic Identity Management: The challenge of a citizen-centric approach beyond technical design. *International Journal on Advances in Intelligent Systems*, 3(1/2): 12–23.

Strauß, S. and Nentwich, M. (2013) Social Network Sites, Privacy and the Blurring Boundary between Public and Private Spaces. *Science and Public Policy* 40(6): 724–732.

Sun, Y., Edmundson, A., Vanbever, L. and Li, O. (2015) RAPTOR: Routing attacks on privacy in Tor. In *Proceedings of the 24th USENIX Security Symposium, Washington D.C.*, 271–286. www.usenix.org/system/files/conference/usenixsecurity15/sec15-paper-sun.pdf.

Sweeney, L. (2002) k-Anonymity: A model for protecting privacy. *International Journal on Uncertainty, Fuzziness and Knowledge-based Systems*, 10(5): 557–570. https://epic.org/privacy/reidentification/Sweeney_Article.pdf.

Tynan, D. (2016) Facebook v Adblock: The anti-ad empire strikes back. *Guardian*, August 11, www.theguardian.com/technology/2016/aug/11/facebook-advertising-changes-adblockers-strike-back.

Warren, S. D. and Brandeis, L. D. (1890) The Right to Privacy. *Harvard Law Review*, 193(IV), No. 5., December 15, 1890, http://faculty.uml.edu/sgallagher/Brandeisprivacy.htm.

Waters, J. K. (2004) The ABCs of Identity Management. *CSOOnline*, January 1, www.csoonline.com/article/2120384/identity-management/the-abcs-of-identity-management.html.

Wolchok, S., Hofmann, O. S., Heninger, N., Felten, E. W., Halderman, J. A., Rossbach, C. J., Waters, B. and Witchel, E. (2010) Defeating Vanish with Low-Cost Sybil Attacks Against Large DHTs. In *Proceedings of the 17th Network and Distributed System Security Symposium (NDSS), San Diego, February 28–March 3*. www.internetsociety.org/sites/default/files/wol.pdf.

Wright, D. and De Hert, P. (eds.) (2012a) *Privacy Impact Assessment*. Law, Governance and Technology Series 6. Dordrecht: Springer.

Wright, D. and De Hert, P. (2012b) Introduction to Privacy Impact Assessment. In Wright, D. and De Hert, P. (eds.), *Privacy Impact Assessment*. Law, Governance and Technology Series 6. Dordrecht: Springer, 3–32.

Wright, D. and De Hert, P. (2012c) Findings and Recommendations. In Wright, D. and De Hert, P. (eds.), *Privacy Impact Assessment*. Law, Governance and Technology Series 6. Dordrecht: Springer, 445–481.

Wright, D. and Kreissl, R. (eds.) (2015) *Surveillance in Europe*. London/New York: Routledge.

Zuiderveen-Borgeswius, F. J. (2016) Informed Consent: We can do better to defend privacy. *IEEE Security and Privacy*, 13(2): 103–107.

Zyskind, G., Nathan, O. and Pentland, A. (2015) Enigma: Decentralized computation platform with guaranteed privacy. White paper. *ArXiv ePrint*, Cornell University. https://arxiv.org/abs/1506.03471.

7 Toward an identifiability-based framework for privacy impact assessment

As discussed in the previous chapter, PIA is an important instrument to improve the effectiveness of privacy protection. However, current approaches are relatively diverse with several limits in scope. There is thus a certain demand to enhance the modalities of PIA. Yet there is no conceptual framework that takes the role of identifiability explicitly into account, which would be vital to come toward a common understanding of privacy impacts, applicable for multiple domains. On a more general level, this demand results from a classic problem of privacy protection: the inherent difficulty to comprehend the mechanisms of privacy intrusion. This problem stems from a relatively static view on privacy including a rather narrow focus on personal data or information. The dynamics of ICTs and expanding identifiability aggravate this problem.

A central part of every PIA concerns the analysis of personal information flows, which basically enable the emergence of a privacy impact. Existing PIA guidelines, irrespective of whether they are very detailed or rather general, thus mainly focus on personal information. This is obviously essential. However, a critical issue is the fact that due to ICTs and digitally networked environments, it becomes increasingly difficult to determine what personal data or more precisely personally identifiable information (PII) *exactly* is. Legal definitions (see also Chapter 3) are reasonably kept broad and provide important minimum standards, but ICTs challenge their meaning in socio-technical practices. Consequently, the operationalization of PII, which is vital to properly implement PIA, can be very difficult. When analyzing a personal information flow, the focus typically is on information directly related to the person, processed within the systemic boundaries of a single information system. Considering the complexity of digital technology, PIA models of this kind may be insufficient to grasp the scope of a privacy impact. Because, in fact, personal information is often not processed by a single information system anymore, but rather by multiple information systems, which are increasingly networked and constantly process information in manifold ways. Moreover, as highlighted with the identity shadow, it is not always clear what kind of information counts as personal information or to what extent technology-generated information refers to the identity of a person as well. Hence, there are not merely explicit types of PII, i.e., information directly related to a person such as name, address, ID number, biometric information, etc., but also implicit ones. Approaches that consider only explicit types of PII are likely to neglect other forms of identification and thus risks of identifiability. Technological design and socio-technical practices further complicate these issues. Therefore, there is demand for a deeper conceptual understanding of the emergence of a privacy impact. A more systematic PIA approach with emphasis on identifiability and different types of identifiable information could contribute to overcoming some of the existing limits. I therefore suggest a basic PIA framework which comprises identifiability as the core determinant of the emergence of a privacy impact. This allows for a more systemic perspective on privacy impacts, which is vital to improve the quality of PIA as well as of privacy protection concepts.

Detecting and assessing privacy impacts

In general, identifiability is the condition which results in an individual being identified (directly or indirectly) based on a set of PII (ISO 2011: 2). Therefore, it is understood here as the initial condition of a privacy impact. At its core, the processing of identifiable information can be regarded as a main trigger for the occurrence of a privacy impact. In this respect, a privacy impact is a (possible but not inevitable) result of a process (or a chain of processes) in which identifiable information is employed, for one or several application contexts. As soon as an individual is directly or indirectly involved in the information processing chain, her identifiability is enabled. This process chain can comprise one or several socio-technical systems. The extent to which privacy is affected by a socio-technical system thus depends on the capability of this system to process identifiable information. A narrow view of a technology or application as an isolated information system leaves opaque whether and how the information may flow into another context or system. Therefore, in line with the boundary control function of privacy, it is important to consider the number of systems and application contexts involved. The complexity of information processing is likely to increase with the number of information systems, which may intensify the risks of privacy intrusion as ISD further decreases. A major reason is that each system may entail the creation of additional identifiable information and thus extend the identity shadow, which can be exploited for further purposes. Furthermore, each system can be intruded into or misused and the more systems available, the higher the realm of possibilities for intrusion. To assess privacy risks and the corresponding demand for protection mechanisms thus requires transparency and verifiability of information processing and of the technological systems involved. A perspective on the meta-architecture of a socio-technical system in which identifiable information is processed contributes to this and facilitates the analysis of the extent to which privacy is affected. This is vital to come toward more systematic conceptualizations of PIA.

Figure 7.1 sketches a general PIA framework with an emphasis on identifiability and identifiable information. This simplified model illustrates the interplay of basic elements of a socio-technical system determining a privacy impact, such

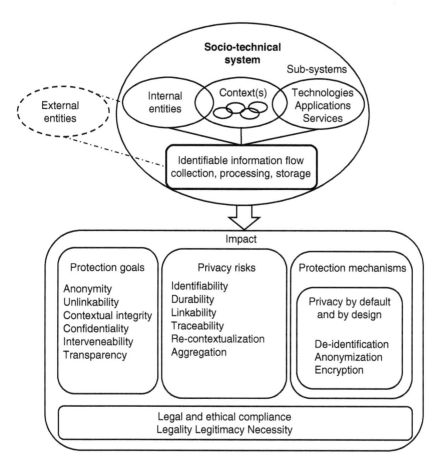

Figure 7.1 Identifiability-based framework for PIA.

as (1) the information flow, i.e., the amount and type of personally identifiable information being processed, (2) the entities gathering and using this information, (3) the context(s) of processing (varying in space and time), and (4) the number and type of (sub-)systems and how they process the identifiable information. These factors are interwoven and primarily affect identifiability, entailing additional privacy risks.

At the core of this framework is the flow of identifiable information, which is determined by the modalities of information processing (i.e., how the information is collected, stored, transmitted, used, etc.). These modalities affect the life cycle of identifiable information, shaped by the interplay of entities, the contexts in which the information is used as well as the design of the socio-technical system including its sub-systems (e.g., applications, databases, services and technologies involved). A variable number of entities can be involved in the socio-technical system with different functions and roles: e.g., system operator, provider of technologies, applications or services, information processing software agents, etc. Besides these internal entities there can also be external entities such as third parties with information access or to whom information is transferred for additional purposes (e.g., contractors of the operating entities, advertising companies, law enforcement agencies' external systems, etc.). These entities employ technologies, applications, services, etc. as well, which may automatically gather and process identifiable information. Hence, among the entities involved are not necessarily institutions or individuals only, but also technical systems or informational agents (e.g., algorithms gathering information, software bots and the like). Considering a general increase in machine learning, (semi-)automated systems and autonomic computing with progress in the field of artificial intelligence, such machine entities are likely to gain in importance in the coming years.

This setting as a whole affects the occurrence of privacy impacts, including the extent to which privacy is exposed to different risks. Above all, the primary risk is identifiability, which entails a number of additional risks. All these risks are interwoven and can further reinforce identifiability, which then may further exacerbate other risks again. The occurrence of a privacy risk resulting from identifiability does not necessarily imply that a person's identity is unambiguously revealed. The fact that identifiable information about a person has already been gathered can be a sufficient condition for a privacy impact. The basic reason is that this information links to an individual's identity and thus may be used to take actions or decisions affecting the person and interfering with her privacy.

The extent to which a socio-technical system provides identifiability of an individual is determined at least by the following core factors:

a   the amount of (personally and technically) identifiable information
b   the durability (or persistence) of identifiable information, determining its temporal availability
c   the linkability of identifiable information, enabling information from separated contexts to be cross-linked
d   and traceability allowing trails of an individual's identity to be reconstructed (e.g., to trace an individual's movements, behavior, actions, relationships, etc.).

Durability fosters traceability and linkability because the longer identifiable information is available, the more traces and the more options for cross-linking information may occur; linkability may extend durability because combined information may undermine temporal limits. Similar is true for traceability as, e.g., even deleted information may leave reproducible traces.[1] These factors are thus interrelated, can affect each other mutually and shape the condition of identifiable information. They represent risks as they enable privacy intrusion in many respects. The storage and retention modalities in particular can be critical because privacy is likely to be increasingly endangered when identifiable information is accessible for longer periods of time. It makes a significant difference whether identifiable information is available only for a limited time-span (such as a dynamic IP address changes after a certain period of time), or whether this information is stored, temporarily or permanently available, separated or linked with other information, as well as whether information is bound to a context or traceable without any limits.

There are (at least) two major risks emerging from the interplay of these conditions: re-contextualization or secondary use, i.e., the use of information for additional privacy-affecting purposes; and aggregation, i.e., the combination or linkage of information from different sources. Aggregation also enables de-anonymization or re-identification by combining different types of information to create (quasi-)identifiers (as highlighted in Chapter 5). This can result in profiling, e.g., the use of information to recognize patterns about particular people and create identity profiles.

Thus, a privacy impact is shaped by a variety of issues resulting from the modalities of information processing. It can make a qualitative difference what type of information that is, how this information is gathered and processed, whether its availability is limited in time or it is stored and used for other purposes, what technologies are involved, etc. In practice, the purposes for collecting and using information often differ or feed into additional purposes beyond the initial processing context. For instance, the primary purpose for collecting identifiable information may be user registration to enable access to a service including an identification/authentication procedure for securing a transaction, to fulfill a legal obligation or for CRM. But there can be other, additional purposes involved such as third-party access for commercial purposes, profiling or surveillance activities, etc. (as shown in Chapter 5). Secondary use is particularly problematic when it occurs without the informed consent of the individuals concerned. A person might prefer to avoid information provision to a service if secondary use is foreseen, such as for targeted advertising, profiling, etc. Hence, secondary use can lead to breach of confidentiality as individual users may not be aware of all contexts in which their information is used. Moreover, (as discussed in the context of limited user control), informed consent is often insufficient to prevent unintended further use; particularly when the individuals concerned find themselves in an accept-or-leave situation. But insufficient privacy protection is a risk not merely for the individuals concerned but also for the institution responsible for the information processing. Lacking protection of information processes can reinforce security risks such as unintended disclosure to external entities. From a wider perspective, this may lead to a reduction in system stability, when, e.g., information systems, applications, etc. are vulnerable to abuse, attacks, data loss, data breaches, or identity theft. This is another reason why privacy protection is not to be misinterpreted and falsely reduced to an issue of individual concern only. This aspect also highlights that privacy and security are often complementary and on the same side of the coin.

In order to address privacy risks and stem uncontrolled privacy impact, protection goals are crucial. A general precondition for the proper processing of identifiable information is its compliance with legal regulations. However, as privacy is not merely a legal but an ethical issue, ethical compliance is an essential requirement as well. It is thus vital that the protection goals are informed by a combination of these basic requirements. A PIA process can serve many different objectives of the organization conducting it. However, irrespective of specific strategic objectives, there are some fundamental protection goals to reduce privacy risks. As security is an important, related issue as well, it is crucial to find a proper balance. In information security there are three typical security goals, i.e., confidentiality, integrity and availability, aiming to ensure that information is authentic, comprehensible, confidential and protected from unauthorized access (Hansen *et al.* 2015; Bieker *et al.* 2016). These objectives largely correspond with goals of privacy protection in cases where the processing of identifiable information is necessary. However, a focus only on these three is not sufficient to reduce privacy risks regarding identifiability. To some extent, there can be conflicts with privacy protection. For instance, availability of information to authorized entities may be in conflict with minimum disclosure to achieve a high level of confidentiality. To extend the scope of protection goals with respect to privacy and data protection issues, Hansen *et al.* (2015) suggest unlinkability, transparency and intervenability as three additional protection goals for privacy. This six-goal approach is promising to enhance the development of protection mechanisms in accordance with PbD. A problem is, though, that full achievement of each goal at the same time is often not possible. Thus, it can be challenging to properly balance different goals (ibid.; Bieker *et al.* 2016). However, to some extent, tensions can be avoided by a stronger emphasis on identifiability and the introduction of contextual integrity (Nissenbaum 2010, as discussed in Chapter 3) instead of availability. Therefore, availability is not considered as a protection goal in the proposed framework because it misleadingly suggests information disclosure. In fact, it means that information is available for authorized use only. Contextual integrity covers this aspect as it implies information is properly processed for a particular purpose only accepted by the individual concerned and not for others. This includes secure handling of this information within this application context.

The primary protection goal in this framework is to process only a minimum amount of identifiable information, i.e., non-identifiability, which equals anonymity. This is in line with the basic privacy principles of data minimization, and purpose and usage limitation. The basic aim is thus to minimize identifiability, reduce corresponding risks and allow for anonymity and pseudonymity wherever possible. Even though this goal is not fully achievable in many contexts, it makes sense to use it as an ideal condition or best-case scenario serving as a fundamental reference point for further objectives. These are confidentiality, contextual integrity, intervenability, transparency and unlinkability. As explained in Chapter 3, *unlinkability* is a crucial requirement to avoid identifiable information being aggregated and cross-linked from multiple contexts. Depending on its implementation, unlinkability is the basis to allow for anonymous and pseudonymous information processing. *Integrity* in a technical sense means to ensure that information is reliable, authentic and correct (Bieker *et al.* 2016). As already mentioned, it is meant here in a broader sense in line with Nissenbaum's (2010) concept of contextual integrity, which is preserved when informational norms are respected so that information is not used for purposes other than those for which the individual has given her consent. *Confidentiality* means that identifiable information is kept confidential and not disclosed to non-authorized entities. Confidentiality thus includes unobservability, i.e., measures to avoid an individual being traceable by her information (Solove 2006; McCallister *et al.* 2010; Hansen *et al.* 2015; Bieker *et al.* 2016). *Intervenability* primarily incorporates ISD and control of the individual concerned so that she can intervene when necessary, and enforce changes and corrections to her information. Practical examples are privacy settings, deletion of information, or revocation of consent. In addition, intervenability is crucial for supervisory authorities such as DPAs to intervene, e.g., in cases of privacy violations. Finally, *transparency* means that all privacy-affecting information processing activities are understandable and open to scrutiny. Transparency is thus a precondition for accountability so that it is comprehensible and verifiable whether the responsible entities appropriately handle and process the information (Hansen *et al.* 2015; Bieker *et al.* 2016).

In order to achieve these goals and reduce privacy risks, protection mechanisms have to be set up. This basically refers to the implementation of privacy by design and by default (as presented and discussed in Chapter 6). Useful guidance about the implementation of common safeguards can be found in IT security standards and frameworks (e.g., BSI 2008; McCallister *et al.* 2010; ISO 2011; EuroPriSe 2017). Typical controls include organizational as well as technical measures such as authentication, encryption methods, guidelines, operational access restriction procedures, organizational norms, physical controls, privacy and security policies, and role and access management. The concrete requirements of protection mechanisms and their usefulness obviously depend on the particular application context, the organizational setting, etc. Furthermore, social practices and the privacy culture in an organization also affect the level of protection. However, irrespective of details, control and protection measures should incorporate basic privacy principles (e.g., ISO 2011; OECD 2013; EuroPriSe 2017), which can be seen as core requirements to achieve protection goals and address the risks. In particular the commonly accepted OECD privacy principles for fair information practices are important guidelines, such as data minimization and avoidance, purpose limitation, minimum retention and storage duration and deletion of unnecessary data, etc. (OECD 2013). These principles are mentioned in most privacy frameworks and also in the European Privacy Seal "EuroPriSe", which provides detailed descriptions about privacy controls in accordance with EU legislation (EuroPriSe 2017).

Altogether, effective protection mechanisms contribute to privacy-preserving processing, retention and storage modalities to limit unnecessary collection, disclosure, retention, sharing and use of identifiable information. For the achievement of technical protection, the implementation of privacy by design and by default is essential. Wherever possible, information should be de-identified and, thus, anonymized. De-identified information means that its capacity to identify a person is removed, e.g., by deletion, masking or obscuring identifiable parts of an information set (e.g., of an identifier). Techniques to reduce the risk of re-identification can be reduced by, inter alia, generalization so that information is grouped and made less accurate, replacing selected values with average values, by erasing parts of identifiable information, or adding noise to the information (McCallister *et al.* 2010). Technically, this can be achieved with cryptography, which provides several methods for de-identification and anonymization. With the use of pseudonyms (see, Pfitzmann and Hansen 2010, as outlined in Chapter 3), different levels of linkability can be established so that application contexts that may require identification can be protected from misuse as identifiers are not easily linkable. With methods of encryption, the risk of unlimited information disclosure can be reduced (for technical PbD concepts see Chapter 6).

Hence, in general, there are many protection mechanisms available to improve privacy protection. However, a crux is that it is often unclear how and what kind of identifiable information is being processed. This hampers analysis of the mechanisms and practices that may induce a privacy impact as well as the development and deployment of effective safeguards. The proposed framework for PIA with a focus on identifiability can contribute to improving this situation. A core piece of this framework is the analysis of the flow of identifiable information. In order to comprehend this flow, the following section suggests a general typology of identifiable information to grasp the specific characteristics of identifiability.

A typology of identifiable information

The analysis of flows of personal data or of PII, is a core task of every PIA process. However, a lack of common understanding about the basic types of this information and their indistinct relation to (digital) technology impede this task, and thus the assessment of privacy impacts. The crux is that ICTs complicate the determination of what counts as PII because, as shown, digital information offers myriad ways to identify a person with and without her involvement. There is as yet no generally valid typology that appropriately considers the role technology has on identifiability and identifiable information. As discussed previously in Chapter 6, typologies such as the seven types of privacy (Finn *et al.* 2013) or Solove's (2006) description of privacy-affecting activities focus instead on personal information and do not sufficiently address identifiability in a broader sense. The term "personal information" implies information originating from a person; the term "identifiable" (or, synonymously, identity) information is conceptually broader, even though it refers to the identity of a person as well. The relevance of this distinction for PIA, particularly as regards technology, will be discussed in the following.

While every kind of personal information is a type of identifiable information, not every type of identifiable information necessarily results directly from a person. As shown in Chapter 5, technology-specific information may enable various forms of implicit identification. Technology usage may automatically generate identifiable information which can be used to identify a person, even though this person did not provide the information directly. It is often sufficient to have some piece of information relating to a particular person gathered from technologies. Identifiable information is generic and context-dependent. In one particular context, information might not refer to one's identity. However, linked to another, it can then become PII due to this linkage of contexts. Information aggregation is thus is a potentially privacy-intrusive practice. The more data is available, the easier it is to find patterns out of it, which can be used for identification purposes and thus privacy intrusion. Through aggregation, identity patterns can be refined, which is particularly fostered by ICTs. Hence, the identifiability of the individual grows with the amount of identifiable information and its usage contexts. Taking these dynamic characteristics of identity and (personal) information more into account may contribute to improving privacy protection in general.

Current privacy standards focus mainly on PII. Standard guides to protect PII such as of the US National Institute of Standards and Technology define PII broadly as

> any information about an individual maintained by an agency, including (1) any information that can be used to distinguish or trace an individual's identity, such as name, social security number, date and place of birth, mother's maiden name, or biometric records; and (2) any other information that is linked or linkable to an individual, such as medical, educational, financial, and employment information.
>
> (McCallister *et al.* 2010: 1)

The ISO/IEC 29100:2011 privacy framework[2] offers a similar definition of PII as "any information that (a) can be used to identify" a natural person "to whom the information relates, or (b) is or might be directly or indirectly linked to" (ISO 2011: 2). According to this framework, there are at least four instances where information can be seen as identifiable information:

> if it contains or is associated with
>
> - an identifier which refers to a natural person (e.g., a social security number);
> - an identifier which can be related to a natural person (e.g., a passport number, an account number);
> - an identifier which can be used to establish a communication with an identified natural person (e.g., a precise geographical location, a telephone number);
> - or if it contains a reference which links the data to any of the identifiers above.
>
> (ISO 2011: 7)

240 Toward an identifiability-based framework

Hence, information does not necessarily consist of an identifier to be understood as PII. Also, a specific characteristic which distinguishes a natural person from others (e.g., biometric data) can be considered as PII (ibid.). An identifier can be used directly for identification while a characteristic can be used for identification in combination with other information. For example, a name is an identifier; eye color is a characteristic which alone does not identify a person, unless she is the only person in a crowd with this eye color. The combination of eye color and other body-specific characteristics may allow a particular pattern to be found that makes an individual uniquely identifiable in a certain context. Moreover, if characteristics are linked to an identifier, then the degree of identifiability increases. But other information, which contains neither an identifier nor a specific characteristic, can also relate to a person and enable identification. The quality of identification inter alia depends on the uniqueness of the identifiable information in relation to its environment. For instance, an identifier consisting of a two-digit number (ranging from one to ten) is obviously insufficient to uniquely identify a person in a group of 100 people. This is a matter of statistics and mathematics and concepts like k-anonymity (Sweeney 2002), t-closeness (e.g., Li *et al.* 2007) or differential privacy (Dwork and Roth 2014), which deal with this issue from a technical perspective (see also the discussion on PbD in Chapter 5). Irrespective of the technical aspects, this dependency on environmental factors affects identifiability. Therefore, the quality of identifiable information may alter with a changing socio-technical environment. In general, identification is closely related to pattern-recognition techniques, as any type of identifiable information can be suitable to explore (unique) patterns which may then serve identification purposes. Given these issues, it can be challenging to grasp the exact amount of identifiable information, particularly when ICTs are involved in the processing.

Although the outlined definitions and standards are essential, there is a general lack of coherent guidelines on how to assess PII and in particular as regards technology-induced identifiable information. Existing typologies of PII suffer from reductionist perspectives which only frame information as PII which "actually identifies a specific individual" in a specific context (Schwartz and Solove 2011: 49). Hence, they are mostly limited in scope and do not mirror contemporary technology and socio-technical practices. As a consequence, risks of de-anonymization or re-identification and use of technology-specific identifiable information often remain unrecognized. A further issue is that the types of identifiable information are not conceptually grasped but derived mainly from legal frameworks only. With different national legal frameworks, the understanding of personal information can also differ. Nevertheless, at least in Europe, the GDPR offers an important baseline as its definition of personal data (in Article 4(1) GDPR) includes direct and indirect identification and considers identifiable information as privacy relevant (see also Chapter 3). However, for conducting PIAs, this baseline can be of limited use, especially when aiming for ethical compliance that goes beyond legal requirements.

Most PIA approaches provide some guidance on how to assess personal data, such as CNIL (2015b), which differs between common and sensitive personal data. Although this distinction is legally important it is limited in scope and can be ambiguous. For instance, the mentioned examples of common data are among others civil status, identity, identification data, financial situation, connection data such as IP addresses, location data, etc. Data listed as perceived to be sensitive are, e.g., biometric data and bank data. And sensitive data in a legal sense are, e.g., philosophical, political, religious and trade-union views, sex life, health data, racial or ethnic origin (CNIL 2015b). Also, additional distinctions between content and non-content and/or metadata (data about data), referring to the peculiarities of digital information processing are not appropriately considered in PIA. Such a distinction was inter alia used in the abandoned EU Directive on the retention of telecommunications data (as mentioned in Chapter 5). Proponents argued that, as no content of communications was gathered but only metadata, the individual's right to privacy would not be violated. However, critics highlighted that metadata provides deep insights into personal communications and a separation between content and non-content is not feasible in socio-technical reality. Not least as, e.g., NSA surveillance practices make heavy use of metadata (Greenwald 2014; Schneier 2014). In his rulings the EU Court of Justice made clear that the retention of metadata is deeply privacy-intrusive (CJEU 2014/2016). This case underlines that ICTs reinforce diminishing boundaries between different types of personal and non-personal information, which challenges the determination of the extent to which privacy is affected. It generally makes sense to consider metadata in PIA. However, metadata are either unconsidered or vaguely associated with PII. In the ISO privacy framework (ISO 2011), for instance, metadata are only incidentally mentioned as an example of information not easily visible to the user, such as properties of a document. Overall, the role of metadata for PIA is rather ambiguous. A stronger consideration of metadata in PIA is relevant but not sufficient as it is conceptually too broad. Overall, existing typologies of identifiable information for PIA are relatively erratic and not systematic. Furthermore, there is a lack of approaches explicitly considering identifiable information resulting from technology usage. There is thus demand for updated concepts of PII. Accordingly, the following section suggests four basic dimensions of identifiability to grasp the different types of identifiable information.

Four basic dimensions of identifiability

As shown, there is a broad range of possibilities to directly or indirectly, explicitly or implicitly, identify individuals. ICTs reinforced identifiability and stimulate a further expansion thereof which may span across a multiplicity of socio-technical contexts. These conflating contexts further complicate privacy protection. Therefore, making the boundaries between different contextual identity layers or sub-systems more visible, i.e., increasing the transparency of explicit and implicit identification processes, is an important step toward more effective privacy concepts. To achieve this requires a deeper understanding of identifiability and the emergence of identifiable information. Identifiable information does not necessarily originate from the individual concerned but can also result from technology usage without direct involvement of that individual. Hence, it can be difficult to even detect such types of information due to the largely lacking options to categorize it as a type of PII. Consequently, potential privacy impacts of the corresponding information processing may be unrecognized. Therefore, I argue for a more detailed consideration of these types of information in PIA processes based on a distinction between personal and technical identifiability (bearing in mind that both are intrinsically linked). Consequently, a typology of identifiable information should not merely comprise PII (as discussed above) but also information related to the technologies that are involved in the processing of PII, i.e., technically identifiable information—TII. Although both types are strongly interrelated it is reasonable to explicitly consider identifiable information emerging from technology.

TII can be defined as any information resulting from the employment or use of a technology that refers or relates to an individual and can be used to (directly or indirectly) identify the individual. Technology primarily means ICTs. As will be shown, this distinction between PII and TII can be of practical use, and support the improvement of PIAs. However, these two types alone are not sufficient to improve the general understanding of how identifiability and thus how identifiable information emerges. From a theoretical stance, the dynamics of identifiable-information processing in general may be characterized by a set of basic dimensions which may be valid for personal and technological entities alike. Such basic dimensions could improve the theoretical understanding of identifiability, which supports the enhancement of PIA as well as PbD approaches. I thus further suggest the following four basic dimensions or meta-categories of identifiable information.[3]

As illustrated in Figure 7.2, the dimensions are not isolated but interrelated and thus also represent layers. The basic rationale for these dimensions is informed by the dialectical character of identity with its relatively static or stable items as well as its dynamics (what Ricoeur (1992) called *idem* and *ipse*, see Chapter 3). However, given the complex dynamics of ICTs, a distinction between stable and dynamic information alone is of limited analytical value. The dynamic issues of (digital) identities in particular complicate the analysis of identifiable information. More reasonable therefore is to find dimensions that determine the composition of identifiable information with respect to these dynamic issues. In this regard it is of particular interest what the reference point of identifiable information is and what it describes (e.g., substantial details of a particular person, a spatio-temporal setting, relations or interactions the person is linked to); how identifiable information occurs; how technology may refer to the individual entity (a person) represented by that information; and how the dynamics of technology may alter this information or create more. As a result, four basic dimensions of identifiable information can be detected, namely substantial, spatio-temporal, relational and interactional.

These dimensions can be explained from a system-theoretical perspective. Similar to a system, which is dynamic by nature, characterized by the interplay

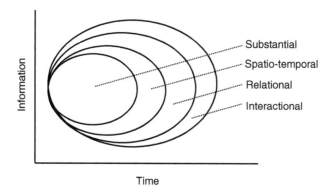

Figure 7.2 Four basic dimensions of identifiable information.

and relations of its elements, an individual can also be abstractly framed as a systemic entity that consists of some substance or core, has relations to others, and interacts with its environment in different spatio-temporal contexts. The same is true for the technologies and applications that are used to process information about the individual. These items can be seen as sub-systems of a socio-technical system related to the individual. As far as these sub-systems process information related to the individual, for each of these systems, the substantial, spatio-temporal, relational, and interactional information they use or produce is of interest, if it links to the individual's identity. It has to be noted that this approach is by no means to be misinterpreted as a reductionist view on identity or individuality, which is completely rejected here. The benefit of these categories is that they allow both types to be considered—PII and TII alike, as well as the dynamics and relations in between. In the following, options are presented on how to categorize PII and TII with these dimensions. Indeed, given the dynamics of digital information, a distinct, completely unambiguous mapping providing a comprehensive list of identifiable information is hardly feasible. Nevertheless, the proposed typology contributes to facilitate the analysis of identifiable information. It represents a concretization of the identity shadow problem as presented in Chapter 5. This typology can also be useful to detect types of information which may be unrecognized yet, though privacy relevant.

Personal identifiability and corresponding identifiable information

As regards PII, these dimensions can be used to structure how a person can be represented by her identifiable information. Briefly speaking, a person has a substantial, unique identity which is involved in multiple different contexts. Identifiable information thus can reveal who a person is, where a person is located at a certain time, whom a person is related to, what a person does and/or how she interacts, and so on. The substantial dimension corresponds with the relatively durable/stable[4] type of identity—*idem*. The other three types can be more variable, and thus refer instead to the dynamic type of identity—*ipse*. During her lifetime, an individual's identity is involved and thus represented in many different spatio-temporal, relational and interactional contexts where she can be identified by information referring to her; e.g., being at a certain place at a certain time; being related to other people, associated with different organizations, etc.; information about individual behavior and actions, etc. In combination, these four dimensions are basic determinants of the representation of an individual identity. Hence, they shape the identifiability of a person.

1   Substantial includes information about the "substance" of an individual person. Regardless of whether identifiable information is dynamic, every individual person can be described by a set of information which can be used to represent her unique identity in a certain context. Or in other words: the information can be used to substantially identify her. As a member of society, a person is identified in a variety of domains and thus has a social, economic and political identity. These identities are usually represented by some kind of unique identifier to substantially identify the person. The first dimension is thus called substantial and comprises all information that allows for unique identification of an individual person (at least in a certain context). Consequently, basic characteristics about a person but also different types of identifiers fall into this category. This includes information that directly refers to this very person such as (a) *body-specific characteristics* (eye color, hair color, height, size, weight, gender, etc.), biometric features (e.g., facial and bodily appearance, fingerprint, iris structure, DNA, voice[5]); but also (b) *person-specific information* used to represent one's social, economic or political identity such as full name, social security number, credit card number, passport number, driving license ID, bank account number, customer ID, etc.[6]

2   The second dimension is called spatio-temporal. It comprises all information that refers to the spatial and/or temporal occurrence of an individual such as age, date of birth, place of birth, home address, postal code, nationality, ethnic origin, location of living, location of work, current location.

3   The third dimension is called relational and addresses all information about relationships of an individual such as personal status (married, single), employment status, employer, family and relatives, friends, personal contacts and associations, etc.

4   The fourth dimension, interactional, comprises all information about personal interests, behavior and actions, communications, expression, etc. including sensitive information such as political activities, religious beliefs, sexual preferences, etc., resulting from or relevant for interactions with others.

Technical identifiability and corresponding identifiable information

All the types of PII mentioned can be represented and processed by technical means. The processing of identifiable information by ICTs makes this information reproducible, which leads to the emergence of digital identity. Technology can extend or enrich identifiable information in manifold ways. Therefore, a digital identity representation is likely to expand. It could be argued that some of the types of PII mentioned involve technologies as well, such as social security, passport, credit card number, etc. This is true, but these kind of identifiers basically serve formal identification purposes, directly related to the person. Therefore, these forms are assigned to PII and not to TII (although in some practical contexts a clear distinction may not always be achievable). Technical identifiability and TII address information of a virtual nature and/or which has virtual processing contexts.

TII typically serves to identify a technical device in the first place. This device, in turn, refers to a person. While identifiable information in the physical or analog world refers to a kind of physical object that has matter or substance (a natural person, a document representing this person, etc.) this is not necessarily the case in digital environments, which process information about virtual representations of the original objects. Hence, the technology (or set of interrelated technologies) applied to process identifiable information can entail the creation of additional identifiable information. For example, a typical online user session may request some kind of information for user authentication. At the same time, it involves at least a computing device (e.g., PC, laptop, smartphone) and a web browser to access a website, service, application, etc. Each of these systems bears some kind of identifiable information which can refer to the individual user. Hence, in this example, three technical systems are involved where each may provide identifiable information. With the number of sub-systems involved, the amount of TII is likely to increase. This aspect is crucial for the understanding of technical identifiability.

The virtual, non-physical processing of identifiable information complicates the conducting of PIA. Metaphorically speaking, every ICT usage can throw an identity shadow which may expand, as discussed in Chapter 5. Besides PII, technology-specific identifiable information can also be used in various ways for privacy intrusion, e.g., by advanced techniques of de-anonymization and re-identification such as digital fingerprinting. It is thus important to consider these technology-specific types of identifiable information as well. It has to be noted that just as with PII, the following description cannot be a comprehensive list of all types of TII either. The types and amount of TII can vary with technologies, applications, etc. But these basic dimensions allow different applications, technologies, etc. to be viewed from the same analytical lens, to gain a more detailed picture of identifiable information and its impact on privacy. Against the background of a growth in converging or hybrid technologies, conglomerates of interrelated applications, etc., it is likely that the complexity of PIA will further increase. This typology can support dealing with this complexity.

TII can be categorized with the same four basic types—substantial, spatio-temporal, relational and interactional:

1   Substantial here means identifiable information that originates from those technologies, devices or applications that are primarily involved in the processing of PII. Basically, this includes information applicable to substantially identify an individual based on a technical artifact (an application and/or technical device) she makes use of. A general guiding question to explore this information is, e.g.: what kind of technologies and applications (hard- and software) are employed and how do they identify a particular user? Typical are (predetermined or generated) unique identifiers. In some cases, it may be useful to distinguish between (a) *application-specific* and (b) *device-specific* information. Basic examples of *application (or service-) specific* information are user credentials (usernames, pseudonyms, e-mail address, phone number, etc.), as well as particular identification numbers (e.g., Google or Facebook ID, user session ID, etc. but also other unique identifiers of a digital identity). Particular cases are external IDM services such as social logins (see Chapter 4). They process substantial identifiable information (e.g., a Facebook ID) but originate from and refer to an external entity, i.e., the social media platform they originate from (they are thus also part of relational TII, see below). *Device-specific information* typically includes identifiers of technical devices, (e.g., IP address, MAC address, SIM-card ID, IMEI of mobile phone, smart card number, what kind of device is used, whatever identifiers are used to establish a user session).

2   Spatio-temporal means temporal and spatial information about the (primary) usage context of a technology, application or service, e.g., about where and when a service was used. Typical examples are geo-location, date, time and duration of usage, (timestamps), time zone, last login, duration of user session, date and time of user activity (e.g., postings), time or similar information about when and from which device a person used a particular application, etc. Information of this kind may be, e.g., stored in log files, usage protocols and the like. Depending on the number of additional technologies or applications involved in the original usage context as well as related contexts, various forms of spatio-temporal information may be gathered. These types are described as relational.

3   Relational basically means information (or metadata) about technologies or applications (and/or sub-systems) that are additionally related to a usage context, either directly or indirectly. Typical examples are the employed computing device, databases and other repositories processing and storing information; or technologies which predetermine an application such as a Web browser in the case of an online service, or integrated social media plugins or logins, or the social graph (see Chapter 4). An example of increasing relevance concerns "*apps*", i.e., micro-programs, typically used to enrich smartphones (but also other computing devices) with additional features. Basically, apps can extend the functionality of a system, and thus

its relations to other systems. They may also process PII and TII and share them with external sources (e.g., username, phone number, geo-location, etc.). In some contexts it can make sense to differentiate further between *internal* and *external* relations: *internal* relations include all features and applications that are directly involved in a usage context; *external* relations may comprise features resulting from external sources or applications with interfaces to other external systems for third-party services. Relational TII comprises information available from the related sub-systems. Depending on the number of sub-systems, there can be myriad ways to gather additional TII and use fingerprinting techniques to create quasi-identifiers.[7] Therefore, configuration details of, e.g., a user's computing device can be assigned to this type, which can be read out to gather identity patterns. For instance, details about the operating system (e.g., type and version), language settings, particular software installations, screen resolution and color depth, installed fonts, plugins, information about Web camera or microphone, etc. In the case of an online service, a variety of information can be gathered (e.g., http header information[8]), web browser data (e.g., bookmarks, referrer, history of visited sites, configuration, information from cookies, browser settings and user preferences such as cookie settings, adblocker settings, list of fonts, list of installed plugins, storage settings[9]); further examples are metadata of digital objects such as documents, specific settings for image representation (e.g., pictures rendered with HTML), and so on. Even the list of favorite wi-fi networks as well as the list of installed apps might be exploited in this regard.

4   Interactional refers to information that occurs during an application context or results from a user interaction. This can be content-specific information, i.e., information that represents the content of a communication or interaction; such as typical information occurring in social media usage, ranging from comments, postings, photos, videos or audio, a digital voice pattern, textual messages, e-mail content, contacts and interaction partners, social media content shared links and "likes", etc.; but also metadata about communications such as information about involved communication parties, time and number of messages, duration of calls or chats, location of the involved parties, etc. Moreover, even hardware information, e.g., generated while a user interacts with a computing component (e.g., keyboard, mouse, touchpad/screen, etc.), can be used to gather unique patterns for fingerprinting (e.g., Norte 2016) to identify a particular user.

Practical scope and limits of the typology

The description of the different types of TII highlights that there are numerous forms of additional identifiable information. ICT usage often involves a conglomerate of many interrelated technologies, entailing enormous complexity. Therefore, the different types of TII can overlap, and a clear-cut distinction is not feasible in many cases. This is particularly true in online services, where,

Toward an identifiability-based framework*

usually, multiple different technologies and applications are involved. A detection of the exact amounts of TII can thus be enormously challenging. The depth of information gathered by these types depends heavily on the technology or application etc. explored. Also, the assignment of information may vary with the primary focus of the analysis. Nevertheless, a basic distinction can be useful to gain a more detailed picture of how identifiability emerges from technology and the socio-technical practices in which it is applied, not least because it can help to reveal how a person might be identifiable by TII, even though she does not directly provide personal information when using a technology, etc. This can support the exploration of what types of identifiable information are necessary and what types could be avoided with respect to data minimization and privacy. The distinction between PII and TII facilitates revealing what information types emerge directly from an individual's identity attributes and what types result from technologies or applications. For instance, in several PIA models (e.g., CNIL 2015a/2015b), IP addresses are deemed as personal data; in others (e.g., ICO 2014), they are unconsidered. In each case, it remains rather vague to what extent they are privacy relevant. The suggested typology allows specifying it as a device-specific type of TII and eases its recognition in PIA.

To provide a more practical notion of the typology, the following examples sketch a brief mapping against the types of PII and TII:

- A common e-mail application may process:

  substantial PII—(a) gender, (b) personal name

  spatio-temporal PII—contact details (affiliation, address, phone number, etc., as, e.g., provided by the signature)

  relational PII—associated institution, message receivers/communication partner(s)

  interactional PII—content of communication

  substantial TII—(a) e-mail account ID, (b) IP address, MAC address (if access is via phone, in addition eventually also IMEI, sim-card ID)

  spatio-temporal TII—timestamp, geo-location

  relational TII—e-mail header information (e.g., IP address and domain of involved e-mail servers, eventual additional digital fingerprinting info (e.g., cookies, http header information, type of submitted document, etc.))

  interactional TII—message content, textual structure and patterns (e.g., writing style).

  Hence, even a typical e-mail application contains a significant amount of personally as well as technically identifiable information.

- The most prominent example with extensive arrays of PII and TII is social media:

  substantial PII—(a) gender, photo (facial appearance, eye color), (b) personal name spatio-temporal PII—date of birth/age, place of birth, home address, postal code, nationality, language, location of living, location of work, current location

relational PII—friends, family, personal status, employment status

interactional PII—personal interests, hobbies, education

substantial TII—(a) username/ID (e.g., Facebook, Google, Twitter, etc.), pseudonyms, e-mail, phone number; (b) IP address, MAC address (if access is via phone, and eventually IMEI, SIM-card ID)

spatio-temporal TII—date and time of logins

relational TII—internal: mapping of social networks, groups involved or associated with (social graph); external: social plugins, i.e., websites visited and signed into with social media ID

interactional TII—content produced, shared or "liked" (such as uploaded documents, images, etc.) posts, comments, search terms, videos watched, music listened to, favorite films, music, books, etc.

- Similar, though even more complex mappings may be gathered, e.g., for a smart metering application:

substantial PII—(a) gender, (b) personal name of consumer, energy contract and billing details (e.g., customer ID, payment method)

spatio-temporal PII—home address, phone number, details about energy demand and power connection

relational PII—number of people in household

interactional PII—energy-consumption behavior patterns

substantial TII—(a) account ID, eventual user credentials (e.g., username, password) for an online application, (b) ID of energy device/smart meter, IP address, MAC address (if access is via phone and eventually IMEI, sim-card ID)

spatio-temporal TII—usage data, e.g., date and time stamps of energy demand, frequency of usage; amount of provided energy and power, etc.

relational TII—data and function of individual consumers

interactional TII—usage patterns (e.g., hours of use, number and type of occupants/devices, i.e., how many computers, TVs, washing machines, etc.).

These examples demonstrate that the amount of PII and (particularly) TII can vary significantly, obviously depending on the assessed technology or application. But there are also several types relevant in each case, when online applications are involved, which may be an indicator for PbD demand. In practical terms, when conducting a PIA, mappings are likely to be less detailed because there is no need to explore all potential types of TII. For PIA, only those types of identifiable information are relevant which are factually gathered and processed by the analyzed application or system, and used for explicit or implicit identification purposes. For instance, when a user's IP address is not gathered by an application or linked to the user, it is less problematic in this regard. Ideally, with respect to data minimization, the amount of TII processing is kept to a minimum, so that only information inevitably required for the application is gathered.

From a wider point of view, the categories of TII in particular may contribute to technology development with respect to PbD and privacy-by-default mechanisms, as those types of information requiring particular protection may be easier to detect. In this regard, the typology also corresponds with the notions of PIA and PbD as proactive tools to detect privacy risks early and define corresponding protection measures. As it is impossible to completely map all types of identifiable information, a basic typology can help in considering the extent to which additional identifiable information may emerge (e.g., during development), for instance from the development of new technologies or the integration of additional sub-systems. Considering further progress of ICTs and recent trends such as "smart" technologies, ambient intelligence, big data, artificial intelligence, machine learning, etc., the emergence of additional identifiable information and further expanding identifiability is likely. To name just one example, smart home apps may create detailed profiles of their users and their embedded environments (e.g., heating temperature, energy consumption preferences, number of people in the household, etc.). As a consequence of these developments, privacy impacts may also further intensify.

The primary aim of the suggested typology is to improve the theoretical understanding of identifiability, which can facilitate the analysis of identifiable information flows crucial for PIA. To some extent, the typology might be relevant from a legal perspective as well. However, it has to be noted that a high degree of caution is required when considering the different types of information in legal contexts. Because simply extending the list of legally relevant types of information is probably not the right way of dealing with the problems resulting from identifiability, the typology as such is instead an attempt to better grasp the functions and origins of identifiable information with respect to enhancing privacy protection. Obviously, the practical implementation and applicability depend heavily on the particular system and contexts a PIA is carried out for. The practicability of the typology thus needs to be explored in future work including empirical testing. Nevertheless, there are some basic steps relevant in each PIA process. The next section provides a general overview on how to carry out a PIA process based on the identifiability-based framework presented, which takes the proposed typology into account.

How to carry out an identifiability-based PIA process

The previous sections presented and discussed a general framework for PIA with an emphasis on identifiability and different types of identifiable information. The presented framework can improve the conceptual and theoretical backing of PIA as it is not limited to specific technologies. The typology of identifiability is an additional value as it sheds light on different types of identifiable information, and thus gives a more detailed picture of a privacy impact. This section briefly outlines how this framework may be practically applied in a prototypical PIA process, sketched in Figure 7.3.

The basic steps of this process are informed by existing PIA approaches (as discussed in Chapter 6; e.g., Raab and Wright 2012; ICO 2014; CNIL 2015a; Bieker *et al.* 2016; EuroPriSe 2017) and adapted to the general identifiability-based framework presented. These phases of the process build on each other, although the particular steps in the assessment phase are not necessarily iterative. Some tasks may overlap or complement each other. Documentation is important

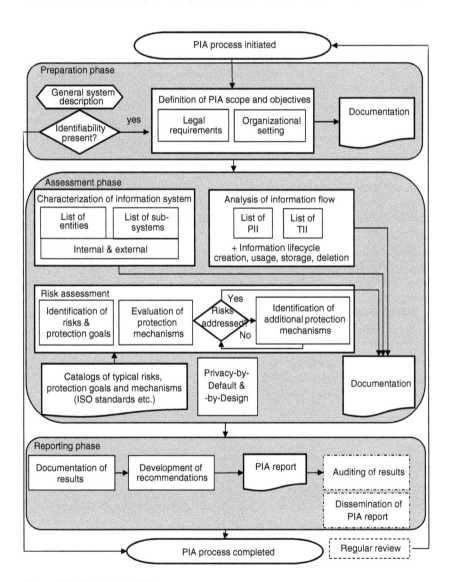

Figure 7.3 Prototypical PIA process.

in each phase to feed the subsequent phases and prepare the PIA report, which is the final outcome of the process.

Preparation phase

Initially, the system, application, etc. of interest needs to be briefly described including its general function and purpose. This short description is the starting point to determine the general requirements and circumstances for the PIA process. Basically, there are many reasons to conduct a PIA, e.g., the assessment of an existing service or product, the development of a new or the improvement of an existing socio-technical system, etc. At this stage, it is also useful to know whether a PIA, a privacy audit or a similar procedure has already been conducted. Ideally, there is corresponding documentation available such as a previous PIA report, an auditing document, etc.

As identifiability is the primary risk, the initial task is to determine whether identifiability is present, i.e., is a person identifiable by any of the information being processed. A guiding question in this regard is, for instance: *Does the system/application/program etc. process information that refers or relates to an individual person?*

If there is no possible clear negation of this question, then a general precondition for PIA is present. In the next step, the scope and objectives of the assessment should be defined. First of all, this means checking whether a PIA is legally required (e.g., by the GDPR and/or national laws) or carried out on a voluntary basis.[10] This is followed by a clarification of the organizational setting including the objectives of conducting the PIA, such as: ensuring privacy compliance, improving the level of privacy protection, fostering transparency and accountability of the product/service/system, etc. Furthermore, who is responsible for the PIA process needs to be determined (e.g., name and role of team members). Ideally, there is a particular person to whom the function of a data protection officer is entrusted (as, e.g., intended in Article 37 GDPR) with the task and the corresponding resources (such as team members from the IT department, product development and quality management) to conduct a PIA process.

Assessment phase

System characterization

In this main phase, the system that processes identifiable information is described in more detail. This includes a description of the purpose(s) and characteristics of information processing, of the main internal and external entities as well as the sub-systems involved in the processing. The result of this description is an overview on the function and purpose of the system, relevant actors and their roles as well as basic components (e.g., applications, databases, software interfaces or technologies) that determine how and in what domains identifiable information is processed. This should include information about integrated data repositories (e.g., databases, registers, etc.) to outline the general system architecture and processing modalities. Already the number of entities and sub-systems involved can be an indicator of eventual risks of re-contextualization and secondary use, because secondary use, for instance, might be more likely with a high number of external entities and sub-systems involved. Typical internal entities are the departments that process personal information (e.g., billing, contracting, CRM, finance, product development, etc.); typical external entities are service providers or third-party contractors with access rights, etc. (e.g., advertising companies, data analysts, marketers, security authorities, etc.).

An entity description may contain, e.g., name, short description of function or role (data controller, data processor,[11] provider, third-party contractor, as, e.g., specified in Article 4 GDPR), relation (internal or external) and purpose of involvement in the information processing system. As privacy and data protection regulation are yet not harmonized internationally, it is also relevant in which country an entity is located and whether EU law is applicable or not. As entities are mostly involved by the provision or use of an integrated sub-system (e.g., a cloud computing infrastructure, a database, an external service, etc.), in many cases, entities and sub-systems may be grouped in one list. Table 7.1 briefly exemplifies a description of entities involved (in the example of a web service).

Analysis of information flow

A core task of the assessment phase is the analysis of the flow of identifiable information. Ideally, this task also includes the information life cycle and the processing modalities from collection/creation, usage, storage to deletion. A useful starting point is a general but not detailed overview on how information is processed and enters the system. The general aim of this system description is to show how the system processes identifiable information: i.e., what are the origins, locations and destinations of the information, to what extent does the individual provide this information and which entities are involved in the

Table 7.1 Example list of entities involved in information processing

Entity name	Role	Relation (internal/ external)	Purpose	Related sub-system or interface
Controlling department	Data processor	Internal	Quality assurance	Controlling software
Customer care company	Data processor	External	CRM	Customer database
Facebook	Data controller	External	Identity management, user authentication	Facebook Connect

processing? It is thus important to describe the modalities of identification or authentication; i.e., whether and how an individual is identified. In the case of online systems or applications, it is particularly important to consider third-party services in this description, for instance external IDM services such as social logins and social plugins (see Chapter 4). Is there some kind of IDM approach, e.g., a standardized user registration and login procedure, is this an internal part of the system or an external service (e.g., an integrated social media profile such as of Facebook or Google), is there a centralized or decentralized user profile, etc.? The utilization of typical tools such as basic-use case descriptions, data flowcharts, workflow diagrams or similar can help to illustrate how personal information flows within the system and its components. Such an overview is also useful to show the interplay of entities, system components and personal information (process information of this kind is generally important for IT management and thus may be available at least in larger companies). It should also be checked and described whether a service serves the basic systems' purpose or an additional purpose and whether a purpose is necessary and legitimate; because every additional purpose may cause additional privacy impacts.

This overview can support fulfilling the main task, i.e., to reveal and list the different types of identifiable information. Basically this means applying the typology of identifiability by mapping which types of PII and TII are actually processed. This is particularly important as most PIA approaches focus merely on personal information and leave other relevant types of information unregarded (as discussed in the previous chapters). Practically, both types of information (PII and TII) are usually gathered in one or several databases or similar repositories. It is thus important to consider these repositories in the analysis. It can help to check the structure of user forms and user interfaces, because these determine, e.g., what information is prompted from the user or stored in her data record. For PII and TII alike, it is generally important whether the processing is necessary and legitimate. Particularly relevant is exploring how and for what purpose(s) the information is gathered and stored, whether third parties can use the information, etc. As TII is often a general by-product of technology usage, it is relevant to grasp how the information is generated and stored, as well as whether this is required for the processing context, for technical reasons or is avoidable. This is a crucial difference because eventual technical requirements may indicate a demand for PbD. The four basic categories of identifiable information (substantial, spatio-temporal/contextual, relational and interactional) and their sub-categories (as described previously) can be used as reference points to detect the amount of identifiable information. For practical use, PII and TII may be coded as shown in Table 7.2.

The codes of PII and TII can then be used to categorize the amount of information. The necessity for a detailed map depends on the concrete system being examined. In practice, a strict and detailed mapping may often be difficult and also not necessary for the objective of a PIA. For practical reasons, it can thus be sufficient in many cases to differ between PII and TII without the extra work of a more detailed additional categorization. Nevertheless, these basic

Table 7.2 PII and TII categorization

PII	TII
P1: substantial PII	T1: substantial TII
P1.1 body-specific	T1.1 application-specific
P1.2 person-specific	T1.2 device-specific
P2: spatio-temporal PII	T2: spatio-temporal TII
P3: relational PII	T3: relational TII
P4: interactional PII	T4: interactional TII

categories can be used as guiding questions to explore the composition of identifiable information. For example: *What information is used to substantially identify a person? Is any body-specific or biometric information gathered? What identifiable information is gathered from technical hardware devices, applications, sub-systems involved? What information is stored that refers to a particular application context?*

Overall, the typology can contribute to gaining a more detailed picture of where identifiable information originates from, how it is processed, etc. This can also help to identify eventual demand for additional protection mechanisms as well as to pre-detect information with an as-yet marginal but potentially higher relevance. For instance: *Are there any further types of identifiable information being processed which are expected to have a future privacy impact?* This can be useful, for example, in the case of a planned additional system feature (e.g., an integration of biometrics, or an additional technical user device such as a smart watch, a body badge, etc.).

The mapping of the amount of identifiable information and its processing modalities is an important indicator of the risks individual privacy may be exposed to. Creating a list of identifiable information is thus crucial for the assessment of these risks. Table 7.3 exemplifies a possible, practical way to gather PII and TII.

The example illustrated in Table 7.3 may be a fictional online shop. The mapping raises some privacy questions, e.g., why the social security number is involved, which is probably not necessary for the purpose. As it is shared with third parties, this may be a critical issue regarding legal privacy compliance. The gathering of an IP address may not be problematic as it is neither permanently stored nor used for a particular purpose. The processing of a facial image can be problematic as it is gathered from an external source as well as shared with third parties. This example also indicates eventual difficulties as regards informed consent as a user may have accepted the terms of use on Facebook but may not be aware that a completely different service uses her photo for CRM including third-party access. Geo-location indicates that this information here may be a sole by-product. Processing could be avoided when the application does not automatically gather this type of information by default.

Table 7.3 Example description of identifiable-information processing

Description of information			Source/processing modality	Storage duration	Purpose of use	Third-party access/ secondary use?
Main type	Category	Item				
PII	P1.2 P2 P2 P1.2	Name and surname Date of birth Address Social security no.	Provided by user	Unlimited	Billing, technical requirement	Yes Yes No Yes
TII	T1.1	User identification no.	Generated by application	Unlimited	Technical requirement	No
TII	T1.1	E-mail address	Provided by user	Unlimited	CRM	Yes
TII	T1.1	Username	Provided by user	Unlimited	Technical requirement	No
TII	T1.2	IP address	Automatically gathered from device	Temporary: after session expires	Undefined	No
PII	P1.1 (T4)	Facial image	External source (e.g., social media)	Unlimited	CRM	Yes
TII	T2	Geo-location	Automatically gathered from application (e.g., user's web browser)	Temporary	Undefined	No

Risk assessment

Based on the system characteristics and the analysis of the information flow, risks and protection goals can be identified as well as measures to mitigate these risks. This includes a target-performance comparison, i.e., an evaluation of the existing protection mechanisms and their suitability to address the risks and goals. This phase can be backed by existing standards and catalogs of typical risks and protection goals (BSI 2008; McCallister *et al.* 2010; ISO 2011; Hansen *et al.* 2015; Bieker *et al.* 2016). An integral part of this phase is also an evaluation of eventual additional protection mechanisms, when existing protection is lacking or insufficient to address the risks. Particularly relevant issues are protection mechanisms that provide privacy by default and privacy by design.

It has to be noted that risk basically means here that individual privacy is affected. This goes beyond the legal requirement to conduct PIA, where a risk may be seen as a potential violation of legal compliance only. However, as this PIA approach is broader, it is crucial to assess the information processing from the individual's perspective. As shown and highlighted in the PIA framework, the primary risk of identifiability entails a number of further basic risks and threats, such as unlimited availability, linkability and re-contextualization. General protection goals help to tackle these risks. These goals are to be understood as an ideal standard setting to achieve privacy protection. Ideally, anonymity and pseudonymity are provided as far as possible. However, full anonymity is often not feasible without challenging the main purpose of information processing. Therefore, the protection goals aim to minimize the risks by providing basic conditions for secure information processing so that identifiable information is largely protected from misuse. Although there is a number of basic risks and protection goals that are of general relevance, each information system differs in functioning and purpose. Hence, the implementation of the risk assessment process, the effectiveness of protection mechanisms and eventual need for additional safeguards depend heavily on the system and its processes as a whole. It is thus important that the risk assessment takes into account the system characterization and the flow of identifiable information. The list of PII and TII and the processing and storage modalities provide several indications of privacy risks and threats. For instance, the risk of unlimited availability is shaped by storage modalities. The longer identifiable information is available and stored, the higher the associated risk. Limited storage and retention duration thus contributes to reducing risks of this kind. A related issue concerns access to information and processing modalities. A centralized database containing a full record of personal information bears a higher risk than a de-centralized storage concept with separated pieces of information. The direct use of global identifiers valid in multiple datasets (e.g., in separated databases, etc.) amplifies the risk of linkability and data aggregation across multiple contexts. Secondary use and access to information by third parties affect the risk of re-contextualization.

All these aspects are relevant to identify the risks and protection mechanisms. General guiding questions are, e.g.: *What kinds of risks is identifiable information exposed to? How and with what protection mechanisms are these risks addressed? Is the processing of identifiable information in accordance with common privacy and data protection principles (data minimization, purpose limitation, etc.)? What are the existing protection mechanisms and how suitable are they to mitigate the risks? How is data protected from illegal or unintended access? Is PbD considered in the information processing context and in what form? Is identifiable information encrypted, pseudonymized, anonymized or deleted?*

There are many options to assess the severity of risks, e.g., with scales from high, medium to low or similar. A further option is to assess the protection level related to a risk with categories, e.g., (4) high, (3) appropriate, (2) sufficient, (1) insufficient, (0) missing; as shown in Table 7.4. This mapping can indicate to what extent the protection mechanisms contribute to mitigating the risks. The results of the risk assessment indicate eventual need for the implementation of additional safeguards. A simple example to compare risks and controls may look as follows.

The concrete realization of a risk assessment procedure depends heavily on the scope and aims of the PIA. A standard application with a low amount of PII and TII has different requirements than a large-scale application that processes sensitive information (e.g., in the health sector). But in any case, for the evaluation of protection mechanisms it is vital to create use cases. The involvement of legal as well as IT experts is important in this regard. Moreover, to avoid organizational blindness, including standard users can be vital to gain the perspective of an individual concerned on privacy intrusion. A potential side-effect of user involvement is a usability evaluation, which can support service provision.

Table 7.4 Example description of risks and protection mechanisms

Risk type	Description of risk	Protection mechanism	Current protection level
Linkability	Identifiers are directly used and refer to full data records, also to external entities	Unlinkability, pseudonymization, encryption	3
Durability	Data access is not restricted	Access management	2
Durability	Data storage is unlimited	–	0
Aggregation	Data from multiple sources is aggregated and centrally stored	Anonymization	4
Re-contextualization/ purpose extension Traceability	Secondary use, e.g., TII to track users' geo-location without informed consent	Informed consent or usage limitation	1
Traceability	Individual user behavior is monitored for profiling activity	–	0

Reporting phase

Finally, all assessment results are documented in the PIA report. This report ideally also provides recommendations on risk mitigation and improvement or implementation of protection mechanisms. For quality insurance, an optional auditing to evaluate the PIA report by an independent authority (e.g., DPA or external data protection officer) can be useful to detect and handle eventual conflicting interests and facilitate the implementation of protection mechanisms. This audit can also be linked to a certification procedure such as the European Privacy Seal.[12] A public dissemination of the PIA report contributes to improving accountability and transparency of information processing, enables public scrutiny, and may support reputation management. Depending on the particular function of the PIA, this document serves as a reference guide for privacy compliance, a discussion paper for development (e.g., to improve product or service quality and security by integrating PbD) as well as input information for a further PIA process. Ideally, a PIA process is continuously revised and conducted in a defined period of time, e.g., every five years or if the system or its purpose has significantly changed by, e.g., new features or technologies.

Notes

1 The secure erasure of data on digital storage components (e.g., hard disk drives) is an issue in computer science. Typical, secure approaches are overwriting information with random values as a simple virtual deletion is insufficient. Data on modern storage devices such as solid-state disks is more difficult to erase. For more details, e.g., Wei *et al.* (2011).
2 This ISO framework is an international privacy standard that supports people and organizations in dealing with organizational and technical privacy issues of ICT systems.
3 It has to be noted that these dimensions are an attempt to theoretically grasp the emergence of identifiability without claiming comprehensiveness.
4 It is described as relatively stable, because these types of information can also change, though rather occasionally and over longer periods of time.
5 Against the background of increasing applications with embedded voice recognition (such as in digital assistants), voice patterns are gaining in importance.
6 Although these identifiers involve technology, they serve formal identification purposes directly related to the person. Therefore, these forms are assigned to PII and not to TII.
7 There are some awareness-raising tools such as "am I unique?" (https://amiunique. org) or https://panopticlick.eff.org, which calculate a user's browser fingerprint based on information a user automatically provides via a typical web browser.
8 Details about http header fields can be found at www.w3.org/Protocols/rfc2616/rfc2616-sec14.html.
9 Even information with temporal limits such as that stored in the cache can be used for fingerprinting; see, e.g., https://kazuho.github.io/http-cache-fingerprint/.
10 Detailed guidance for legal requirements with respect to the GDPR can be found, e.g., in EuroPriSe (2017).
11 Basically, the controller determines the purpose of processing or adds additional purpose, while a processor acts on behalf of the controller. In practice, the distinction between controller and processor can be difficult. For a discussion on these issues, see, e.g., WP29 (2010).
12 www.european-privacy-seal.eu.

References

All URLs were checked last on October 23, 2018.

Bieker, F., Friedewald, M., Hansen, M., Obersteller, H. and Rost, M. (2016) A Process for Data Protection Impact Assessment under the European General Data Protection Regulation. In Rannenberg, K. and Ikonomou, D. (eds.), *Privacy Technologies and Policy. Fourth Annual Privacy Forum (APF)*, LNCS 9857. Frankfurt/Heidelberg/New York/Dordrecht/London: Springer, 21–37.

BSI—Bundesamt für Sicherheit in der Informationstechnik (2008) *BSI Standard 100-2: IT-Grundschutz Methodology*. Version 2.0. Bonn, Germany. www.bsi.bund.de/Shared Docs/Downloads/EN/BSI/Publications/BSIStandards/standard_100-2_e_pdf.pdf?__blob=publicationFile&v=1.

CJEU—Court of Justice of the European Union (2014) The Court of Justice Declares the Data Retention Directive to be Invalid. Press release no. 54/14. Luxembourg, April 8, 2014. Judgment in Joined Cases C-293/12 and C-594/12 Digital Rights Ireland and Seitlinger and Others. http://curia.europa.eu/jcms/upload/docs/application/pdf/2014-04/cp140054en.pdf.

CJEU—Court of Justice of the European Union (2016) The Members States May Not Impose a General Obligation to Retain Data on Providers of Electronic Communications Services. Press release no. 145/16, Luxembourg, December 21, 2016. Judgment in Joined Cases C-203/15 Tele2 Sverige AB v Post-och telestyrelsen and C-698/15 Secretary of State for the Home Department v Tom Watson and Others. http://curia.europa.eu/jcms/upload/docs/application/pdf/2016-12/cp160145en.pdf.

CNIL—Commission Nationale de l'Informatique et des Libertés (2015a) *Privacy Impact Assessment (PIA): Methodology (how to carry out a PIA)*. June 2015 edition. www.cnil.fr/sites/default/files/typo/document/CNIL-PIA-1-Methodology.pdf.

CNIL—Commission Nationale de l'Informatique et des Libertés (2015b) *Privacy Impact Assessment (PIA): Tools (templates and knowledge bases)*. June 2015 Edition. www.cnil.fr/sites/default/files/typo/document/CNIL-PIA-2-Tools.pdf.

Dwork, C. and Roth, A. (2014) The Algorithmic Foundations of Differential Privacy. *Foundations and Trends in Theoretical Computer Science*, 9(3–4): 211–407.

EuroPriSe—European Privacy Seal (2017) *EuroPriSe Criteria for the Certification of IT Products and IT-Based Services*. "GDPR ready" version, January 2017. www.european-privacy-seal.eu/AppFile/GetFile/e5ed7122-74b1-4f75-a5af-fb0c317bd20b.

Finn, R. L., Wright, D. and Friedewald, M. (2013) Seven Types of Privacy. In Gutwirth, S., Leenes, R., De Hert, P. and Poullet, Y. (eds.), *European Data Protection: Coming of Age*. Dordrecht: Springer, 3–32.

GDPR—General Data Protection Regulation (2016) Regulation (EU) 2016/679 of the European Parliament and of the Council of 27 April 2016 on the Protection of Natural Persons with Regard to the Processing of Personal Data and on the Free Movement of Such Data, and Repealing Directive 95/46/EC (General Data Protection Regulation). http://eur-lex.europa.eu/legal-content/EN/TXT/HTML/?uri=CELEX:32016R0679&qid=1485427623759&from=en.

Greenwald, G. (2014) *No Place to Hide: Edward Snowden, the NSA and the surveillance state*. London: Hamish Hamilton/Penguin Books.

Hansen, M., Jensen, M. and Rost, M. (2015) Protection Goals for Privacy Engineering. In *Proceedings of the 2015 IEEE Security and Privacy Workshop, May 21–22, San Jose*, 159–166. http://doi.ieeecomputersociety.org/10.1109/SPW.2015.13.

ICO—UK Information Commissioner's Office (2014) *Conducting Privacy Impact Assessments: Code of practice.* Version 1.0. https://ico.org.uk/media/for-organisations/documents/1595/pia-code-of-practice.pdf.

ISO—International Organization for Standardization (2011) *Information Technology—Security Techniques—Privacy Framework.* ISO/IEC 29100:2011(E). First edition 2011–12–15.

Li, N., Li, T. and Venkatasubramanian, S. (2007) t-Closeness: Privacy beyond k-anonymity and l-diversity. In *Proceedings of the 23rd IEEE International Conference on Data Engineering (ICDE)*, 106–115. doi: 10.1109/ICDE.2007.367856.

McCallister, E., Grance, T. and Scarfone, K. (2010) *Guide to Protecting the Confidentiality of Personally Identifiable Information (PII). Recommendations of the National Institute of Standards and Technology (NIST), special publication 800-122.* US Department of Commerce. www.nist.gov/publications/guide-protecting-confidentiality-personally-identifiable-information-pii.

Nissenbaum, H. (2010) *Privacy in Context: Technology, policy, and the integrity of social life.* Stanford: Stanford University Press.

Norte, J. C. (2016) Advanced Tor Browser Fingerprinting. Blogpost, March 6, http://jcarlosnorte.com/security/2016/03/06/advanced-tor-browser-fingerprinting.html.

OECD—Organization for Economic Co-Operation and Development (2013) *The OECD Privacy Framework.* OECD Publishing. www.oecd.org/sti/ieconomy/privacy-guidelines.htm.

Pfitzmann, A. and Hansen, M. (2010) *A Terminology for Talking About Privacy by Data Minimization: Anonymity, unlinkability, undetectability, unobservability, pseudonymity, and identity.* Version 0.34. http://dud.inf.tu-dresden.de/literatur/Anon_Terminology_v0.34.pdf.

Raab, C. D. and Wright, D. (2012) Surveillance: Extending the limits of privacy impact assessment. In Wright, D. and De Hert, P. (eds.), *Privacy Impact Assessment.* Dordrecht: Springer, 363–383.

Ricoeur, P. (1992) *Oneself as Another.* (Translated by Kathleen Blamey). Chicago: University of Chicago Press.

Schneier, B. (2014) Metadata = Surveillance. *Schneier on Security*, March 13, www.schneier.com/blog/archives/2014/03/metadata_survei.html.

Schwartz, P. M. and Solove, D. J. (2011) The PII Problem: Privacy and a new concept of personally identifiable information. *New York University Law Review*, 86: 1814–1894.

Solove, D. J. (2006) A Taxonomy of Privacy. *University of Pennsylvania Law Review*, 154(3): 477–560.

Sweeney, L. (2002) k-Anonymity: A model for protecting privacy. *International Journal on Uncertainty, Fuzziness and Knowledge-based Systems*, 10(5): 557–570. https://epic.org/privacy/reidentification/Sweeney_Article.pdf.

Wei, M., Grupp, L. M., Spada, F. E. and Swanson, S. (2011) Reliably Erasing Data from Flash-Based Solid State Drives. In *9th USENIX Conference on File and Storage Technologies, San Jose, February 15–17.* www.usenix.org/legacy/events/fast11/tech/full_papers/Wei.pdf.

WP29—Article 29 Data Protection Working Party (2010) Opinion 1/2010 on the Concepts of "Controller" and "Processor". 00264/10/EN WP 169. http://ec.europa.eu/justice/article-29/documentation/opinion-recommendation/files/2010/wp169_en.pdf.

8 Is effective treatment of privacy possible?

Summary and concluding remarks

Privacy, identity and identification are inextricably intertwined. This fundamental nexus is present in analog and in digital environments or contexts alike. We as individuals become frequently identified in social, economic, political or technological domains; and we are affected and governed by the processing of various informational representations of our identities. Essentially, practices of identification involve the processing of identifiable information referring or relating to a specific person. Identification is thus a basic condition for the emergence of a privacy impact. But even just the possibility of processing information that refers or relates to the identity of a person can cause privacy risks. Moreover, the realm of possibilities of intruding into privacy expands with technology. Therefore, as argued, socio-technical identifiability is a crucial determinant of a privacy impact and lacking control thereof is a core problem of contemporary privacy protection.

As outlined in Chapter 1, this problem is a bit like a chronic disease: it appears every now and then, often with only minor symptoms. At some point, however, it breaks out on a large scale, with correspondingly serious consequences. The current public debate about how the exploitation of social media data endangers democracy can be seen as an indicator among many of a larger break out. The recent data scandal around Facebook and Cambridge Analytica showcased how easily social media, and user profiles in general, can be misused for questionable practices (e.g., for targeted political campaigning akin to surreptitious advertising aimed at influencing or manipulating voter behavior). Indeed, this debate needs to be thoroughly explored and discussed, which cannot happen in this final chapter here. But it should at least be obvious with this book that information about our identities is not just occasionally but extensively exposed to various uncontrolled usage purposes. Some uses may be not be problematic; some, e.g., that mentioned, threaten even the core processes of democracy. But irrespective of particular cases, there is a general commonality: the processing of identity information is largely uncontrolled and can therefore easily be misused. This harms privacy and can even damage the foundations of society.

Uncontrolled identifiability can thus be seen as a sort of serious digital disease that privacy protection is suffering from. This situation is likely to worsen with the ongoing digital transformation of society, which involves several socio-technical transitions altering societal functions and processes in many respects. Through ICTs and digital technology, society is increasingly pervaded and shaped by various forms of networked environments. It thus incrementally transforms into a highly networked society. Embedded in this far-reaching transformation is the changing role of privacy and identification. Identification practices significantly altered with technology. This also had an effect on the scope and functioning of privacy. Given the peculiarities of ICTs and, fundamentally, of digital information, technology usage extends the representation of personal identities. These developments increasingly challenge traditional notions of privacy and of personally identifiable (or identity) information. In contrast to analog forms of identification, digital identification can comprise multiple, dynamic contexts in which identifiable information is processed. These multiple contexts or (identity) layers are often and increasingly beyond any control. There are myriad ways to gather, re-contextualize or reproduce personal information. Moreover, there are various options to use other, non-personal types of information for identification as well. Hence, the notion and conceptualization of personal information as such has changed through informatization and digitization. As the boundaries between personal and non-personal information diminish, it is thus increasingly difficult to even determine what personal information exactly means and comprises.

Altogether, individuals are largely vulnerable to and defenseless against privacy intrusion. With growing numbers of digitally networked environments and the corresponding changes in socio-technical practices, identifiability expands significantly. As a result, the effective protection of privacy becomes even more burdensome and challenging. On the one hand, this concerns individuals who already have very limited possibilities to exercise ISD. Hence, the options for individuals to control the processing of their information could further erode. Moreover, on the other hand, even for privacy-aware institutions, it becomes increasingly difficult to protect personal information flows from misuse. Consequently, the efficacy of privacy protection in general is likely to continue to decrease. Reasons for this problem can be found in insufficient technology design and the related usage practices, but also in volatile conceptualizations of privacy which complicate protection measures overall. Apparently, privacy is a relatively abstract concept with various roles and meanings. This is one reason for complications as regards its protection. Therefore, it is crucial to reconsider what protecting privacy means in essence in order to achieve appropriate levels of protection with respect to socio-technical change.

Privacy: a permanent "versus them"? Exaggerated conflicts and underestimated complementarities with other concepts

Chapter 3 highlighted how privacy, identity and identification are intrinsically linked. Privacy is not "just" a fundamental human right but a cultural universal, as Westin (1967) highlighted. Privacy as such fulfills a vital societal function: it has an inherent boundary control function, regulating the interplay between private and public spheres. At its core, this interplay is determined by information. Consequently, privacy protection basically regulates informational relations and boundaries between individuals and other entities. ISD is thus an essential concept of this boundary control function of privacy. It involves the individual's capacity to control the processing of information about her (see Chapter 3). ISD thus contributes to self-determined maintenance, disclosure and performance of personal identity. This is crucial as, ideally, privacy provides a domain (i.e., one's particular, private sphere) where the individual can act in a self-determined way, free from interference. Privacy thus represents a constitutive framework for autonomy, enabling self-determination, vital for identity development. At the same time, identity constitutes the private sphere of a particular individual because, otherwise, privacy would have no subject or benchmark. In the same manner, identity is the socio-technical construct shaping the interactions of an individual with others and her environment. Privacy enables self-determined, free action and participation of individuals in society. Therefore, it is an enabler of other rights such as freedom of expression and thought, of movement, association, etc. (Solove 2006; Nissenbaum 2010; Cohen 2012). Consequently, the private and the public spheres are by no means opponents because they complement each other. Privacy enables regulation of the interactions between individual identities and society. This is not to be misinterpreted as a decoupling of the individual from her environment; on the contrary, this contributes significantly to a self-determined involvement in society. Therefore, privacy is not merely a private but also a public value—essential for democratic processes at the individual as well as at societal levels.

However, there are certain tensions with concepts that are partially conflicting. These tensions and conflicts challenge the public value of privacy and are a great barrier to effective protection. Particular tensions result from the misleading trade-off between privacy and security (Solove 2011; Strauß 2017). Further controversies exist with transparency: notions of post-privacy question the necessity for privacy due to increasing technical and societal transparency. In these controversies, privacy is framed as a concept in contradiction to security as well as to transparency. These narrow framings assume that privacy would be in permanent conflict with these other concepts. This jeopardizes the public value of privacy. In fact, though, there is no permanent contradiction in each case. As argued in Chapters 3 and 5, the assumed perpetual trade-off between privacy and security is a common fallacy, which reinforces securitization and privacy-intrusive surveillance practices supported by corresponding technologies. Indeed, privacy intrusions are foreseen by the law, but as exceptional options to protect democratic principles in the interests of the public, but not as a permanent necessity as suggested by the trade-off. In the trade-off logic, security is falsely presented as a dominant value frequently endangered by privacy. This misleadingly justifies a reinforcement of privacy-intrusive security and surveillance practices in the sense of a proceeding securitization.

Metaphorically speaking, a constructed security continuum generates an expanding privacy vacuum, reinforced by technology. To some extent, the rationales of post-privacy and of securitization overlap: both misleadingly reduce privacy to a form of secrecy aimed at hiding information. This logic is a fallacy because privacy comprises much more than personal secrecy or confidentiality (Solove 2011). Privacy is not least a public value requiring contextual integrity, so that personal information is processed for a particular purpose in accordance with legal and ethical norms (Nissenbaum 2010). This refers to the need for responsible handling of personal information by processing entities. However, a reductionist framing of privacy as a form of secrecy widely overrules this need for responsible actions. In fact, security and transparency of information processing are major requirements of privacy protection to allow for more accountability of processing entities. For ISD to be viable, the individual needs to know, e.g., what personal information is collected, stored and processed for what purpose, and by whom. ISD thus implies transparency and control of information processing. Accordingly, opacity undermines accountability and scrutiny of (personal) information processing and thus effective privacy protection.

Altogether it is therefore important to reconsider that, even though privacy obviously has several differences with the public sphere, security and transparency, these are *functional but not fundamental differences*. Hence, misconceptions about privacy and its alleged antagonists complicate the development of appropriate protection measures. Such misconceptions can lead to flaws in technology design, which then cause additional problems. There is already heavy pressure on privacy and ISD due to the dynamics of ICTs and of the related socio-technical practices. This pressure intensifies with a lack of solid, privacy-friendly technology design and appropriate measures. In this regard, the functional difference between privacy protection and identification can be critical: privacy implies the existence of informational frictions so that personal information is not disclosed or accessible to others without the intention and control of the individual concerned. Identification implies establishing an informational link between different entities and, thus, crossing informational boundaries. Actually, privacy protection implies regulation of these boundaries. Therefore, these different functions are not necessarily incompatible. However, several issues and tensions occur due to technology: digital technology and identification practices foster seamless information flows and complicate the provision of self-controlled informational frictions, i.e., unlinkability (as a crucial concept of technical privacy protection). Moreover, these dynamics of ICTs and digital identification benefit the dynamics of securitization and economization, which together reinforce privacy risks.

Networked identities on the rise

As shown in Chapter 4, digital identification emerged within a wider socio-technical transition, including various transformations in social, economic, political and technical domains. In a relatively short period of time, ICTs became increasingly interactive, interconnected and deeply integrated in society. They are not merely tools of information and communication anymore; they are deeply embedded *in* and have a substantial impact *on* societal structures. Visions of pervasive computing and similar ideas suggesting hyper-connectivity have become more concrete in recent years. Analog and digital environments increasingly converge, where ICTs represent socio-technical artifacts connecting both worlds. They foster networking structures, connectivity and further growth in digital information processing. This includes extended digital representations of our identities and changing identification practices. The connecting function of identification enables links between different entities serving social, economic, political as well as technical purposes. This function is embedded in and reinforced by various socio-technical developments: different forms of identification are involved to establish and maintain socio-technical networking structures; socio-technical systems generally include technical identification mechanisms as two or more entities require some processing of identifiable information about each other to establish connections; finally, individuals and institutions are also increasingly networked by various technologies processing their information. The growth in networking structures also affects the handling of digital identities: formerly rather isolated user profiles and other forms of identity representations embedded in socio-technical systems are increasingly networked as well. Social media platforms prominently highlight how interactive and interconnected online identities have become. They are thus a blueprint for the networking dynamics of digital identities.

These socio-technical transformations entail different modes of personal as well as technical identification and boost the amount of identity information. To deal with the growing complexity and foster control of digital information processing, concepts of IDM gained in importance. Basic aims include improving efficiency and security of identification processes to handle digital identities. IDM is an integral part of ICTs and online services serving various purposes, e.g., to conduct transactions in e-commerce and e-government, to manage user profiles of online platforms, etc. There is a general trend of increasing IDM, digital identity representations, personalization and thus different forms of identification, which entail and foster network dynamics. Online platforms providing social plugins and logins highlight how far-reaching digital identity information can be cross-linked and aggregated over multiple application contexts. All these practices affect the relationship between individuals and institutions in public and private sectors.

While technological progress triggered a general demand for IDM, its implementation is mainly driven by a number of interrelated economic and political interests. Policy makers in Europe as well as in other countries highlight IDM as a tool of governance to improve administrative procedures and especially to stimulate the digital economy. Digital identification serves a variety of economic purposes including, e.g., CRM, personalization, profiling, service efficiency, service-for-profile business models as well as targeted advertising. Online platforms highlight the enormous economic value of identity information and, thus, exploit it commercially. Furthermore, IDM is closely related to a number of security objectives ranging from securing online services, issues of cyber security, fighting identity fraud, crime and terrorism and thus national security. Hence, regimes of the digital economy and of the security sector are strong drivers of digital identification.

Trends of a further expansion of digital identification practices result from a complex interplay of technological, economic and socio-political factors: ICTs generally extend the representation of (digital) identities, reinforced by a convergence between analog and digital environments. Social media demonstrates this expansion of digital identities serving various commercial interests. But besides social media, identity information is also used for a number of economic, political and security purposes. Initially, IDM was used for formal identification to conduct e-transactions, though its scope extended with ICT diffusion and usage. Today, formal and informal, explicit and implicit identification overlap in many respects. Trends to further expand identification, such as questionable plans to integrate social media profiles into formal identification procedures (e.g., for national security purposes such as border control or law enforcement) highlight that digital identities increasingly enter "real world" contexts, closely related to different modes of governance and control.

The control dilemma of privacy: shaped by securitization, economization and increasing information asymmetries

Control over (digital) identity information is a crucial issue for privacy as well as for identification, though for different reasons. Protecting privacy aims to shield individuals from unintended and uncontrolled identification. This implies protecting information which directly or indirectly represents the identities of individuals. Identification includes the processing of this information to determine the identities of individuals, distinct from others. Uncontrolled processing of identity information challenges privacy protection as well as identification. The increasing importance of IDM can be seen as an attempt to regain control over digital information, though mainly to improve security. As argued in Chapter 5, this can lead to a further loss of control from a privacy perspective; in particular, as there is a lack of effective privacy features. There is thus a certain privacy control dilemma of digital identification: on the one hand, in line with various institutional modalities of power and control, the identities of individuals become increasingly gathered, recorded, measured, predicted and scored; or put simply our identities become more and more transparent in socio-technical systems and exposed to various forms of control. On the other hand, these systems, including numerous processing contexts and usage purposes of identity information, become increasingly opaque and uncontrollable for the individuals concerned.

Indeed, (digital) identification serves many vital societal functions, and is a basic instrument of social, economic and political governance. Nevertheless, it also represents a control mechanism which can be critical for privacy. In general, the striving for control involves a quest for security and stability of a matter. This applies to political and administrative power, national security as well as economic growth. Identification is used as a means toward this quest with the basic aim to reduce uncertainty and improve security in particular settings by gaining knowledge about individuals' identities. Compared to security and economic interests, privacy protection plays a rather marginal role in the implementation and usage of IDM or related digital identification practices. Given the strong influence of the digital economy and the security domain, including their self-dynamics, we can thus speak of an *economization* and *securitization of digital identification.*

As shown, several empirical examples highlight that identity information is treated as a valuable economic factor for digital markets. Likewise, identity information flows into a wide array of security and surveillance practices driven by the logic of securitization: digital identification is also framed as a tool of security governance, increasingly linked to various forms of preventive risk detection. Economic and political actors of surveillance often overlap here, together shaping the surveillant assemblage (Haggerty and Ericson 2000). The Snowden files (Greenwald 2014) bear prominent examples of this complex interplay of private enterprises and security authorities gathering identity information from ICTs. However, the nexus between surveillance and digital identification is not limited to this case. Irrespective of the usage purposes in particular, the various examples ranging from commercial exploitation to different forms of surveillance underline that the broad availability of digital identity information stimulates desires to use this information. Consequently, the almost unlimited options to gather identity information intensify risks of function and mission creep, i.e., the incremental extension of usage purposes and surveillance practices. The indistinct mix of economic and security objectives that digital identification practices often relate to underlines this aspect.

Hence, there is often a rather thin line between surveillance and (digital) identification. Apparently, its close relationship with surveillance does not imply that identification is a means of surveillance and control in any case. In brief, surveillance is privacy-intrusive when it involves the processing of identifiable information. Identification is privacy-intrusive when it breaches legal or ethical privacy norms such as a violation of contextual integrity. Therefore, the processing of identity information beyond control of the individual concerned affects her privacy. A critical issue of identification lies in imbalanced control over identity information and lacking ISD, hampering privacy protection. In this regard, there are certain observable overlaps between panopticism and identification as regards their basic mechanisms, which entail information asymmetries. A central functionality of panoptic power (mostly inherent to surveillance) is the creation and maintenance of information asymmetries for the benefit of the entity exercising this power. Also, identification can create information asymmetries, when the individual person lacks control over being identified and has little or no knowledge about the use of her information. Considering these overlaps is also relevant to really comprehend the modalities of so-called "new" technology-aided forms of surveillance.

Identity information is generally used by a variety of different actors for various reasonable purposes ranging from carrying out administrative procedures, stimulating economic development as well as for political objectives. In many cases, the processing of identity information is primarily controlled by institutional/organizational actors (e.g., businesses, public sector institutions, security authorities, social media providers, etc.). This is particularly the case in digital environments as individuals often lack control over the technologies and systems processing their information, provided or employed by institutional entities. Thus, at its core, the privacy control dilemma is determined by information asymmetries and agency problems resulting from imbalanced control over identity information, reinforcing institutional power. The presented perceptions of citizens on privacy, security and surveillance largely confirm this. More precisely, the processing of identifiable information beyond individual control is a basic trigger of privacy-affecting information asymmetries. Agency problems hamper ISD and bear risks of moral hazard. Hence, information is used at the cost of the individual's privacy. As shown, information asymmetries concerning digital identities can entail many forms of social control, profiling, discrimination as well as manipulation. Developments toward extensive scoring systems bear many serious risks. The Chinese credit scoring system, which generates scores for all citizens, is a drastic example of the abuse of identity information to reinforce panoptic power. These and many other developments stimulate automated forms of control (akin to the core feature of the panopticon). Consequently, there is a certain risk that individual identities are reduced to quantifiable patterns of information. Already today, semi-automated algorithms processing identity patterns for price discrimination, profiling, risk calculation, scoring, etc. demonstrate that this risk is not merely theoretical, also in Western countries. There is already evidence of algorithms reinforcing social disparities including stereotyping and social sorting; and the big data paradigm supports tendencies to extend scoring and other forms of automated risk calculation (Strauß 2018). Given the dynamic features of digital identity representations and the incremental extension of identification practices, information asymmetries, and thus privacy risks, can easily intensify as long as there are no effective protection measures.

A crucial issue which reinforces information asymmetries of identification is that identity is likely to grow over time: basically, identity has narrative characteristics which are naturally volatile in analog environments. However, technology reduces this volatility as identity information and the aggregation thereof can make the narrative of identity explicitly visible and reproducible. Consequently, digital identity representations can be reproduced and processed in multiple contexts, decoupled from the individuals they originate from. ICTs demonstrate this in many respects with various forms of explicit and implicit identification which are uncontrolled, extensive and, therefore, critical for privacy. There is thus a general increase in identifiability which further reinforces privacy-affecting information asymmetries. Consequently, uncontrolled socio-technical identifiability has been identified as a core issue of contemporary privacy protection. As demonstrated with the identity shadow, digital identities can be exposed to several uncontrolled contexts of information processing. Hence, besides explicit forms of identification, technology usage generates various types of information suitable for implicit identification. Explicit forms of identification can entail a quasi-obligation for individuals to provide identity information; implicit forms of identification benefit from the broad availability of digital information related to individuals. The latter is facilitated by the design of most ICTs conveying what I call *identifiability by default* mechanisms. This provides various ways to gather quasi-identifiers and create "digital fingerprints"; used inter alia for large-scale profiling and the creation of identity graphs. The crux is that digital information processing can entail multiple contextual identity layers. Moreover, there are several trends of expanding identifiability as basically every technology usage can lead to an extended representation of an individual's identity. The increasing use of biometric technologies including fingerprint scanners, and facial and speech recognition systems highlights that diminishing informational boundaries even affect the privacy of the human body. New technologies make a further expansion of the identity shadow and thus of identifiability very likely.

Revitalizing privacy as public value instead of privatization

Revitalizing privacy protection and tackling the problem of expanding sociotechnical identifiability requires action on several fronts, including social, political, economic and technical measures. More specifically, there is need to enhance ISD and individual privacy controls, and most importantly more effective safeguards, implemented by information processing entities. This includes technical as well as organizational measures. As argued in Chapters 6 and 7, fostering the combination of PbD and PIA is crucial in this regard to raise the effectiveness of privacy protection overall. Both concepts can also stimulate economic incentives to protect privacy instead of abusing it by monetizing identity information. Currently, this is among the core barriers to effective privacy protection besides mass surveillance and rampant activities in the realm of security. The GDPR of the EU is an important stepping stone to strengthen privacy regimes in Europe and, in the longer run, also in other countries. To unfold this potential requires effective implementation of PbD and PIA.

As argued, improving privacy protection implies a means to compensate information asymmetries resulting from socio-technical identifiability. The fact that identifiability triggers privacy impacts does not imply that every form of identification is privacy-intrusive or harmful. Identification practices are vital for the functioning of society. But an explicit consideration of identifiability when assessing privacy impacts is beneficial in improving the theoretical understanding of privacy protection as well in improving the effectiveness of safeguards. The analysis of the prospects and perils of PbD and privacy-enhancing approaches (in Chapter 6) revealed that there are several technical concepts to protect identifiable information: cryptography has always been a backbone of information privacy and security, ranging from content encryption, providing unlinkability to different anonymization techniques; and novel approaches such as differential privacy, or concepts employing blockchain technology (e.g., Ethereum) fostering decentralized information processing can improve PbD, e.g., in the realm of big data and pervasive computing. From a systemic perspective, PbD represents an approach to foster the boundary control function of privacy. It aims to provide mechanisms to create informational frictions so that different socio-technical systems can be decoupled with respect to privacy protection. Encryption technology is an important means to achieve this. Hence, basically, there are several promising approaches to revitalize the boundary control function of privacy in the networked society.

However, there are also various barriers to the effective implementation of PbD. First, the misuse of informed consent can be very problematic as it often forces individuals to fully accept the privacy conditions of, e.g., a service. In such cases, even the most sophisticated PbD concept can be of limited effect, because when services are based on a "take it or leave it" approach, individuals are more or less enforced to fully accept the terms of use and thus privacy intrusions. Second, the effectiveness of PbD suffers from a still relatively high complexity of technical tools, which complicates individual handling and thus ISD. Privacy controls are often limited in scope as only skilled users can properly handle them. In this regard, there are certain privacy divides between skilled and standard users. Furthermore, there are tendencies to discriminate against users of privacy tools (e.g., by blocking access to online services or complicating registration without real ID). Third, barriers to PbD result from a certain tendency to what can be called *privatization of privacy:* this means that the responsibility to protect privacy is mainly shifted to the individual. A consequence of this is that privacy becomes a sort of luxury good while institutional responsibility is neglected. As an individual can hardly control all the processing contexts of her identity information, privacy protection reaches its limits.

Therefore, PbD aiming to enhance individual privacy controls is essential but not enough to relativize the privacy control dilemma and improve the level of protection. Hence, also here, agency problems become apparent. To reduce these problems and foster PbD requires a revitalization of the public value of privacy. This implies a shared responsibility between individuals and institutions. For PbD, this means that the processing of identifiable information is to be avoided as far as possible. But technical solutions are not enough to ease this problem. There is thus demand for a combination of regulatory, organizational and technical measures to reduce privacy-affecting information asymmetries. This requires more transparency and accountability of information processing entities to achieve a shared responsibility regarding privacy protection. Basically, the GDPR is a promising regulatory approach in this regard as it fosters the relevance of PbD as well as of PIA. This new regulation partially satisfies the long-standing claim of privacy advocates to make PbD and PIA a legal requirement. But, apparently, the law cannot give procedural guidance on their implementation. To effectively implement PbD requires knowledge about the functioning of information processes including the technologies and applications involved. PIA is essential in this regard as it can support institutions in identifying their demand and requirements to implement PbD. In the longer term, PIA and PbD can complement and reinforce each other, leading to more effective privacy standards on a global level.

Taming identifiability with privacy impact assessment and a general typology of identifiable information

As PIA is an important precondition for PbD, its functions and scope were examined in Chapter 6 in order to develop a refined approach, as presented in Chapter 7. The results revealed that existing PIA approaches are often either tailored to a specific issue or offer rather general organizational steps with limited guidance to explore privacy impacts; some focus more on legal compliance, others more on risk assessment. This great diversity of PIA concepts is partially plausible as a PIA process needs to be specified with respect to particular institutional settings. However, a main barrier to the effective implementation of PIA results from a lack of common understanding of the emergence of a privacy impact. Consequently, the implementation of appropriate privacy safeguards (PbD) is hampered as well. As argued, identifiability is a core determinant of a privacy impact. Therefore, a general, identifiability-based PIA framework was proposed in Chapter 7. This framework can support the analysis of those information flows which are relevant to grasp privacy risks and develop corresponding protection.

The framework has no legal focus, although it can help with compliance checks, as this requires knowledge about the processing of identifiable information in all ways. In this framework, identifiability represents the initial privacy risk from which further risks can emerge (i.e., aggregation of information, durability, linkability, re-contextualization and traceability). These risks can then be addressed by basic protection goals (anonymity, confidentiality, contextual integrity, intervenability, transparency, unlinkability) and suitable PbD approaches. To grasp privacy risks requires a deeper understanding of the amount of identifiable information being processed. Privacy intrusion due to ICTs is not limited to personal information anymore. As argued, technology altered the role and generation of personal information so that the boundary between personal and non-personal, or personally and technically identifiable information, blurs. Neglecting this fact can significantly hamper privacy protection. Existing privacy standards often focus on PII only and rather neglect information resulting from technology usage. Therefore, I argue for introducing an additional type of information, i.e., *technically identifiable information* (TII).

As highlighted with the identity shadow (in Chapter 5), technology offers many options for implicit identification (including de-anonymization, re-identification, etc.) based on information which is not perceived as PII. Hence, there is a growing demand for PIA as well as PbD concepts incorporating TII. Contemporary privacy protection requires a deeper, process-oriented understanding of (digitally networked) information. I thus suggest an *alternative typology of identifiable information*, which explicitly takes PII as well as TII into account. This can improve PIA of a particular technology or application. The typology is based on four basic dimensions of identifiable information: *substantial, spatio-temporal, relational* and *interactional*. These layers allow not merely PII but also TII to be considered when analyzing privacy-relevant information flows. The rationale of these dimensions is that information processing can involve multiple socio-technical (sub-)systems. Awareness and knowledge about these systems and their dynamics is relevant to assess and reduce the risks of implicit identification (e.g., unintended third-party access, hidden profiling, etc.).

In light of the GDPR, PIA can be expected to gain in importance within the coming years. Although PIA is only mandatory under certain conditions (as regulated in Article 35 GDPR), public and private institutions have to evaluate and document their privacy-relevant information processes in order to act in compliance with the law and to avoid penalties. A PIA approach enabling more knowledge about identifiable information has several benefits in this regard: it contributes to improving transparency, accountability and legitimacy of information processing, which supports institutions in providing privacy compliance; it helps to respect the privacy principles of data minimization and purpose binding, because it eases evaluation of what types of information are necessary for a particular purpose and what types can be avoided; processing entities can proactively protect their information and improve security of their processes; the implementation of PbD is fostered as more effective safeguards can be developed, which contributes to improving information security as well as raising the general level of privacy protection. This is also relevant in light of increasing security threats of cyber-attacks, which demonstrate the vulnerability of socio-technical systems. More transparency and protection of identifiable information also correspond with the partial complementarity between privacy and security.

Primarily, the proposed framework is a contribution to improving the theoretical understanding of privacy impacts and their assessment, which is of practical relevance as well. Therefore, the major steps of this framework were sketched in a prototypical PIA process, exemplifying how it could be used in practice to analyze socio-technical systems and their impact on privacy. The presented typology of identifiable information is a core part of this process. It is an attempt to support a more systematic analysis of privacy-relevant information processes, which is an integral part of PIA. Indeed, given the high complexity of digital information processing, it can be challenging to detect the different types of PII and TII. Therefore, a clear assignment may not always be achievable in practice. Depending on a specific usage context, the practical employment of this typology may thus require refinement or simplification. This framework and the typology of identifiable information also suggest demand for further research to evaluate and test its practicability. In any case, a more systematic incorporation of PII and TII supports raising privacy awareness and gaining a more detailed picture of privacy-relevant types of information. This can facilitate the development of PbD and related technical privacy concepts, ideally in cooperation with technology vendors, providers and operators. An additional value can be to detect hidden impacts inherent to technology which may imply security risks as well. In the longer run, there is thus potential to stimulate the creation of better standards for PIA and PbD. The framework may contribute to tapping this potential.

Better standards for privacy protection to improve the quality of ICTs, digital products, services and information processes are in all ways required to tackle the various challenges privacy protection encounters. The proposed framework is only a small contribution in this regard. There are several other issues such as the remaining problems of informed consent, third-party usage of identifiable information, general increase in biometric identification including facial and speech recognition, extensive profiling and preventive surveillance practices, etc. to name just a few. Not least, the outlined problem of an increasing privatization of privacy needs a wider paradigm shift to revitalize the public value of privacy beyond PIA.

A stronger systematic consideration of TII when designing and assessing technologies (or, basically, socio-technical systems) is particularly important in light of continuing technological progress that further boosts digital networking and visions of pervasive computing. Furthermore, there is an incremental but accelerating increase in (semi-)automated systems, artificial intelligence, machine learning algorithms, etc. Therefore, additional privacy problems concerning the processing of identifiable information by machine entities can be expected. Intensifying challenges to privacy and increasingly also to human autonomy are thus likely. Already today, there are various algorithms capable of (semi-)autonomous identification based on a set of identity criteria for various activities including influencing, nudging, predicting, profiling, scoring, social sorting, etc. As a consequence, information about human identities may be increasingly processed by technological agents on an automated basis. This bears serious risks of bias, stereotyping, discrimination, etc. and can lead to many conflicts between (semi-)autonomous systems and human autonomy; especially when automatically gathered identity information is used to take automatic decisions. This has serious impact on the individual as well as on society as a whole. Regulation to prevent automated decision-making is already strained and it is an open question whether it offers sufficient protection. Hence, there are a number of issues suggesting further research and sound regulation are required.

To ensure that privacy protection has a stable, future-proof foundation requires a solid privacy regime on a global level, including a mix of regulatory, technical, economic and political measures. This involves the need to foster the public value of privacy and of anonymity as its pivotal point. Because, as a matter of fact, the large-scale exploitation of our identities (regardless of whether online or offline, digital or analog) for extensive, uncontrolled purposes jeopardizes privacy and free, self-determined identity development. This is not "just" a problem of some privacy advocates but has negative effects on social, political and economic security and thus, ultimately, on the stability of society. Although the fundamental role privacy fulfills in society is of enduring value, the continuity of its protection is at stake when protection mechanisms lack effectiveness to deal with socio-technical practices. We should be very aware that a loss of privacy and anonymity causes serious damage to the development of our identities and to the foundations of our society.

References

Cohen, J. E. (2012) *Configuring the Networked Self: Law, code, and the play of everyday practice.* Yale: Yale University Press.

Greenwald, G. (2014) *No Place to Hide: Edward Snowden, the NSA and the surveillance state.* London: Hamish Hamilton/Penguin Books.

Haggerty, K. D. and Ericson, R. V. (2000) The Surveillant Assemblage. *British Journal of Sociology,* 51(4): 605–622.

Nissenbaum, H. (2010) *Privacy in Context: Technology, policy, and the integrity of social Life.* Stanford: Stanford University Press.

Solove, D. J. (2006) A Taxonomy of Privacy. *University of Pennsylvania Law Review,* 154(3): 477–560.

Solove, D. J. (2011) *Nothing to Hide: The false tradeoff between privacy and security.* New Haven/London: Yale University Press.

Strauß, S. (2017) A Game of Hide and Seek? Unscrambling the trade-off between privacy and security. In Friedewald, M., Burgess, P. J., Čas, J., Bellanova, R. and Peissl, W. (eds.), *Surveillance, Privacy, and Security: Citizens' perspectives.* London/New York: Routledge, 255–272.

Strauß, S. (2018) Big Data: Within the tides of securitisation? In Saetnan, A. R., Schneider, I. and Green, N. (eds.), *The Politics of Big Data: Big data, big brother?* Oxon: Routledge, 46–67.

Westin, A. (1967) *Privacy and Freedom.* New York: Atheneum.

Index

accountability 1, 11, 71, 145, 151, 158, 195, 205–210, 237, 252, 259; improving of 11, 67, 207–210, 214, 216, 252, 259, 265, 271, 273; lack of 71, 145, 149–151, 160–161, 206; precondition for 209–210, 237; relevance of 1, 11, 49, 67–68, 151, 158, 161, 195, 206
agency problems 145–149, 162, 199, 205, 208, 214, 269, 271
agency theory 145
aggregation of information 40, 44–45, 144, 220–222, 233–235, 239, 257, 269, 272
algorithm 70, 101, 108, 147, 149–151, 173, 234, 269, 274
algorithmic authority 149
algorithmic power 149
anonymity 3, 37, 41–45, 92, 162, 173, 191–194, 197–198, 204–205, 236, 240, 257, 272, 274
anonymization 139, 148, 164–165, 171, 190–192, 202, 204, 233, 238, 258, 271
artificial intelligence 83, 85, 173, 234, 250, 274
assessing privacy impacts 232, 270
asymmetric information 145
asymmetry of power 129, 142–146
autonomy 10, 26, 30, 32, 47, 50, 52–55, 65, 71, 81, 126, 264, 274

big brother 139
big data 5, 85, 87, 131, 137, 139, 144, 148, 150–151, 170–171, 190, 193, 209, 250, 269, 271
biometrics 37, 89, 113, 171–174, 217–219, 255
Cambridge Analytica 2, 98, 100, 102, 150, 200, 264
citizen(s) 7, 10, 33–35, 42, 51, 54–58,

63–66, 68, 70, 96, 110, 113, 127–128, 135–136, 148–152, 154–161, 269
cognition: process of 23–25
conditional identification 131
confidential 192, 222, 236–237
confidentiality 69, 49–50, 161, 220–222, 233–237
connectivity 5, 70–71, 81–87, 166, 266
content production 102, 149
contextual integrity 8, 71, 167, 176, 198, 236–237, 265, 268, 272
Convention 108, 47–48
convergence between analog/physical and digital/virtual 4, 85, 112–113, 173, 176, 219, 267
cryptography 192–193, 223, 238, 270

Dark Web dilemma 204
data mining 44, 70, 98, 105, 218
data protection 2, 7–8, 11, 24, 45–48, 56–58; authorities 68, 173, 209; by design 208 (*see also* privacy by design); framework 7, 48; impact assessment 224–225, 229, 260 (*see also* privacy impact assessment); law 2, 30, 38, 46–49, 57, 201, 210; officer 214, 224, 252, 259; principles 30, 208, 258 (*see also* protection standards); reform 2, 211; regime 56, 209, 211
de-anonymization 139, 164–165, 171, 202, 235, 240, 272
de-identification 191, 233, 238
democracy 1, 42, 50–51, 64–65, 69, 123, 141, 146, 262
democratic society 2, 44, 47, 49, 51, 54, 57, 59–60, 141, 205, 212, 264
dialectical character of identity 242
differential privacy 191, 240, 271
digital identification: emergence of 9, 26,

40, 72, 114, 126, 134, 188; major
drivers of 92, 267; political and
economic interests of 26, 94, 133;
spiral of 156
digital identity 6, 24–25, 39, 72–78, 89,
94–96, 101, 112, 126, 137, 149, 164,
167–170, 178, 206, 245, 266–269
digitization 68, 85–96, 263
dignity 50, 52, 57, 60
dimensions of identifiable information
242–243, 273
discrimination 66, 130, 135, 140, 145–150,
175, 207, 269, 274
dynamics of socio-technical systems 18,
82

echo chamber 149
economization 10, 100, 113, 128, 134,
137, 147, 198, 205, 15, 267–268
effectiveness of privacy protection 2, 6,
23, 27, 72, 160, 209, 214, 231, 270
effectiveness of security measures 63, 135,
154, 155, 156, 207
electronic/digital panopticon 128–131
electronic/digital surveillance, surveillance
and technology 140–143
emergence of privacy impact 3, 9, 11, 71
encryption 2, 190–194, 202–203, 237–238,
258, 270
ethical: aspects 2, 4–7, 11, 111;
compliance 205, 233, 235–236, 240;
norms 6–10, 19–21, 49, 62, 69, 71,
205, 237, 265, 268; problems and risks
59, 64, 141, 149, 161, 205
Europe vs. Facebook 214
European Convention on Human Rights
215
evolutionary system 19–20, 23
explicit identification 94, 168–170

facial recognition 172–174
fair information practices 48
filter bubble 100, 149
Foucault, Michel 139
freedom 34, 42, 52–57, 61, 64–65, 154,
217, 264
fundamental rights 50, 57, 63–65, 135, 217

General Data Protection Regulation
(GDPR) 2–3, 46–49, 58, 208–209,
212, 214, 240, 252–253, 259, 270–273
governance 19, 26, 35, 61, 88, 126,
128–132, 136, 143, 146, 151, 193, 207,
266–268

Government Communications Headquarter
(GCHQ) 133, 176
graph theory 103, 105, 171

hard identification 40, 89, 197
how surveillance affects privacy 130–133
human condition 5–6
human-centered security 61
human right 1, 42, 57, 54, 60–64, 110,
135, 158, 191, 204–205, 212
hyper-connectivity 84, 86, 266

idem 32, 53, 175, 242, 244
identifiability 3–4, 11, 41–42, 45, 128,
143–144, 161–168, 176, 188–191, 200,
205–210, 219–223, 231–238, 255;
dimensions of 223, 241–247;
expansion of 167, 176, 170–176, 231,
251, 265, 270; risks related to
233–235; socio-technical 11, 200, 210,
262, 269–270; technical 245
identifiability-based framework for PIA 233
identifiability by default 163–166, 188,
200, 270
identifiable information 3, 7, 11, 21, 25,
36–37, 40–43, 46, 162–163, 166–171,
188–195, 207–210, 219–223, 231–250,
252–258, 262–263, 266–268
identification system 7, 24, 88, 145–146,
151, 197
identification: connecting function of 25,
34, 41, 92, 107, 128–129, 166, 266;
different qualities of 39–41; domains
and features 34; modalities of 37–38,
40, 131, 254
identifier 25, 37–39, 44, 46, 57, 92–95,
163–169, 171, 191–196, 238; domain-
specific 164; global 196, 257;
protection of 191–192; quasi-identifier
166–168, 171, 235, 247, 257, 260; role
of 38–39, 88–90, 239–240, 244–247,
270; sector-specific 196; technical 167,
179, 246, 269; unique 39, 44, 57,
89–91, 195–196, 201, 240, 244
identity graph 105, 138
identity layers 167–170, 241, 263, 270
identity management (IDM) 6, 26, 58, 81,
87, 89, 93, 194
identity shadow 11, 162–168, 171, 188,
196, 198, 200, 207, 231–232, 243, 245,
268–270, 272
implicit identification 7, 11, 41, 163,
167–170, 202, 207, 219, 239, 241, 249,
267, 269–273

For Product Safety Concerns and Information please contact our EU
representative GPSR@taylorandfrancis.com
Taylor & Francis Verlag GmbH, Kaufingerstraße 24, 80331 München, Germany

www.ingramcontent.com/pod-product-compliance
Ingram Content Group UK Ltd.
Pitfield, Milton Keynes, MK11 3LW, UK
UKHW020931180425
457613UK00012B/316